Human Rights & Social Justice

Muzafer Assadi

Professor and Director
Department of Political Science
University of Mysore, Mysore-06, India

SERIALS PUBLICATIONS
NEW DELHI (INDIA)

First Published - 2011

ISBN: 978-81-8387-462-5

Published by

SERIALS PUBLICATIONS
4830/24, Prahlad Street, Ansari Road
Darya Ganj, New Delhi-110002 (India)
Phone : 23245225 Fax : 91-11-23272135
E-mail: serials@sify.com

Contents

Preface .... *vii*

- Investigating Iran's Legal Texts Concerning the Prohibition of Torture *1-9*
  Gholam Hossein Masoud
- Contemporary Changes in Coal Mining Society in West Bengal *11-15*
  Sribas Goswami
- Child Labour in Rural Areas– A Case Study of Carpet Industry in Amritsar *17-23*
  Seozy Bhatia
- Analysis the Socio- Economic Aspects of Child Labor in the Districts of Upper Sindh Pakistan: A Case Study of Child Laboring in Donkey Cart Riding *25-41*
  Muhammad Haroon Bahlkani
- Euthanasia and Its Legality and Legitimacy from Indian and International Human Right Instruments Perspectives *43-54*
  Tushar Kumar Biswas & Arnab Sengupta
- Unfolding Terrorism *55-63*
  Kaustav Roy & Chandrajit Mukherjee
- Humanitarian Intervention and the UN Charter Regime: Sovereignty, Human Rights and Peace *65-84*
  Japheth Afwayi Khamasi
- Offence of Rape and Relevancy of Consent: An Analysis With Special Reference to India *85-92*
  Arun Kumar Singh
- Social Security in India: The Legislative Support *93-104*
  Ashish Kumar Pandey
- Police Reform: A Long Awaited Task *105-119*
  Avinash Kumar
- Private Law and Environmental Regulation: Between Protection and Prevention *121-129*
  Scott Nicholas Romaniuk
- Protecting Child Rights– An Inevitable Agenda *131-140*
  Avinash Kumar

- Prison Conditions and Prisoners' Rights in Punjab: A Study of the Role of Punjab State Human Rights Commission *141-155*
  Satnam Singh Deol
- Sexual Harassment of Women at Workplace *157-167*
  R. N. Mangoli
- Taking Risks Ethically *169-179*
  John D. Haskell
- Sex Work, HIV/AIDs and Sexual Rights in Africa: The Nigerian Experience *181-216*
  Ebenezer Durojaye, Olubayo Oluduro & Uju Okeke
- "Protection of Human Rights, Act 1993– Human Rights Courts in India" *217-240*
  Sujesh Somanathan
- "Consumer Right Transcending into a Human Right" *241-253*
  Arya Tripathy & Astha Sharma
- Female Criminality and Prisonisation in Karnataka *255-269*
  Nandini G. Devarmani & M. G. Huddar
- Women Behind Bars and their Rights – An Evaluation *271-282*
  Nandini G. Devarmani & M. G. Huddar
- The Unlawful Activities Prevention (Amendment) Act, 2008: Anarchy Codified? *283-290*
  Akshaya Iyer
- Educational Development of Muslims in Maharashtra: Analysis from Policies, Commissions and Educational Schemes in India *291-301*
  Dhaneswar Bhoi
- Problems of Women Entrepreneurs in Karwar Taluka of Uttar Kannada District *303-319*
  Maya S. Gaonkar
- Right to Education and Problems in it's Implementation: A Case Study of Women's Education in Jammu and Kashmir *321-341*
  Fayaz Ahmad Bhat & Fouzia Khurshid
- Foeticide – A Threat to Society *343-353*
  Nirmala Devi

Index *355-374*

Preface

The present volume is collection of twenty-four research articles/research papers based on Human Rights which have now acclaimed a world wide prominence and need of the hour. These research papers now present a world perspective furnishing voluminous information in form of statistical tables, new theories, facts and cases, in regard to wide spread violence and wars in the world. These research papers are written by national and international eminent established authors and subject experts. These papers contain a complete picture of various laws and legislations passed by various government in the world. These papers also details the various conventions and covenants and Human Rights Instruments formulated and being got implemented by the apex body of world nations viz United Nations. We can witness the violations of human rights in Afghanistan, Kosovo, Palestine, Jammu and Kashmir, Sri Lanka, and several African Countries and all over the map of the world. These papers not only emphasis on Human Rights but also touch many other interesting subjects like, Euthanasia, Humanitarian Intervention, Social Security in India, Socio-Economic aspects of Child Labor, Child Rights, Prisons Conditions, Sexual Harassment, Consumer Rights, Problems of Women Entrepreneurs, Education problems in the state of Jammu and Kashmir, and a lot more.

Mr. Gholam Hossein Masoud, Head Faculty of Law, Najab-Abad Islamic Azad University, Iran, comprehensive disusses Iran's Legal Texts concerning the Prohibition of Torture while obtaining confession. He disusses International Conventions and Agreements and related articles therein which advocates human rights like Universal Declaration of Human Rights (UDHR), International Covenant on Civil and Political Rights (ICCPR), Cairo Declaration on Human Rights in Islam, convention against Torture and Other Cruel Inhuman or Degrading Treatment or Punishment. He also squeezes the essence of Geneva Convention. He brings forth three major personalities (Commandants) like Hajji Mirza Aghassi, Amir Kabir, Mirza Hussein Khan Sepahalar, who first advocated prohibition of torture for obtaining confession. He mentions various Iran's Constitutional article in favour of prohibiting torture in confession. Full consideration for human rights is detailed by several human rights instruments and constitutional framework. A very Knowledgeable and information study on the legal instruments in Iran on human rightr.

Sribas Goswami's study paper entitled 'Coal Mining Society in West Bengal' is a valueable and informative paper which discusses contemporary changes in the field of mining which have taken place recently. These changes are the fresh and latest in the field. A brief history of coal industry in West Bengal is presented. Also defined industrial relations (IR) culture, industrial relations in coal mines society. In view of the information furnished undoubtedly proves that industrial relations index in West Bengal, Cola mines in particular has moved towards positive directions from its earlier stage. Researchers in this field will surely find rejuvenating information in industrial relations culture which is a departure from the past history of industrial relations in West Bengal.

Seozy Bhatia's paper on Child Labor in Rural Areas, is a very current topic of the day and not only is a serious concern of the governments of the concerned country but the also concern of United Nations, which is an apex body of world Nations and who tirelessly working to eradicate the Child Labor from map of the world. Here the author cites the case study of Carpet Industry in Amritsar in particular. International Labor Organization (ILO) a constituent part of UNO, is specially taking serious initiatives to labor problems in the countries of the world including Child Labor in the world. UN Commission on Human Rights drafted the convention on the rights of child (CRC) and India has ratified the same. Child Labor affects lives of many millions of Children all over the world. The study examines child labor in various states in India, causes of the child labor, relations between child labor and female literacy, and work participation across Indian States. Finally critically studies programs and policies relating to elimination of child labor. The study revealed that there is higher incidence of child labor in the states of Andhra Pradesh, Rajasthan, Karnataka and on the contrary the states of Haryana, Punjab, Maharashtra and Gujarat have lower incidents of child labor. Strategies of various non-Government organizations towards eradication of child labor are also discussed. It is also found out that the socio-economic and working conditions of the child labor are not healthy. Child labor has serious effect on the education, mental and physical growth of the children. The paper provides all the relevant cases and information in a very exhaustive manner to study.

In yet another useful study on child labor, Muhammad Haroon Bahlkani analyses the socio-economic spects of child labor in the district of Upper Sind Pakistan: A case study of Child Laboring in Donkey Cart Riding. Child labor, in Pakistan, is prevalent in all sectors of economy. Major sectors absorbing child labor in the Pakistan are manufacturing, transport, trade, agriculture, construction, donkey card riding and services. Child labor is found in sports industry, Surgical goods industry, cottage industry, chemical industry, power looms, footwear industry, fisheries, carpet weaving, engineering and iron shops, furniture and fixtures. Child labor is abundantly involved in construction industry. The paper details important national laws pertaining to child labor as Factories Act, West Pakistan Shops and Establishment Ordinance, Employment of Children Act, Bonded Labor System Abolition Act, Punjab Compulsory Education Act etc. The study also analyses Child labor legislation in Pakistan. It carries intensive details of child labor absorbed in Donkey Cart Riding. This a very absorbing and comprehensive article on the children in Donkey Cart Riding and other various industries.

The next most interesting article by Tushar Kumar Biswas and Arnab Sengupta is the EUTHANASIA which means in Greek- 'an easeful death'. It describes the practice of bringing about death in a manner that causes the least amount of suffering to the patient. The concept of Euthanasia has been a matter of significant controversy over the recent past both in India as well as in other parts of the globe. Suppose a Women 'X' has been suffering brain damage and has become dependent on a feeding tube and there is no living will on her part. Her husband is praying before the Court to discontinue the tube feedings on the contrary her natal family wants to continue with the life support- what type of decision would one can expect from the courts in India? There are numerous such examples where the patient is neither lives or dies and no hope of life. The article pleads legal and constitutional means and decisions. One should rather revert to this very interesting article which imparts knowledge and increasing one's information in regard to such cases. Constitution of India provides Right to Life and no person should be deprived of his life. The concept of Euthanasia is discussed under (1), Voluntary Euthanasia (2) Non-Voluntary Euthanasia (3) In-Voluntary Euthanasia. The article discusses in details Indian Legal System in this regard and cites several cases decided by the apex legal body in the country. It also examines Euthanasia under International Human Rights instruments and its legitimacy to Right to Life under International Convention on Political Rights, (ICCPR), Universal Declaration of Human Rights (UDHR) etc. In this regard UK House of Lords Select Committee's verdict is of noteworthy and its view are enlightening.

Japheth Afwayi Khamasi, in his research paper 'Humanitarian Intervention and the UN Charter Regime—' examines the initiatives of world apex body-United Nations to save the nationals of various nations from human rights violations. In this realistic paper which defines humanitarian intervention is an unilateral intervention for protection of another state's nationals for human rights.

One of the cornerstones of the UN is the sovereign equality of all its member states. It takes effective measures for the prevention and removal of threats to the peace, and for the suppression of acts of aggression or other breaches of the peace. Also ensures measures to strengthened universal peace and to achieve international cooperation in solving international problems and in promoting and encouraging respects of Human Rights and fundamental freedoms. The paper examines various articles of the charter individually for establishment of world peace and security. Various other points discussed are – Priority over Sovereignty over Human Rights, Sovereignty and Principle of Non-Intervention, limits of domestic jurisdiction and the correlative duty of non-interference, relationship between Non-Interference and Human Rights, humanitarian intervention within the framework, peace as a controlling norm of the Charter. Human Rights violations, Peace the absence of force, NATO's Part etc. are discussed. In short the research paper is a very analytical study with legal framework of the Charter.

Ashish Kumar Pandey of Banaras Hindu University's research paper examines social security in India with all its pros and cons, It briefly discusses evolution of term social security and details ILO's convention No.102: Social Security Minimum Standards 1952, where nine branches of social security are discussed. It further state need for social security, developing of social security system in India, factors that influence statutory social security system in India, constitutional provisions of social security under various articles of ILO. It also discusses Workmen's Compensation Act, 1823, Employees State Insurance Act, 1948, Employees Provident Fund Act, Employees Pension Scheme and various benefits available under the scheme, Payment of Gratuity Act, 1972. The paper brings forth a fact that social security legislation of our country suffer from certain defects as uneven scope, inadequacy of benefits, duplication and overlapping provisions and different administrative authorities for implementation and enforcement over all it is detailed exhaustive study of social security.

RN Mangole, Asst Prof, PG Dept in Criminology and Forensic Science, Karnataka University, Dharwad discusses an important topic viz. Sexual Harassment of Women at workplace. The paper has touched all the minute problem related to the harassment of women at workplace. The ethical and moral values of society have decreased toward women since the Vedic times through ancient times, medieval times and to date in the modern period. There was a time when women were worshipped and its was said in the Vedic Literature that "Yatra Naryantu Pujyente ramente tatra devta:. Today the position of women have entirely changed and they play a very crucial role in the socio-economic development of a country. Sexual harassment is taken place everywhere and at the workplace. Sexual harassment affects all women in some form or the other particularly at workplace. The objective of the study is- to understand problems of sexual harassment in Indian Society, causes of increasing sexual harassment in the society, to know remedial measures taken against sexual harassment of women at workplace, also to know existing laws combating against sexual harassment. It also examines various human rights instruments which advocate elimination of sexual harassment in whatever form they exist like Convention on Elimination of Discrimination against Women (CEDAW), National Commission for Women, Various Indian Penal Code's sections, etc. The study also covers the eye opening cases of sexual harassment as - Of Ms Asha Rajora, Technical Assistant in Herbal Research and Development Institute, Gopeshwar (Uttaranchal) whre services of Director, Dr.JS Rawat were terminated, second case is of Mrs. Rupan Deol Bajaj, IAS

Officer, in which Shri KPS Gill, former DG Punjab Police was involved and subsequently he was awarded three month rigorous imprisonment by chief judicial Magistrate shri Darshan Singh, third case is of Nalini Netto, a Senior IAS officer. The paper has a very remedial impact for persons involved in sexual harassment. The details are interesting to study. Full details of existing laws against sexual harassment in India are justiciably streamlined. Sexual Harassment and Domestic laws under IPC-1860, is also discussed. Various other legislations where several provisions against sexual harassment are provided, are mentioned. It also critically examines various clauses under UN Convention on Sexual Harassment like CEDAW, Nairobi Forward, Vienna Declaration, Declaration on the Elimination of Violence against women (DEDAW), Beijing Declaration, and Inter-American Convention on Prevention, Punishment and Eradication of Violence against women.

In view of the constraints of space and time, it is undoubtedly not possible to examine all the rest of the research papers in the present volume. But it is rest assured that all the undiscusseed paper contain valueable information and other facts and figures related to the concerned subject of the topic. All the twenty four study papers on Human Rights and Human Rights Violations, and social justice are full of immense information which can be used all the time for various research work. These papers have been widely acclaimed at national and international level while circulated through "Indian Journal of Human Rights and Social Justice" by the Serial Publications, New Delhi. Now these scattered knowledge has been gathered together for the benefit of Indian and Foreign readership and scholars engaged in research work on subject of Human Rights and Social Justice. The papers in form of book will be better utilized by the students, research scholars and information centres and libraries of social sciences.

Muzafer Assadi

Professor and Director

Department of Political Science

University of Mysore, Mysore-06, India

Investigating Iran's Legal Texts Concerning the Prohibition of Torture

Gholam Hossein Masoud*

INTRODUCTION

Article 38 of Iran's constitution[1] stipulates that "all forms of torture for the purpose of extracting confession or acquiring information are forbidden. Compulsion of individuals to testify, confess, or take an oath is not permissible; and any testimony, confession, or oath obtained under duress is devoid of value and credence. Violation of this Article is liable to punishment in accordance with the law".

This Article is compatible with international conventions and is supported by a historical background from inside the country. In this , we review both of these two aspects, and then, we consider the correct terms by which a confession obtained according to Iran's legal system.

International Conventions and Agreements

Universal Declaration of Human Rights[2]

Article 5: "No one shall be subjected to torture or to cruel, inhuman, or degrading treatment or punishment."

Article 14: "(1) Everyone has the right to seek and to enjoy in other countries asylum from persecution."

"(2) This right may not be invoked in the case of prosecutions genuinely arising from non-political crimes or from acts contrary to the purposes and principles of the United Nations."

International Covenant on Civil and Political Rights[3]

Article 7: "No one shall be subjected to torture or to cruel, inhuman or degrading treatment or punishment. In particular, no one shall be subjected without his free consent to medical or scientific experimentation."

* *Faculty of Law, Najaf- Ābād Islamic Āzād University, Iran, (E-mail : marajabi63@gmail.com)*

The Cairo Declaration on Human Rights in Islam[4]

Article 20: "It is not permitted without legitimate reason to arrest an individual, or restrict his freedom, to exile or to punish him. It is not permitted to subject him to physical or psychological torture or to any form of maltreatment, cruelty or indignity. Nor is it permitted to subject an individual to medical or scientific experiments without his consent or at the risk of his health or of his life. Nor is it permitted to promulgate emergency laws that would provide executive authority for such actions."

The Declaration on the Protection of All Persons from Being Subjected to Torture and Other Cruel, Inhuman or Degrading Treatment or Punishment[5]

Article 3: "No State may permit or tolerate torture or other cruel, inhuman or degrading treatment or punishment. Exceptional circumstances such as a state of war or a threat of war, internal political instability or any other public emergency may not be invoked as a justification of torture or other cruel, inhuman or degrading treatment or punishment".

Article 4: "Each State shall, in accordance with the provisions of this Declaration, take effective measures to prevent torture and other cruel, inhuman or degrading treatment punishment from being practiced within its jurisdiction."

Convention against Torture and Other Cruel, Inhuman or Degrading Treatment or Punishment[6]

Article 1: This article defines the term "torture". It means "any act by which severe pain or suffering, whether physical or mental, is intentionally inflicted on a person for such purposes as obtaining from him or a third person, information or a confession punishing him for an act which he or a third person has committed or is suspected of having committed, or intimidating or coercing him or a third person, or for any reason based on discrimination of any kind, when such pain or suffering is inflicted by or at the instigation of or with the consent or acquiescence of a public official or other person acting in an official capacity. It does not include pain or suffering arising only, inherent in or incidental to lawful sanctions." This article does not include any international instrument or national legislation which does or may contain provisions of wider application.

Article 2: This article demands frankly each State Party to take effective legislative, administrative, judicial or other measures to prevent acts of torture in any territory under its jurisdiction, and emphasizes that no exceptional circumstances whatsoever ,or an order from a superior officer or a public authority, may be invoke as a justification of torture.

Article 3: This article obliges any State Party not to expel, return or extradite a person to another State where there are substantial grounds to believe that he would be in danger of being subjected to torture.

Article 4 : This article demands each State Party to ensure that all acts of torture are offences under its criminal law, and to make these offences punishable by appropriate penalties which take into account their grave nature.

Article 5 : This article demands each State Party to take measures as may be necessary to establish its jurisdiction over the offences referred to in Article 4.

Articles 6, 7, 8, and 9 : These articles describe how to prosecute, arrest, and expatriate any individual who has committed any offences referred to in Article 4. All States Parties shall afford one another the greatest measure of assistance regarding fulfilling the above mentioned procedure.

Articles 10 and 11 : These two articles put all States Parties under obligation to ensure that education and information regarding the prohibition against torture is fully included in the training of law enforcement personnel and other officials who may be involved in the custody, interrogation or treatment of any individual subjected to any form of arrest ,detention or imprisonment. All States Parties shall include this prohibition in the rules or instructions issued in regard to the duties and functions of any such persons.

Articles 17 to 20 : These articles deal with all measurements to carry out this convention and establishing a Committee against Torture which investigates the received reports from all States Parties, members of the United Nations.

There are two important points in this convention to take into account:

(a) The first point, revealed at the first glance to this convention, is that if injuries and suffering, physically or mentally, are results of any individual's act who occupies no formal job and authority in government, his/her act will be subjected to laws and articles dealing with offenses, assaults and batteries. Also, if any official or agent in government, due to his/her personal relations or benefits and not because of his/her posts in the government, or because of executing his/her formal duties, tortures another person, the articles of the convention of 10th December 1984 doesn't cover his/her acts[7].

(b) The second point to consider about torture is that in addition to banning and forbidding torture, this convention deals with stabilizing the executive guarantees and sanctions and establishing an investigative discipline in order to fulfill the articles in the best manner. It presumes that global society is permitted to supervise the commitments which any State Party is bound to, and all peoples have the right to prosecute and pursuit any torturer in any territory of the States bound to this convention and even it is foreseen to force any proven torturer to compensate any losses.

Convention on the Rights of the Child by General Assembly Resolution of 20 November 1989[8]

Article 37: "States Parties shall ensure that No child shall be subjected to torture or other cruel, inhuman or degrading treatment or punishment... No child shall be deprived of his or her liberty unlawfully or arbitrarily."

Quadruple conventions known as Geneva Convention[9]

Common Article 3 in all Four Conventions

No one shall be subjected to torture or to cruel, inhuman or degrading treatment or punishment.

Article 99 of the third Geneva Convention[10]

> "No prisoner of war may be tried or sentenced for an act which is not forbidden by the law of the Detaining Power or by international law, in force at the time the said act was committed."

"No moral or physical coercion may be exerted on a prisoner of war in order to induce him to admit himself guilty of the act of which he is accused."

Charter of International Court of Justice

The given charter says in article 38 of its B clause that considering the international common law, any torture is forbidden.

Other Adopted Conventions and Agreements by Legal Agencies Related to United Nations

During the conference of international law association held in 1984, some of major issues about human rights were introduced as rights which can not be ignored even in emergency situations. These rights, known as "Paris Minimum Standards", are not violable from the viewpoint of the given association's members even by resorting to Article 4 of International Covenant on Civil and Political Rights. Apart from Paris Minimum Standards, this point is affirmed by Article 11 of American Convention on Human Rights, and Article 27 of European Convention on Human Rights, that is, some issues and subjects of human rights must not be ignored including executing Article 7 of International Covenant on Civil and Political Rights, Article 5 of African Charter on Human and Peoples'[11] Rights, and Article 5 of American Convention on Human Rights.[12] Article 5. Right to Humane Treatment:

"1. Every person has the right to have his physical, mental, and moral integrity srespected.

2. No one shall be subjected to torture or to cruel, inhuman, or degrading punishment or treatment. All persons deprived of their liberty shall be treated with respect for the inherent dignity of the human person.

3. Punishment shall not be extended to any person other than the criminal.
4. Accused persons shall, save in exceptional circumstances, be segregated from convicted persons, and shall be subject to separate treatment appropriate to their status as unconvicted persons.
5. Minors while subject to criminal proceedings shall be separated from adults and brought before specialized tribunals, as speedily as possible, so that they may be treated in accordance with their status as minors."

By the way, clause 2 of Article 15 of European Convention on Human Rights doesn't admit any limitations for living right and forbidding torture.[13]

Iranian Commandments[14]

The Command of Hajji Mirza Aghassi

The Command of Hajji Mirza Aghassi (chancellor of the Ghajar dynasty) can be considered as the first Iranian command to declare the legal prohibition of torture for obtaining confession. This command was issued in 1845 for regional governors.

Amir Kabir's Command (State Charter)

Amir Kabir (another chancellor of the Ghajar dynasty) declared the legal prohibition of torture for regional governors in 1849.

The Command of Mirza Hussein Khan Sepahsalar

This command, (which was issued in the second half of 19th century) like the two previous ones, forbade the act of torture, although the executive officers didn't pay much attention to it.

Confession without Torture

To prove that anybody is guilty and has committed any offence, some reasons must have been acquired for it. Obtaining reasons to prove anybody guilty is achieved in several ways:

1. *Confession:* it means that somebody says that I have committed such an act. In legal classic definition, it is informing of a right against oneself and for other.
2. *Attestation:* it means that somebody says that I have seen or heard that a person has done such an act or said such words.
3. *Oath:* A solemn promise, usually invoking a divine witness for affirming the truth of one's words.

The three issues mentioned above are of the oldest manners to obtain the reasons, specially the first which has been the most popular one in all human history.

One of the most common ways to obtain confession is to persecute and torture someone and often the persecution is so hard and cruel that such person confesses the crimes which he/she has never committed, just because of getting rid of persecution. This action is called "torture". Torture is in fact a cruel and inhuman manner to obtain information and there is no measure for it.

Iran's Constitution defines this manner of obtaining reasons as vicious and unaccepted and the reasons obtained herewith are void. Article 38 of Iran's Constitution[15] mentions that it is not permitted to force a person to testify, confess, or swear, and affirms that such testimony, confession, and swear is void.

> "All forms of torture for the purpose of extracting confession or acquiring information are forbidden. Compulsion of individuals to testify, confess, or take an oath is not permissible; and any testimony, confession, or oath obtained under duress is devoid of value and credence. Violation of this article is liable to punishment in accordance with the law."

In this Article there are two criticized actions: torture and constraint. Here, we provide brief definitions for both of them.

Torture is any act by which severe pain or suffering, physically or mentally, is intentionally inflicted on a person to obtain information or a confession. In public view, torture is a cruel, intolerable pain or suffering, but in legal definition, practicing any harm and pain is considered as torture and there is no need to severity. Torture is usually practiced to obtain but if it is done in order to obtain testimony or swear or oath, it is also considered as torture. Torture is usually done by various tools and nobody likes to be tortured, except mental patients.

Constraint means forcing somebody to commit an action despite of his/her willingness; for instance, tying a person and injecting narcotic drug into his/her vein. Though injecting drug is considered as a crime, because he/she had no freedom and control to avoid it, so he/she is not responsible for it. According to Article 38 of the constitution, if the evidences or reasons, which may be accepted by court, are obtained by torture, so they are void and not used to convict a criminal.

Sometimes the confession is obtained by an inhuman manner but is not considered as torture or constraint. For instance, when inspectors give promise and hope to help the criminal and thus provoke him/her. I don't say it is correct and the confession obtained herewith is without any difficulty. Even it may not be a real reason and evidence, but such an action is not torture and constraint, and may be covered by the first part of Article 129 of Iran's Criminal Procedure Code. It is useful to say here that confession is not always a good reason for conviction. It may be a confession but improper. It may a defendant taking part in a given crime and he/she accepts the accusation, but this confession doesn't in fact correspond with the truth. For example, in the case of shooting at a victim, the defendant confesses the act of shooting but in fact the victim is dead by the shot of another Sometimes a person confesses falsely to release another. At times, it is seen that the defendant accepts the accusation altogether in a confession obtained by force.

Article 578 of Iran's Islamic Penal Code[16] is a good executive guarantee for Article 38 of Iran's Constitution. It says that:

> "If an officer, juridical or non-juridical, uses torture in order to obtain confession and the defendant dies under torture, he will be punished as a and the person commanding the torture will be punished as a commander of murder".

According to Article 243 of Iran's Principals Criminal Procedure[17], only the confession which is obtained before the judge is valid, and if it is obtained before other persons it is only useful as a background and not as a reason to prove the crime. The verdict no. 1025 of Iran's supreme court is among those evidences which show that confession is not considered as the prime reason to affirm an accusation, where there are scientific reasons leading the judge to the truth. Where there is a disagreement between the confession and an expert's vision, only the is valid and the confession is void.

Article 129 of Iran's Criminal procedure code says that:

> "Inspiring questions, or constraining the defendant is forbidden."[18]

Inspiring question is the question which implies a message so that the defendant begins to talk and narrates the event and then reaches in his/her speaking to a point that has no resort but confession. By weakening and influencing on defendant's will, it can not be assured that the obtained confession is absolutely truthful. Usually, the defendant tries to demonstrate that he/she is innocent and to deceive the inspector, while the inspector tries to make the defendant confess. Considering the police power and the defendant's invulnerability, finding the truth will be difficult because of this imbalance of power and the inspiring question. The confession and the information obtained herewith and recorded in the files can mislead the judges.

Professor Enrico Eltavilla cites in his book, Judiciary psychology, that during the occupation of Italy, an American narrated the behavior of American inspectors which were against the emotions of the supreme judges: the prosecuting attorney threatens the defendant to confess, misleads him/her by inspiring questions, disturbs him/her by hostility and irony, abuses and wishes him/her hell agony. I witnessed some inspection processes in the United States and declare that it is the most arbitrary, cruel, and strange trial which could be in any judiciary procedure. I saw an officer shaking the gun used during the crime. This act is complementary to police torture. However, I add that the special methods of torture will encounter with the resistance of the judge who has an informed conscience[19].

Yet, one of these two issues must be chosen: prohibition of torture and of obtaining the reasons by torture and constraint, or imposing torture tools and constraint. The best choice is the first which is affirmed by Iran's Constitution. This point deserves our attention that few can imagine themselves in a usual and ordinary situation as a defendant, and while reading the confession, can think of how it has been obtained. Usually what is ignored is the nature of obtaining the confession.

How correct is the confession obtained by inspection?

Considering that enactment of laws does not necessarily guarantee the repression of torture, It seems that the United Nations should perform constant and efficient supervision on global execution of Human Rights, including prohibition of torture and take essential measures to inform the people world wide.

Some points must be taken into account in order to accept a confession:

(1) Confession to any crime must be immediate and direct by the defendant, not in the form of citation by others, or even by his/her attorney.

(2) Confession and its content must be clear not vague or brief. In some cases a defendant might confess a crime, but seeks excuses such as ignorance, collusion, tricks, and being deceived, all of which led him/her to the crime, or that he/she was forced to commit a crime. In these cases, it deserves that the judge explains the elements of crime to the defendant so that he/she understands fully his/her charges in order to answer clearly, openly, and without ambiguity. But if it is of no use, the judge must consider the defendant's statements as a denial of his/her confession.

(3) If we notice that confession has been obtained by force and without freedom and discretion, then, the confession is void.

(4) The attorney must not dictate the confession to the defendant. In some cases, the attorney inspires the defendant that there is no remedy but confession, because there are evidences against him/her in the hand of judge, therefore, confession can be a sign of good faith. In some cases, even though the defendant has not committed any crime, he/she is encouraged to confess.

(5) Whenever confession is obtained by promising the defendant to extenuate his/her punishment, it will be unacceptable.

Notes and References

1. *Available at http://www.servat.unibe.ch/icl/ir00000_.html#A038_*
2. *Available at http://www.unhchr.ch/udhr/lang/eng.htm*
3. *Available at http://www.unhchr.ch/html/menu3/b/a_ccpr.htm*
4. *Available at http://www.religlaw.org/interdocs/docs/cairohrislam1990.htm*

5. *Available at http://www.unhchr.ch/html/menu3/b/h_comp38.htm*
6. *Available at http://www.unhchr.ch/html/menu3/b/h_cat39.htm*
7. Ardebili Mohammad Ali, "Torture," *Juridical Research Journal of Shahid Beheshti University*, No. 9, 1991, pp. 181-215.
8. *Available at http://www.unhchr.ch/html/menu3/b/k2crc.htm*
9. *Available at http://usmilitary.about.com/library/milinfo/genevacon/blart-99.htm*
10. *Available at http://en.wikisource.org/wiki/Third_Geneva_Convention#Article_99*
11. *Available at http://ushttp://www.africa-union.org/official_documents/Treaties_%20Conventions_%20Protocols/Banjul%20Charter.pdf*
12. *Available at http://www1.umn.edu/humanrts/oasinstr/zoas3con.htm*
13. *Available at http://www.oireachtas.ie/documents/bills28/acts/2003/a2003.pdf and http://www.hri.org/docs/ECHR50.html*
14. Ardebili Mohammad Ali, "Torture," *Juridical Research Journal of Shahid Beheshti University*, No. 9, 1991, pp. 181-215.
15. *Available at http://www.servat.unibe.ch/icl/ir00000_.html#A038_*
16. Zeraat Abas, *Iran's Islamic Penal Code*, Tehran, 2003, p. 423.
16. Zeraat Abas, Mohajeri Ali, *Principals Criminal Procedure*, Tehran, 2003, Vol. 1, p. 309.
17. *Ibid.*, p. 213.
18. Enrico Eltavilla, *Judiciary psychology*, Translated into the Persian by Mehdi Keynia, Majd Pub., Tehran, 1996, vol. 2, p. 131.

Contemporary Changes in Coal Mining Society in West Bengal

SRIBAS GOSWAMI*

Changes are natural. Everything under the sky is changing. Coal mining society comprising of huge heterogeneous work force is also under the process of change. Industrial relation culture in the coal mining industry has undergone havoc change. Right from the pattern of mining with the old industrial relation culture to its modern mining supported by the sophisticated technology having matching workforce is one of the important aspects of change.

The relationship between Employer and employee or trade unions is called Industrial Relation. Harmonious relationship is necessary for both employers and employees to safeguard the interests of the both the parties of the production. In order to maintain good relationship with the employees, the main functions of every organization is to avoid any dispute with them or settle it as early as possible so as to ensure industrial peace and higher productivity. Personnel management is mainly concerned with the human relation in industry because the main theme of personnel management is to get the work done by the human power and it fails in its objectives if good industrial relation is not maintained. In other words good Industrial Relation means industrial peace, which is necessary for better and higher productions and productivity. This study is a comparison between pre independence and post independence era of IR aspects in coalmines.

In 19th century a number of coalmines came in to being where Brtishers played a major role. There after came Bengal Coal Company, Equitable coals company etc the major coal giant in the coal industry. Later on Karam Chand Thapper (KCT), Haridas Mundra, and Karnani Groups etc- the national companies came to play a major role in coal mining industry in West Bengal. Work forces were hired from the then central province. Under ground coal cutting job was hazardous and wages of the miner were negligible. There was no sufficient legislation to protect the interest of coal miners. In such scenario the relation between the work force and mine owners was very much strained – almost like master slave relation.

* *Lecturer in Sociology, Serampore College, Hoogly, W.B.*

Now the Industrial Relation culture has undergone changes. The feudal culture has been substituted by the corporate culture having well-organized HRD wing. The department of Human Resource Development in Coal India has been set up to deal with the development of existing Human Resources also, it is looking ahead with clear perspective to all-round growth of manpower to fulfill demand of production vis-a-vis technology. With the change in the scenario with reference to status of mine, specifically in ECL (mostly cover the territory of West Bengal) the vision of the company, health of organization - profit & loss, criteria for raising productivity, cost parameters and criteria for excellence in performance for survival of the company are being changed. And this way new industrial relation - democratic in nature is developed gradually through bilateral relation between employer and employee.

OBJECTIVES OF STUDY

This study was persuaded with the following objectives:

1. To identify the quality of changes in Industrial relation culture.
2. Relevance of changes in contemporary society in West Bengal.
3. To ascertain the aspects of progressive transformation of IR culture.
4. To know the direction of changes in industrial relation in coal mines.

METHODS OF STUDY

For the present study secondary sources are used for data collection. Content analysis method is also used for this purpose. However to understand the present scenario through participant observation the executives and workers of coalmines were interviewed. For this purpose the samples were selected randomly in several collieries in ECL.

FINDINGS

Various Aspects of Changes in Industrial Relation in Coal Mining Society in West Bengal

Coal is said to be Black Diamond- the terminology aptly given to coal. The coal being the base of many industries contributes a lot towards the GDP of the country. At the time of inception of the industry coal mining was not as easy as it is present day. It was hazardous. Underground coal mining through pits or inclines was fraught with danger of explosion for explosive gas like Carbon Monoxide, Methane. There was danger of inundation, roof falling, air blasting etc. Almost all the underground mining was death trap. Incidence of accidents was kept suppressed at that time. The workforce was hired from outside Bengal as because the local people were not interested for job in the coal mining industry. Before them mining job was hazardous and laborious. They preferred only white colour job. At that time workers from central province came as underground miners. They were gradually called Gorokhpuria loaders - in short GKP loaders. Also miners from Bilashpur known as Bilashpuria loaders– in short BP loaders were hired. Such workers lost their identity and they were recognized through their token number. All such loaders used to come in a group and there was a group captain who used to control these miners. Sometimes these miners used to flee from the mines since the underground job was very difficult. The wages of such miners were very low. There was no sufficient legislation to protect their interest or right of the miners. The relation was just strain between employer and employee like between capitalist and workers in the process of production. Government attitude was to follow laissez-faire policy in this regard. It's a pre independent scenario.

In order to protect the interest of workmen to improve the industrial relation Government had taken certain initiatives. In 1923 The workmen compensation act, in 1926 Trade union act and Payment of wages act 1936 came in to being. But these pieces of legislation were almost kept in the book without any implementation. This scenario of coal mining society before independence will help in understanding the aspect of industrial relation at that time. In such situation the relation between the labour force and the mine owner were very much strained. The work force was illiterate and the owners were totally reluctant to provide the basic amenities like education, health care and good wages. There was no provision of good accommodation, safe drinking water. Surrounding environment was totally unhygienic. Almost unlettered, exploited as if destined to suffer, working mass in one side and wealthy mine owner living on the blood of thousand bereaved in other with antagonistic contradiction was the picture behind the dismal strained industrial aspect.

Only after independence the industrial relation scenario in the coal mining industry had started changing very fast. People got freedom after a prolonged foreign rule. The wave of freedom started penetrating all sphere of society of Bengal. Society in coal industry could not be the exception. A number of legislation namely Industrial disputes act 1947; Minimum wages act 1948, CMPF act, Mines act 1952, etc. came into existence. As if these pieces of legislation would bring about total emancipation of the working masses and that too overnight. Suppressed anguished was now released giving rise to militant trade unionism with its ugly instruments of intimidation, gherao etc to force the management to yield to even its unethical demand. The role of trade unionism stared changing. The industrial relation got changed. Strike could be called at grass root level and on a trivial issue. The workers also resorted to wildcat shrike. So the industrial relation was not up to the mark and in which union took upper hand.

Coal mining industry was nationalized in 1971(cocking coal) and in 1973(non cocking coal) and it was thought of that there would be very good industrial relation good enough to bring remarkable changes in coal mining industry. Public sector industry signed wage agreement one after another thereby ameliorating lot of its workers. The coal mining people were getting very good pay packets matching that of the standard business houses. Coal mining society had changed itself substantially by this time- their skill had developed, now they had multifolded rights. Their trade union was all-powerful having backing of state and central statesman. Now pattern of strike had changed. Gherao etc was the story of past days.

So there has been marked shift in quality of industrial relation from the earlier to later phases. Earlier quality of IR was feudal type- strained where the mine owners were all in all and workers had no right to establish their reasonable demand. After independence the IR got changed where there was almost balance of power between the workforces. But still there was room for improvement in IR. Still true democracy was not established in IR aspect. Only after nationalization of coal mines the system of participatory management gradually emerged as a controller of industrial relation. The problems were sought to be solved by mutual negotiation since the government itself controlled the industry.

The western part of west Bengal had witnessed the industrialization before independence. Durgapur steel plants with other allied industries had history of planned growth. Having large percentage of literacy they maintain a good industrial relation but unlike these industries coal industry as a compact industry practically came into existence only after its nationalization where illiteracy was still a curse. So the pattern of industrial relation was different from the other industries of West Bengal. Coal industry was good paymaster. As such it had influenced the consuming capacity of the masses particularly in Asansol, Durgapur urban area. Still its workers have not been able to rise to occasion like their counterpart in other industries. They failed to play a progressive role in industrial relation culture in their own industry.

Now in IR aspect management is providing training matching with its technology and environment irrespective of cadre. The management is analyzing the project requirement. Personnel in skilled and non-skilled categories are being trained for optimum utilization of capital, technology and HR input. Suitable inputs are being given to all the new entrants to the critical skilled areas and the basic courses, while immediate action have been taken to conduct refresher courses for those who are occupying skilled position.

Thus changes in the production and productivity have taken place with the change in technology and industrial relation. Through basic and technical training programmes industrial relation is gradually improving in coal mining society in West Bengal.

In ECL we can understand the present aspect of IR culture adopted by the employer's side. These are promoting and developing congenial labour management relations. They are enhancing the economic status of the worker by improving wages, benefits and by helping the worker in evolving sound budget and regulating the production by minimizing industrial conflicts through state control. The management has given effort to socialize the industry by providing an opportunity to the workers to have a say in the management and decision-making. The management is also keen to improve upon workers skill with a view to solve their problems through mutual negotiations and consultation thereby maintaining industrial democracy.

In West Bengal employers' organizations are desirous of associating themselves with different government agencies taking into consideration the general, social, public and economic issues affecting employers and workers relations. In West Bengal Eastern Coal Fields Ltd has taken part in developing many rural projects in the surrounding villages such as community development in the form of constructing community well, clubs, hospitals, schools, rural roads and play grounds. The ECL management has extended facilities of electrification in many villages. A good percentage of coal mines workers reside in the surrounding villages of the mines who continuously share their views with the masses of coal mining society. All these happened for very good industrial relation.

CONCLUSION

Undoubtedly the industrial relation index in West Bengal, coal mines in particular has moved towards positive direction from its earlier stage. Through a zigzag path of evolution it has come to its present democratic form which can match itself with other sophisticated industries of West Bengal. Coal mining society can well expect a bright industrial environment in the days which are not far of. Industrial peace will bring about total prosperity which will influence not only the coal mining society but social life of West Bengal as a whole.

References

Akhauri, R.K. (1969), Labour in Coal Industry in India.

Lahiri Dutta Kuntala and Soma Lahiri, The Occupational Structure of Mining Towns of West Bengal, Vol. 16, No.1.

Lahiri Dutta Kuntala (2001), Mining and Urbanization in the Raniganj Coal belt.

Murty, B. S. and S.P. Panda (1988), Indian Coal Industry and Coal Miners.

Prasad, Maheswari (1986), Social Aspects of Mining Towns of the Tribal Region.

Child Labour in Rural Areas–
A Case Study of Carpet Industry in Amritsar

SEOZY BHATIA*

INTRODUCTION

The problem of child labour in the developing world has drawn considerable attention recently. According to child labour (Prohibition and Regulation Act, 1986), "Child is a person who has not completed his fourteenth years of age. Any such person engaged for wages, whether in cash or kind, is a child worker". According to International Labour Organization (ILO), there are 250 million working children in the world in the age group of 5-14 years. (Ashagrie 1998), with most of them being in the developing countries. In absolute numbers, child labour is most prevalent in Asia, which accounts for 60 per cent of all child labour force, with India as one of the main contributors.

In November 1989, the government of India ratified the Convention on the Rights of the Child (CRC) drafted by the United Nations Commission on Human Rights. The convention draws attention to four sets of rights, namely, the right to survival; right to protection; right to participation; and the right to development. The phenomenon of child labour is inimical to all these rights and both the central government and the various state governments have incorporated eradication of this social evil into their respective social welfare agenda. The translation of intent into implementation presumably cannot proceed very far without a prior assessment of the magnitude and causes of the problem; and it is to this rather elementary question that the present paper is addressed.

Further, child labour affects lives of many million of children. They often work in deplorable conditions that exploit them, prevent their education and jeopardize their health and safety. The cost is high, both for the victims who reach adult-hood impaired and for societies which degrade their human resources. According to Weiner (1991), the number of working children in India could be anywhere between 13 to 44 million, depending on how one defines

* *Senior Research Fellow, Punjab School of Economics, Guru Nanak Dev University, Amritsar, Punjab, India, (E-mail: seozy_bhatia_2007@yahoo.co.in)*

child labour and the manner in which data are used. Hence, India is obviously a good case to study the problem of child labour.

Broadly, the objectives of the study are:

1. The extent of child labour in various states in India;
2. Studying the causes of child labour;
3. Working out correlation between child labour, female literacy and work participation across Indian states;
4. Studying the nature and use of child labour in carpet industry in Amritsar and its surrounding villages and policy implications thereof and;
5. Finally examining programs and policies relating to elimination of child labour.

CAUSES OF CHILD LABOUR

Human resources constitute men, woman and children and act as both producers and consumer, who determine the quality of economic development. When children – the vital component of human resources – work as workers, their work interferes with their education, recreation and rest. Thus their capabilities remain unutilized or underutilized. The wastage of this resource further perpetuates the vicious circle of poverty as shown in the following diagram.

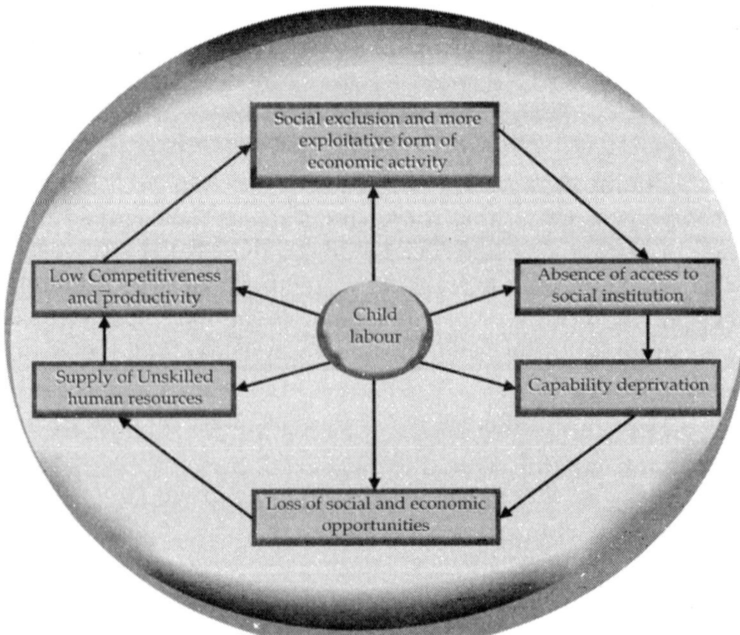

Effects of Child Labour Perpetuation of Vicious Circle of Poverty

A review of the factors resulting in the prevalence of child labour indicates that poverty is the main reason why children work. It is commonly said that poorer the family, the poorer the district, the poorer the country, the higher would be the incidence of child labour. When the people are deprived of threshold facilities like nutrition, sanitation, health and shelter, there is not much of an option left for them between work and non work. Deprivation in this case acts as a propelling push factor. Then this deprivation results in exclusion, it leads to vulnerability, to ignorance and also to physical weakness and lack of property assets. Hence, children living in these deprived families receive the shock effect of this deprivation and society becomes passive towards them.

While poverty is a major factor, there are many other related causes, such as economic instability, migration, discrimination, criminal exploitation, traditional cultural practices, a lack of decent work for adults, inadequate social protection, no strong constitutional provisions, a lack of schools and the desire for consumer goods.

Co-relation between Child labour, literacy, income and work participation across states.

Table 1

State	*Child Labour*	*P.C. Domestic Product*	*Female Literacy*	*W.P.* *All*	*W.P.* *Female*
Andhra Pradesh	17.8	10313	24.8	81.0	72.4
Karnataka	13.9	11910	34.6	74.9	61.3
Himachal Pradesh	13.6	10942	51.5	79.9	72.9
Rajasthan	12.2	8819	15.0	77.6	67.2
Tamil Nadu	10.4	13108	42.8	74.8	64.7
Madhya Pradesh	8.7	7635	22.1	76.5	63.0
Orrisa	7.4	6105	30.5	65.3	45.7
Maharashtra	6.5	15070	39.7	77.7	70.5
West Bengal	5.1	10376	40.7	58.9	28.5
U.P.	5.0	5770	22.9	61.9	34.7
Gujarat	4.1	12975	36.1	73.2	57.9
Bihar	3.7	3399	19.7	56.6	26.9
Punjab	2.7	15390	43.9	58.7	32.4
Assam	2.6	5989	52.1	54.5	23.9
Haryana	2.6	14075	43.9	58.7	32.4
Kerela	0.8	11046	81.7	53.4	32.5

Note: Domestic product in Rs; other columns in %ages
Source: NSS 50th round, 2002

The cases of Andhra Pradesh, Orissa, Madhya Pradesh, Rajasthan and Karnataka show that they have higher incidence of child labour and lower level of per capita state domestic product. On the contrary, Haryana, Punjab, Maharashtra and Gujarat have comparatively lower incidence of child labour associated with higher level of state domestic product.

If we observe correlation between child labour and female literacy then we find that with increase in female literacy, woman become aware of ill effects of child labour and thus there is negative correlation between child labour and female literacy. States having low literacy generally have the most acute child labour problems. It has been often stated that education can bring the dramatic exploitation of child labour to an end.

Table 1 also shows that work participation has strong influence on the prevalence of child labour. In general, one observes a positive correlation between the two indicators. The two outliers are Maharashtra and Gujarat. The states with the low female work participation are also states with low level of child labour.

CASE STUDY

A specific case may help to illustrate the general state of affairs. The study is primarily based on a detailed study of 30 child carpet weavers in Amritsar and in its two surrounding villages - Chhadi and Rajasansi. The data was obtained by the investigating using a structured questionnaire. Our survey revealed that 67 per cent of the sampled child workers were below the age of 12 years. The minimum age at which they joined the labour force was 8 years. They worked from 7:00am to 7:30pm in the summer and from 9:00am to 5:00pm in the winter, in each case with an hour for lunch. They took from one to six months to learn the craft and were paid from Rs. 5 to Rs. 15 per day. Majority of them joined the labour force due to their families facing financial problems. Further, child workers spend their wages either for meeting family expenditure, paying off debt and for self consumption. Majority of them had never been to school. Inspite of their liking for studies, they have to leave it due to their poor economic background, marriage, illness etc. and started working on looms at a very tender age. Further high percentage of them belong to lower caste and were found residing in Kuchha houses.

The conditions of loom-sheds were fairly squalled. Weavers sat cross - legged in front of the work, without moving for many hours. As a result, children complained of swelling of lower limbs and severe pain in joints. They also come into contact with woolen fluff causing skin troubles, scabies and respiratory ailments. Poor light is an additional problem which they face, which impacted the eye - sight of children. Thus, the mere physical conditions in which they have to work were so grim that it virtually constitutes their physical abuse cramped conditions, harsh work, inadequate lightening, long working hours, strain on the eyes and tender hands speak volume. But, employers have no feeling of guilt about employing children but they 'were proud to have discovered a profitable activity'.

POLICY IMPLICATIONS

Certain policy implications followed from the study:

1. As poverty of the family is the main reason for the child labour, all out effort should be made by the government to improve the economic conditions of the poor. Some programmes should be initiated whereby the children of the poor should be selected by the government, semi government and other social organizations for giving them education.
2. Education should not be degree oriented alone rather they should be given some vocational and technical training, thus enabling them to acquire some skill. This will help them to stand at their own in the later life also. This will also prevent the parents to put their wards to work.
3. Poor people should also be made aware of the benefits of small family norms.
4. Inspite of many child labour legislations in carpet industry, child labour exists. There seems to be problem at the level of implementation. Law enforcing machinery should be strengthened so that the law is implemented in true letter and spirit.
5. As problem of child labour is a complex socio economic phenomenon, it calls for a multiplicity of actions both by government and non government social organization including individuals. It is only these all out efforts which can reduce and eliminate the child labour.

Initiatives to Eliminate Child Labour

The eradication of child labour depends on the commitment of government at two imperatives - enforcement of existing legislations, and the creation of meaningful alternatives for the present army of children in the workforce. Besides, it requires a combination of concreted government action and extensive community involvement.

The constitution of India lays down Article 24, 45, 39-C. Thus if these provisions are laid down then they have a potential for a total elimination of child labour and for protection of children from any form of exploitation.

Article 24 prohibits the employment of children below the age of 14 in factories or mines or in other hazardous jobs.

Article 39 C provides protection against exploitation of children and youth.

Article 45 states that primary education must be given to all the children below 14 years of age.

Moreover, we have UN convention on the Rights of Child (CRC) which has prescribed a set of rights for the child that have been loosely categorized by many as survival, protection development and participation rights.

Further, NGO's have following strategies in mind to eliminate this evil:

- Mobilizing and creating awareness
- Providing education
- Providing early childhood care and education (ECCE)
- Facilitating intra household adjustments
- Social labeling
- Advocacy for legal and institutional reforms
- Assuring work and income for parents.

Punjab prospers but the plight of child labour remains pathetic as the state fails to address the issue of compulsory primary education. Ministry of Labour recently issued a notification banning children below 14 years from working in residencies and in hospitality sector. The prohibition was brought into force by adding those areas in list of hazardous occupations, where child labour is prohibited. The ban has been imposed under Child Labour Prohibition and Regulation Act 1986 and was effective from 10 Oct, 2006.

According to official data, around 2051 and 2316 children were working in industrial cities in Ludhiana and Amritsar respectively. In Punjab National child labour projects each at Amritsar, Jalandhar and Ludhiana have been undertaken under National Child Labour Policy. These projects are fully funded by the Govt of India and total cost is approximately Rs. 8 crore. Under these projects children working in hazardous processes are put into informal schools, where they are their provided education upto 5th level.

Further, poverty - alleviation programmes must have strong linkages with education and child labour. The problem is to be addressed with a wider framework of poverty reduction. Hence, until society progresses and enough opportunities arise that allow all children to go to school and live happily, the problem of child labour cannot be eliminated completely.

Thus, the problem can be solved by a movement for consciousness and awakening amongst the people to realize the damage done to their wards due to working. So, children should be allowed to blossom as "what is done to children they will do to society". Let us hope our government and state governments put their efforts towards this direction so that our country can be labeled as 'Child labour - FREE Country' in the world.

CONCLUSIONS

This paper concluded that the socio-economic and working conditions of the child labour were not healthy. They were deprived of the basic facilities of life like education and health. Children were forced to join labour force due to poverty. Child labour has negative effect on the education, mental and physical growth of the children. Thus, it calls for a multiplicity of actions both by government and non-government social organization including individuals, to end up this evil otherwise employers may go to various extremes to exploit young children up to the hilt.

References

Ashagree, K. (1998), Statistics on Working Children and Hazardous Child Labour in Brief, International Labour office, Geneva.

Mustafa and Sharma (1997), Child Labour in India–A Bitter Truth, Deep and Deep Publications, New Delhi.

S. N. Thripathy, Child Labour in India.

Weiner, M. (1991), The Child and the State in India, Oxford University Press, Delhi.

Analysis the Socio- Economic Aspects of Child Labor in the Districts of Upper Sindh Pakistan: A Case Study of Child laboring in Donkey Cart Riding

MUHAMMAD HAROON BAHLKANI*

"There is no trust more sacred than the one the world holds with children. There is no duty more important than ensuring that their rights are respected, that their welfare is protected, that their lives are free from fear and want and that they can grow up in peace."

– Kofi Annan

INTRODUCTION

Child labor is prevalent in Pakistan in all sectors of the economy, though it mostly exists in the informal sector of employment and in the home-based industry. Pakistan is a developing country with per capita income of US$ 480 and 12 per cent of the population lives below an income of US$ 1 per day. Pakistan has introduced legislation to eliminate child labor. Pakistan as a member of the ILO has signed a number of conventions. Even though various conventions and seminars have been held in the country, the problem still exists.

The major sectors absorbing child labor in the country are manufacturing, transport, trade, agriculture, construction, donkey cart riding (most of the rural districts of Pakistan) and services. Child labour in the manufacturing sector (small scale and informal sector) is found in the sports industry, surgical goods industry, cottage industry, chemical industry, power looms, footwear industry, fisheries, carpet weaving, engineering and iron shops, furniture and fixtures. In the construction sector child labour is engaged in stone quarrying, building and road construction, steel shops, and the brick kiln industry. In the transport sector, child labor is found in auto workshops, service stations, and in garages as helpers, porters, loaders, and cleaners,. In the trade sector, it is found as shop assistants and street vendors. The agriculture sector absorbs child labor in fisheries, forestry, dairy and poultry farming, and agricultural labor. In the services sector child labor is found as domestic servants, cobblers watch makers,

* District Officer SW, Community Development Department, (E-mail: bahlkani72649@yahoo.com)

electricians, mechanics, painters, tin packers, paper pickers, and trash pickers. It is found in hotels and restaurants as service boys, in laundry shops, barber shops, tailoring and embroidery shops as well.

Pakistan is essentially an agrarian economy, with most people depending on some form of agricultural activity for their livelihood. Within this context, it is common to find children playing an important economic role within the family. In the rural areas, agriculture is the main occupation, absorbing more than three-quarters of child labour. In urban areas, about three-fifths of child labour is engaged in production activities. Moreover, the rural and urban areas have different socio-economic conditions, so the determinants of child labor vary to some extent.

In Pakistan children aged 5-14 are above 40 million. During the last year, the Federal Bureau of Statistics released the results of its survey funded by ILO's IPEC (International Program on the Elimination of Child Labor). The findings were that 3.8 million children age group of 5-14 years are working in Pakistan out of total 40 million children in this age group; fifty per cent of these economically active children are in age group of 5 to 9 years. Even out of these 3.8 million economically active children, 2.7 million were claimed to be working in the agriculture sector. Two million and four hundred thousand (73%) of them were said to be boys.

During the year 2008 and 2009 the government of Pakistan carried out a series of consultation of tripartite partners and stakeholders (Labor Department, trade unions, employers and NGOs) in all the four provinces. The objective was to identify the occupations and the categories of work, which may be considered as hazardous under the provisions of ILO Convention 182. As a result of these deliberations, a national consensus list of occupations and categories of work was identified, which is given below:

1. Nature of occupation-category of work.
2. Work in carrying dust sand, stone, cement, bricks.
3. Work with fruit and vegetable markets.
4. Work with live electrical wires over 50V.
5. Work in grain markets.
6. Mixing or application or pesticides insecticide/fumigation.
7. Sandblasting and other work involving exposure to free silica.
8. Work with exposure to ALL toxic, explosive and carcinogenic chemicals.
9. Work with exposure to cement dust (cement industry).
10 Work with exposure to coal dust.
11. Manufacture and sale of fireworks explosives.

12. Work at the sites where Liquid Petroleum Gas (LPG) and Compressed Natural Gas (CNG) are filled in cylinders.
13. Work on glass and metal furnaces.
14. Work in the cloth printing, dyeing and finishing sections.
15. Work inside sewer pipelines, pits, storage tanks.
16. Stonecrushing.
17. Lifting and carrying of heavy weight specially in transport industry (15kg and above).
18. Work between 10 pm to 8 am (Hotel Industry).
19. Carpetwaving.
20. Working to carry heavy loads, people from one place to another place.
21. All scavenging including hospital waste.
22. Tobacco process (including Niswar) and Manufacturing.
23. Deep fishing (commercial fishing/ sea food and fish processing.
24. Sheepcasing.
25. Horse/Donkey Cart Pushing in rural; areas of Pakistan.
26. Surgical instrument manufacturing especially in vendor's workshop.
27. Bangles glass, furnaces.

Now we can easily imagine in the light of above mentioned facts and figures how the nation's future namely children are deprived of pleasures of life, ignorance has reduced their abilities of thinking right or differentiating between right and wrong, as well as their life-chances, to their non-access to education. It is true that child Labor is not an isolated phenomenon.

It is an outcome of a multitude of socio-economic factors and has its roots in poverty, lack of opportunities, high rate of population growth, unemployment, uneven distribution of wealth and resources, outdated social customs and norms and plethora of other factors. According to the United Nations Development Program (UNDP) the daily income of 65.5% people of Pakistan is below 2 U.S. dollars a day. According to the Asian Development Bank (ADB) Report, 47 million people in Pakistan are leading lines below the line of poverty, whereas the Social Policy Development Centre (SDPC) Karachi has stated in one of its reports that the ratio of poverty in Pakistan was 33% during 1999 that increased in 2001 and reached 38%. The ratio of poverty in the current year is around 30%.

The estimates of child labour in Pakistan vary widely. Hussain [1985] estimated 14 million child workers, which makes 40 per cent of the child population of the country. Cochrane *et al* [1990] have calculated 31 per cent child labour force participation for boys and 7 per cent for girls in the age group 10-14 years. Ahmed [1991] referred to the *Economic Survey 1988-89* and put the number of working children around 2.194 million in the age group 10-14 years, of which 2.01 million are actually working and 0.184 million seek work. He stated that the actual figure must be much higher as children less than 10 years of age are not covered by this official estimate. Sathar [1993] has estimated 19 to 25 per cent of male child workers and 22 to 32 per cent of female child workers in the country.

Mahmood *et al* [1994] have estimated the magnitude of child labour in the country in the age groups of 5-9 years and 10-15 years. The children in the age cohort 5-9 years are most vulnerable to child labour, their physical, mental and conceptual development being critically jeopardized. In the age group of 5-9 years, 39 per cent of the total population of children in this age group works. In the age group of 10-15 years, 77 per cent of the population of children works. For the entire age cohort of children 5-14 years, 58 per cent are working. This gives a child labour force of 19 million, of whom 7 million are below the age of 10 years, and another 12 million are between the ages of 10-14 years.

The estimates of child labour vary widely due to lack of systematic data collection and availability of micro-based data only. As most of the research work is based on case studies covering a few villages, a city, a sub-national area, at best a province, state or an equivalent region.

The latest nation-wide survey of child labour was undertaken in 1996, by the Federal Bureau of Statistics in collaboration with the Ministry of Labour, Manpower and Overseas Pakistanis, and International Programme on the Elimination of Child Labour (IPEC) as a component of the International Labour Organization (ILO). The survey was the first of its kind in Pakistan. According to the survey, there are 40 million children in the age group of 5-14 years, which is close to one-third (30 per cent) of the total population of the country. More than 50 per cent of the children are in the age group of 5-9 years. Among them the male children outnumbered female children with a sex ratio of 106 to 100. In both age groups of 5-9 and 11-14 years, again male out-numbered female with a sex ratio of 107 and 105 to 100, respectively. The majority of the children, i.e. 28.7 million (72 per cent) live in rural areas. Rural areas have relatively higher male/female sex ratio than urban areas.

Among the 40 million children aged 5-14 years, 3.3 million, i.e. 8.3 per cent are economically active. According to the survey the volume of child labor is about 3.3 million of which 2.4 million (73 per cent) are boys and 0.9 million (27 per cent) are girls. The quantum of child labour increases with age, i.e. the older the child, the higher is the rate of labour force participation. The volume of male child labour is about 2.1 million in the age group of 10-14 years which is about seven times greater than the level of 0.3 million in the age group of 5-9 years. Similarly the volume of female child labour in the age group of 10-14 years (0.6 million) is about three times greater than in the age group of 5-9 years (0.2 million). It is also noted that male child labourers outnumbered female child labourers in both rural and urban areas. The ratio of rural areas in child labour is about eight times higher than that of urban areas. This may be due to unpaid farm activities performed by family members in the rural areas.

The provincial distribution indicates that the volume of child labour in the Punjab is about 1.9 million, which is about three-fifths (60 per cent) of the total child labor in the country. Next stands NWFP, which has about 1 million child laborers, and then Sindh with 298.30 hundred child laborers. The lowest figure of 13.72 hundred is for Balochistan, where less number of households has reported child labor.

NATIONAL LAWS PERTAINING TO CHILD LABOUR

The Constitution of Islamic Republic of Pakistan states: "No child below the age of fourteen shall be engaged in any factory or mine or in any other hazardous employment." Also, "All forms of forced labour and traffic in human beings is prohibited." A number of laws contain provisions prohibiting child labour or regulating the working conditions of child and adolescent workers. The most important laws are:

- The Factories Act 1934.
- The West Pakistan Shops and Establishments Ordinance 1969.
- The Employment of Children Act 1991.
- The Bonded Labour System Abolition Act 1992.
- The Punjab Compulsory Education Act 1994

Child Labor Legislation in Pakistan

Although the UN Convention deals with all the aspects of children's rights, there are six provisions, which apply directly to working children. These include the right to be protected from economic exploitation (Article 32), the right to be protected from abuse (Article 19), right to access to primary education, the right to be protected from all forms of harm, neglect and sexual abuse (Article 34), and the right t Collectively, these provisions try to protect children from adversity that accompanies child labor by shielding them from risks and abuses they encounter daily due to their vulnerability and unequal bargaining power. Despite Pakistan's ratification of the Convention, none of the above is observed in the case of child workers in auto workshops as is evident from the results.

After signing the 1990 International Convention on the Rights of the Child, the Government of Pakistan repealed the obsolete Employment of Children Act 1938 and enacted a new law called the Employment of Children Act 1991.o be protected from all forms of exploitation (Article 36).

Part 1 of the Act defines children as persons below the age of 14, which is at variance with the convention that regards all persons below 18 as children.

Part 2 of the 1991 Act prohibits the employment of children in any occupation and process related to transport or ancillary operations, manufacturing of matches, crackers and fire works, making carpets, cement, cloth dyeing and weaving, mica, soap, wool cleaning, building and construction, slate and pencil (making and packing), agate products and toxic substances such as pesticides, chromium, benzene, asbestos, etc. However, the catch is that the above prohibition exempts cases where any of these hazardous occupations are carried on by a person with the help of his family members.

Part 3 of the Act permits child employment in occupations other than those mentioned above and attempts to regulate the conditions of work of children. Thus they are prohibited from working between 7 p.m. and 8 a.m. The maximum working hours permitted is seven with a break of at least one-hour after three hours of continuous work. No overtime is allowed, nor is a child allowed to take up two jobs simultaneously. A working child is entitled to at least one weekly holiday. All establishments employing children are required by this law to notify the government about the nature of work and working conditions. These establishments are expected to conform to health and safety standards prescribed by the government and to ensure clean and hazardous free working conditions for children.

Part 4 of the 1991 Act prescribes for breach of any provision of the act by employers. These include imprisonment for a period extending to one year and a fine of up to twenty thousand rupees. While these penalties are more severe than those provided under the earlier child labor legislation, they are mild when we consider the impact on the health, safety and psyche of the child when the provisions are violated. Moreover, they are not enforceable against family members and unregistered establishments.

Manufacturing units employing less than 10 persons on a regular basis do not fall within the definition of factories and are not regulated by the factories act. Thus, the Employment Act of 1991 may at best help reduce the number of children employed in hazardous occupations in the formal sector where the overwhelming proportion of working children is actually employed.

There is substantial child labor legislation in Pakistan, including the Employment of Children Act 1991 which established a minimum age and conditions of work in some occupations and bans child labor altogether in others. However, on the one hand these various laws and Acts have largely been ignored, and on the other many are so vague that they have left wide open room for legally perpetrated abuses.

The legislation for the protection of children lacks adequacy. The constitution prohibits the employment of children under the age of 14 in factories, and hazardous employment. There has so far not been a single court ruling interpreting the word "hazardous" under this article. Moreover, labour laws do not include labor in the agricultural sector and informal sector, where the majority of child labor is employed.

The penalty for employing children or for violating the regulatory provisions of the law is mild. The Workman's Compensation Act 1923 provided for Rs. 15,000 in case of death or injury to an adult labourer. For children the compensation is Rs. 4,000. Persons pledging children for work are fined Rs.50, those who accept a pledged child are fined Rs. 200.

Determinants of Child Labor

Several formal models [Levy (1985), Rivera-Batiz (1985) and Sharif (1994)] of the household economy take into account the economic contribution of children to household income to explain the decision of supply of child labor by parents.

Although the data on the remuneration of child workers is scarce and investigations on child labor supply have found mixed evidence, the general conclusion seems to be the same that the children are paid less than adults, even when they perform the same task [Bequele and Boyden 1988; Jomo 1992]. The effect of lower earnings on child labour depends on the wage elasticity of child labour supply, and here too the evidence is mixed. Some studies find that employers have no difficulties recruiting children even at very low wages, while others find elasticity's in the range of 0.8 to 1.0, although elasticity seem to be lower for older children [Levy 1985; Rosenzweig 1981]. Still low wages of children is a cause of demand for children as workers.

Many researchers have focused on the determinants of schooling attendance to analyze the reasons for child labor, even recognizing that school attendance is not the "inverse" of child labour. Children who are not enrolled in school are not necessarily involved in child labour activities, while many children who are enrolled in school also work, either in household enterprises or after school hours. In some cases schooling problems contribute to child labour. The inaccessibility of schools or their poor quality often spurs parents to engage their children in work. And many children may have to work in order to afford the direct costs associated with school attendance, such as fees and school books. Cost of schooling enhances the supply of child labour [Abdalla 1988].

Schooling facilities negatively affect the supply of child labour. Schooling facility is a function of the cost of schooling, government expenditures on education, private schooling system, the quality of education, and job orientation of education and the distance of school from home.

Keywords

Donkey cart riding, child labor, bonded labor.

METHODOLOGY AND SURVEY

Objectives

The study is carried out to ascertain:

1. Socio-economic background of child labour and the parents/ employers in donkey cart riding industry.
2. The reasons why these children work and the reasons for leaving school
3. The element and the extent of exploitation, i.e. working hours, midday break, physical punishment, amount of payment, and mode of payment, etc.
4. The utilization of children's income as contribution towards family income
5. The extent of awareness concerning children's rights amongst the children and their employers
6. Recommendations for effective solutions of the issue

Data Collection

A comprehensive interview schedule was developed. It comprised various dimensions of the issue involved in the problem of child workers in donkey cart riding in many districts of upper sindh. To take an in-depth understanding of various issues and to investigate the unexpected aspects of the problem, the technique of Focus Group was involved.

Child's Perspective

A structured interview schedule was developed. It had questions pertaining to various dimensions of the issue of child labour in donkey cart pushing , such as demographic information, school history, reasons for leaving school, previous work history, duration of present job, reasons for working and economic aspects, psychological environment, and working conditions, etc.

Parents/ Employer's Perspective

The structured interview also included a part to investigate the perspective of employers of the children or the owners of the donkey carts. The employers were asked the reason for employing children, wage structure and pattern, the benefits provided to the child in addition to wages, leisure, etc. The survey was conducted in 6 districts of upper sindh of Pakistan. kashmore, Jacobabad, shikarpur, sukkuir, kamber ,larkana . The districts surveyed were of rural areas and the sample was selected randomly.

The children were classified into three categories according to their age group, i.e. less than 8 years, 9 to 11 years, and 12 to 14 years.

The data was selected through interviewing the children individually through the structured interview schedule. Preferably the employer was not allowed to be present while interviewing the child. Similarly, by interviewing the owner of the donkey cart the information was collected. The response rate was more than ninety per cent.

RESULTS AND DISCUSSION

An analysis of child labor in donkey cart pushing industry reveals that:

- Child labour in donkey cart riding is 30 per cent i.e. a relatively higher incidence of child labour in this category.
- There is extensive violation of the Convention on the Rights of the Child and Employment of Children Act 1991.
- Child labor also exists in authorized workshops, i.e. either the companies and corporations do not have their code of conduct regarding child labour or do not obey it.

The detailed results are shown in the tables. The age groups of the sample are shown in Table 1. The average statistics of the child laborers are discussed in Table 2. The working conditions are discussed in Table 3. Table 4 and 5 gives information about the perspective of the father/head of household of working children. Household size of the child laborers is shown in Table 6. The reasons for leaving school and starting work is shown in Table 7.

Table 1
Child Labor in Age Groups

Age Group (Years)	*No of Children (Percentage)*
-8	12.5
9-11	37.5
12-14	50.0

It is evident from the above table that child labor participation in auto-workshops increases with increase in age.

Table 2
Average Statistics of the Children

Age	*11 Years 01 Month 13 Days*
Income	Rs. 32.88 per week
Daily Working Hours	11.45 Hours
Duration of Midday Break	27.17 Minutes
Working Experience of Children	2 Years 01 Month 04 Days
Time to Complete the Training	1 Year 11 Months 19 Days
Distance of Work place From Home	3.5 K.m
Completed Years of Schooling	3.9 Years

It was found that the wages were paid weekly and no child have taken an advance as against many other forms of child labor, like child labor in carpet weaving, in brick kilns and in agriculture. It shows:

- There is no bonded child labor in donkey cart riding
- Under market forces employers do not give advance due to abundance of supply of children as compared to demand
- The parents or children do not take advance due to the perception that the job is apprenticeship type, moreover they consider skill acquirement is better than education from the point of view of employment, as formal education does not guarantee a job.

All the above factors keep the wages of children low.

The number of hours that children work is critically important. Fatigue is a major cause of accidents and can impair intellectual development.

Average years of child's experience estimated in the present study are two years. According to the parents, it needs approximately one more year on average to complete the training. This means the total duration of training is three years. Such a long period of training with a long working day for a skill suggests a number of possibilities that may be

- The trainee is dull, not interested in the skill, unable to learn properly or the learning is very difficult.
- The skill master is not interested in their learning, unable to teach, intentionally delays the period.
- The major part of the job is work, not learning.

Most of the child workers come from far distances, as the average distance from home to work place is 3.5 kilometers. The average completed numbers of years of schooling by working children indicates that the majority of the children have not completed the primary level of education.

Table 3
Percentage Statistics of Children

(Children)	*(Percentage)*
Beaten up by the parents/Employer	95.65
Live in the Work place	7.5
Occasionally Live in the Work places	4.5
Enrolled in Formal Education	Nil
Fathers/parents are employers	94.16

The factors which contribute to make work hazardous are the age of the child, the hours and conditions of work, and the physical and psychological strain of the activity. A large majority of child workers (95.65 per cent) accepted that the parents/employers beat them up.

The data reveals that 7.5 per cent of the child workers do not go back to their home everyday and sleep in the workplace, while 4.5 per cent of children have to live in work places occasionally due to workload. They are provided only a little place to sleep; none of the children is enrolled in formal education. This means that child labour in donkey cart riding have such difficulties that to combine education with work is not possible. A number of likely reasons are:

- Children have no time to attend lessons due to long working hours.
- Non-availability of teachers and informal education.
- Fatigue does not make it possible for the children to think about education.

Table 4
Occupation of Father

Type of Occupation	*Percentage*
Landless Farmers	90
Employers	2
Wage Earners	3
Self-employed Non-agriculture	2
Farmer with Land ownership	3
Government Employee	Nil
Total	100.00

The highest number of children, that is 90 per cent, comes from households where fathers/head of the households are engaged in farming having no any land. It may be inferred that the job is not secured or the source of income is not secured. So the households supply their children as laborers. Second highest proportion (3) comes from the farmers with land ownership. This is not surprising because all these households have a small piece of land, as they have the capital, so their source of income should be secured. But the small holding of land is insufficient to support the family so the children are supplied as laborers. Moreover, the seasonal conditions in the income of the farmers support the option of child labour. These conditions lead to the decision of the head of the households to engage their children in skill acquiring as against engaging them in agriculture. The fluctuation in income enhances the supply of child labour, the point is supported by the evidence that child labor supply is nil from the households having head of the household as government employee.

As concerns the land-less farmers, they should supply child labour more as compared to the farmers with land ownership, due to the fact that households with no capital are relatively more vulnerable and poor. In fact, these farmers may have more desire to engage their children in such type of work but their landlords do not spare the children. The landlords keep them engaged in unpaid activities.

Table 5
Education of Fathers

Years of Education	*Percentage*
Nil (Illiterate)	90
1-5	5
5-8	2
9-10	2
11-12	1
13-14	Nil
Total	100.00

The highest proportion of child labour (90 per cent) comes from illiterate families. In the present study the average completed years of education of fathers is illiterate.

Table 6
Households (Who Supply Child Labour) with Children

No of Children	*Household (Percentage)*
1	0.00
2	4.16
3	0.00
4	5.10
5	12.50
6	16.66
7	20.83
8	12.50
9	4.16
10	4.16

The results in the table show another reason to leave school and put the child to work that is larger families. The size of the family was mostly large in the survey. It is found that 20.83 per cent of the working children come from families having 7 offspring. Similarly 16.66 and 12.5 per cent come from households with 6 and 5 children respectively. The more the children, the more the parents are unable to provide them better options that are why they choose to work. The study gives the clue that the families with large number of children cannot afford schooling expenditures of all the children so some children work to support themselves and school going children of the household. It is also calculated in the present study that the average number of children per household (who supply child labour) is 5.95. Lloyd [1994] described that the larger household size increases the probability of child labour. It may be concluded that inadequacy of a family planning programme can also be attributed to the existence of child labour.

Table 7
Reasons for Leaving School

Reasons	*Children (Percentage)*
Lack of Resources	90
Lack of Interest in Education	5
Beaten up by the Teacher	3
Parent's Preference for Work	2
Total	100

Since schooling is the main factor demanding time, it stands to reason that the cost of schooling would be an important determinant of the likelihood of child work [Siddiqi and Patrinos 1995].

Siddiqi and Patrinos [1995] view schooling as the most important means of drawing children away from child labour. The type and amount of work a child performs can directly affect school performance. The more vigorous and time consuming the work, the more likely that the child will score poorly on tests, miss school, and repeat grades. The children who work continuously from a very young age are also more likely to drop out of school after having completed only a minimum level of education.

Harsh attitude of teachers, high schooling cost and lack of interest in education propels dropouts and so the supplies of child labour [Chand 1983]. Children are forced to work due to lack of education facilities [Ahmed 1991]. Lack of schooling facilities propels child labour [Bonnet 1993]. Children work because of non-availability of schools compounded by the poor quality of education [Bequele and Boyden 1988]. The extreme poverty of households contributes to low school enrolment rates. The parents commented that since schooling did not guarantee better jobs for their children, it is better to send them to work [Salazar 1988].

In the survey, children who had left school were asked to highlight the reason for leaving school. Most of them replied that it was due to lack of resources. The second reason given was the lack of interest in education. Some children revealed the reason for leaving the school as being beaten up by the teacher. The above two reasons reveal that at least their parents had attempted to educate them but did not succeed.

There are 2 per cent children who work because their parents removed them from school and preferred work, which indicates the helplessness of these children. They are expected to accept the double authority of fathers, as a parent as well as the master employer.

CONCLUSION

Child labor engaged in donkey cart riding is considered to be source of earning for poor families so the wages are comparatively lower than other types of child labour. The finding matches the results of other studies.

Growing children are eager to learn about the world, about its dynamics and its wonders, its customs and its rules. They absorb information with miraculous ease, as if knowledge itself were fuelling their development, learning from the world around them, from school, from play, from parents, from teachers, from other children and sometimes also from work. What kind of learning, however, is a child to imbibe from work in donkey cart with long daily working hours with a short midday break, beaten up by the parents or employer, and sleeping in work places in isolation from the family? The situation violates most of the rights in the Convention on the Rights of the Child and basic humanity.

The general observation indicates the poor health of the children, bad, smoky, dusty and dirty surroundings of the work places.

It has also been found that the income of these children is not fully utilized in the household expenditures; only 45 per cent of them give their salary to their mothers or fathers. They only partly contribute to their families.

The majority of the children left school due to poverty, lack of interest in education and harsh attitudes of the teachers.

The lower value of Standard Deviation of wages of children shows that the employers have fixed the wages collectively so the market forces work for the uniformity of wages in donkey cart pushing industry.

None of the children believe that schooling is good. This indicates that the working children are unaware of their exploitation and work seemed to them an opportunity to earn for livelihood.

In the conclusion end, I will repeat the great words of *Scottish Singer-Song writer* Donovan Leitch:

Some of us believe in communism,
some of us believe in capitalism,
some of us believe in spiritualism,
some of us believe in materialism
some mothers believe in heavy dandy,
some fathers believe in understanding.
Some of us believe in total freedom,
some of us believe in laying the rules on.
But the children believe in friends,
For the children of the world,
Every boy and girl,
All they'll know is what we teach 'em,
Most of us fail when we try to reach 'em
For the children believe in having friends

– **Donovan**

RECOMMENDATIONS

Finding out about child labor to determine the exact magnitude, nature and effects, a thorough qualitative analysis of the specific groups of child labor and their working and living conditions also needs to be done. Training on design management and evaluation of child labor projects and programmes are proposed.

Child labor schools should be established for donkey cart pusher kids to enroll their children and monthly compensation including free dress and free text books should be provided by government as well as NGO sector to reduce the child laboring in rural areas. This will also motivate the parents that by getting monthly compensation. Scholarship, they will enroll their school aged kids in schools instead of donkey cart riding.

Promoting the welfare and development of the children, protecting the working child and providing health and social welfare services are proposed. Moreover, withdrawing, rehabilitating, offering alternatives and/or compensating child laborers are also required.

The study proposes the elimination of the economic, social and physical exploitation of child laborers. It stresses on the provision of protection from performing work that hampers their physical and mental development. Advocating effective laws and their enforcement and assisting in identification of contraventions of the law, to control factors that generate the demand for child labour as well as that generate the flow of children into the workforce is required.

Education should be in easy access to the poor and financial support in the shape of less expensive education should be provided. Physical punishment of all sorts should be strictly prohibited in educational institutions and the offender be given appropriate penal punishment. The rights of the child should be made a part of the teacher's training curriculum and also be given exposure in school curriculum. Motivation of school teachers should be improved through improvement in salaries, working conditions, housing, etc. and arrangements for training and supervision of their work.

The schools should develop strategies with which the illiterate parents should not feel left out. A more encouraging and supportive attitude towards the children, whose parents are not educated is proposed. Parents with children between 5 to 7 should be given special encouragement to send their children to schools.

NGOs working for the rights of children should concentrate on this segment of neglected children. They should design campaigns to make the public, policy makers and parents aware of the serious repercussions on a child's future once exposed to physical, sexual or economic abuse.

Employer's organizations can play an important role by helping business and industries using child labor to improve their efficiency and competitiveness through production and personnel practices that increase incentives for adult workers and decrease reliance on children. Firms need to establish their own codes of conduct that prohibit the direct and indirect employment of children.

Civic sense should be created for parents through workshops and seminars. Due to donkey cart riding by school aged kids create lot of traffic problems, and major accidents in which innocent labor children are killed. Therefore it is also recommended to start traffic safety classes for children, their paretnts and common citizen should be initiated at government level.

Awareness seminars, workshops, walks should be initiated by NGOs and philanthropists.

References

Abdalla, Ahmed (1988), "Child Labour in Egypt: Leather Tanning in Cairo", in Bequele and Boyden (ed) Combating Child Labour. ILO, Geneva.

Ahmed, Manzooruddin (1991), "Child Labour - A Time to Reflect" UNICEF, Pakistan and Govt. of Balochistan, Pakistan.

Ali, Karamat and Abdul Hamid (1999), "Major Determinants of Female Child Labour in Urban Multan (Punjab-Pakistan)", Department of Economics, Bahauddin Zakariya University, Multan. Processed.

Awan, Saeed A. and Abid Ali Khan (1992), "Child Labour in Carpet Weaving Industry in Punjab", UNICEF, Punjab in collaboration with Center for the Improvement of Working Conditions and Environment, Lahore.

Bequele, A. and J. Boyden (eds) (1998), "Combating Child Labour" ILO, Geneva.

Bonnet, Michel (1993), "Child Labour in Africa", *International Labour Review,* (Geneva) 132(3):371-389.

Chand, Raja (1983), " An Explanatory Study of Fifty Children Working in Auto Workshops", Department of Social Work, University of the Punjab, Lahore.

Chaudhry, M. A. K. (1998), "Child Labour–Facts And Fiction", *Lahore Journal of Economics* (Lahore) 2(2).

Cochrane, S., V. Kozel and H. Alderman (1990), "Household Consequences of High Fertility in Pakistan", *World Bank Discussion Paper # 111*. The World Bank, Washington, D.C.

Grootaert, Christiaan (1998), "Child Labour in Cote d' Ivoire: Incidence and Determinants", *Policy Research Working Paper # 1905*. The World Bank, Washington, D.C.

Hafeez, Sabeeha (1979), "Some Aspects of Child Labour in Pakistan", Department of Sociology, University of Karachi, Karachi.

Hafeez, Sabeeha (1991), "The Changing Pakistan Society", Royal Book Company, Karachi.

Hamid, Shahnaz (1994), " A Micro Analysis of Urban Child Labour: Some Determinants of Labour and Its Conditions", *The Pakistan Development Review,* (Islamabad) 33 (4). Part II Winter.

Hussain, Akmal (1985), "Child Labour in Lahore", A Survey Sponsored by Sayyed Engineers, Lahore.

Hussain, Akmal (1998), "Child Workers in Hazardous Industries in Pakistan", *The Lahore Journal of Economics,* (Lahore) 2(2).

Jahangir, Asma (1989), "Children in Pakistan - The Defacto Situation" in Child Abuse in Pakistan, Report of the Seminar organised by Pakistan Paediatric Association NWFP (Peshawer) with the collaboration of UNICEF.

Jomo K. S. (ed), (1992), *Child Labour in Malaysia,* Varlin Press, Kuala Lumpur.

Khan, Shaheen (1982), "Compelled Child Labour in Punjab: A Case Study", Punjab Economic Research Institute, Lahore.

Khan, Shaheen (1982), "Labour Force Participation of Children: A Case Study", *Pakistan Social and Economic Review,* Summer.

Levy, Victor (1985), "Cropping Pattern, Mechanization, Child Labour and Fertility Behavior in A Farming Economy: Rural Egypt", *Economic Development and Cultural Change,* 33.

Lloyd, Cynthia B. (ed,), (1994), "Investing in the Next Generation: The Implication of High Fertility at the Level of the Family", *Research Division Working Paper # 63.* New York Population Council, New York.

Moazam, Mahmood (1994), "Why Do Children not Go to School in Pakistan–Some Estimates and A Theoretical Framework", *The Pakistan Development Review,* (Islamabad) 33 (4):581-592. Part II. Winter.

——NCCR and UNICEF, 1998, "Enforcement of Employment of Children Act 1991 in North West Frontier Province", Pakistan. National Coalition on Child Rights (NCCR) and UNICEF, Peshawer.

Rivera-Batiz, F. L. (1985), "Child Labour Patterns and Legislation in Relation to Fertility", Mimeo: Department of Economics, Indiana University, Bloomington.

Rosenzweig, Mark R. (1977), "The Demand for Children in Farmhouses", *Journal of Political Economy.*

Salazar, Maria Cristina (1988), "Child Labour in Colombia: Bogota's Quarries and Brickyards", in Bequele and Boyden (ed.) Combating Child Labour. ILO, Geneva.

Sathar, Zeba A. (1993), "Micro-consequences of High Fertility: The Case of Child Schooling in Rural Pakistan", in Cynthia B. Lloyd (ed) Fertility, Family Size and Structure: Consequences for Families and Children. Proceedings of Population Council Seminar, New York 9-10 June, 1992. New York Population Council, New York.

Sharif, Muhammad (1994), "Child Participation, Nature of Work and Fertility Demand: A Theoretical Analysis", *Indian Economic Journal,* 40 (4).

Euthanasia and Its Legality and Legitimacy from Indian and International Human Right Instruments Perspectives

TUSHAR KUMAR BISWAS* & ARNAB SENGUPTA*

INTRODUCTION

I am the master of my fate; I am the captain of my soul

William Ernest Henley

Euthanasia is a Greek word which literally means 'an easeful death'. It describes the practice of bringing about death in a manner that causes the least amount of suffering to the patient. The concept of euthanasia has been a matter of significant controversy over the recent past both in India as well as in other parts of the globe. Let us take some hypothetical situations in order to understand the complex issues surrounding to euthanasia. A woman say 'X' who has been suffering brain damage and became dependent on a feeding tube and there is no living will on her part. Her husband is praying before the Court to discontinue tube feedings but on the contrary her natal family wants to continue with the life support what type of decision would one expect from the courts in India? Let us take another fact situation 'P' was born prematurely and suffered brain damage. Although, he was not dying, he often needed ventilation. The likelihood was that he would be blind and deaf and unable to speak. The question arises as to what should be done if in future ventilation is needed?

Then again coming back to the problems of developing countries like India where there may be the cases of shortage of bare necessities of life such as adequate nutrition, clothing and shelter over the head and facilities for reading, writing and expressing oneself in diverse forms and life is solely dependent on the mercy of other in many cases. Keeping such situation in the background,

* *Senior Associate member of "Society for Security Laws & Financial Markets", at the West Bengal National University of Juridical Sciences, Kolkata.*

now the question is if any person is suffering from intolerable pain of incurable diseases and the person does not have sufficient means to continue his treatment whether in such cases euthanasia should be allowed? What will be the implications if in such cases euthanasia is allowed? Most importantly from the legal point of view the question which arises whether the right to life includes right to die under the constitution of India as well as under the international human rights instruments?

The constitution of India also provides about the right to life and it unequivocally provided that no person shall be deprived of his life or personal liberty except according to procedure established by law[1]. What is the meaning of right to life and whether it includes right to die will be discussed in the subsequent chapter.

For the purpose of the present paper, the concept of euthanasia can be interpreted under the following heads:

(i) *Voluntary Euthanasia:* People concerned to legalize the termination of life on medical grounds have always concentrated on Voluntary Euthanasia (This implies that the patient specifically requests that his life be ended.) It is generally agreed that the request must come from someone who is either; (a) in intolerable pain or (b) who is suffering from an illness which is agreed as being terminal. It may be prior to the development of the illness in question or during its course. In either case it must not result from any pressure from relatives or those who have the patients in their care.[2] Both active and passive euthanasia can be termed as forms of voluntary euthanasia.

(ii) *Non-Voluntary Euthanasia:* Seen by some as sub-variety of voluntary euthanasia. This involves the death, ostensibly for his own good, of someone who cannot express any views on the matter and who must therefore use some sort of proxy request that his/her life be ended. As Glover points out, this form of Euthanasia is that which most intimately concerns the medical profession. Selective non-treatment of the new-born or "the doctor may be presented with demented and otherwise senilely incompetent patients. In practice, non-voluntary euthanasia presents only as an arguable alternative to non treatment."[3]

(iii) *Involuntary Euthanasia:* It involves ending the patient's life in the absence of either a personal or proxy invitation to do so. The motive 'The relief of suffering' may be the same as voluntary euthanasia-but its only justification – "a paternalistic decision as to what is best for the victim of the disease." In extreme cases it could be against the patient's wishes or could be just for social convenience. It is examples of the latter which serve as warnings as to those who would invest the medical professional with more or unfettered powers over life and death.[4]

There is also the distinguishment between active and passive euthanasia. In active euthansia there is a positive act which is intended to kill while in passive euthansia there is an omission to an act, equally intentionally, allowing the patient's death to occur.[5] This distinction may at times be a very superficial one. It may be difficult to conclusively say whether a conduct is to be regarded as an act or omission. For example, the doctor knows that if the life support system is not made available to a patient, he will not survive. But in order to do so he must switch off the ventilator. For a layman the conduct of switching off the ventilator would be an act, but court held it to be an omission.[6]

It is to be noted that active euthanasia is not expressly permitted in any part of the world. Active euthanasia, which is a deliberate act to end the life of the patient, is prohibited in almost everywhere. The distinction appears to be grounded in a belief that to kill someone is more morally blameworthy than simply to allow her to die. This position has ancient religious and philosophical roots[7].

For the purpose of the present paper, emphasis will mainly be given to the concept of voluntary euthanasia and its legal implications from Indian context and under various international human right instruments. The permissibility of euthanasia under Indian and international human rights instruments will be also discussed subsequently.

UNDERSTANDING EUTHANASIA FROM THE INDIAN LEGAL PERSPECTIVES

Indian position regarding euthanasia is somewhat complex and complicated in many respects. The constitution of India simply says that no person shall be deprived of his life or personal liberty except according to procedure established by law. Two important questions require immediate consideration for the purpose of the present paper i.e. what is the meaning of life? And whether right to life includes right to die under the constitution of India? A Constitution Bench of Supreme Court in *Kharak Singh v. State of UP*[8] held that right to life means something more than 'mere animal existence'. It was held that the word 'life' in Article 21 means right to live with human dignity and the same not merely connote continued drudgery. It takes within its fold "some of the finer graces of human civilization, which makes life worth living" and that the expanded concept of life would mean the "tradition, culture and heritage" of the concerned person.

In *State of Himachal Pradesh v. Umed Ram*[9], it was observed that the right to life embraces not only physical existence but the quality of life as understood in its richness and fullness by the ambit of the Constitution; and for residents of hilly areas access to road held to be access to life itself, and so necessity of road communication in the reasonable condition was held to be a part of constitutional imperatives, because of which the direction given by the

Himachal Pradesh High Court to build road in the hilly areas to enable its residents to earn livelihood was upheld.

Subsequently in the case of *CESC Ltd. v. Subhash Chandra*[10] it has been opined by a minority Judge (J. Ramaswamy) that physical and mental health have to be treated as integral part of right to life, because without goods health the civil and political rights assured by our Constitution cannot be enjoyed.

Therefore, the analysis in the context of Indian constitution shows that the term 'life' has a very wide connotation and it does not merely confined to merely animal existence which it inter alia includes the right to live with human dignity, physical and mental health etc.

Now let us shift to the next legal question i.e. whether right to life includes right to die in India? The rationale behind the question is if it is proved that right to life includes right to die, then there would little or no impediments for holding at least voluntary euthanasia legal.

In *RC Cooper v. Union of India*[11], it was held that what is true of one fundamental right is also true of another fundamental right. It was then stated that it is not, and cannot be, seriously disputed that fundamental rights have their positive as well as negative aspect. For example, freedom of speech and expression includes freedom not to speak. Similarly, the freedom of association and movement includes freedom not to join any association or move anywhere. So too, freedom of business includes freedom not to do business. Whether, therefore, it is to be understood that logically it must follow that the right to live will include right not to live i.e., right to die or to terminate one's life?

Indian Penal Code, 1860 (hereinafter referred to as IPC) makes attempt to commit suicide punishable[12]. It is to be noted hereby that intention to commit suicide is an essential ingredient in order to constitute an offence under IPC.

As discussed earlier about voluntary Euthanasia where we have seen that people concerned to legalize the termination of life on medical grounds have always concentrated on Voluntary Euthanasia and this implies that the patient specifically requests that his life be ended. Now if a doctor who assists a patient to terminate his/her life upon his request can be punished for abetment.[13]

The first in point of time is the decision of a Division Bench of Delhi High Court in *State v. Sanjay Kumar*[14] where the court observed as follows:

It is ironic that Section 309 IPC still continues to be in our Penal Code.... Strange paradox that in the age of votaries of Euthanasia, suicide should be criminally punishable. Instead of the society handing its head in shame that there should be such social strains that a young man (the hope of tomorrow) should be driven to suicide, compounds its inadequacy by treating the boy as a criminal. Instead of sending the young boy to psychiatric clinic it gleefully sends him to mingle with Criminals.... The continuance of Section 309 IPC is an anachronism unworthy of a human society like ours. Medical Clinics for such social misfits certainly but police and prisons never. The very idea is revolting. This concept seeks to meet the challenge of social strains of modern urban and competitive economy by ruthless suppression of mere symptoms - this attempt can only result in failure. Need is for human, civilized and socially oriented outlook and penology.... No wonder so long as society refuses to face this reality its coercive machinery will invoke the provision like Section 309 IPC which has no justification right to continue remain on the statute book.

Later on the Division Bench of Bombay High Court in *Maruti Sharipati Dubai v. State of Maharashtra*[15] took the view and that section 309 of IPC was ultra virus being violative of Article 14 and 21 and was therefore struck down[16].

Close on the heels was the decision of a Division Bench of Andhra Pradesh High Court in *C. Jagadeeswar v. State of Andhra Pradesh*[17], in which on the High Court being approached against the conviction of the appellants under Section 309, inter alia, on the ground of the section being violative of Articles 14 and 21 of the Constitution, the Bench held that the section was valid as it did not offend any of these articles and the Bombay view was dissented to.

P. Rathinam/Nagbhusan Patnaik vs. Union of India and another[18] case, the Supreme Court of India held that Section 309 of the Penal Code deserves to be effaced from the statute book to humanise our panel laws. It is cruel and irrational provision, and it may result in punishing a person again (doubly) was has suffered agony and would be undergoing ignominy because of his failure to commit suicide. Then an act of suicide cannot be said to be against religion, morality or public policy, and an act of attempted suicide has not baneful effect on society. Further, suicide or attempt to commit it causes no harm to others, because of which State's interference with the personal liberty of the concerned persons is not called for.

Subsequently the Supreme Court of India in *Smt. Gian Kaur Vs. State of Punjab*[19] case while holding sections 306 and 309 I.P.C. to be constitutionally valid observed that when a man commits suicide he has to undertake certain positive overt acts and the genesis of those acts cannot be traced to, or be included within the protection of the 'right to life' under Article 21. The significant aspect of 'sanctity of life' is also not to be overlooked. Article 21 is a provision guaranteeing protection of life and personal liberty and by no stretch of imagination can 'extinction of life' be read to be included in 'protection of life'. Whatever may be the philosophy of permitting a person to extinguish his life by committing suicide, we find it difficult to construe Article 21 to include within it the 'right to die' as a part of the fundamental right guaranteed therein. 'Right to life' is a natural right embodied in Article 21 but suicide is an unnatural termination or extinction of life, and therefore, incompatible and inconsistent with the concept of 'right to life'. With respect and in all humility, we find no similarity in the nature of the other rights, such as the right to 'freedom of speech' etc. to provide a comparable basis to hold that the 'right to life' also includes the 'right to die'.

INTERNATIONAL HUMAN RIGHTS INSTRUMENTS AND LEGITIMACY OF EUTHANASIA

There are number of international human rights instruments which deal with the right to life and liberty of persons whether in the form of conventions or declarations, which gives birth to a legitimate ground to analyse euthanasia in their varied context. The Universal declaration of human rights (hereinafter referred to as UDHR) gives quite a wide understanding of life. The reason for discussing UDHR is that now it is an accepted fact that the UDHR has acquired the character of customary international law though it is nothing but a declaration and not a treaty. UDHR provides everyone the right to life, liberty and security of person.[20] Everyone has the right to a standard of living adequate for the health and well-being of himself and of his family, including food, clothing, housing and medical care and necessary social services, and the right to security in the event of unemployment, sickness, disability, widowhood, old age or other lack of livelihood in circumstances beyond his control.[21] Everyone has the right freely to participate in the cultural life of the community, to enjoy the arts and to share in scientific advancement and its benefits.[22] It also emphasises upon the free and full development of individual's personality.[23]

On the other hand the European Convention on Human Rights contain provisions regarding right to life and as well as the exceptions of it[24]. The said convention also provides provision relating to liberty of person[25] as well as lays down general principle of law that there shall be no punishment without law[26]. There has been some consideration on assisted suicide under Article[27] 8 of the European Convention on Human Rights. In *R v/s UK*[28] the European Commission considered the admissibility of a complaint of a member of voluntary euthanasia society who had been convicted and sentenced to 18 months imprisonments for aiding and abetting suicide and for conspiring to aid and abet suicide. The contention of the applicant was that his conviction under section 2 of the Suicide Act, 1961 constituted a violation of his right to respect for private life contrary to Article 8 of the Convention. Arguments were also raised that the offering assistance to those who wants to commit suicide falls within the domain of private life. The commission held that the acts of aiding, abetting are excluded from the concept of privacy and cannot be described as falling into the sphere of private life protected under Article 8 of the convention[29].

The International Covenant on Civil and Political Rights (hereinafter referred to as ICCPR) also provides about right to life[30]. The right to life is the most significant of all human rights. The existence and operation of other human rights are predicated on the effective guarantee of the right to life[31]. Dinstein puts it thus:

> "Civilized society cannot exist without protection of human life. The inviolability or sanctity of life is, perhaps, the most basic value of modern

civilization. In the final analysis, if there were no right to life, there would be no point in the other human rights".

Its importance is underlined by the fact that it is one of the non-derogable rights referred to in Art 4(2) which cannot be suspended notwithstanding life-threatening national emergency. Commentators have noted the use of the term "inherent" as adding significance[32]. Dinstein argues that the term "inherent" suggests that the framers of the ICCPR regarded the right to life as part of international customary law; it raises interesting issues as to whether there is any difference in terms of its ambit compared with Art 6.1 ICCPR. The intention of the majority of delegates in the General Assembly's Third Committee was, apparently, to entrench the natural law basis of the right to life. It has also been observed that the location of "the inherent right to life" in the first sentence of Art 6(1) extends beyond the draft prepared in 1954 by the Human Rights Commission[33] and also beyond the comparable texts adopted in regional human rights conventions.

The upshot of this is that the fundamental nature of the right and the degree of significance accorded to it by those responsible for including it in relevant international treaties and the institutions seeking to interpret it have implications for its interpretation. The Human Rights Committee has resolved that the right to life ought not to be given a narrow construction[34]. A further issue arises as to whether the right is discretionary or mandatory. If it is mandatory, it is inalienable and accordingly incapable of waiver irrespective of the wishes of the beneficiary of the right. If it is discretionary, the right-holder is capable of waiving the right. The characterization of the right as discretionary or mandatory is the "crux of the problem of voluntary euthanasia unfortunately no clear guidance on this issue is available and the matter is still inconclusive[35].

So it is evident that the international instruments of human right recognises a very wide range of rights of persons some of which discussed above have a causal connection with euthanasia or in other words they are in some way or other connected with the matter of euthanasia.

UNDERSTANDING THE ARGUMENTS AGAINST EUTHANASIA

Among the arguments that can be raised against euthanasia, moral and religious arguments take primacy especially in a country like India. Not only in case of euthanasia but also in other matters moral and ethical standard in India always occupies a very high position. For example there were moral impediments in patenting living organism in India. Indian tradition is well known for worshipping animals and plants. Indian worship cows and plants such as *tulsi, neem*, etc. perhaps Indian considers certain plants and animals as a form of God. For an Indian patenting of such plants and animals would be like patenting and owing God[36].

Hinduism also views the practice of euthanasia negatively. Unless one has been born into the warrior class of the kshatriyas, where one is expected to kill if it protects society from evil, to kill is considered to be negative karma and to go against the principle of ahimsa. Again, each moment of a being's life is an opportunity to improve karma and move closer to moksha or liberation. To deprive oneself or another of that opportunity would obviously therefore be negative. Furthermore, while one is living at the grihasta or householder stage, it is one's religious duty or dharma to care for one's elders also. Euthanasia would deprive a Hindu of the opportunity to fulfil his religious duty.[37]

The concept of euthanasia can be negatively construed from the point of view of medical professional ethics. From the medical professional's point of view, it has to be acknowledged that like every profession, medicine has its own set of professional ethics. These would essentially be based on the relationship of trust between a medical practitioner and his patient. However, the set of ethics and morals would be of a much higher standard because of the inherent nature of the work that is performed by the medical fraternity. Medicine and religion have been intertwined from the earliest times with priests performing the role of physicians as well[38].Medical ethics based on religion have a clear sense of fundamental values. In the Christian tradition these include a strong belief that human life is a divine gift which cannot be disposed of by mortals.[39] In the light of this it is often seen as wrong to interfere with the manifest destiny which has been prepared for man.

Not only in India but also in the universal context, what makes the issue of euthanasia so morally contentious is the enormous value which we place upon human life. Augustine and Thomas Aquinas professed the view that whoever deliberately took away the life given to them by their Creator showed the utmost disregard for the will and authority of God and jeopardized their salvation, thereby encouraging the Church to treat suicide as a sin.[40]

CONCLUSION

Consideration of physician assisted suicide or euthanasia as a matter of policy rather than right requires a shift of perspectives[41]. Legally speaking there should not have any bar under the constitution of India so far as the matter relates to voluntary euthanasia is concerned. The matter has been dealt at length in *P.Rathinam/ Nagbhusan Patnaik vs. Union of India and another*[42] case by the Supreme Court. What the Supreme Court of India had done subsequently *Smt. Gian Kaur Vs. State of Punjab*[43] case was nothing but giving effect to the policy consideration of the government under the veil of 'sanctity of life'. Considering India is a country where corruption is rampant[44]almost in every sphere and the liabilities of the medical professionals are very less[45] (if not nonexistent) legalising euthanasia will create a further avenue for corruption which in effect may have the potential to jeopardise the life of citizens. Finally the concern which was expressed by the UK House of Lords Select Committee which reported in 1993 can be taken into consideration in order to conclude from Indian perspectives as well:

> "We do not think it is possible to set secure limits on voluntary euthanasia. It would be impossible to frame safeguards against non-voluntary euthanasia if voluntary euthanasia were to be legalised. It would be next to impossible to ensure that all acts of euthanasia were truly voluntary and that any liberalisation of the law was not abused. Moreover, to create an exception to the general prohibition of intentional killing would inevitably open the way to its further erosion, whether by design, by inadvertence, or by the human tendency to test the limits of any regulation. These dangers are such that we believe that any decriminalisation of voluntary euthanasia would give rise to more and more grave problems than those it sought to address."

Notes

1. Article 21 of the Constitution of India.
2. J. K. Mason, *et al,* Law and Medical Ethics, 529 (2002) *see also* Penney Lewis, The Empirical Slippery Slope from Voluntary to Non-Voluntary Euthanasia, 35 J.L. Med. & Ethics 197; W. Wright, "Historical Analogies, Slippery Slopes, and the Question of Euthanasia," *Journal of Law, Medicine & Ethics,* 28 (2000); D. A. J. Richards, "Constitutional Privacy, The Right to Die and the Meaning of Life: A Moral Analysis," William & Mary Law Review 22 (1981)
3. *Id;*
4. *Id., See also* Eugenie Anne Gifford, Artes Moriendi: Active Euthanasia and the Art of dying 40 UCLA L. Rev. 1545, 3 (1993).
5. M Stauch, M., et al, Text Cases & Materials on Medical Law, 643 (2006).
6. Lord Goff held it to be an omission in Airedale NHS Trust v. Bland [1993] AC 789.
7. *See Generally* Eugenie Anne Gifford, Artes Moriendi: Active Euthanasia and the Art of dying 40 UCLA L. Rev. 1545, 3 (1993).
8. MANU/SC/0184/1978 : 1978CriLJ1741, *see also* Board of Trustees Port of Bombay v. Dilip Kumar, MANU/SC/0184/1982 : (1983)ILLJ1SC ; Vikram Dev Singh v. State of Bihar, MANU/SC/0572/1988 : AIR1988SC1782 ; and Ram Saran v. Union of India, MANU/SC/0406/1988 : AIR1989SC549.
9. MANU/SC/0125/1986: [1986]1SCR251.
10. MANU/SC/0466/1992 : (1992)ILLJ475SC.
11. MANU/SC/0074/1970 : [1971]1SCR512.
12. Section 309. Attempt to commit suicide. Whoever attempts to commit suicide and does any act towards the commission of such offence, shall be punished with simple imprisonment for a term which may extend to one year {Subs.by Act 8 of 1882, s.7, for "and shall also be liable to fine"} [or with fine, or with both].
13. Section 306 reads as under: Abetment of suicide - If any person commits suicide, whoever abets the commission of such suicide, shall be punished with imprisonment of either description for a term which may extend to ten years, and shall also be liable to fine. Section107. Abetment of a thing.

    A person abets the doing of a thing, who —

First—Instigates any person to do that thing; or,

Secondly—Engages with one or more other person or persons in any conspiracy for the doing of that thing, if an act or illegal omission takes place in pursuance of that conspiracy, and in order to the doing of that thing; or

Thirdly —Intentionally aids, by any act or illegal omission, the doing of that thing.

Explanation 1—A person who, by wilful misrepresentation, or by wilful concealment of a material fact which he is bound to disclose, voluntarily causes or procures, or attempts to cause or procure, a thing to be done, is said to instigate the doing of that thing.

14. (1985) *Crl. Law Journal*, 931, in which the court was seized with the question as to whether the invest taxation of the case under Section 309 should be allowed to continue beyond the period fixed by Section 368 Cr. PC Some loud thinking was done by the Bench on the rationale of Section 309. Sachar, J., as he then was, observed as aforesaid for the Bench.
15. (1987) Crl. L J 743, speaking through Swant, J., as he then was, on being approached for quashing a prosecution launched against the petitioner under Section 309 of the Penal Code on the ground of unconstitutionally of the section.
16. The Bombay High Court held Section 309 as violation of Article 14 also mainly because of two reasons. First, which act or acts in series of acts will constitute attempt to suicide, where to draw the line, is not know - some attempts may be serious while other non-serious. It was stated that in fact philosphers, moralists and sociologists were not agreed upon what constituted suicide. The want of plausible definition or even guidelines, made Section 309 arbitrary as per the learned Judges. Another reason given was that Section 309 treats all attempts to commit suicide by the same measure without referring to the circumstances in which attempts are made
17. (1983) Crl. L J 549
18. AIR1994SC1844, 1994(2)ALT(Cri)1, 78(1994)CLT796
19. AIR1996SC1257, 1996(1)ALD(Cri)102, 1996(1)ALT(Cri)535
20. Art. 3 of UDHR
21. Art. 25(1) of UDHR
22. Art. 27(1) of UDHR
23. Art. 29(1) of UDHR
24. Article 2 Right to life
    1. Everyone's right to life shall be protected by law. No one shall be deprived of his life intentionally save in the execution of a sentence of a court following his conviction of a crime for which this penalty is provided by law.
    2. Deprivation of life shall not be regarded as inflicted in contravention of this Article when it results from the use of force which is no more than abso-lutely necessary:
       (a) in defence of any person from unlawful violence;
       (b) in order to effect a lawful arrest or to prevent the escape of a person lawfully detained;
       (c) in action lawfully taken for the purpose of quelling a riot or insurrection.
25. Article 5 of the European Convention on Human Rights

26. Article 7
27. Article 8 Right to respect for private and family life
    1. Everyone has the right to respect for his private and family life, his home and his correspondence.
    2. There shall be no interference by a public authority with the exercise of this right except such as is in accordance with the law and is necessary in a democratic society in the interests of national security, public safety or the economic well-being of the country, for the prevention of disorder or crime, for the protection of health or morals, or for the protection of the rights and freedoms of others.
28. (1983) 33 DR 270.
29. *See also* Margaret F.A. otlowski, Voluntary euthanasia and the common law 197(2007).
30. Art 6(1) every human being has the inherent right to life. This right shall be protected by law. No one shall be arbitrarily deprived of his life.
31. Human rights and euthanasia, Human Rights and Equal Opportunity Commission, Sydney, December 1996. Available at *http://www.hreoc.gov.au/pdf/human_rights/euthanasia.pdf*, last visited on June 15, 2010.
32. Nowak, p 105; Dinstein in Henkin (ed.), p 115 as cited in Human rights and euthanasia, Human Rights and Equal Opportunity Commission, Sydney, December 1996. Available at *http://www.hreoc.gov.au/pdf/human_rights/euthanasia.pdf*, last visited on June 15, 2010.
33. Article 6 of the text enacted by the Human Rights Commission (1954), in E/2573, 66
34. Gen C 6/16 paras 1, 5: "It is a right which should not be interpreted narrowly" (6/16 1); as cited in Human rights and euthanasia, Human Rights and Equal Opportunity Commission, Sydney, December 1996. *http://www.hreoc.gov.au/pdf/human_rights/euthanasia.pdf*, last visited on June 15, 2010
35. *Id;*
36. *See generally* Dr. N.S Sreenivasulu, Et al , Biotechnology & Patent Law Patenting Living Beings, 222 (2008)
37. Seegenerally,*[http://www.walkdenhighschool.org.uk/Departmental/*ReligiousStudies/Hinduism/Abortioneuthsuic.pdf], last visited on May 15, 2010.
38. J. K., Mason, Et al, Law and Medical Ethics, 5 (2002).
39. *Id.*, 5.
40. Available at *http://en.wikipedia.org/wiki/Suicide_Act_1961*, last visited on May 20, 2010.
41. Ezekiel J. Emanuel, PHYSICIAN-ASSISTED SUICIDE: FACING DEATH AFTER GLUCKSBERG AND QUILL: ARTICLE: The Future of Euthanasia and Physician-Assisted Suicide: Beyond Rights Talk to Informed Public Policy, 82 Minn. L. Rev. 983, 9 (1998)
42. AIR1994SC1844, 1994(2)ALT(Cri)1, 78(1994)CLT796
43. AIR1996SC1257, 1996(1)ALD(Cri)102, 1996(1)ALT(Cri)535
44. India stands ahead in terms of corruption. As per the worldwide Corruption Perceptions Index (CPI), prepared by independent international agency, Transparency International, India ranks 74th. U.S. is at 20th position. Ranking is based on the least corrupted countries.

Available at *http://www.siliconindia.com/shownews/India_ahead_in_corruption-nid-44081.html,* last visited on July 2, 2010.

45. A long list of defences are available under the Indian penal Code, 1861 apart from that in Dr. Suresh Gupta v/s Government of NCT of Delhi and another case (AIR 2004 SC 4091) the Supreme Court of India observed that for fixing criminal liability on a doctor or a surgeon the standard of negligence required to be proved should be so high as can be described as gross negligence or recklessness ....mere in inadvertence or some decree of want of adequate care and caution may create a civil liability but would not suffice to hold him criminally liable.

Unfolding Terrorism

KAUSTAV ROY* & CHANDRAJIT MUKHERJEE*

INTRODUCTION

> *"Terrorism is the intentional generation of massive fear by human beings for the purpose of securing or maintaining control over other human beings".*[1]

Terrorism has occurred throughout history for a variety of reasons. Its causes can be historical, cultural, political, social, psychological, economic, or religious – or any combination of these. In general, democratic countries have provided more fertile ground for terrorism because of the open nature of their societies. In such societies citizens have fundamental rights, civil liberties are legally protected, and government control and constant surveillance of its citizens and their activities is absent. By the same token, repressive societies, in which the government closely monitors citizens and restricts their speech and movement, have often provided more difficult environments for terrorists. But even police states have not been immune to terrorism, despite limiting civil liberties and forbidding free speech and rights of assembly.[2]

ROOTS LEADING TO THE MENACE

Terrorism is frequently argued to be the product of poverty and poor levels of economic development in countries. Examining the distribution of terrorist attacks and casualties due to terrorism across the states of India, this article demonstrates that the phenomenon of terrorism is not a clear product of poor economic development but rather exacerbated by unresolved and poorly managed political conflict. Poorer states in India are not necessarily more prone to terrorism, but states that have outstanding and poorly addressed political disputes do experience a disproportionately high level of terrorist activity. This examines six sources of political conflict that contribute to terrorism in India – separatist movements, ethnic conflict, communal conflict, the presence of scheduled castes and tribes, high population growth, and the phenomenon of stateless areas – and makes several observations on the successes and failures

* B.A.LL.B.(Hons.), Dr. Ram Manohar Lohiya National Law University, Lucknow.

of Indian counterterrorism policy. Society is, in its simplest description, overlapping social groups composed of individuals with social roles, privileges and obligations implicit in their own cultural values and norms. Each social group undergoes the process of social integration and disintegration simultaneously. Social disintegration is the aggregate of personal disintegration. Disintegration causes three basic types of reactions: aggression, acquiescence or retreat.

It is not poverty, religion or culture that is a major cause of terrorism, but alienation from rapidly changing societies. The rapid development puts high demands on the ability of communities and people to adapt. Not being able to cope with a changing environment can cause distress and insecurity. This can alienate people from the societies they live in. In changing situations, people look for familiar 'anchors' to cling on to. 'Religion, culture and traditions can provide stability, but in the hands of extremists they become a tool for radicalization, hatred and resistance to change', the Prime Minister claimed. Societies must promote political and economic freedom in order to remain innovative and competitive. 'If they don't, differences in relative wealth and modernity will be catalysts of envy and friction.'[3]

The discussion of this issue without referring to the historical fact that backed the terrorist particularly in India and that is the partition of India on the basis of religion. The consequential event that again ignited the fundamentalist approach and communal riots followed by the demolition of BABRI MASJID. The Babri Masjid demolition in Ayodhya on December 6,1992 is seen by many as a cause of fuelling terrorism and is considered as one of the prime reasons for the serial bomb blasts in Mumbai on March 12,1993. The serial bomb blasts in Mumbai in March 1993 is considered as a reaction to the totality of events in December 1992 and January 1993 in Ayodhya and Mumbai "by angry, frustrated and desperate young Muslims keen to seek revenge for the perceived injustice done to, and atrocities perpetrated on them, or to others of their community." Justice Sri Krishna noted that "the Muslims perhaps felt that the government and the police, instead of protecting their interests, had actually acted against their interests by joining hands with communal elements which took a lead in the riots.[4]

TERRORISM AND HUMAN RIGHTS

"The promotion and protection of human rights for all and the rule of law is essential to all components of the Strategy, recognizing that effective counter-terrorism measures and the promotion of human rights are not conflicting goals, but complementary and mutually reinforcing"[5]

Today, both the world at large and India in particular, face daunting challenges in the task of protecting human rights of common people regardless of the country they belong to. No country in world can be said to be free from the deadly scourge of terrorism. With the grim spectre of terrorism continuing to target innocent and defenseless people, the task has been ever challenging for the institutions around the world. A peaceful society rest on the pillars of justice and individual accountability. The concern for justice has been the paramount objective of this topic while dealing with vexed issue of terrorism. These are turbulent times in many parts of world. It has become apparent that in many ways, the world has become complicated, to say the least. The destinies and the interests of the nations and their citizens have become interlinked to such an extent that, invariably, the action of the one has adversely affected the other, leading to strife and suffering. In all such tragic situations, it has been mostly the common people, men, women and children whose rights have been violated. This is the greatest challenge, which all of us are faced with. In their constant endeavor for better future, nations and their citizens should always respect the human rights of the people who could be affected in the process. But experience has shown that more often it is not so. The result is that innocent people all over the world, irrespective of their colour, religion and creed, have suffered the most. It is important to understand the nature of terrorism and the way or the manner in which terrorism is treated by the world and the countries deploying the counter-terrorist measures belong to which school of thought.[6]

Human rights are relevant to terrorism as concerns both its victims and its perpetrators. The concept of human rights was first expressed in the 1948 Universal Declaration of Human Rights, which established "recognition of the inherent dignity and inalienable rights of all members of the human family." The innocent victims of terrorism suffer an attack on their most basic right to live in peace and security.[7]

The right to life, which is protected under international and regional human rights treaties, such as the International Covenant on Civil and Political Rights, has been described as "the supreme right" because without its effective guarantee, all other human rights would be without meaning. As such, there is an obligation on the part of the State to protect the right to life of every person within its territory and no derogation from this right is permitted, even in times of public emergency. The protection of the right to life includes an obligation on States to take all appropriate and necessary steps to safeguard the lives of those within their jurisdiction. As part of this obligation, States must put in place effective criminal justice and law enforcement systems, such as measures to deter the commission of offences and investigate violations where they occur; ensure that those suspected of criminal acts are prosecuted; provide victims with effective remedies; and take other necessary steps to prevent a recurrence of violations. In addition, international and regional human rights law has recognized that, in specific circumstances, States have a positive obligation to take preventive operational measures to protect an individual or individuals whose life is known or suspected to be at risk from the criminal acts of another individual,12 which certainly includes terrorists. Also important to highlight is the obligation on States to ensure the personal security of individuals under their jurisdiction where a threat is known or suspected to exist. This, of course, includes terrorist threats. Terrorism clearly has a very real and direct impact on human rights, with devastating consequences for the enjoyment of the right to life, liberty and physical integrity of victims. In addition to these individual costs, terrorism can destabilize Governments, undermine civil society, jeopardize peace and security, and threaten social and economic development. All of these also have a real impact on the enjoyment of human rights. Terrorism aims at the very destruction of human rights, democracy and the rule of law. It attacks the values that lie at the heart of the Charter of the United Nations and other international instruments: respect for human rights; the rule of law; rules governing armed conflict and the protection of civilians; tolerance among peoples and nations; and the peaceful resolution of conflict. Terrorism has a direct impact on the enjoyment of a number of human rights, in particular the rights to life, liberty and physical integrity. Terrorist acts can destabilize Governments, undermine civil society, jeopardize peace and security, threaten social and economic development, and may especially negatively affect certain groups. All of these have a direct impact on the enjoyment of fundamental human rights.[8]

A LOOK INTO THE VAROUS LEGISLATIONS THAT HAVE BEEN INCORPORATED TO COMBAT TERRORISM

After the Independence of India, political parties and people in power have formulated special legislation's in order to crush the vote of dissent and to deal with their political opponents. The legislation's may be in the form of Maintenance of Internal security Act,1971, followed by National Security Act, 1980 and in similar terms Public Safety Act, as operational in Jammu & Kashmir. Later on taking shelter under special circumstances, the political party at the helm of affairs in New Delhi framed special legislation called, Terrorist and Disruptive Activities (Prevention) Act (TADA), 1985 and Prevention of Terrorism Act (POTA), 2002.

A study of these laws would disclose that the legislature had the sole object of suppressing the voices of dissent or to deal with the political opponents so that they do not become people's movements. These legislation's have been from time to time framed and misused in the beginning in one state or the other, but when the majority of the Indian citizens chose to not to raise their voice against such repressive laws, these laws were misused in the whole of the country. For example, TADA, enacted in the year 1987 when it was originally introduced and passed in the Parliament, the excuse was to contain the elements that demanded a separate home land for the Sikhs and were considered by the interested parties to be a threat to national security. In the garb to contain the movement, the Act which was introduced mainly for Punjab was by and large misused in all the states till it was finally allowed to lapse and die its own death in April, 1995, but before its death, it ruined lives of thousands of innocent citizens, not only in Punjab, but also in various parts of the Indian State. In Punjab, more than fifteen thousand people were booked under TADA most of them were Sikhs and falling in the age group of 18-25 years. Though the Act is no more in force after April, 1995, but even today in the State of Punjab there are around fifty cases of TADA being tried in the various courts. So, the misuse of TADA continues unabated, even after the death of the Act.[9] TADA faced unprecedented protests from civil rights groups. They said the law violated fundamental rights and gave police unbridled powers with little accountability. In 1994, the Supreme Court, however, upheld the law[10], stating "freedom of individual must take second place to the requirement of safety of citizens." The Court directed specific modifications to temper the law. An important direction was the constitution of Screening or Review Committees to periodically scrutinise cases registered under the Act. Despite these safeguards, there were allegations of abuse of law by the executive (police) from different parts of the country, including from states not affected by terrorism.[11]

Similarly, POTA enacted in the year 2001 by government ordinance, soon after the September 2001 attack on New York's World Trade Center. The Bharatiya Janata Party-dominated coalition government subsequently seized on the December 2001 attack on the Indian Parliament, to whip up anti-terrorist and anti-Pakistan sentiment, which proved pivotal in steamrollering POTA through parliament. Like the US Patriot Act, POTA discarded the fundamental right of accused to due process and presumption of innocence. Persons arrested under POTA could be held for 30 days before authorities had to produce them in a special court of law. Human rights organisations have shown that on numerous occasions the authorities used this 30-day period to extract "confessions" through threats and torture. POTA detainees were burned with cigarette butts, raped, forced to drink urine, and subjected to electric shocks. That POTA's authors gave a green light to such techniques is underscored by the legislation's setting aside of the Indian judicial system's normal rules of evidence. Under POTA, a person's confession to a crime that he had not formally been charged with could be used by the prosecution as evidence in the court of law. Under Section 49 (7) of POTA, bail was almost impossible to obtain, since the courts were allowed to grant bail to POTA detainees only if they concluded they were unlikely to be found guilty of the charges against them. POTA was used by the government, writes Human Rights Watch, "against political opponents, religious minorities, Dalits [or ex-untouchables], tribals and even children". Even India's official Human Rights Commission condemned POTA, declaring that "existing laws are sufficient to deal with any eventuality, including terrorism, and there is no need for a draconian POTA".[12]People's Union for Civil Liberties (PUCL) challenged the constitutional validity of POTA, before the Supreme Court. The Court upheld the Constitutional validity of POTA[13], but with several caveats to check its possible arbitrary use by police. The court held that the "protection and promotion of human rights under the rule of law is essential in the prevention of terrorism", involving "court's responsibility" and that if human rights are violated in the process it will be "self defeating". The judgment pointed out that "lack of hope for justice provides breeding grounds for terrorism" and, therefore, in the fight against terrorism "human rights" will have to be respected. In the wake of allegations of misuse and abuse of POTA and an electoral promise by the Congress, the law was repealed on September 21, 2004.[14]

India has had and continues to have a veritable spectrum of draconian laws that are supposedly aimed at stopping terrorism. The Armed Forces Special Powers Act (AFSPA) is one of them. The wording of the AFSPA enacted by Parliament in 1958 is indeed blood curdling to even read let alone act out. The act states that any commissioned officer, warrant officer, non-commissioned officer or person of equivalent rank in a disturbed area may fire upon or use force even to the point of causing death if he is of the opinion that it needs to be done to maintain public order. He may arrest, without a warrant, any person against whom a reasonable suspicion exists and may use the above mentioned force to effect the arrest, as well as enter and search without warrant any premises to make any such arrest or if reasonable suspicion exists. Any person arrested under this Act is to be taken to the nearest police station and placed in custody without any delay. If this weren't enough already, the Act gives sweeping immunity to anyone acting under it. It states verbatim "Protection to Persona acting under Act: No persecution, suit or other legal proceeding shall be instituted, except with the previous sanction of the Central Government, against any person in respect of anything done or purported to be done in exercise of the powers conferred by this Act."[15] There has long been international criticism of the AFSPA. Over 10 years ago, in 1997, the United Nations Human Rights Committee expressed concern over the "climate of impunity" provided by the act. Since then, the UN Special Rapporteur on extrajudicial, summary or arbitrary executions (2006), the Committee on the Elimination of Discrimination against Women (2007) and the Committee on the Elimination of Racial Discrimination (2007), have all called for an end to the AFSPA.[16]

Thangjam Manorama- one of the many victims of this draconian legislation was allegedly raped, tortured, and killed by the paramilitary forces while she was in custody created a lot of furore in Manipur. She was arrested on the suspicion of being a militant and no such incriminating evidence was found during a search of her house. Emotions ran high all over the State as people thronged curfew-bound streets, defying rubber bullets and tear gas shells, in protest against the atrocities committed by security forces and demanding the immediate withdrawal of the Armed Forces (Special Powers) Act (AFSPA).[17] Human rights activist Irom Chanu Sharmila, has been on a continuous fast for the past nine years demanding complete withdrawal of the Armed Forces Special Powers Act 1958.[18]

The recent public outburst in Jammu and Kashmir regarding the withdrawal of this legislation from the valley portrays its draconian nature. The Kashmir valley in India has witnessed more than 15 deaths in June alone, all of them caused by Indian security forces firing upon the protesting crowds. These crowds were comprised largely of teenagers pelting stones at the security forces especially in and around areas of old Srinagar, the capital of Jammu and Kashmir. Most of these deaths occurred when security forces opened fire on crowds protesting similar murderous firings unleashed on common citizens by the security forces. The list of the dead includes minors, the youngest being just nine year old. The government have overworked to save the officers guilty of killing, maiming, abducting and torturing common citizens by using the worst provisions of the notorious Armed forces (Special Powers) Act 1958 (AFSPA) imposed in the area since July 1990. The state has clinically and systemically foiled any attempts made by the civil society members to bring the question of grave injustices and human rights violations committed by the security forces in Kashmir. Only change is that Indian state engaged in a shadow war with heavily armed and a well-trained militant outfit is thus waging a war with stone pelting teenagers now. And its security forces are apparently scared, very scared. What else will explain the hurriedly organised press conference by Lt Gen B S Jaswal to refute the demands of scrapping AFSPA by none other than Omar Abdulla, the Chief Minister of Jammu and Kashmir. Lt Gen Jaswal termed provisions of AFSPA as 'pious' to him and to the 'entire Indian army'. Only that, India is a democracy and not a theocracy. And that legality should be the sole criterion to retain or scrap an act and not religiosity or piousness!

The road to peace can only be taken if the government of India pulls its act together and brings the officers responsible for firing at and killing innocent civilians under the ambit of the law while stripping them of the immunity offered under the AFSPA and does away with archaic colonial and brutal laws like AFSPA made for disturbed lands.[19]

CONCLUSION

Terrorism associated with any religion, cult or belief remains terrorism and has to be fought by tooth and nail. Terrorism is adopted as the weapon of the weak. It poses serious threats to the democracy of a nation, but it is important to recognise that the response ought to be within the rule of framework for it to be effective and legitimate.

During the discourse of writing this article we understood and analysed the debate between the protection of human rights and procedures for the implementation of anti-terror legislations. The bone of contention is that a balance should be maintained between national security and human values. In concurrence to this ongoing debate Herbert Packer[20] designed a two pillar model consists of (a) crime control mechanism and (b) duo process mechanism.

These two are alternative weapons to combat with terrorist activities in different situations in the national interest. In order to construct solid human rights culture required to root out terrorism, there is a need to bridge the gulf between human rights, norms and their application in reality. Human Rights law gives a fair balance between legitimate national or security concerned and fundamental freedoms in each cases. These balances are reflected in ICCPR, European Convention for the protection of human right and fundamental right, African Charter on human rights, Convention on human right and fundamental freedom, the American Convention on human right and the Arab charter of human rights.

The UN Counter terrorism Committee has played a significant and worldwide role in combating the scourge since its creation. In this article, we made the study on the crucial subject of human being and its violations through the menace of terrorism. This article also tries to explain the concept of terrorism and its quagmire in today's era. The major terrorist incident shows the extent of terrorism and the need for adequate prevention. Our composite efforts can make this world a better place to live.

Notes

1. Cooper, H.H.A. (2001), Terrorism: The Problem of definition revisited. *American Behavioral Scientist*, 44: 881-93.
2. Terrorism," page 1, Microsoft® Encarta® Online Encyclopedia 2007 *http://encarta.msn.com* © 1997-2007 Microsoft Corporation. All Rights Reserved.
3. Jan Peter Balkenende, 'The Causes Of Terrorism'<*http://ianwestbrook.blogspot.com/2005/02/causes-of-terrorism_23.html*>accessed 3August 2010.
4. I.A.Ansari, 'Babri Masjid Dispute: Rule of Law and Building Confidence'<*www.jstor.org/stable/4411497*> *accessed 2 Septemeber, 2010*
5. United Nations Global Counter-Terrorism Strategy (General Assembly Resolution 60/288, annex). Human Rights, Terrorism and Counter- Terrorism. < *http://www.ohchr.org/Documents/Publications/Factsheet32EN.pdf*> accessed 2 April 2010.
6. Saurabh Dhawan, 'Terrorism and Human Rights: Role of the Security Personnel and the Police' < *http://www.legalserviceindia.com/article/l271-Terrorism-And-Human-Rights.html*> accessed 2 April 2010.
7. Amy Zalman, 'Human Rights and Terrorism : An overview'.< *http://terrorism.about.com/od/humanrights/a/Human_Rights.htm*>accessed 10 April 2010
8. Note 30 *supra*
9. 'POTA – another tool for oppression', <*http://www.lfhri.org/Pages/Library/POTA.htm*> accessed 5 April 2010.
10. *Kartar Singh v. State of Punjab* 1994 SCC Cr. 899

11. Wilson John & P.V. Ramana, 'Effective legislation critical for fighting terror'(Observer Research Foundation Policy Brief No. 5,2006) <*www.observerindia.com/cms/.../py060831_1162551713391.pdf*> *accessed* 3 September 2010.
12. Kranti Kumara , 'Repeal of India's draconian anti-terrorism law' <*http://www.wsws.org/articles/2004/nov2004/ind-n27.shtml*> accessed 2 September 2010
13. *PUCL v. Union of India* (2004) 9 SCC 580
14. Note 3 *supra*
15. Sriram, 'India's Draconian Armed Forces Special Powers Act'<*http://www.sacw.net/hrights/sriram08102004.html*> accessed 28 August 2010
16. 'India: Repeal Armed Forces Special Powers Act' (Human Rights Watch,2008)<*http://www.hrw.org/english/docs/2008/08/18/india19628.htm*> accessed 24 August 2010
17. Sushanta Talukdar, 'Manipur's Protests', *Frontline* Vol. 21, Issue 17, August 14-27, 2004.
18. 'Irom Sharmila Freed' *The Hindu*,(8 March 2008). <*http://www.hindu.com/2009/03/08/stories/2009030857230100.htm*> accessed 3 September 2010.
19. Avinash Pandey Samar, 'AFSPA And Political Violence In Kashmir'<*http://www.countercurrents.org/samar180710.htm*> accessed 21 September 2010.
20. Herbert L. Packer was a distinguished professor of law at Stanford University. Two of his most famous works are the article "Two Models of the Criminal Process" (113 U. PA. L. Rev. 1, 1964) and *The Limits of the Criminal Sanction* (Stanford: Stanford University Press, 1968). The two models in the first reference are the "crime control model," which is designed to protect the rights of law-abiding citizens by stressing efficient apprehension and punishment of criminals, and the "due process model," which is designed to protect the rights of the accused by presenting formidable impediments to carrying them past each step in the legal process.

Humanitarian Intervention and the UN Charter Regime: Sovereignty, Human Rights and Peace

JAPHETH AFWAYI KHAMASI*

INTRODUCTION

It has been asserted that even if, in principle, force could be used to defend human rights in extreme cases in principle, as a matter of law, such a proposition is untenable because it cannot be reconciled with the priority that the Charter accords to state sovereignty and peace. However, the possible existence of a right to humanitarian intervention does not rest on the assumption that human rights have achieved the status of jus cogens which somehow override the Charter's clear commitments to sovereignty and peace. The issue is not a competition of norms but whether they can be accommodated simultaneously.

The requisite burden is not to show that human rights protection necessarily trumps sovereignty and peace but to demonstrate that the overriding goals of sovereignty and peace within the Charter and international law generally do not preclude or prohibit the use of force in cases of extreme humanitarian need. The maintenance of sovereignty, the pursuit of peace, and the use of force in cases of extreme humanitarian need are not necessarily mutually exclusive goals.

DEFINITION OF HUMANITARIAN INTERVENTION

The "Classical" humanitarian intervention entails unilateral intervention for protection of another state's nationals from human rights violations.

The term 'humanitarian intervention' normally denotes armed interference by one or several states in the internal affairs of another state, without its prior consent or the authorization of the United Nations Security Council, to prevent a situation where the most basic rights of the people of that state is being violated. The doctrine is controversial because it violates the most fundamental principle of international law, namely the principle of sovereignty. This

* *Research Scholar, Department of Studies and Research in Law, Manasagangotri, University of Mysore, Mysore, Karnataka, India.*

principle is the very founding matter of international law, in that states are in principle only bound by what they consent to.

Humanitarian intervention can briefly be described as the interference of one or more states in the domestic affairs of another state by means of armed force, with the intention of making that state adopt a more humanitarian policy.[1]

STATE SOVEREIGNTY AS A CONTROLLING NORM OF THE CHARTER

Purposes of the Charter

It is beyond doubt that one of the cornerstones of the UN is the sovereign equality of all its member states.[2] Moreover, sovereign equality is a principle intimately connected to the prohibition on the use of force. However, Article 1 of the Charter further provides that its purposes, amongst others, are:

> "To take effective collective measures for the prevention and removal of threats to the peace, and for the suppression of acts of aggression or other breaches of the peace;
>
> To take measures to strengthen universal peace; and to achieve international co-operation in solving international problems and in promoting and encouraging respect for human rights and fundamental freedoms."

These are the overarching parameters of the Charter and the framework in which its legal obligations must be interpreted: state sovereignty, international peace and security, and the promotion of respect for human rights. This reflects the principle that the rules of international law, in toto, can be explained as a constantly changing and dynamic interplay between the rules underlying the principles of sovereignty and those governing the other fundamental principles of international law.[3]

THE PRIORITY OF SOVEREIGNTY OVER HUMAN RIGHTS?

While a case could be made in favour of employing force in defence of human rights in extreme circumstances, given that the defence of human rights is one purpose of the Charter, it has been consistently asserted that such an argument would ultimately fail because it cannot be reconciled with the priority that the instrument accords to state sovereignty.[4] It has been further argued that one cannot resist the conclusion that the promotion of human rights ranks far below the protection of national sovereignty as an organizational goal.[5]

However, others have maintained that the Charter succeeded in elevating human rights from a subsidiary role to a primary one both for the United Nations and in international law in general,[6] noting that the purposes enumerated in the instrument place the respect for human rights and fundamental freedoms on exactly the same level of importance as the maintenance of peace and security.[7] Even if the human rights provisions in the Charter were originally aspirational or vague, perhaps not intended to provide a legal rationale for enforcement, much less any mandate for military intervention without Chapter VII authorization,[8]constitutions, domestic and international, cannot be fettered forever by the rigid rules imposed by its creators.[9] Such provisions need to be interpreted in light of contemporary standards and meanings.[10]

Even if the prerogative of state sovereignty has traditionally taken precedence over human rights, where large scale human rights violations tantamount to threats to international peace and security are concerned, the order of priority between the prerogatives of state sovereignty and the requirements of human rights has since been reversed.[11] This proposition is consistent with the well-settled principle of international law that grave violations of human rights fall outside the parameters of exclusive sovereign control. Once human rights violations assume the nature of crimes against humanity, for example, they become a matter of international interest.[12]

SOVEREIGNTY AND THE PRINCIPLE OF NON-INTERFERENCE

"Sovereignty" can be loosely defined as the power to govern without external control. Ian Brownlie has described one of the corollaries of state sovereignty and equality as a duty of non-intervention in those areas within the exclusive jurisdiction of another state.[13] Article 2(7) of the Charter codifies this guarantee of sovereign equality of states by prohibiting interference by the UN in matters which are essentially within the domestic jurisdiction of any state. While Article 2(7) is concerned with the delimitation of competence between UN organs and states,[14] it may be also viewed as a codification of the more general principle of non-interference as between sovereign states. This principle of non-interference is an essential subcomponent of the prohibition on the use of force.

LIMITS OF DOMESTIC JURISDICTION AND THE CORRELATIVE DUTY OF NON-INTERFERENCE

Article 2(7) is qualified by the phrase, "in matters which are essentially within the domestic jurisdiction of any other state," which confirms that the principle of non-intervention is not absolute and, in terms of its wider context and history, no longer impenetrable.[15]As the parameters of domestic jurisdiction depend on the development of international law, international law contained in multilateral conventions removes the subjects regulated in these conventions from exclusive domestic jurisdiction.[16] Even states who have traditionally contested this assertion, claiming instead that the sphere of domestic jurisdiction is independent of international law, have in more recent times accepted that compliance with international obligations concerning the rights of persons are matters of legitimate international concern and, consequently, do not constitute exclusively an internal affair of the respective state.[17]

Therefore, the argument that human rights are, in all cases, of a subsidiary character to the guarantee of state sovereignty ignores the fact that "international law does not require that respect for the sovereignty and integrity of a State must in all cases be given priority over the protection of human rights and human life, no matter how serious the violations of those rights perpetrated by that State."[18] There are limits to the discretion states enjoy as a matter of their personal and territorial supremacy. Interference in a state's affairs may be permissible where it "renders itself guilty of cruelties against and persecution of its nationals in such a way as to deny their fundamental rights and to shock the conscience of mankind."[19]

In relation to the human rights provision articulated in Article 1(3) of the Charter, the Report of the Rapporteur, Subcommittee I/I/A of the San Francisco Conference stated that if "such [human] rights and freedoms were grievously outraged so as to create conditions which threaten peace then they cease to be the sole concern of each state."[20] The gravity and nature of the violations at issue are critical as lesser human rights infringements would constitute matters which largely fall within the domestic jurisdiction of the state.[21]

THE RELATIONSHIP BETWEEN NON-INTERFERENCE AND HUMAN RIGHTS: THE CHANGING FACE OF SOVEREIGNTY

Since the latter half of the twentieth century, both the reality and legal conception of sovereignty have been profoundly affected by the emergence of the customary and conventional human rights scheme.[22] The concept of sovereignty requires a more balanced and complex interpretation as growth of the international human rights regime supports the view that the state itself is the subject of obligations in addition to having an entitlement to rights.[23] As a concept, sovereignty has been continuously redefined and modified, emerging presently as more of a "ticket for admission" to international fora rather than as a formula for shielding exclusive areas of national concern.[24] In fact, the tendency of all international activities in recent times has been towards the promotion of the common welfare of the international community with a corresponding restriction of the sovereign power of individual States.[25]

Justices of the International Court of Justice have expressed similar sentiments regarding the erosion of the concept of absolute sovereignty, finding that new international law must "limit absolute international sovereignty of States according to the new requirements of life of peoples and must yield to the changing necessities of that life."[26] Former UN Secretary-General Perez de Cuellar echoed a similar view in his 1991 Annual Report, stating that "the principle of non-interference within the essential domestic jurisdiction cannot be regarded as a protective barrier behind which human rights could be massively or systematically violated with impunity."[27]

In the aftermath of NATO's intervention in Kosovo, the Netherlands's delegate also stated in the Security Council that respect for human rights in contemporary international law may be greater and respect for sovereignty less absolute, as it is generally accepted in international law that "no sovereign state has the right to terrorise its citizens."[28]

HUMANITARIAN INTERVENTION WITHIN THIS FRAMEWORK

Therefore, while the Charter does guarantee the sovereign equality of states, it has not operated as an interference or impediment to the growth of the international human rights regime. A state's treatment of its own citizens is neither insulated nor protected from international scrutiny.[29] This is consistent with the notion that domestic jurisdiction is "essentially relative"[30] and depends on the development of international relations.[31] Areas governed by international conventions to which a state is a party do not fall within the exclusive jurisdiction of that state. What non-interference obligations prohibit is "dictatorial interference" in matters in which each state is permitted, by the principle of state sovereignty, to decide freely.[32] Matters upon which states are permitted to decide freely by virtue of sovereign equality would include the choice of a political, economic, social, or cultural system in addition to foreign policy formulations.[33]

However, there is no doubt that contemporary international law has established that severe violations of human rights are matters of international concern.[34] As such, reconciling human rights protection with the primacy of sovereignty need not be conclusively resolved because the two do not stand in direct contrast. Sovereignty remains unrestricted only in regard to matters within the essential jurisdiction of the state. As the International Court of Justice has articulated, prohibited interventions are those which have "bearing on matters in which each State is permitted, by the principle of State sovereignty, to decide freely."[35] As systematic violations of basic human rights do not fall within the ambit of essential domestic jurisdiction, nor are they matters upon which states are permitted to decide freely, their mode of remedy[36] or protection from outside sources will not, in all cases, necessarily offend the principle of non-interference, it is a principle which operates only in terms of purely domestic matters.

While the Charter did accord priority to state sovereignty and equality, those provisions interpreted within the framework of contemporary international law are not necessarily inconsistent with an intervention to protect the right to life. If Article 2(4) is in principle capable of exception, and humanitarian concerns in cases of massive human rights violations and if crimes against humanity do not belong to the sole province of state sovereignty, then carving out a limited exception to Article 2(4) which permits the employment of limited force for humanitarian purposes is not necessarily inconsistent with contemporary international law. The argument that sovereignty occupies a primordial place in international law, so much so that it operates as a bar to interference in cases of extreme humanitarian need, ignores the well-settled principle that sovereignty shields only matters of exclusive domestic jurisdiction, matters which do not include grave human rights violations.

PEACE AS A CONTROLLING NORM OF THE CHARTER

The Meaning of "Peace"

Following World War II, peace became the supreme goal of the world community,[37] with Article 2(4) formally renouncing the use of force as an instrument of national policy to resolve international disputes.[38] The term "peace" is usually understood to mean the absence of inter-state military conflict or forceful intervention. This has been asserted as another impediment to the emergence of any right to humanitarian intervention, that the supremacy of refraining from armed conflict, in order to "save succeeding generations from the scourge of war"[39] supersedes all other goals.

While this assertion is not without its merits, both the Preamble and Article 1 of the Charter indicate that peace is more than the absence of war.[40] The Dumbarton Oaks Proposals addressed the importance of international co-operation in social spheres, these provisions based on the belief that, "apart from the abolition of war, the maintenance of peace and security required economic and social stability among and within states."[41] Some would likely take issue with this proposition and argue that peace, as understood in the Charter, must strictly mean the absence of military conflict or use of force because it was conceived in the aftermath of World War II's devastation, the goal of the instrument being to "save succeeding generations from the scourge of war."[42] Even if that is how the drafters conceived the meaning of peace, since 1945 peace has been reconceived by the international community.

The absence of military intervention by itself may be too simplistic a manner in which to identify or secure peace; if there is to be perpetual peace in a world of nation states, the individuals who live in them must be free, their human rights must be respected.[43] As stated by former Secretary-General Perez de Cuellar, it is possible for "violations of human rights [to] imperil peace;"[44] a fortiori where the right to life is at stake.

The Relationship between Peace and the Protection of Human Rights

Some scholars have asserted that the protection of human rights within the Charter regime is "subsidiary to the objective of limiting war and the use of force in international relations."[45] In holding peace as the ultimate goal of the international community, it has been argued that it is "protected primarily through respect for the equality of states and the renunciation of war as an instrument of national policy"[46]. While the renunciation of war or inter-state armed conflict may be one necessary component of securing a peaceful co-existence of states, it cannot by itself constitute a sufficient condition. The logical conclusion of such a proposition would mean that Rwanda categorically enjoyed peace in 1994 merely because it was not involved in inter-state armed conflict.

The suppression of widespread human rights violations may be intimately tied to the maintenance of international peace as the "protection of individual rights is not only a valuable goal in itself but also a precondition for long-term domestic and international order."[47] The argument that peace, interpreted as the absence of force, should reign at all costs ignores the reality that peace cannot exist where the fundamental observance of human rights is lacking; the right to life as a human right may not be subordinated to the right to peace as a right. The relationship is one of interdependence.[48]

HUMAN RIGHTS VIOLATIONS: THREATS TO THE PEACE?

Admittedly, cases where human rights violations, in and of themselves, threaten international peace will be rare. Humanitarian catastrophes or widespread human rights violations may entail a threat to international peace and security, [but] they do not necessarily do so.[49] At the same time, while such cases may not be common, it cannot be ignored that the potential for various situations to threaten peace, beyond those of merely employing military force, remains. As such, human rights and international peace cannot always be neatly divorced. This notion has been recognized at various points in history: (i) the Peace Conference following World War I,[50] (ii) Franklin Roosevelt's Four Freedoms Address,[51] and (iii) the Atlantic Charter.[52] In 1954, Former UN Secretary-General Lie also identified economically underdeveloped areas and the struggle of subjugated peoples for fuller freedoms and national independence as potential threats to international peace.[53]

The Security Council is an appropriate organ to look to for indications of international legal developments.[54] Council resolutions demonstrate that a wide variety of situations which do not involve the use of force between states can constitute threats to peace, including the following instances:

- The unilateral declaration of independence by Southern Rhodesia;[55]
- Domestic racial policies in South Africa;[56]
- The repression of the civilian population, particularly the Kurdish peoples, in Iraq;[57]
- The alleged support for state sponsored terrorism by Libya and its refusal to extradite individuals suspected of participation in the bombing over Lockerbie, Scotland;[58]
- The breakdown of the state and human suffering in Somalia;[59]
- The refusal to accept election results in Haiti;[60]

- The presence of civil conflicts in Liberia[61] and Angola;[62] and
- The grave humanitarian situation and impending humanitarian catastrophe in Kosovo, Federal Republic of Yugoslavia.[63]

As a necessary corollary, if these situations can threaten peace, the absence of inter-state military force alone is clearly not a sufficient condition for the existence of peace. The Security Council has expressly articulated that "the absence of war and military conflicts does not in itself ensure international peace and security. The non-military sources of instability in the economic, social, humanitarian and ecological fields have become threats to peace and security."[64] The threat of massive human rights deprivations would therefore constitute a threat to peace as the term has come to be defined through United Nations practice. A literal interpretation of Article 2(4) cannot always sufficiently reflect this principle because it fails to account for the capacity of gross human rights violations to imperil peace; a strict reading of the rule presupposes that the only threat to the right of political independence of a people is that of external and overt invasion.[65]

Through such instruments as the UDHR, Article 56 of the Charter, the International Covenant on Civil and Political Rights[66] and the International Convention on Economic, Social and Cultural Rights,[67] the international community has further demonstrated an overriding commitment to human rights, a goal that is intimately interdependent and connected to that of maintaining peace and security.[68] In fact, some scholars have submitted that the right to peace should take its cue from the "imperative norm" of the right to life.[69] This is not to suggest that human rights somehow occupy greater hierarchical status in the Charter but merely that their promotion and respect is, in some cases, a necessary component for the existence of peace.

PEACE: THE ABSENCE OF FORCE?

Equating peace with the mere absence of force, in every situation, posits the argument as if there were always a stark choice between maintaining peace and protecting human rights, but the concepts are not always capable of separation. There will be times where the preservation of peace is closely tied to the protection of human rights. The argument that the Charter clearly privileges peace over dignity[70] ignores the reality that the two concepts may be intimately interconnected as the securing of peace, broadly understood, will at times potentially rest on the assurance of human dignity. The realization that dignity can be a precondition for peace is necessary in placing this analysis within the reality of international relations. The apparent tension between the relevant Charter provisions can therefore be reconciled, since the legal obligation to maintain peace may, paradoxically, be accomplished through the use of force.

As UN Secretary-General Annan stated following the crisis in Kosovo, the parties who drafted the Charter were experienced in war but were nevertheless aware "that there are times when the use of force may be legitimate in the pursuit of peace."[71] The critical question in a decentralized security system is not whether force was employed but whether it has been applied in support of or against community order and basic policies.[72] The Preamble of the Charter recognizes a similar possibility by stating that "armed force shall not be used, save in the common interest."

The proper question, in terms of assessing the emerging legality of humanitarian intervention, may therefore be whether the use of force is justified as a method to restore peace because once there is large scale loss of life through systematic human rights abuses, peace has already been relinquished. Thus, the inquiry into whether the maintenance of peace need trump the protection of human rights is not proper inquiry as the mere absence of military conflict between states is not sufficient in and of itself for the creation or maintenance of peace.[73] As such, the argument that a right to humanitarian intervention is necessarily precluded by the hierarchical position that human rights occupy in the Charter in relation to the provisions regarding peace, does not itself offer a satisfactory justification to prohibit the emergence of such an exception in international law.

FACTORS OR CIRCUMSTANCES FOR HUMANITARIAN INTERVENTION

The components discussed below are necessary but not sufficient preconditions for the exercise of any right to humanitarian intervention. If such a right were to emerge and crystallize, it would only be capable of being exercised within the following restricted parameters.

Nature of the Right Involved: The Right to Life

Humanitarian intervention would be restricted to cases where the right to life is at stake. A doctrine of humanitarian intervention is inapplicable to human rights abuses in general.[74] Since human rights violations are a common occurrence in the international community, "if it were permissible to remedy them by external use of force, there would be no law to forbid the use of force by almost any state against almost any other."[75] Furthermore, a doctrine of humanitarian intervention which recognized the equal validity of civil and political rights and economic, social and cultural rights would be unable to distinguish between the NATO intervention in Kosovo and the intervention by the Soviet force, in 1968, to end the 'Prague spring' in Czechoslovakia.[76]

The practice of states further reflects that loss of life is the appropriate initial threshold for any humanitarian intervention.[77] This practice is also consistent with the principle that the right the intervening states seek to protect must be one that is both fundamental and universal in nature.[78] The right to life has attained the status of jus cogens,[79] recognized as a "primordial human right"[80] by the international community. As such, the right to life has been considered as "the most prominent and undisputed human right protectable by humanitarian intervention."[81]

Scale of Deprivation or Violations: Humanitarian Catastrophe

As military intervention for humanitarian purposes is an exceptional measure, large scale loss of life must be evident. Only severe threats to life, on a widespread scale, will warrant consideration of a military response.[82] The international community has generally required evidence demonstrating overwhelming humanitarian distress in that the right to life was about to be violated on a massive scale[83] or that there was an "overwhelming necessity to act" to avoid additional loss of life. It has been and should continue to be incumbent on the intervenor(s) "to make the case to other governments and domestic and international public opinion that the violations of human rights within the target state had reached such a magnitude that they shock the conscience of humanity."[84]

The practice of states demonstrates that large scale loss of life is a threshold requirement when considering intervention for humanitarian purposes. In a statement to the House of Commons the Secretary of State for Defence for the UK described this as the presence of an "immediate and overwhelming humanitarian catastrophe" which could only be averted by the use of force.[85] Other NATO member states couched their justifications for intervention in Kosovo in similar terms: (i) the US, Germany, and the Netherlands referred to the "humanitarian catastrophe that engulfed the people of Kosovo;"[86] (ii) Canada stated that its participation was prompted by events that "shocked the conscience of the world;"[87] and (iii) Italy argued NATO was compelled to intervene to halt "ongoing genocide."[88]

While humanitarian intervention should undoubtedly be reserved for cases which involve large scale loss of life, in certain cases such loss of life may be prospective or threatened. Given that the very basis of humanitarian intervention is the protection of humanity, there cannot be a principle forcing the intervening party to wait until the destructive act has been committed. Such intervention being preventative rather than punitive, the existence of the imminent danger is sufficient. Humanitarian intervention may therefore encompass preventative action. As stated by the UK's Permanent Representative to the UN, NATO's action in Kosovo was justified to prevent a humanitarian catastrophe, and evidence demonstrated that such a catastrophe was imminent.[89]

State practice seems to suggest that the decision to intervene may therefore be subject to a test of reasonableness or a good faith determination by the prospective intervenor that human rights violations are in fact imminently threatening, on the brink of evolving into actual mass deprivation. It would create an anomaly in international law to require that an intervening party wait for actual violations to occur prior to taking any preventative action.[90]

There is, of course, the fear that intervening states will be the sole arbiters of the necessity to intervene.[91] Allowing a state or coalition to make its own 'good faith' determination of the circumstances which might permit intervention would necessarily open the door to abusive claims. This is somewhat untenable because states are consistently subject, in their dealings, to some form of sanction for illegal behaviour in addition to an overriding duty to conduct their dealings in good faith.[92]

Furthermore, the idea that international law has no bearing on states' protection of their interests is not reflected in practice. As Christopher Greenwood has suggested, "[i]f governments believe that they are free to do as they please, without regard to international law, when faced with threats to their fundamental interests, they do not explain their actions in those terms."[93] States have consistently demonstrated that they require a basis of legitimacy in which to ground their actions, both to their own citizens and to other states.[94]

Purpose of Military Involvement: Relief of Humanitarian Need and Protection of Persons

States have rejected a doctrine of humanitarian intervention that would include the overthrow of a government "even if that government had been responsible for massive human rights violations."[95] The purpose of every phase of a humanitarian intervention must be the relief of humanitarian need and the protection of the victimized population. Neither territorial or economic goals nor any objectives designed to effect a change of government in the target state may form part of a humanitarian intervention. The overthrow of the target state government clearly goes beyond the parameters of a humanitarian intervention since, unlike massive violations of human rights involving large scale loss of life, the 'choice' of government is wholly an internal matter.[96] It has been suggested that one method of ensuring the intervening state's 'purity' of humanitarian motive may be to require relative disinterestedness of the parties. However, this component is fraught with difficulty as it is highly subjective and the exercise of imputing motives to states is beset with ambiguity.

Nature of Military Involvement: Necessary and Proportionate to Achieving Only Humanitarian Goals

Each component of the intervention must be directed exclusively towards ensuring the success of its humanitarian objectives.[97] Specifically, the method of intervention must be reasonably calculated to end the humanitarian catastrophe as quickly as is possible and involve measures to protect civilians, avoid collateral damage to civilian society, and preclude any punitive or retaliatory action against the target government. Any use of force must be necessary and proportionate to the humanitarian aim of the operation, strictly limited in both time and scope, as described by the UK; it is the employment of the minimum force necessary to achieve humanitarian ends and a withdrawal of forces at the earliest point in time that is consistent with the humanitarian objectives. Once the humanitarian goal has been achieved, the legal mandate for the use of force (or the presence of foreign forces) expires and any continued force or presence will solicit international public censure and become vulnerable to charges of unlawful action.

ATTEMPTS AT PEACEFUL RESOLUTION

Some attempts at peaceful resolution need to be explored as the resort to force cannot be the initial, hasty, or solitary response to humanitarian necessity. As stated by NATO members during the Kosovo crisis, the operation was undertaken as a last resort and after efforts to achieve a negotiated solution had failed.[98] While the international community attempted to reach a negotiated settlement in both Bosnia and Kosovo, both instances ultimately required "the use of force to bring a halt to the planned and systematic killing and expulsion of civilians."[99] There would be certain circularity in insisting that intervening states exhaust every possible avenue prior to intervening. The emergent nature of the situation may have ceased to exist by the time every peaceful avenue is explored, thereby defeating the need to intervene at all.[100] The phrase 'last resort' is commonly employed as an attempt to ensure that force is not resorted to prior to the exhaustion of other alternatives. However, labeling humanitarian intervention as a method of 'last resort' is not entirely accurate or even desirable because:

> ... strictly speaking, there is no such thing as a last resort. No matter how fearful the situation has become, there is always something else that can be tried ... So it would be absurd, in this literal sense, to say that states may turn to war only as a last resort. Literal lastness never comes ...[101]

Instead of characterizing humanitarian intervention as a last resort, it would be preferable to include in its definition situations where intervening parties have explored all reasonable and plausible avenues prior to employing armed force, insofar as time permits.[102]

COLLECTIVE NATURE OF INTERVENTION

In relation to their intervention in Kosovo, NATO states emphasized that their action was justified because it was not taken by one state but by a group of states acting unanimously within the framework of an intergovernmental organization.[103] The collective use of force does imply some checks and balances, both in the decision-making and in action[104] and likely enjoys a greater perception of impartiality and evenhandedness.

Ruth Wedgwood has suggested that NATO should be accorded more deference in its decisions to intervene than should an individual state because it represents the vast majority of the European community and can only make decisions by unanimous consensus under the terms of its Constitutive Charter.[105] In terms of the intervention in Kosovo, "[t]he fact that 19 states with multi-party democratic systems did act collectively is impressive, and the democratic nature of their systems may have helped to place certain restraints on the means used and on the goals of the military operation."[106]

However, the unilateral nature of a humanitarian intervention is nevertheless possible despite the presumption that collective action is more likely to ensure the relative purity of intentions required from the intervenors. A single state is not, in principle, precluded from taking measures as a lack of widespread interest on the part of other States for the ongoing or threatened human rights deprivations should not leave the victims unprotected. Unilateral intervention may be presumptively illegitimate, but the presumption can be overridden.[107] Humanitarian intervention may therefore encompass action taken by a state acting alone.[108]

CONCLUSION

The Charter is a means and not an end. To comply with its aims one must seek the methods of interpretation most likely to serve the natural evolution of the needs of mankind. It is not enough to assert that when "two postulates of justice are in conflict with each other, the higher one prevails."[109] The protection of fundamental human rights should not, for example, be considered more or less important than compliance with the sometimes relative rule prohibiting the use of force. Rather, the answer may be to recognize that the preservation of the human species through the use of force is not necessarily at odds with the Charter. The temporary destabilizing nature of the use of force may, in narrow instances, serve to ensure peace more effectively than restraint. Furthermore, as such cases will undoubtedly be rare and exceptional in nature, the 'order/justice' conundrum tends to exaggerate the threat which the practice of humanitarian intervention might pose to global order.

As Rosalyn Higgins has noted, the role of legal norms is not to remove the potential for abuse.[110] Claims which may be regarded as lawful in exceptional circumstances "should not a priori be disallowed because on occasion they may be unjustly invoked."[111]

Notes

1. Taken from The Oxford Dictionary of Law (Oxford University Press, 4th ed 1997).
2. Charter, Art. 2(1). However, C. Greenwood, "International Law and the NATO Intervention in Kosovo" (2000) I.C.L.Q. 926 at 929, has pointed out, it would be "too rigid a view" to nevertheless assert that general international law and the Charter "rest exclusively on the principles of non-intervention and respect for sovereignty of the State."
3. G. Schwarzenberger, A Manual of International Law, 4th (London: Stevens & Sons, 1960) at 84.
4. C. Chinkin, "The Legality of NATO's Action in the FRY Under International Law" (2000) 49 I.C.L.Q. 910 at 917-918.

5. T. J. Farer, "Humanitarian Intervention: The View from Charlottesville" in Lillich, Humanitarian Intervention and the United Nations (1973) 149 at 190. Farer also notes that a majority of states rejected the proposal to include a bill of rights in the Charter in order to support the assertion that "human rights had only a tenuous place among the concerns of the founding members," citing P. Meyer, "The International Bill of Rights: A Brief History" in P. Williams, The International Bill of Human Rights, xxiii (1981).

6. H. Kindred, International Law, Chiefly as Interpreted and Applied in Canada, 5th ed. (Toronto: Emond Montgomery, 1993) at 590.

7. J.P. Humphrey, "Human Rights: The Necessary Conditions of Peace" (1990) 10 Int'l Rels. 117 at 120.

8. Independent International Commission on Kosovo, Kosovo Report: Conflict, International Response, Lessons Learned (Oxford: Oxford University Press, 2000) at 168 [hereinafter Kosovo Report].

9. Sohn, "Expulsion of Forced Withdrawal from an International Organization", (1964) 77 Harv. L. Rev. 1381 at 1421

10. Alvarez J. in dissent in Competence of the General Assembly, at 18, held that: "It is therefore necessary, when interpreting treaties - in particular, the Charter of the United Nations - to look ahead, that is to have regard to the new conditions, ... A treaty or a text that has once been established acquires a life of its own ... we must have regard to the exigencies of contemporary life, rather than to the intentions of those who framed it ..."

11. A.J. Semb, "The New Practice of UN-Authorized Interventions: A Slippery Slope of Forcible Interference?" (2000) 37 J. Peace Res. 469 at 472- 473, compares the UN's reaction to Vietnam's intervention in Cambodia in 1979 to the Security Council's reaction in 1991 to the Iraqi suppression of the Kurdish population in northern Iraq.

12. UN Doc. S/PV.298 (1991) at 53 (France).

13. I. Brownlie, Principles of Public International Law, 4th ed. (Oxford: Clarendon Press, 1990) at 287. This also includes: (i) a jurisdiction, prima facie exclusive, over a territory and the permanent population living therein; and (ii) the dependence of obligations arising from customary law and treaties on the consent of the obligor.

14. B. Simma, "NATO, the United Nations and the Use of Force: Legal Aspects" (1999) 10 E.J.I.L. 1 at 3; L. Henkin, International Law: Politics and Values (Dordrecht: Martinus Nijhoff Publishers, 1995) at 150. Article 2(7) does not however prejudice the application of enforcement measures under Chapter VII.

15. D. Kritsiotis, "Reappraising Policy Objections to Humanitarian Intervention" (1998) 19 Mich. J. Int'l L. 1005 at 1041. Kritsiotis refers to the works of Grotius and de Vattel to demonstrate that restrictions on sovereigns' treatment of their own citizens existed long before the "classical period of international law." See H. Grotius, De Jure Belli Et Pacis bk. II, ch. XXV, § 8 (1625); E. de Vattel, Le Droit des Gens ou Principles de la Loi Naturelle 210 (J.B.C. Mohr Tübinger, ed., 1959) (1758).

16. Simma, supra note 13 at 152, also referring to the Institute of International Law draft resolution regarding The Protection of Human Rights and the Principle of Non-Intervention in the Internal Affairs of States to the 46th Sess. on the Commission of Human Rights, Article 2 states: "A state acting in breach of its obligations in the sphere of human rights cannot evade its international responsibility by claiming that such matters are essentially within its domestic jurisdiction," UN Doc. E/CN.4/190/ NGO/55.

17. Simma, supra note 13 at 151, citing the CSCE Expert Conference on Minorities in Geneva (1991), the Moscow Meeting of the Conference on Human Dimensions of the CSCE (1991), Fastenrath, ed., Documents on the CSCE (1992), at H.4. China would, however, remain a notable exception to this trend.
18. C. Greenwood, "International Law and the NATO Intervention in Kosovo", (2000) I.C.L.Q. 926 at 929.
19. R. Jennings & A. Watts, Oppenheim's International Law, 9th ed., (Essex: Longmans, 1992) at 442.
20. UN CIO Doc. 723, I/I/A/19 at 10.
21. R. Müllerson, "Human Rights and the Individual as Subject of International Law: A Soviet View" (1990) 1 E.J.I.L. 33 at 39.
22. R. Falk, On Human Governance: Towards a New Global Politics (1995) at 251 cited in Steiner & Alston, International Human Rights in Context: Law, Politics, and Morals, 2d ed., (New York: Oxford University Press, 2000) at 651. at 581.
23. R. Falk, "Sovereignty and Human Dignity: The Search for Reconciliation" in Deng & Lyons, African Reckoning: A Quest for Good Governance (1998) at 12 cited in Steiner & Alston, International Human Rights in Context: Law, Politics, and Morals, 2d ed., (New York: Oxford University Press, 2000) at 651. at 581. at 581.
24. Danish Institute of International Affairs, Humanitarian Intervention: Legal and Political Aspects (Copenhagen, 1999) at 17.
25. Reservations to the Convention on the Prevention and Punishment of the Crime of Genocide, [1951] I.C.J. Rep. at 46 per Guerrero, McNair, Read & Hsu Mo in dissent.
26. International Status of South Africa, [1950] I.C.J. Rep. 128 at 176 per Alvarez J. in dissent, the purpose of the new international law being to bring about international social justice.
27. Human Rights Watch, World Report 2000, (New York: Human Rights Watch, 1999) at xix [hereinafter Human Rights Watch Report]. As noted by former UN Secretary-General Perez de Cuellar in the 1991 Annual Report of the UN Secretary-General, UN GAOR, 46th Sess., Supp. No. 1, UN Doc A/46/1 (1991) [hereinafter Report of the UN Secretary-General], "[t]he fact that in diverse situations the United Nations has not been able to prevent atrocities cannot be accepted as an argument, legal or moral, against the necessary corrective action, especially when peace is threatened. See also V. Lowe, "International Legal Issues Arising in the Kosovo Crisis" (2000) 49 I.C.L.Q. 934 at 941: "no state should be driven by the abstract and artificial concepts of State sovereignty to watch innocent people being massacred ..."
28. UN SCOR, 54th Year, 4011th Mtg., UN Doc. S/PV.4011 (1999) at 12.
29. C. Chinkin, "The Legality of NATO's Action in the FRY Under International Law" (2000) 49 I.C.L.Q. 910 at 918.
30. Nationality Decrees in Tunis and Morocco Case (1923) P.C.I.J. Ser. B., No. 4 at 23-24.
31. The court there was considering domestic jurisdiction as articulated in Article 15(8) of the Covenant of the League of Nations.
32. H. Lauterpacht, Oppenheim's International Law, 8th ed. (London: Longmans, 1955) at 305.
33. Nicaragua v. United States [1986] I.C.J. Rep. (Merits) at para.205 and 258. [hereinafter Nicaragua].

34. Simma, supra note13 at 1-2. Not even the Russian Federation argued that the situation in Kosovo was an internal matter, the dominant view being that the FRY had violated its international legal commitments which "cannot be dismissed as an internal matter." See UN SCOR, 54th Year, 3988th Mtg., UN Doc. S/PV.3988 (1999).

35. Nicaragua, supra note 32 at para. 205.

36. See V. Gowlland-Debbas who notes that the International Court of Justice has juxtaposed the bilateral structure of international law against the idea of a collective interest, finding that states may well have an ergaomnes right or even an obligation to act in matters affecting the international community at large.

37. A. Cassese, International Law in a Divided World, (Oxford: Clarendon Press, 1986) at 137.

38. R. Falk, "The Decline of Normative Restraint in International Relations" (1985) 10 Y.J.I.L. 263.

39. Charter of the United Nations, 26 June 1945, Can. T.S. 1945 No. 7.

40. Simma, supra note 13 at 50, asserting that "[t]hese provisions refer to an evolutionary development in the state of international relations which is meant to lead to the diminution of those issues likely to cause war. ... Article 1(3) indicates that the United Nations' function is to bring about a stabilization of international relations in order to curtail the likelihood of war."

41. Ibid. at 48, citing R. Wolfrum, "International Law of Cooperation", E.P.I.L. 9 at 193-8.

42. See Preamble to Charter, supra note 38.

43. Humphrey, supra note 6 at 118, also referring to I. Kant, Perpetual Peace and Other Essays, trans. T. Humphrey (Indianapolis: Hackett, 1985) 107 et seq.

44. Report of the UN Secretary-General, supra note 26.

45. J. Charney, "Anticipatory Humanitarian Intervention in Kosovo" (1999) 93 A.J.I.L. 834 at 835.

46. S. Chesterman, Just War or Just Peace? Humanitarian Intervention and International Law (2001) at 222.

47. Danish Institute, supra note 23 at 15.

48. B.G. Ramcharan, The Right to Life in International Law (Dordrecht: Martinus Nijhoff, 1985) at 13.

49. S. Wheatley, "The NATO Action Against the FRY: Humanitarian Intervention in the Post-Cold War Era" (2000) 50 N. Ire. L.Q. 478 at 485. See also R. Higgins, "International Law in a Changing International System" (1999) 58 Cambridge L.J. 78 at 95 [emphasis added].

50. Cited by Claude, National Minorities, 4th ed., (New York, 1971) at 14.

51. President Roosevelt, "Wartime Aid to Democracies," The Public Papers and Addresses of Franklin D. Roosevelt, (Washington: 1938-50) vol. 9 at 672, stating that human rights are "the necessary conditions of peace and no distant millennium."

52. Whereby Churchill and Roosevelt agreed that "complete victory over their enemies [was] essential to defend life, liberty, independence and religious freedom and to preserve human rights and justice in their own lands as well as in other lands", (14 August 1941).

53. T. Lie, In the Cause of Peace: Seven Years With the United Nations (New York: Macmillan, 1954) at 436.
54. R. Higgins, The Development of International Law Through the Political Organs of the United Nations (London: Oxford University Press, 1963) at 2, suggests that the UN provides a "very clear, very concentrated, focal point of State practice."
55. SC Res. 232 (16 December 1966).
56. SC Res. 418 (4 November 1977).
57. SC Res. 688 (5 April 1991).
58. SC Res. 748 (31 March 1992).
59. SC Res. 794 (3 December 1992). Secretary-General Boutros Ghali stated in regard to the enforcement action in Somalia that the Security Council had "established a precedent in the history of the UN: it decided for the first time to intervene militarily for strictly humanitarian purposes." [1993] U.N.Y.B. 51.
60. SC Res. 841 (16 June 1993).
61. SC Res. 788 (19 November 1992).
62. SC Res. 864 (15 September 1993).
63. SC Res. 1203, (24 October 1998); SC Res. 1244 (10 June 1999).
64. Security Council Summit Statement Concerning the Council's Responsibility in the Maintenance of International Peace and Security, UN SCOR, 47th Year, 3046th Mtg., UN Doc S/23500 (1992).
65. M. Reisman, "Criteria for the Lawful Use of Force in International Law", (1985) 10 n.2 Y.J.I.L.279 at 283.
66. (1966) 999 U.N.T.S. 171, in force 1976.
67. (1966) 993 U.N.T.S. 3, in force 1976.
68. M.S. McDougal, H. Laswel & L. Chen, Human Rights and World Public Order: The Basic Policies of an International Law of Human Dignity (New Haven: Yale University Press, 1980) at 241.
69. Ramcharan, supra note 47 at 6, also notes that the right to peace is grounded in the principle of prohibition on the use of force. The Preamble to the UDHR, supra note 71, also affirms that "recognition of the inherent dignity and of the equal and inalienable rights of all members of the human family is the foundation of freedom, justice and peace in the world." From this language, Ramcharan has concluded that the right to peace would therefore appear to be a derivative of the right to life rather than vice versa.
70. S. Chesterman, Just War or Just Peace? Humanitarian Intervention and International Law (2001) at 45.
71. UN Press Release SG/SM/7136 GA/9596 (20 September 1999). The Secretary-General of the UN does play a role in the application of the organization's constitutional system and in the recognition of emerging norms: R. Wedgwood, "NATO's Campaign in Yugoslavia" (1999) 93 A.J.I.L. 828 at 830- 831.
72. Reisman, supra note 23 at 284.
73. Danish Institute, supra note 73 at 17, noting that individuals, not only states, are increasingly becoming fundamental subjects of international relations as security and

basic rights of individuals within the state are essential to international stability and peace.

74. Chinkin, supra note 28 at 920-921, has suggested that an appropriate guide might be to look to enumerated crimes in the Rome Statute of the International Criminal Court (1998).

75. L. Henkin, How Nations Behave: Law and Foreign Policy, 2d, ed. (New York: Council in Foreign Relations Press, Columbia University Press, 1979) at 145.

76. S. Wheatley, "The NATO Action Against the FRY: Humanitarian Intervention in the Post-Cold War Era" (2000) 50 N. Ire. L.Q. 478 at 493.

77. Legality of the Use of Force (Provisional Measures), "Oral Pleadings of Italy" (11 May 1999), I.C.J. Doc. CR 99/19 at 6: Italy argued that the aim of NATO's operation in Kosovo was "the protection of the right to life." Bosnia and Herzegovina stated in Security Council debates at the time of the NATO intervention in Kosovo that military action may be "the only option available to save innocent lives," UN SCOR, 54th Year, 3988th Mtg., UN Doc. S/PV.3988 (1999) at 12.

78. W.D. Verwey, "Humanitarian Intervention under International Law" (1985) 32 Netherl. Int'l L. Rev. 357 at 410.

79. Spec. Rapporteur of UN Commission on Human Rights, UN Doc. A/37/564 at para. 22.

80. Ramcharan, supra note 68 at 7.

81. Verwey, supra note 77 at 369. There have been academic suggestions that even such a minimalistic grounding is not without its difficulties as even the right to life may not be absolute, citing for example, Article 2(2) of the European Convention of Human Rights (1950). However, while Article 2(2) and its similar counterparts in other international conventions do permit suspensions of the right to life in certain situations (e.g. to effect lawful arrest, in the event of public emergency, or in action lawfully taken for the purposes of quelling a riot or insurrection) the right to life is nevertheless generally perceived as non-derogable in the international community.

82. Human Rights Watch Report, supra note 26 at xviii.

83. Verwey, "Humanitarian Intervention" in A. Cassese, The Current Legal Regulation of the Use of Force (Dordrecht: Martinus Nijhoff, 1986) 57 at 71.

84. N. Wheeler, Saving Strangers: Humanitarian Intervention in International Society (New York: Oxford University Press, 2000) at 34, paraphrasing M. Walzer [emphasis added].

85. G. Robertson, Secretary of State for Defence, U.K., H.C., Parliamentary Debates, vol. 328, (25 March 1999) at cols. 616-614. UK FCO Note, supra note 203, states that it must be objectively clear that there is no practicable alternative to the use of force if lives are to be saved.

86. Legality of the Use of Force (Provisional Measures), "Oral Pleadings of the United States" (11 May 1999) I.C.J. Doc. CR 99/24 at para. 1.7.; Legality of the Use of Force (Provisional Measures), "Oral Pleadings of Germany" (11 May 1999) I.C.J. Doc. CR 99/18 at para. 1.3.1; Legality of the Use of Force (Provisional Measures), "Oral Pleadings of the Netherlands" (11 May 1999) I.C.J. Doc. CR 99/20, para. 40.

87. Legality of the Use of Force (Provisional Measures), "Oral Pleadings of Canada" (11 May 1999) I.C.J. Doc. CR 99/16 at para. 27.

88. "Oral Pleadings of Italy," supra note 85 at 6.

89. UN SCOR, 54th Year, 3988th Mtg., UN Doc. S/PV.3988 (1999) at 12.

90. J.F. Metzl, "*Rwandan Genocide and the International Law of Radio Jamming*" *(1997)* 91 A.J.I.L. 628 at 648, notes, however, that "international practice does not seem to condone or even accept humanitarian intervention to prevent genocide before it occurs."

91. Wheatley, supra note 75 at 504, referring to Fairley, "State Actors, Humanitarian Intervention and International Law: Re-opening the Pandora's Box" (1980) 10 Ga. J. Int'l & Comp. L. 29 at 61.

92. Cassese, supra note 36 at 153-154.

93. C. Greenwood, "International Law and the United States' Air Operation Against Libya" (1987) 89 W. Virg. L. Rev. 933 at 957; see also Higgins, supra note 22 at 248: "[t]here are a variety of important decision-makers, other than courts, who can pronounce on the validity of claims advanced ..."

94. O. Schacter, International Law in Theory and Practice (Dordrecht: Martinus Nijhoff, 1991) at 110.

95. Greenwood, supra note 17 at 35. See also H.G. Schermers, "The Obligation to Intervene" in Delissen & Tanja, Humanitarian Law of Armed Conflict: Essays in Honour of Frits Kalshoven, (Dordrecht: Martinus Nijhoff, 1991) at 590, which posits similar parameters regarding intervention stating that no intervention would be permissible where (i) the sole reason for intervention is that a target state changes its government or that it no longer fits in the block in which it used to belong, or (ii) the intervention serves the power politics of another state. In a similar vein, A. D'Amato, "The *Invasion of Panama Was Lawful Response to Tyranny" (1990) 84 A.J.I.L. 516 at 519,* asserts that "there is no Wilsonian principle of international law that permits intervention to impose a democratic form of government in another state, any more that there is a Brezhnev Doctrine in international law that permits intervention to impose of restore a socialist or Communist form of government."

96. Nicaragua, supra note 32 at paras. 205 & 258.

97. Newman, "Realpolitik and the CNN Factor" in Bourantonis & Wiener, eds., The UN in the New World Order: The World Organization at Fifty (Basingstoke: Macmillan, 1995) 190 at 204-5.

98. "Oral Pleadings of Italy," supra note 85; "Oral Pleadings of Germany," supra note 208 at para. 1.3.1; Legality of the Use of Force (Provisional Measures), "Oral Pleadings of the Netherlands," supra note 208 at para. 40.

99. Report of the Secretary-General Pursuant to General Assembly Resolution 53/35 (New York: UN Secretariat, 1999) at para. 503.

100. See M.J. Bazyler, "Re-examining the Doctrine of Humanitarian Intervention in Light of the Atrocities in Kampuchea and Ethiopia" (1986) Stan.J.I.L. 547 at 606-7: "There may be instances where resort to other alternatives may be futile or where it may even compound the tragedy. ... In such severe situations, nations may use the minimum necessary force to intervene without first taking the time to try other, less drastic measures."

101. B. Orend, Michael Walzer on War and Justice (Cardiff: University of Wales Press, 2000) at 98.

102. *Ibid.* at 98. Where time permits, it may be appropriate to exhaust multilateral remedies. Falk has also suggested that, in the context of humanitarian intervention, "a recourse to force should be clearly presented as the consequence of an energetic, good faith attempt

via flexible diplomacy to find a peaceful solution," R. Falk, "Kosovo, World Order, and the Future of International Law" 93 A.J.I.L. 847 at 855.

103. A. Cassese, "A Follow-Up: Forcible Humanitarian Countermeasures and Opinio Necessitatis" (1999) 10 E.J.I.L. 791 at 794.

104. A. Pellet, "Brief Remarks on the Unilateral Use of Force" (2000) 11 E.J.I.L. 385 at 387.

105. R. Wedgwood, "NATO's Campaign in Yugoslavia", (1999) 93 A.J.I.L. 828 at 833.

106. Roberts, "NATO's 'Humanitarian War' over Kosovo" (1999) 41 Survival 102 at 102 & 107.

107. M.J. Smith, "Humanitarian Intervention: An Overview of the Ethical Issues" (1998) 12 Ethics & Int'l. Affs. 63 at 77.

108. This last component of the overall framework of a justified humanitarian intervention, collectivity of action, is therefore not necessary in all cases but its presence would surely add more presumptive legitimacy to such an operation.

109. Kelsen, "Will the Judgment in the Nuremberg Trial Constitute a Precedent in International Law?" (1947) 1 Int'l Leg.Q. 153 at 165, cited by the Supreme Court of Canada in R. v. Finta (1994) 112 D.L.R. (4th) 513.

110. Higgins, supra note 53 at 316, has pointed out "... there have been countless abusive claims of the right to self-defence. That does not lead us to say that there should be no right of self-defence today." See also Greenwood, supra note 76 at 931.

111. *Ibid.* at 248.

Offence of Rape and Relevancy of Consent: An Analysis With Special Reference to India

ARUN KUMAR SINGH*

INTRODUCTION

Rape is a heinous crime which does not only affect physically the victim but create mental agony. It is a weapon that distorts a woman's sexuality, restricts her freedom and violates her human rights. It leaves a woman feeling exposed, humiliated and traumatized. Rape is a word originated from Latin word *rapine or rapio* which means to carry off or to overcome. It is an offence which is punishable under section 376 of Indian Penal Code. It is an act by which men keep women in State of fear. Consensual intercourse is valid in India but the consent must be voluntary. The husband and wife's relationship is a fiduciary relationship and is based on *utmost good faith.* But the provisions of exception of section 375 of the Indian Penal Code is being misused which provides legality for marital rape. The exclusion of married women from the purview of rape, if sexual intercourse has been committed by her husband without her will or consent, reflects the law maker's view of a wife as being her husband's private property. Women who are raped by their partners are likely to suffer severe psycho logical consequences such as anxiety, depression, intense fear etc. Marital rape is serious problem and millions of women are facing such problems. On account of matrimonial consent she cannot retract from sexual intercourse unless they are judicially separated or court has forbidden the Judiciary. The 1979, Convention on the Elimination of the All Forms of Discrimination Against Women (CEDAW) and the Beijing Declaration directs all states to take all appropriate measures to prevent discrimination against women besides taking step to protect honor and dignity of women. India is also signatory of this convention. None the less sexual abuse of women in Indian society is on increase. This paper aims to discuss the shortcomings of the provisions of section 375 of the Indian

Penal Code, 1860. It is also tried to highlight the role of judiciary. Lastly paper mentions certain suggestions to achieve the required objectives.

* Assistant Professor, Department of Law, North-Eastern Hill University, Shillong, Meghalaya, 793022.

STATUTORY PROVISIONS

Macaulay when drafted the Code, the provisions were called 'Clauses'. Under clause 359 he propounded that "A man is said to commit rape who except the case here after excepted has sexual intercourse with a woman under the circumstances falling any of the following descriptions:[1]

(i) Against her will.

(ii) Without her consent

(iii) With her consent but consent is obtained by putting her in fear of death or hurt.

(iv) With her consent when the man knows that the consent is given because she believes that he is a man to whom she believes herself to be married.

(v) With or without her consent when she was under the age of nine years.

The exception of this clause was that sexual intercourse by a man with her wife was in no case rape. But in above provision the age of consent of wife was very low and that was of nine years only. In 1860 the Indian Penal Code came into existence. In this Code the word 'clause' has been replaced by the word 'Section'. Section 375 of the Indian Penal Code, 1860, provides about the rape[2] and section 376 provides the punishment of rape[3]. A new section has also been inserted by the amendment of 1983 to provide punishment to those husbands who are living separately with their wives and commits sexual intercourse forcibly.[4] At the initial stage the age of consent for the wife was ten years. The age of consent for wife increased from time to time. It was amended in 1891 and 1925 where the age of consent for the wife became 12 years and 13 years respectively. By the amendment of 1891 the explanation clause has been inserted in section 375. Again amendment took place in the section by which the age of consent for wife increased for fifteen years. By the Criminal Law Amendment Act, 1983 a new clause 'fifthly' is inserted in the section 375. Before that only five clauses were there in the section.

RELEVENCY OF CONSENT UNDER SECTION 375 OF THE INDIAN PENAL CODE, 1860

Consent is an important word which provides protection to the offender but women giving consent must be in position to give consent. If she is of sound mind and attaints the age of 16 year will be competent to give her consent. In case of wife attained the age of fifteen years, her consent is immaterial whether she has given her consent or not, the husband will not be liable for rape. But if the age of wife is less than fifteen years but more than twelve years it is rape but punishment is lesser than other[5]. Similarly if the wife's age is less than twelve years and husband commits sexual intercourse with her that is the rape and is punishable for the same punishment as if rape is committed against any other woman under section 375 of the Indian Penal Code. Consent has no place there.

Now the question is that once consent is given by the woman who has attained the age of 16 years or more, how far it shall be deemed to be in existence. For example, suppose sexual intercourse is going on between male and female with consent, meantime if woman withdraws her consent due to any reason but male continues intercourse. Is the subsequent act of sexual intercourse (after withdrawn of consent by female) will amount to rape? The consent for sexual intercourse in the above situation was voluntarily given by the female and the sexual intercourse was started with the voluntary consent of the parties. Another issue for debate is regarding thirdly of section 375[6]. If consent of women for sexual intercourse is given because of some greed or promise, not because of hurt or death created by the male, and subsequently promise is not performed by the male, Then will the sexual intercourse done under that promise amount to rape or not?

Marital rape is the serious form of domestic violence. It is an abuse of power by which husband attempts to show dominance over his wife. It may be in the form of battering rape where women receive physical and sexual violence in the relationship, or obsessive rape in which assault involves torture and/or perverse sexual act. So far as the exception of section 375 of Indian Penal Code is concerned it provides validity to marital rape[7]. Because it is preserved by the law as well society that the husband cannot be guilty of rape committed by himself upon his lawful wife for their mutual matrimonial consent and contract. The wife has given herself to the husband which she cannot retreat. This notion establishes that once woman is married she cannot refuse sex with her husband even if she is not willing for that if her age is not less than 15 years. This exception provides husbands with license for rape their wives. It is violation of her human rights as well as Article 21 of the Constitution of India[8] because right to life under Article 21 of the Constitution includes right to life with human dignity.[9] However, safeguards have been provided to the wife whose age is less than 15 years[10] and the wife who is judicially separated from the husband[11].

One more thing is required to pay attention is that if wife's age is less than fifteen years age (may be of one day less than fifteen years) and non consensual intercourse is committed against her is rape and if she attain the age of fifteen years his consent is immaterial and non consensual intercourse against her is not rape under the section 375 of Indian Penal Code.

Under the Hindu Marriage Act, 1955[12] as well as special Marriage Act, 1957[13] on one hand the law prevents a girl from marrying if her age is less than eighteen years even if she has attained the age of fifteen years. But on the other hands it legalizes non-consensual intercourse with the wife who is just of fifteen years old.

It is clear from the section 375 of Indian Penal Code that if the sexual intercourse with unmarried woman is committed by a man without her consent, it amounts rape. But subsequently if he offers for marriage with the girl and girl is ready for marriage with him, will the previous act of man be legalized after marry with her and not be covered under the purview of rape? If not then after the marriage their life cannot move smoothly, because rape is non compoundable offence under section 320 of Criminal Procedure Code, 1974. So once the act was done without the consent of girl it cannot be compounded even if the parties are agreed to sum up the case.

JUDICIAL APPROACH

Acknowledging the need to provide protection to the basic human rights and guarantee from sexual exploitation of women the Court has played very crucial role. Absence of consent beyond reasonable doubt was not easy to prove by the victim. The *Mathura rape case*[14] caused widespread reaction in the country which compelled the parliament to enact the Criminal Law (Amendment Act,) 1983, as a result of which rape committed on a woman while in custody is punishable under clause B-D of section 376 of Indian Penal Code, 1860. Criminal Law (Amendment) Act, 1983 brought a change in burden of proof regarding sexual intercourse. By this Act, 114-A is inserted in the Indian Evidence Act, 1872. It states that if girl says that the sexual intercourse is committed without her consent the Law shall presume that consent of women is absent and burden of proof will lie on the male that the consent of woman was present there.[15] Before the insertion of this section it was not very easy for the female to prove that consent of her was not present. Sometimes, if no injuries on the body of woman are found, prove that the concept of woman was present there.

Supreme Court of India in case of *Rafiq v State of UP*[16] upheld the conviction of accused for the rape of a woman working in a village welfare organization. The contention of the accused was that there was no injury on the body of the victim. So it is not rape because it reflects consent. The Court held that corroboration as condition for judicial reliance on testimony of victim was not a matter of law but a guidance of prudence under given circumstances.

In *Bhogibhai case*[17] Court started that in India refusal to act on the testimony of victim of sexual assault in the absence of corroboration as rule is adding insult to injury. We should not see the evidence of girl or woman who complains for rape or sexual molestation with the spectacles fitted with the lenses tinged with doubt disbelief and suspension. If we do so we justify the wrong activity of the males in male dominated society. The Court also said that in Indian Society hardly a girl or woman be reluctant even to admit that any incident which is likely to reflect on her chastity had ever occurred. Because she has fear in the mind that disclosing of incident can also be risk of losing the love and respect of family members, neighbours, relatives and husbands.

The court adopted similar view in case *Kewalchand Jain's* case.[18]The Court held that a victim of sexual offence could not be put in the place of accomplice her evidence should be given same weightage as of the evidence of an injured person of physical violence. Her evidence should not be compelled to be corroborated because ordinarily a woman will not come forward to impose allegation against any male for her chastity. The Court stated that a raped woman suffers tremendous sense of shame and fear of being shunned by society and her near relatives including husband[19]. It is not very easy to prove that the consent of woman was present or not, the story is fabricated or true. In a leading case Rajasthan High Court held that sometimes it is found that the story is fabricated. In this case the woman was raped by his brother in-law in day time in a cattle shed near public way.[20] High Court stated that the husband was with her during the interviewing period of two days and therefore, it could not be ruled out that all the injuries had been received by her while cohabiting with her husband because duration of injuries did not tally with the time of the occurrence and acquitted the accused. The Supreme Court reversed the judgment of the High Court and convicted the accused for rape. The Court stated that it was not possible to believe that when a married woman had sex with her husband in the privacy of her bed room she would suffer abrasion on her body and veginal walls[21]. The Court said that the evidence of rape-victim woman should be given same weight age as an injured witness. She should not be seen in suspicious eye that the statement of her is fabricated.

In case of *Bodhisatwa Gautam v Subha Chakraborty*[22] the Supreme Court stated that rape is a crime against basic human rights and a violation of the victims most cherished of fundamental rights namely right to life contained in Article 21 of the Constitution. Justice Sagir Ahmad observed that unfortunately women in our country belong to a group of society who are in disadvantaged position on account of several social barriers and impediments and have therefore been tyranny of the hands of men. The Court said that women also have right to be respected and treated as equal citizens under the Constitution of India. Their honour and dignity cannot be touched or violated. In this case the consent of girl was obtained under the influence that he would marry her. That is why she had given her consent. The Court held this is not a valid consent and it amounts to rape. The Court took one step forward and ordered to pay the compensation to the victim. The Court held that the consent obtained under the misrepresentation or fraud is not voluntary consent under section 375 of the Indian Penal Code, 1860.

Giving consent and submission of her chastity are two different things. A woman is said to consent only when she freely agrees herself while in free and unconstrained possession of their physical and moral power to act in manner she wanted.[23] The consent implies the free and untrammeled rights to forbid or withhold what is being connected to.[24] It is a voluntary and consensus acceptance of what is proposed to be done by others.[25] Submission differs from consent because submission may be under compulsion also. So we can say that all consent involves submission but all submission does not involve consent. Submission under compulsion does not exempt accused from liability.

In *Rao Harnam Singh's case*[26] Shruti the deceased and his husband Kalu Ram were residing in the house of Harnam Singh. One day a party was going on for the celebration of one police officer's transfer, in whose office Kalu Ram was also working. Kalu Ram was asked to produce his wife to Rao Harnam Singh and his guests for eve enjoyment. Firstly she refused but under the compulsion and pressure of the husband agreed because husband was asked to resign from the office. She was ravished by three persons including Harnam Singh and died. High Court held that when volitional faculty is vitiated by duress cannot be deemed to be a valid consent even if no resistance has been created by the victim at the time of sexual intercourse.

In case of *State of Punjab v Gurmit Singhv*[27] The Supreme Court held that even if the girl is shown to be habitual sex. The Court should not describe her to be loose character.

In *State of Maharashtra v Madhukar N Mardikar*[28] the Supreme Court held that the unchaste of women does not make her open to any and every person to violate her person as and when he wishes without her consent. She is equally entitled to protect her persons. If there is an attempt to violate her person against her will she is entitled to protection of law. Merely on the ground that she is of easy virtue her evidence cannot be rejected.

CONCLUSION AND SUGGESTIONS

The rape is such type of worst crime which not only violates the victim's privacy and personal integrity but also cause serious physical and psychological damages. The murderer destroys the physical frame of the victim where as a rapist degrades the soul of helpless female. Although Judiciary play a vital role to control rape by way of punishing the accused but it has its own limitations. So there is need of substantial change in the law of sexual offences to make them gender neutral and remove inequalities. Consensual intercourse with women of sixteen years old is not rape. Once it is given up to what extent it shall be deemed to be in existence is not clear in the section 375 of the Code. It should be clearly mentioned in the section. The exception of section 375 should be deleted and sexual intercourse with his lawful wife, who is of fifteen years age or more, without her consent should also be included as marital rape. The age of consent should increase from sixteen to eighteen because in most of the laws the consent age for marriage is eighteen years. In Place of using word rape the word sexual assault should be used and every type of penetration should be included in the purview of sexual assault. Apart from the above rarest of the rare principle should be followed in certain cases of rape such as rape by father to his daughter or brother to his sister and they should be punished for the life imprisonment. Mere declaration of conduct as an offence of rape is not sufficient but it is required to sensitize the society towards sexual offences.

Notes

1. Susan Brownmiller,*'Against Our Will'* Peguin Book,*1976*, p. 17see also Nitish Nawsagary,Offence of Rape under the Indian Penal Code, NCLJ, Vol. VIII, 2003, pp. 78-79.

2. Section 375 of Indian Panel Code, 1860 provides, A man is said to commit rape who except in the case here in after excepted has sexual intercourse with a woman under circumstances falling under any of the six following descriptions:

   First: Against her will

   Secondly: Without her consent

   Thirdly: With her consent, when her consent has been obtained by putting her in whom she is interested in fear of death or of hurt.

   Fourthly: With her consent when the man knows that she is not her husband

   Fifthly: With her consent when at the time of giving such consent by reason of unsoundness mind or intoxication or the administration by him personally or through another of any stupefying or unwholesome substance she is unable to understand the nature and consequence of that to which she gives consent.

   Sixthly: With or without her consent when she is less than sixteen years of age.

   Explanation: Penetration is sufficient to constitute sexual intercourse.

   Exception: Sexual intercourse by a man with his own wife not being under fifteen years of age is not rape under Indian Penal Code.

3. Section 376 provides "Whoever, except in the cases provided for by section(2), commits rape shall be punished with imprisonment of either description for a term which shall not be less than seven years but which may be for life or for a term which may extend to ten years and shall also be liable to fine unless the women raped is his own wife and is not under twelve years of age, in which case, he shall be punished with imprisonment of either description for a term which may extend to two years or with fine or with both.

4. Section 376-A provides "Whoever has sexual intercourse with his own wife, who is living separately from him under a decree of separation or under any custom are usage without her consent shall be punished with imprisonment of either description for a term which may extend to two years and shall also be liable to fine.

5. Section 376 provides that whoever commits rape with his wife not below the age of twelve years shall be punished with the description for a term which may extend to two years or with the fine or both.

6. Thirdly of section375 provides "With her consent, when her consent has been obtained by putting her in whom she is interested in fear of death or of hurt".

7. *Exception:* Sexual intercourse by a man with his own wife not being under fifteen years of age is not rape under Indian Penal Code.

8. Article 21 0f the Constitution of India provides "No person shall be deprived of his life or personal liberty except according to the procedure established by law."

9. Francis Coralie Mullin v Administrator, Union Territory of Delhi, AIR 1981 SC 746

10. Section 376 of Indian Penal Code, 1860

11. Section 376-A of the Indian Penal Code,1860

12. Section 5(iii) of the Hindu Marriage Act, 1955 ,provides that a marriage between two Hindus can be solemnized if bridegroom has attend the age of twenty one years and bride has completed the age of eighteen years.

13. Section 4 clause (c) of the Special Marriage Act, 1954 provides that a marriage between two persons may be solemnized if at the time of marriage the male has completed the age of twenty one years and female has completed the age of eighteen years.

14. *Tukaram v State of Maharashtra,* AIR 1979 SC 185
15. In a prosecution for rape under clause (a)-(e) and clause (g) of subsection(2) of section 376 of the Indian Penal Code where sexual intercourse by the accused is proved and the question is whether it was without the consent of the woman alleged to have been raped and the states in her evidence before the Court that she did not consent, the Court shall presume that she did not consent.
16. AIR 1981 SC 96.
17. *Bhogibhai Hirjibhai v State of Gujrat* AIR 1983 SC 753.
18. *Kewalchand Jain v State of Maharashtra,* AIR 1990 SC658.
19. *Ibid* at 665 para 18
20. *State of Rajasthan v Shri Narayan Koyalti* AIR 1992 SC 2003
21. *ibid* at 2008 para5
22. (1996) 1SCC 490
23. K D Gaur, *A Text Book on the Indian Penal Code,* Universal Law Publishing Co. Ltd., 2004 p.592.
24. *Ibid.*
25. *Ibid.*
26. *Rao Harnam Singh Sheoji Singh v State* AIR 1958 Punj.123
27. (1996)2SCC384
28. (1991)1SCC 57

Social Security in India:
The Legislative Support

Ashish Kumar Pandey*

INTRODUCTION

Social Security manifests the "natural desire of communities for protection from life's problems, from uncertainty, from disease and deprivation. It is the protection which society provides for its members through a serious of public measures against the economic and social distress that otherwise would be caused by the stoppage or substantial reduction of earnings resulting from some specific contingencies such as sickness, maternity, old age, employment injury, invalidity unemployment, and death, the provisions of medical care, and the provision of subsidies for families with children" *(ILO, 1998)*. The concept of social security based on 'cradle- to- grave' philosophy, which envisages social protection to the needy from the pre-natal (pre-birth and maternity benefits) to posthumous care (death/ funeral benefit).

ILO Convention No. 102, Social Security Minimum Standards 1952, covers nine branches of social security, i.e. medical care, sickness benefit, maternity benefit, unemployment benefit, old-age benefit, employment injury benefit, family benefit, invalidity benefit, and survivor's benefit *(Punekar, 1978)*.

EVOLUTION OF SOCIAL SECURITY

The general notion of social security is as old as the history of man. Stories of Bible tell us how, during the years of famine, Joseph tried to tide over the situation by making use of surplus stocks of grain which he had stocked during the earlier years of plenty. The oldest institution of social security is family that includes the extended family. Industrial revolution in the Europe has seen the growth of urban and industrial centre that affected the rural joint families. When individual was unable to take care of his own needs, the society realized the importance of protection for the individual and his family. In Great Britain Poor Laws were enacted to provide minimal food and shelter in a workhouse to the poor. Private saving, compensation by employers, mutual aid or mutual

* *Research Scholar, Faculty of Commerce, B.H.U. Varanasi- 221005, (E-mail: apapandey95@gmail.com)*

benefit, private insurance and life insurance are some of the evolutionary forms of social security efforts.

NEED FOR SOCIAL SECURITY

Social security has evolved out of man kinds quest for protection from hazards arising out of vagaries of nature and from arising out of life and work in modern societies. With the advent of industrial revolution in Europe a new class of "workers" emerged. Broken away from their families and villages they were totally dependent on wages for subsistence. In due course, a comprehensive social security system was developed covering all eventualities from conception and birth till death like pre-natal and maternity benefits, paid leave, medical care, pensions, unemployment benefits, family's allowances and old age pensions, etc.

DEVELOPMENT OF SOCIAL SECURITY SYSTEM IN INDIA

Social security is provided in two forms- institutionalized form and non-institutionalized form. In India, the non-institutionalized form of social security has been in existence since time of immemorial and joint families, panchayats (guilds), religious and charitable institutions have continued to provide assistance to the needy for various common risks, misfortunes, and calamities. Kautilya's Arthashatra and Manusmriti bear testimony to the fact that the social structure in those days was so evolved and codes so designed as to provide security to all people *(Singh, 2007)*. It has been very aptly observed that, in ancient India joint Hindu family was the unit of social organization and was also the original cell for security and first line of defence, which could cope only with limited misfortunes. In case of larger calamities, appeal was made to the guilds or the neighbors. The main purpose was to provide collective security of life and property, freedom from want and misery, and security against common risks. However, organized social security measures in statutory form are only of recent origin.

In the Indian context, the statutory social security system is influenced by the following factors:

- In the early phase of industrialization, there was a need to promote the commitment of the workforce to industrial and urban life.
- A policy of corporate paternalism envisaged the provision of a variety of benefits, both to promote loyalty of employees and as a part of non-union strategy.
- The welfare state concept emerged in the post independence ere which encouraged a serious welfare and protective legislations based on relevant International Labor Organization Conventions. Several of the social security and welfare measures have become statutory obligations of employers. The pressure by the trade unions further enhanced and rain forced the governmental measures for social security.

CONSTITUTIONAL PROVISIONS

Labour is in the concurrent list of our Constitution allowing a limit autonomous of States to frame legislations for achieving their socio-economic objectives like employment. Constitution of India is yet to recognize Social Security as a fundamental right and envisaged by the Constitution of India in terms of the Directive Principles of State Policy. The following provisions of the Directive Principles of the State Policy refer to the State's obligation for social security *(Dev, 2001):*

- *Article 38* : "The state should strive to promote the welfare of the people by securing and protecting as effectively as it may a social order in which justice- social, economic and political shall inform all the institutions of the national life."
- *Article 39* : "Right to adequate means of livelihood."
- *Article 41* : "The state shall within the limit of its economic capacity and development, make effective provisions for securing the just and humane conditions of work, public assistance in case of unemployment, old age sickness, disablement, and other cases of undeserved wants."
- *Article 43* : "The state should endeavor to secure work to all workers, a living wages condition of work ensuring a decent standard of life."
- *Article 47* : "The state should regard the raising of the level of nutrition and the standard of living of its people and the improvement of public health as among its primary duties."

Legislative Support: In India, labour laws have been codified in consonance with the above Directive Principles of State Policy and thoughts of great leaders like Mahatma Gandhi, Pt. Nehru and Sardar Vallabh Bhai Patel etc., the universal Declaration of Human Rights and other principles recommended by International Labor Organization from time to time. It may be desirable to note that the social security scheme provide protection and safeguards, and security in a statutory form against various risks and contingencies in workers' life. Some of the important labour laws relating to social security are as follows:

1. The Workmen's Compensation Act, 1923.
2. The Employees' State Insurance Act, 1948.
3. The Employees' Provident Funds and Miscellaneous Provisions Act, 1952.
4. The Maternity Benefit Act, 1961.
5. The Payment of Gratuity Act, 1972.

The existing labour laws enacted for providing social security, as mentioned above, can be broadly divided into two categories, namely, the contributory and non-contributory. The contributory laws are those which provide for financing of the social security programmes by contribution paid by workers and employers and in some cases supplemented by contribution/ grants from the Government. The important contributory schemes includes Employees' State Insurance Scheme framed under the Employees' State Insurance Act, 1948 and the Provident Fund, Pension and Deposit Linked Insurance Schemes framed under the Employees' Provident Funds and Miscellaneous Provisions Act, 1952. The major non-contributory laws are the Workmen's Compensation Act, 1923, the Maternity Benefit Act, 1961 and the Payment of Gratuity Act, 1972.

The major objectives in the of specified risks and the laws under which they are covered are as shown below in the Table 1.

Table 1
Risks Covered Under Social Security Legislations in India

Risks	*Legislations under which covered*
Disablement	I. Workmen's Compensation Act, 1923.
	II. Employees' State Insurance Act, 1948.
	III. Payment of Gratuity Act, 1972.
Death	I. Workmen's Compensation Act, 1923.
	II. Employees' State Insurance Act, 1948.
	III. Employees' Provident funds & Misc. Provisions Act, 1952.
	IV. Payment of Gratuity Act, 1972.
Maternity	I. Employees' State Insurance Act, 1948.
	II. Maternity Benefit Act, 1961.
Sickness	I. Employees' State Insurance Act, 1948.
Old Age or Retirement	I. Employees' Provident funds & Misc. Provisions Act, 1952.
	II. Payment of Gratuity Act, 1972.
Funeral	I. Employees' State Insurance Act, 1948.

Source: Aspects of Labor Welfare & Social Security by A.M.Sarma, Himalaya Publishing House, New Delhi.

Workmen's Compensation Act, 1923

With increased industrialization when accidents became more frequent, workers raised protests against the callous attitude of the employer, and this gradually set in motion the reformatory movement for the improving the lot of depressed class of workers. Reforms were starting the prevailing Common Law. The various enactments enacted by the Government of England also affected the reformatory movement in India. In 1921, the government made proposals for the grant of compensation and circulated them for opinion. The proposals received general support and as a result, the Workmen's Compensation Act was passed in March, 1923 and was put into force on July 1, 1924.

The Workmen's Compensation Act, 1923 is the first organized social security legislation in India *(Sinha, 2004)*. It has made the employer liable for any injury suffered by the worker by arising out of and during the course of employment and in certain limited circumstances for occupational diseases. The Act favour the workers rather than the employer, and has made almost imperative for the employer the payment of compensation to a worker in all cases of personal injury suffered by him during the course of employment and in cases of occupational diseases. The basic principle of the Act is social justice[1]. The main object of the Act is, to provide social justice and social security to the workers through imposing an obligation upon employers for the payment of compensation.

The Act extends to the whole of India including the State of Jammu and Kashmir. The Act applies to workers employed, otherwise than in a clerical capacity, in railways, factories, mines, plantations, ports, coaling ships at docks, construction, maintenance and repairs of roads & bridges and other hazardous occupations and employment specified in Schedule 2 of the Act. The Act however does not apply to members serving in armed forces of Indian Union, and employees covered under the provisions of the Employees' State Insurance Act, 1948, as disablement and dependents' benefit is available under this Act (*Goswami,* 2008).

The Act makes provisions for the payment of compensation in two cases, first in case of personal injury caused to a worker by accident arising out of and in the course of employment and secondly in case of occupational diseases. The Workmen's Compensation Act, 1923 provides for compensation to the workmen or their survivors in cases of industrial accidents and occupational diseases, resulting in disablement or death. Minimum amount of compensation for death and permanent total disablement have been fixed at Rs. 80000 and 90000 respectively. Maximum amount for death and permanent total disablement can go up to Rs. 4.56 lakh and Rs. 5.48 lakh respectively depending on age and wages of workman.

Employees' State Insurance Act, 1948

The Employees' State Insurance Act, 1948 is a pioneering measure in the field of social insurance in India. The Act was passed on April 19, 1948 which is being implemented on the all India basis, is a landmark in the realm of social security in India.

The promulgation of ESI Act, 1948 it is an integrated need based social insurance scheme that would protect the interest of workers in contingencies such as sickness, maternity, temporary or permanent physical disablement and death due to employment injury resulting in loss of wages or earning capacity. The Act also guarantees reasonably good medical care to workers and their immediate dependents.

The main object of the Employees' State Insurance Act, 1948, is to evolve a scheme of socio-economic welfare. For fulfillment of this objective, the Act provides certain benefits to employees in form of cash benefits and medical care in cases of sickness, maternity and employment injury.

The Act extends to the entire country except the State of Jammu and Kashmir. The Act applies to all non-seasonal factories using power and employing ten or more employees, and, to non-power using manufacturing units and establishments employing twenty or more employees. The provisions of the Employees' State Insurance Act, 1948, however, are not applicable to factories or establishments run by the State Governments/Central Government, whose employees are otherwise receipt social security benefits (substantially similar or superior) under any other Act. The Act, also, does not apply to a mine or railway running shed, and specified seasonal factories. The existing wage-limit for coverage under the Act, is Rs.10,000/- per month (with effect from 1.10.2006). The provisions of the Employees' State Insurance Act, 1948, however, are not applicable to factories or establishments run by the State Governments / Central Government, whose employees are otherwise receipt social security benefits (substantially similar or superior) under any other Act. The Act, also, does not apply to a mine or railway running shed, and specified seasonal factories.

The ESI Scheme is operated in 783 Centres situated in 29 States/ UTs. As on 31 March, 2009, 12.93 million insured persons and about 50.20 million beneficiaries are covered under the Scheme. The number of employments and establishments covered by the end of the year had gone up to 3, 94,332. Health and medical care facilities are provided to the employees through a network of 148 hospitals, 42 annexes and 1388 dispensaries throughout the country by the end of March, 2009.

The ESI Scheme is mainly financed by contributions from the employers and employees. The rates of the employers' and the employees' share of contribution are 4.75% and 1.75% respectively. The State Governments' share of the expenditure on the provision of medial care is to the extent of 12.5% (1/8th within the per capita ceiling). The Corporation has prescribed a ceiling on the shareable expenditure on medical care. From 1st April, 2007, the ceiling on expenditure per insured person family unit has been raised to Rs. 1000/- per annum. All capital expenditure on construction of ESI hospitals, and other buildings including their maintenance is borne exclusively by the Corporation.

Employees' Provident Funds & Miscellaneous Provisions Act, 1952

Prior to India's independence in 1947, there was no compulsory provident fund scheme for industrial and commercial workers of the country. Some paternalistic employers had introduced their own provident fund schemes. Although, there was the Provident Fund Act of 1925, it only provided for the regulation of certain provident funds and statutory benefits as well as immunities in respect thereto, but it did not provide for the compulsory creation of any provident fund.

The Labour Investigation Committee of 1946 recommended that provident funds wherever existed should be compulsory. The 9th session of Indian Labour Conference in 1948 discussed the question of compulsory provident fund scheme for industrial workers. The subject of compulsory provident fund scheme was once again discussed at the 12th meeting of the Standing Labour Committee in 1950. Thus, toeing the recommendations of the Indian Labor Conference and the Standing Labour Committee, the Government of India promulgated the Employees' Provident Funds ordinance on 15 November 1951. The ordinance provided for the institution of compulsory provident funds scheme for the employees serving in factories and other industries. The ordinance was subsequently replaced by the Employees' Provident Funds Act (later re-named Employees' Provident Funds & Miscellaneous Provisions Act) passed on 4th March 1952.

The Act provides a scheme for the institution of provident fund for specified classes of employees. On a review of the working of the scheme over the years, it was found that provident fund was on doubt an effective scheme for old age and survivorship benefit, but in the event of the pre- mature death of an employee, the accumulations in the fund were not adequate sufficient or enough to render long term financial protection to his family. This lacuna led to the introduction of the Employees' Family Pension Scheme 1971. In 1976, the Act was amended with a view to introducing Employees' Deposit Linked Insurance Scheme, a measure to provide an insurance cover to the members of the provident fund in covered establishments without payment of any premium. Furthermore, the Act was amended in 1995 providing for Employees' Pension Scheme in liew of (in stead of) the existing Employees' Family Pension Scheme, 1971. Thus, three schemes have been framed under the Employees' Provident Funds & Miscellaneous Provisions Act, 1952.

The Act provides for the compulsory institution of contributory provident funds, pension funds and deposit linked insurance funds for employees. The act aims to ensure a retrial benefit to secure the future of the employee after retirement and early death.

The Act extends to the whole of India except the State of Jammu & Kashmir. As on 31st March 2009, the Act applied to every establishments/factories engaged in 186 Industries/classes of Establishments employing 20 or more persons (5 or more in the case of cinema). However, it does not apply to the co-operative societies employing less than 50 persons. The existing wage-limit for coverage under the Act is Rs. 6500 per month. Presently, three schemes are operated under the Act namely-

I. Employees' Provident Fund Scheme, 1952.

II. Employees' Deposit Linked Insurance Scheme, 1976.

III. Employees' Pension Scheme, 1995.

Employees' Provident Fund Scheme, 1952, which came into force w.e.f. November 01, 1952. At the end of March, 2009, 5.73 lakh establishments with 47.07 million subscribers were covered under the Employees' Provident Fund Scheme.

Employees' Deposit Linked Insurance Scheme, 1976, which came into force w.e.f. August 01, 1976. All the employees who are the member of the Provident Fund are members of this scheme also. Under the scheme, employers are required to pay contribution to Insurance Fund @ 0.5% of the pay of the employees pay i.e. basic wages, dearness allowance including cash value of food concession and retaining allowance, if any. During the year 2008-2009, a sum of Rs.368.40 crores comprising of employers' contribution was deposited. During the year 2008-2009, 21146 claims were settled and an amount of Rs. 48.43 crore was disbursed. At the end of 2007-2008, the EPFO had cumulative investments of Rs. 7155.33 crores under this Scheme.

The Employees Pension Scheme is compulsory for all the persons who were members of the Family Pension Scheme, 1971. It is also compulsory for the persons who have become members of the Provident Fund from 16-11-1995 i.e. the date of introduction of the scheme. The Employees' Pension Scheme, 1995 provides the following benefit package:

- Superannuation Pension.
- Early pension.
- Permanent Total Disablement pension.
- Widow or Widower's pension.
- Children pension/ orphan pension.
- Nominee pension or Dependent parent's pension.

Superannuation pension will be payable on attaining the age of 58 years and on completion of 20 years of service or more. Early pension can be taken at a reduced rate between 50-58 years of age, on completion of 10 years Pensionable service or more. No pension for less than 10 years of service lump sum withdrawal benefit is paid in such cases. As on 31 March 2009, there were 18, 05,012 members, 5,97,940 spouses, 5,20,625 children, 13,226 orphans and 7,620 nominees receiving pension under the Scheme. Total amount disbursed among the pensioners during the year was Rs. 2,727.97 crore through the nationalized banks and post offices.

The Scheme is financed by transferring 8.33% of the Provident Fund contribution from employers' share and by contribution @ 1.16% of basic wages by the Central Government. All accumulations in the ceased Family Pension Fund constitute the corpus of the Pension Fund. During the year 2007- 2008, Rs. 9,012.46 crore were received as Pension Fund contributions, out of which Rs. 8,022.48 crore were collected from Employers' share and Rs.990 crore were contributed by the Central Government.

Maternity Benefit Act, 1961

In order to reduce the disparities relating to maternity protection under different state enactments, the Central Government passed the Maternity Benefit Act in 1961. By the end of the year 1972, the Act has been extended to the whole of the Indian Union *(Goswami, 2008)* and applies to every establishments belonging to government and to every establishment wherein persons are employed for the exhibition of equestrian, acrobatic and other performances. The Act is however no applicable to the employees covered under the ESI Act, 1948.

Maternity Benefit Act is a piece of social labour legislation enacted to promote the welfare of working women. The Act prohibits the working of pregnant women for a specified period before and after delivery. It also provides for maternity leave and payment of certain monetary benefits for women workers subject to fulfillment certain conditions during the period when they are out of employment on account of their pregnancy.

The Act regulates the employment of women workers before and after childbirth and provides for maximum 12 weeks of maternity leave, medical bonus and certain other benefits. Of this 6 weeks of must be taken prior to the date of delivery of child and 6 weeks immediately following that date. To be entitled the maternity benefit a woman worker must have actually worked for not less than 80 days in the twelve months immediately preceding the day of her expected delivery.

The Payment of Gratuity Act, 1972

Gratuity is a lump sum payment made to a worker or his heirs by the company on termination of his service due to retirement, retrenchment, invalidity or death. Before the codification of the Payment of Gratuity Act, 1972, there was no Central Act to regulate the payment of gratuity to industrial workers, except the Working Journalists Conditions of Service and Miscellaneous Provisions Act, 1955. A proposal for Central Legislation was discussed in Labour Ministers' Conference held at New Delhi in August 1971 and also discussed in the Indian Labor Conference held in October 1971. Keeping in view the Payment of Gratuity Bill 1971, introduced in the Lok Sabha on 10 December, 1971. The Bill was passed on August 21, 1972 as "Payment of Gratuity Act, 1972" and came into force from September 16, 1972.

The main object of the Act is to help the workman and his heirs after retirement, whether retirement is resulting of the rules of superannuation or physical disablement or impairment of vital part of the body and on death.

The Act extends to the whole of India except the State of Jammu and Kashmir. The Act applies to every factory, mines, oil field, plantation, ports, Railways Company and shop or establishment, in which 10 or more employees are employed, or were employed on any day of the preceding twelve months.

The Act is applicable to employees other than apprentices drawing wages not exceeding Rs. 3500 per month.

The Payment of Gratuity Act, 1972 provides for a scheme of compulsory payment of gratuity to employees engaged in factories, mines, oil fields, plantations, ports, railway companies, motor transport undertakings, shops or other establishments.

Section 4 of the Act confers a right of the every employee, other than apprentice irrespective of his wages is other than apprentice is entitled to receive gratuity after he has rendered continuous service for five years or more. Gratuity is payable at the time of termination of his service either

- on superannuation or
- on retirement or resignation or
- on death or disablement due to accident or disease.

Termination of services includes retrenchment. However, the condition of 5 years continuous service is not necessary if services are terminated due to death or disablement. In case of death of the employee, the gratuity payable to him is to be paid to his nominee, and if no nomination has been made then to his heirs.

For every completed year of service or part thereof in excess of six months, the employer pays gratuity to an employee at the rate of 15 days' wages based on the rate of wages last drawn by the concerned employee. The amount of the gratuity payable to an employee shall not exceed Rs. 3,50,000.

All these legislations are the results of the intense struggles and lobbying of trade unions. Over a period, benefits under various legislations have been improved, particularly in terms of coverage, income ceiling for eligibility and quantum of contributions by employers and benefits to worker. Over and above these legislative provisions, collective agreements at the enterprise / industry level have provided for further improvements in many of the benefits covered by the legislations referred to above.

Administrative Arrangements

The Workmen's Compensation Act is being administered exclusively by the State Governments/Union Territory administrations. In the administration of the Employees' State Insurance Act, the Central Government and State Governments share the responsibilities. Cash benefits under the ESI Act are administered by the Central Government through the Employees' State Insurance Corporation (ESIC), whereas the medical care under the ESI Act is being administered by the State Governments and Union Territory Administrations. The Employees' Provident Funds & Miscellaneous Provisions Act is administered by the Central Government through the Employees' Provident Fund Organization (EPFO). The provisions of the Maternity Benefit

Act are being administered by the Central Government through the Chief Labour Commissioner (Central) in case of mines and circus industries and by the State Governments in factories, plantations, and other establishments. The Payment of Gratuity Act is being administered by the Central Government in establishments under its control, and also establishments having branches in more than one state, major ports, mines, oil field and railways, and by the respective State Governments and Union Territory Administrations in all other cases.

Need of an Integrated Social Security Scheme

Integration means bringing the different social security schemes under the same roof. The process of integration refers to the fusion of different agencies into one agency, which will be responsible for providing all these benefits to the beneficiaries, which the different agencies were providing previously *(Bhatnager, 1984).*

India still does not have an integrated scheme of social security with the result that similar are being disbursed under the various schemes. Differential rates of benefits are in vogue for the same contingency under different social security schemes. This leads to unnecessary and avoidable waste of money and effort. For instance, maternity benefit is provided under the ESI Act, 1948 and Workmen's Compensation Act, 1923. Thus, we find there is a lot of duplication of efforts and money in meeting these contingencies. The Study Group *(1957-58)* appointed by the Government of India has recommended for integration of various social security measures with a unified scheme of contribution and administration, providing for medical care and coverage against sickness, maternity, employment injury, old age and death. The Group also recommended for integration of ESI Scheme and EPF Scheme under one agency which called the "Organization" and the coverage under the scheme should be made co-existent.

CONCLUSION

One of the most striking features of social security is its rapid progress and improvement throughout the World. As a mechanism for meeting human needs, social security programmes have achieved near universal acceptance. Even among the newest of the emerging countries and among those with least economic development, it is a rare nation which does not have at least one social security program in operation. Extension of coverage, higher levels of benefits, new benefits for less privileged sections and innovative benefit provisions are the highlights of recent development.

As in the case with some other countries, the statutory social security schemes in India cater only for a small proportion of population. A vast majority of labour force in the unorganized and agricultural sector are beyond the benefits of organized social security schemes. However, the problem of limited coverage has become a matter of concern to social security policy makers, who recognize that the exclusion of ordinary people from modern forms of social protection is undesirable. Further, there is absence of comprehensive social security policies which can co-ordinate different schemes and ensure that their various objectives are complementary.

On the whole, the social security legislations of our country suffer from certain defects as uneven scope, inadequacy of benefits, duplication and overlapping provisions and different administrative authorities for implementation and enforcement. Inspite of certain drawbacks, social security schemes can contribute towards social protection if they are adequately supported with resources, carefully designed to meet local needs, and integrated into a national policy committed to providing adequate social protection to the excluded majority.

Notes

1. V.V.Giri, loc. Cit., p. 133.

References

Bhatnager, D. (1984), 'Labour Welfare & Social Security Legislation in India', Deep & Deep Publications, New Delhi, p. 121.

Dev, S. M. (2001), 'Social & Economic Security in India', Institute for Human Development, New Delhi, pp. 61-62.

Government of India (GOI), 'Report of the Study Group on Social Security', 1958 Delhi, 1958, para 5.4.

Government of India (GOI), Ministry of Labour & Employment, Annual Report on Social Security (2008-09), New Delhi.

Goswami, V.G. (2008), 'Labour and Industrial Laws', Central Law Agency, Allahabad, p. 385-86

Goswami, V.G. (2008), 'Labor and Industrial Laws', Central Law Agency, Allahabad, p.168.

International Labour Organization, 'World Employment Report', (1997-98), Geneva - Decent Work, Geneva, 1998.

Punekar, S. D. (1978), 'Labour Welfare, Trade Unionism & Industrial Relations', Himalaya Publishing House, Bombay, p. 133.

Singh, B. D. (2007), 'Labour Laws for Managers', Excel Books, New Delhi, pp. 257-58.

Sinha, P. R. N. (2004), 'Industrial Relation, Trade Unions and Labour Legislation', Pears on Education, Delhi, p. 428.

Police Reform:
A Long Awaited Task

Avinash Kumar*

PROLOGUE

Police is the first agency in the administration of criminal justice system. They are the entry point of the criminal justice system. To an average man the police represent the law. The responsibility of mainstream law and order is also on the police. The offender has first to encounter the police. It is this contact which influence their behavior toward the legal system as such and the society in general.

The primary responsibility of police is to protect life, liberty and property of citizens. It is for protection of these rights that criminal justice system has been constituted assigning important duties to perform the most important among them being maintenance of law order and Investigation of offences.

Investigation is a normal preliminary to an accused being put up for trial for an offence. The word 'Investigation' is defined in section 2(b) of the Criminal Procedure Code as:

> "all the proceedings under the code for the collection of evidence by a police officer or by any other person (other than a Magistrate) who is authorized by the Magistrate in this behalf."

Criminal investigation is simply defined as the evidence collection vis-à-vis a crime, an effort to know the truth and to provide a legal proof against the perpetrators of the crime. The process must establish, beyond 'reasonable doubt': Commission of crime, opportunity to commit crime, *Corpus delicti*, Motive *Modus operandi*.[1] It is basically an art of unearthing the truth for the purpose of successful detection and prosecution. In other words of the Supreme Court in (*H.N. Rishbud v/s State of Delhi*)[2] the investigation generally consists of the following steps:

(1) Proceeding to the spot;

(2) Ascertainment of the facts and circumstances of the case;

* *4th Year Student, The WB National University of Juridical Sciences, Kolkata.*

(3) Discovery and arrest of the suspected offender;

(4) Collection of evidence relating to the commission of the offence which may consist of the examination of:

(a) Various persons(including accused) and the reduction of statements into writing, if the officer thinks fit;

(b) The search of places and seizure of things considered necessary for the investigation and to be produced at the trial; and

(5) Formation of the opinion as to whether on the materials collected, there is a case to place the accused before a Magistrate for trial and, if so, taking the necessary steps for the same for the filing of a charge sheet (u/s 173 of Cr. P.C.)

The standard of police investigation in India remains poor and there is considerable room for improvement. The Bihar Police Commission (1961) noted with dismay that "during the course of tours and examination of witnesses, no complaint has been so universally made before the Commission as that regarding the poor quality of police investigation".[3] Almost in the same vein, the Punjab Police Commission (1961-62) bemoaned poor quality of police investigation. The West Bengal Police Commission (1960-61) also referred to noticeable deterioration in the investigation. The second West Bengal police Commission (1988) reaffirmed the downward trend and observed that during the intervening years the standard of investigation had further gone down. Many cases did remain undetected. It also observed that conviction figures had also gone down.[4]

The Police, as a sub-system in law-enforcement, have a variety of power and authority. Unfortunately there are allegations in some parts of the world against the abuse of authority or assuming pseudo authority by police. They violate the human rights of the people, which range from tattooing the foreheads of suspects or humiliating or torturing under-trials to "take encounters" with people in the pretext of suppressing extremist activities.[5] It is also alleged that they concoct evidence to somehow get a conviction for the accused, and at times incite communal violence for political gains of their political masters. All these are criticisms that have been appearing recently in the media about police atrocities.[6]

According to many political thinkers, the law and order scenario has become a cause for serious concern since political will is totally lacking when it comes to making the police an effective agency for dealing with the present day situation of insurgency and terrorism in some parts of the world. A mega-situation could in all probability be expected to develop in future because of increasing population, unemployment and criminalization with anti-social elements continuing to upgrade the techniques and resources.

PROVISIONS OF LAW UNDER CRIMINAL JUSTICE SYSTEM AND ITS LOOPHOLES

The manner in which police investigation are conducted is of critical importance to the functioning of the criminal justice system. Not only serious miscarriage of justice will result if the collection of evidence is vitiated by error or malpractices, but successful prosecution of the guilty depends on a thorough and careful search for truth and collection of evidence which is both admissible and probative.

Even though investigation is the foundation of the Criminal justice system, it is unfortunate that is not trusted by the laws and the courts. A confession made to a police officer is not admissible as evidence in court of law.[7] This provision, though enacted with good motive, nevertheless, creates unnecessary hardships to the police in prosecution work. There is no harm in making confessions before police officer admissible in evidence though the courts may be extra cautious while dealing with the question of authenticity of such confession. Obviously admissibility of a piece of evidence as relevant is one thing but relying on it is quite another thing. The same holds true in case the statements made to police officer whose admissibility has been barred under Sections 162[8] of the Cr. P. C. There are good reasons, as pointed out by the Supreme Court, for not treating a statement made to the police as a good and highly dependable piece of evidence, but surely there is nothing wrong about its being made admissible before a court of law. There are some officers who justifiably argue that it is not possible to make the police law abiding unless some confidence is reposed in them.

The law Commission therefore recommended that, on experimental basis, confessions made to an officer of the deputy Superintendent level or above may be made admissible provided the officer concerned conducted the investigation himself.[9]

Victims of crimes are sometimes turned away from a police station on the mere ground that the reported crime has occurred in the jurisdiction of some other police station and it is for the victim to go there and make his complaint. This works to the disadvantage of ignorant people and weaker sections in society. The NPC (National Police Commission) has recommended an important amendment to Section 154[10] of Cr.P.C. which would make it incumbent on a police station to register an FIR whether or not the crime has taken place in its jurisdiction and then transfer the FIR to the concerned police station, if necessary.

Section 167(2)[11] of Cr.P.C. provides for a maximum of 15 days in police custody. It is not possible to fully investigate serious crimes having inter-state ramification in this limited period. Moreover as per Section 167 Cr.P.C. the accused is liable to be released on bail if the charge sheet is not filed against him within 90 days from the date of his arrest. It is not always possible to investigate a case comprehensively within this period particularly cases having Inter-State or trans-national ramifications. This results in accused involved in grave victims being enlarged on a bail.

In addition to under Section 167(2) an accused cannot be taken on police custody remand after the expiry of first 15 days from the date of his arrest. This has emerged as a serious handicap in sensitive investigations.

Many times accused are admitted in Hospital during police custody on health grounds and stay there for several days. During this period interrogation of accused is not possible. Thus the police officer is handicapped in investigation.

A Session Court or High Court is empowered to grant anticipatory bail[12] irrespective of the fact whether it has the jurisdiction to hear the matter or not. Further the law does not allow the Public Prosecutor being heard, irrespective of the gravity of the offence. This provision has been often misused by rich and influential people.[13]

Under the Criminal Procedure Code, it is required that whenever the police enter any premises for the purpose of search and seizure[14], they must be accompanied by at least two respectable inhabitants of the locality. Since it is not always possible to find two respectable persons willing to associate with the police for the purpose, the police find themselves in a difficult situation and hence try to observe the formality with the co-operation of some "respectable" persons who might be of dubious character and reputation.[15] Courts being aware of such practices of police treat the evidence produced by search and seizure with utmost suspicion and even genuine prosecution cases are adversely affected in the process.

NEED FOR SEPARATE CADRE OF INVESTIGATING OFFICERS

Law is an important instrument for prevention and control of crime. There have been considerable radical changes in the political, social and economic situation in the country after the enactment of the Indian Police Act, 1861. It needs to be emphasized that the duties of the police as prescribed in Section 23 of the Indian Police Act, 1861 have become totally outdated.

Terrorism, particularly state sponsored terrorism from across the borders, has drastically changed the ambit and role police functions and duties in certain parts of the country. Besides, organized

Crime having Inter-State and trans-National dimensions has emerged as a serious challenge to the State authority. There are several reasons which are the drawbacks of investigation of police cases.

At the first place, there is inadequacy of the investigating staff. The police officers are hard pressed for time with multifarious commitments and thus, not able to devote adequate time for investigational work. A sample survey[16]

done in the six States of the country revealed that on an average, the investigating officer is able to devote only 27% of his time on investigational work, while the rest of the time is taken by other duties connected with the maintenance of law and order, VIP bandobust[17], petition enquires, court attendance, collection of intelligence and other administrative work.[18] According to the National Police Commission, policemen work for long and arduous hours on most days of duty, very much in excess of the normal eight hours.[19] A survey carried out by the National Productivity Council has revealed that the normal working time put in every day by an average subordinate police officer employed in public order or crime investigation duties is 13 hours. Not only are the policemen obliged to work on gazette holidays, they are sometimes not able to avail their normal entitlement of leave every year. These observations by the commission suggest pathetic police strength in the country. Moreover, in the existing set-up, the police function under the executive control of the state government.[20] According to the Commission, the manner in which political control has been exercised over the police in this country has led to gross abuses, resulting in erosion of rule of law and loss of police credibility as a professional organization. The threat of transfer/suspension is the most potent weapon in the hands of the politician to bend the police down to his will. The National Police Commission by a sample survey in six States in different parts of the country found that an average I.O was able to devote only 30% of his time to investigational work while the rest of the time was taken in other duties.[21] The Law Commission of India also categorically recommended separating the investigating agency form the law and order police.

Another important reason for the decline of investigation is lack of effective and timely supervision by the senior officers. There is hierarchy of officers above the SHO who are empowered to monitor and guide the investigation in terms of Section 36 Cr. P. C.[22], namely, Dy. SP, Addl. SP, and Superintendent of Police and even the Range DIG. But most of them do not devote adequate time and energy to supervisory work. Need less to say, supervision ensures proper direction, coordination and control and this helps efficiency. Effective supervision by the District Superintendents of Police and Circle officers also reduces the utilization of opportunities and misuse of coercive powers vested in the officers from the SHO down to the constabulary to the minimum. If the supervision of the District, SP and the CO is lax and ineffective, it is bound to breed inefficiency and corruption in the force.

INADEQUATE TRAINING

The present day crime situation in India is of alarming concern to the police force and enforcement agencies of the Central Government. Crime investigation is a highly specialized and complex matter, requiring a lot of expertise, patience and training. Given the complexity of crime, it is not possible for the police officers themselves to understand various facets of crime and conduct competent investigations all by themselves. To tackle the challenge of terrorism (including narco-terrorism anti terrorist-funding), organized crime, drug trafficking, economic crimes such as bank-scams etc. and crimes having inter-state and trans-national ramifications, new strategies is called for.[23] They would need help of experts from various discipline such as Auditing, Computer Sciences, Banking, Engineering, Revenue Services and so on. The investigating officers can perform their duties properly only when they are properly trained and possess necessary skill and expertise. For example the I.O should be accompanied to the crime scene by an appropriately trained scientific hand, as it is the standard practice in most of the advanced countries is to provide such scientific hands, variously designated as 'Field Criminalist', Scene of Crime Officers' (SOCO), Police Scientists etc., in the permanent strength of each police station. In some cases, these personnel are drawn from scientific cadre, while in some others they are policemen themselves, specially selected for their flair for scientific work and their academic background of science subjects. These personnel are then provided in depth training in crime scene management and in the identification of different types of scientific clues to be looked for in different types of Crimes.

In addition of the above, the specialized squads are necessary for investigating cases of Murder, Burglary, Economic Offences, Forgery, Robbery, Dacoity, Kidnapping for ransom and Automobile thefts etc.[24] the committee suggests the constitution of the following specialized squads at the district level: Homicide Squads, Burglary Squads, Economic Offences and Forgery Squads, Robbery/Dacoity Squads, Kidnapping/Missing Person Squads, Automobile theft Squads and Squads for tracking criminals.[25]

The NPC also felt that during communal riots, adequate interest is not taken in investigation of heinous and serious crimes. For investigation of such cases, special investigating squads under the State CID should be set up comprising officers of proven integrity and impartiality. Vigorous investigation should be followed by prosecution to ensure deterrent punishment to the offenders. However, the withdrawal from trial of cases occurring during communal riots by the State Governments with a view to promoting communal harmony often proves illusory and has to be discouraged. Moreover, emphasis should be given to community policing in such cases. The concept of 'Community policing'[26] is the essence of confidence building measures. In Mumbai, '*Mohalla Committees*' were set up in different areas affected by the communal riots of 1992-93.[27]

Special Investigation Teams have to be constituted to investigate the LWE (Left Wing Extremist) related cases with all necessary resources.[28]

ROLE OF GOVERNMENT

Increasing crime, rising population, growing pressure of living accommodation, particularly, in urban areas, violent outbursts in the wake of demonstrations and agitations arising from labour disputes, the agrarian unrest, problems and difficulties of students, political activities including the cult of extremists, enforcement of economic and social legislation etc. have all added new dimensions to police tasks in the country and tended to bring the police in confrontation with the public much more frequently than ever before.

Considering the far reaching changes that had taken place in the country after the enactment of the Indian Police Act, 1861 and absence of any comprehensive review at the national level of the police system after independence despite radical change in the political, social and economic situation in the country, the Government of India, on 15th November, 1977, appointed a National Police Commission. The Commission was required to recommend measures and institutional arrangements to prevent misuse of powers by the police, by administrative or executive instructions, political or other pressures or oral orders of any type, which are contrary to law, for the quick and impartial inquiry.[29]

In the second report, it was noticed that the crux of the police reform is to secure professional independence for the police to function truly and efficiently as an impartial agent of the law of the land and at the same time to enable the Government to oversee the police performance to ensure its conformity to the law. A supervisory mechanism without scope for illegal, irregular or mala fide interference with police functions has to be devised. The report, inter alia, noticed the phenomenon of frequent and indiscriminate transfers ordered on political considerations as also other unhealthy influences and pressures brought to bear on police and, inter alia, recommended for the Chief of Police in a State, statutory tenure of office by including it in a specific provision in the Police Act itself. Besides the report submitted to the Government of India by National Police Commission (1977-81), various other high powered Committees and Commissions have examined the issue of police reforms, viz. National Human Rights Commission, Law Commission, Ribeiro Committee (1998) , Padmanabhaiah Committee and Malimath Committee on Reforms of Criminal Justice System(2002) . All the Commissions and Committees above noted have broadly come to the same conclusion on the issue of urgent need for police reforms. The Police Commission Report recommended that the investigation task should be beyond any kind of intervention by the executive or non-executive. It was hoped that the Government would examine and publish the report expeditiously so that the process for implementation of various recommendations made therein could start right away. But the recommendations of National Police Commission were not implemented, for whatever reasons[30] or compulsions, and they met the same fate as the recommendations of many other Commissions.

In addition to above, the Government of India in terms of Office Memorandum dated 20th September, 2005 constituted a Committee comprising Shri Soli Sorabjee, former Attorney General and five others to draft a 'New

Police Act' in view of the changing role of police due to various socio- economic and political changes which have taken place in the country and the challenges posed by modern day global terrorism, extremism, rapid urbanization as well as fast evolving aspirations of a modern democratic society. The Sorabjee Committee has prepared a draft outline for a new Police Act (9th September, 2006).

For separation of investigation work from law and order even the Law Commission of India in its 154th Report had recommended such separation to ensure speedier investigation, better expertise and improved rapport with the people without of course any water tight compartmentalization in view of both functions being closely inter-related at the ground level.

JUDICIAL APPROACH ON POLICE REFORMS

Nearly ten years back, in "*Vineet Narain & Ors. v.Union of India and Anr.*"[31] Supreme Court noticed the urgent need for the State Governments to set up the requisite mechanism and directed the Central Government to pursue the matter of police reforms.

However, on 22nd September 2006, the Supreme Court of India delivered a historic judgment, in "*Prakash Singh and Others Vs Union of India and Others*"[32], laying down six practical directives to kick-start the police reform process. The Court's directives are binding on all state governments to frame appropriate legislation. The most important directives of the Supreme Court are Directives 1 and 6 on setting up 'State Security Commissions' and 'Police Complaints Authorities'[33]. But the Supreme Court under its fourth directive ordered the separation of the investigating police from the law and order police to ensure speedier investigation, better expertise and improved rapport with the people.

The transition, however, is not going smooth. The separation of law and order and investigation wing is being opposed by the states citing "*the huge cost involved*" in such exercise. Unfortunately, only ten states (Assam, Arunachal Pradesh, Manipur, Meghalaya, Mizoram, Nagaland, Sikkim, Tripura, Uttaranchal and Goa) have wholly or almost wholly complied with the directions of the Supreme Court. But most states are dragging their feet. The worst offenders are Maharashtra, Tamil Nadu and Uttar Pradesh. Maharashtra has taken the stand that the Supreme Court's directions are "inconsistent with statutory provisions in existence." Tamil Nadu has argued that "courts have no power to pass directions by way of judicial order to affect the legislative autonomy of the state."[34] Uttar Pradesh has set up a Police Reforms Commission to draft a bill that can be passed by the legislature.

Moreover, nine states have passed laws or ordinances to circumvent the implementation of the Supreme Court's directions. These are: Bihar, Chhattisgarh, Haryana, Himachal Pradesh, Gujarat, Kerala and Rajasthan. The Bihar Police Bill 2007 is particularly perverse.

Thus, it is the duty of the respective state governments to enforce the judgment of the Supreme Court in view of the larger interest of the society by giving away all political gains and their personal interests. The Supreme Court's orders, if sincerely implemented, should have far-reaching implications. They would change the working philosophy of the police and transform what has been a 'ruler's police' into a 'people's police'.

CONCLUSION

Public order and crime control are responsibilities of State government, State government takes action to maintain order and deal with crime in their respective jurisdiction. Terrorism and organized crime in many cases have interstate and international ramifications. In these cases, CBI does not have original jurisdiction. It cannot take up all cases due to organizational inadequacies. In view of these shortcomings and their grave implication for national security, it is imperative that India should create Federal crimes and set up a federal investigation agency as has been done in the USA. In this connection, Malimath Committee has remarked, "time has come when the country has to give deep thought for a system of Federal Law and Federal Investigating agency with an all-India Charter. It could have within its ambit crimes that effect national security activities aimed at destabilizing the country politically and economically.[35]

In this regard Central government has proposed to pass a Federal Investigation Agency which will have sweeping powers to prove cases of terrorism anywhere in the country without the prior consent of states. But the states apprehend that the proposed federal agency may usurp their powers and upset the Quasi-federal arrangement envisaged in the constitution.[36]

The directions to the state were aimed at insulating the police from extraneous pressures, give them functional autonomy, making them more accountable, separating investigation from law and order duties in the metropolitan towns, introducing transparency[37] in the selection of police chiefs[38], and giving a statutory minimum tenure[39] to officers posted in the field.

There are a number of other administrative measures which would need to be taken to give greater muscle to the police, we are heavily under policed.[40] The police population ratio in India is 1:694. It is 1:334 in the U.S, 1: 290 in the UK and 1: 416 in New Zealand.

Modernization of police forces should get high priority. The centre has been liberal in releasing the funds. Here also, the state governments have been tardy in properly utilizing them. Training remains a neglected area[41]. As recommended by the 'Administrative Reforms Commission' headed by Verrappa Moily, the deputation to training institutions must be made more attractive in terms of facilities and allowances so that the best talent is drawn as instructors.

Besides, training should focus on bringing attitudinal change in police so that they are more responsive and sensitive to citizen's needs. What is required is public co-operation through 'Confidence Building Measures' by police. In western countries where police gadgetry and forensic science have reached principle of performance, the crime figures are showing ever increasing trend. Police managers and social scientist there are now switching over surer service modules of policing and trying to enlist public co-operation through announcement of police-community programmes and value based policing.

As the first exercise in CBM both politicians and police should honour and respect the laws of the land.[42] Moreover, the concept of Community policing as the essence of confidence building measures should be extended to other aspects of policing like settling petty disputes, prevention and detection of crime and even surveillance over suspicious strangers or visitors to the locality. In exercise of legal statutes police should not under any circumstances, distinguish between the followers of ruling party and the opponents. This is show of executive honesty through neutrality. It manifest rule of law and not rule of ideology.

Thus, the researcher concludes that the wider ramification of different variety of emerging crimes and various loopholes in the Criminal justice system need to be corrected. Moreover the government needs to strengthen the existing police force by providing all sorts of assistance in terms of latest technology and adequate infrastructure during the process of investigation rather than mere focusing on increasing the manpower. The present situation demands the urgent need of police reforms.

Notes

1. B. R. Sharma, 'Scientific Criminal Investigation',1st edition, Universal Law Publishing Co. Pvt. Ltd., 2006.
2. AIR 1995 SC 196.
3. Committee on Reforms of Criminal Justice System, (2003) Mali math Committee Report, p. 88.
4. Ibid.
5. Sohrabuddin Sheikh fake encounter case. [*The Hindu*, 23 July, 2010]
6. The recent enquiry of CBI against the Gujarat Home Minister 'Amit Shah' and other senior police officers of Gujarat in the fake encounter case of Sohrabuddin Sheikh and her wife in 2006, under the supervision of Supreme Court of India. The Hindu, Gandhinagar,(23 July, 2010)
7. Sec. 25 of Indian Evidence Act
8. Statements to police not to be signed: Use of statements in evidence. (1) No statement made by any person to a police officer in the course of an investigation under this Chapter, shall, if reduced to writing, be signed by the person making it ; nor shall any such statement or any record thereof, whether in a police diary or otherwise, or any

part of such statement or record, be used for any purpose, save as hereinafter provided, at any inquiry or trial in respect of any offence under investigation at the time when such statement was made:

Provided that when any witness is called for the prosecution in such inquiry or trial whose statement has been reduced into writing as aforesaid, any part of his statement, if duly proved, may be used by the accused, and with the permission of the Court, by the prosecution, to contradict such witness in the manner provided by section 145 of the Indian Evidence Act, 1872 (1 of 1872); and when any part of such statement is so used, any part thereof may also be used in the reexamination of such witness, but for the purpose only of explaining any matter referred to in his cross-examination.

(2) Nothing in this section shall be deemed to apply to any statement falling within the provisions of clause (1) of section 32 of the Indian Evidence Act, 1872 (1 of 1872), or to affect the provisions of section 27 of that Act.

Explanation: An omission to state a fact or circumstance in the statement referred to in sub-section (1) may amount to contradiction if the same appears to be significant and otherwise relevant having regard to the context in which such omission occurs and whether any omission amounts to a contradiction in the particular context shall be a question of fact.

9. Section 25 of the Evidence Act may be suitably amended on the lines of Section 32 of POTA 2002 that a confession recorded by the Superintendent of Police or Officer above him and simultaneously audio/video recorded is admissible in evidence subject to the condition that the accused was informed of his right to consult a lawyer. See, Shankar Gopalakrishnan, 'Recommendations of the Malimath Committee on reforms of Criminal Justice System', available online at *http://www.pucl.org/Topics/Law/2003/malimath-recommendations.htm* [last visited 21 August 2010].

10. Information in cognizable cases: (1) Every information relating to the commission of a cognizable offence, if given orally to an officer in charge of a police station, shall be reduced to writing by him or under his direction, and be read Over to the informant; and every such information, whether given in writing or reduced to writing as aforesaid, shall be signed by the person giving it, and the substance thereof shall be entered in a book to be kept by such officer in such form as the State Government may prescribe in this behalf.

(2) A copy of the information as recorded under sub-section (1) shall be given forthwith, free of cost, to the informant.

(3) Any person aggrieved by a refusal on the part of an officer in charge of a police station to record the information referred to in subsection (1) may send the substance of such information, in writing and by post, to the Superintendent of Police concerned who, if satisfied that such information discloses the commission of a cognizable offence, shall either investigate the case himself or direct an investigation to be made by any police officer subordinate to him, in the manner provided by this Code, and such officer shall have all the powers of an officer in charge of the police station in relation to that offence.

11. The Magistrate to whom an accused person is forwarded under this section may, whether he has or has not jurisdiction to try the case, from time to time, authorize the detention of the accused in such custody as such Magistrate thinks fit, for a term not exceeding fifteen days in the whole ; and if he has no jurisdiction to try the case or commit it for trial, and considers further detention unnecessary, he may order the accused to be forwarded to a Magistrate having such jurisdiction:

Provided that-

1*[(a) the Magistrate may authorize the detention of the accused person, otherwise than in the custody of the police, beyond the period of fifteen days ; if he is satisfied that adequate grounds exist for doing so, but no Magistrate shall authorize the detention of the accused person in custody under this paragraph for a total period exceeding,-

(i) ninety days, where the investigation relates to an offence punishable with death, imprisonment for life or imprisonment for a term of not less than ten years;

1. subs. by Act 45 of 1978, s, 13, for paragraph (a) (w.e.f, 18-12-1978).

2. Ins. by act 10 of 1990 , s.2 (w.e.f 19-2-1990)

(ii) sixty days, where the investigation relates to any other offence, and, on the expiry of the said period of ninety days, or sixty days, as the case may be, the accused person shall be released on bail if he is prepared to and does furnish bail, and every person released on bail under this sub-section shall be deemed to be so released under the provisions of Chapter XXXIII for the purposes of that Chapter ;]

(b) no Magistrate shall authorize detention in any custody under this section unless the accused is produced before him;

(c) no Magistrate of the second class, not specially empowered in this behalf by the High Court, shall authorize detention in the custody of the police.

1 *[Explanation I.-For the avoidance of doubts, it is hereby declared that, notwithstanding the expiry of the period specified in paragraph (a), the accused shall be detained in custody so long as he does not furnish bail ;].

2*[Explanation II.-If any question arises whether an accused person was produced before the Magistrate as required under paragraph (b), the production of the accused person may be proved by his signature on the order authorizing detention.]

1*[(2A) Notwithstanding anything contained in sub-section (1) or sub-section (2), the officer in charge of the police station or the police officer making the investigation, if he is not below the rank of a sub-inspector, may, where a Judicial Magistrate is not available, transmit to the nearest Executive Magistrate, on whom the powers of a Judicial Magistrate or Metropolitan Magistrate have been conferred, a copy of the entry in the diary hereinafter prescribed relating to the case, and shall, at the same time, forward the accused to such Executive Magistrate, and thereupon such Executive Magistrate, may, for reasons to be recorded in writing, authorize the detention of the accused person in such custody as he may think fit for a term not exceeding seven days in the aggregate; and, on the expiry of the period of detention so authorized, the accused person shall be released on bail except where an order for further detention of the accused person has been made by a Magistrate competent to make such order ; and, where an order for such further detention is made, the period during which the accused person was detained in custody under the orders made by an Executive Magistrate under this sub-section,

1. ins. by Act 45 of 1978, s. 13 (w.e.f. 18-12-1978).

2. Explanation numbered as Explanation II by s. 13, ibid. (w.e.f. 18-12-1978) shall be taken into account in computing the period specified in paragraph (a) of the proviso to sub-section (2): Provided that before the expiry of the period aforesaid, the Executive Magistrate shall transmit to the nearest Judicial Magistrate the records of the case together with a copy of the entries in the diary relating to the case which was transmitted to him by the officer in charge of the police station or the police officer making the investigation, as the case may be.

12. Section 438 of Cr. P. C.
13. See, Supra note. 9 (S. 438 of the Code regarding anticipatory bail be amended to the effect that such power should be exercised by the Court of competent jurisdiction only after giving the public prosecutor an opportunity of being heard).
14. Section 100(4) of Cr. P. C.
15. See, Supra Note. 9 (Presence of witnesses of the locality or other locality or neighborhood is required under different provisions of the existing laws. The committee recommends that such provisions be deleted and substituted by the words "the police should secure the presence of two independent witnesses").
16. Committee on Reforms of Criminal Justice System (Malimath Committee Report), vol. 1, Government of India, Ministry of Home Affairs, March 2003.
17. There are about a 1,000 policemen protecting Chief Minister 'Prakash Singh Badal' and his family. [Times of India, December 17, 2008].
18. National Police Commission, Fourth Report, p. 8.
19. Crime in India(1993) at p. 70
20. Jain Havala case: concerning money laundering to foreign accounts: the Central Bureau of Investigation (CBI) (a national police body equivalent to the RCMP) had leveled the charge that politicians were involved in such money laundering and that investigations into these activities were being influenced. The Court CBI should have come superintendent control over its functions; this case was extremely important in being the first judgment where superintendence and control over police has been indicated.
21. Law Commission 154th report.
22. Powers of superior officers of police: Police officers superior in rank to an officer in charge of a police station may exercise the same powers, throughout the local area to which they are appointed, as may be exercised by such officer within the limits of his station.
23. There are two aspects of modernization. One of them pertains to the use of technology in police working. Use of computers in police working has resulted in networking between police stations and in district headquarters. Video Conferencing has eliminated wastage of time in travel. Computerized fingerprints analysis and Criminal Tracking system has been of great assistance in investigation. DNA technology is also being used in investigation. Most sophisticated technology is used in the VVIP security. See, Satish Sahney, *'Modernising the Indian Police'*, One India One People, Vol. 10/6, 2007, p. 17.
24. National Police Commission Report, vide Para 49.82.
25. *Ibid*
26. Community policing is basically a partnership between the police and the people of that area to ensure that peace prevails and criminality is kept in check.
27. Prakash Singh, *' Ruler's police to peoples police'*, One India One People, Vol. 10/6, 2007, p. 11
28. The special investigation Team has proved their effectiveness in cases like, Parvathipuram conspiracy case, the Secunderabad conspiracy case, and the case of assassination of Late Sri Madhav Reddy and most importantly, the Rajiv Gandhi assassination case. See, A.B.V Rao, *'Investigation of Extremist offenses'*, available online at

http://www.cidap.gov.in/documents/Investigation%20of%20Extremist%20offenses.pdf (last visited on 14 August 2010).

29. M.P. Singh, 'Police *Problems and Dilemmas in India'*, 1st edition, Mittal Publication, New Delhi, 1989
30. The reforms, however, were never carried out because of the combined opposition of political parties.
31. (1998)1 SCC 226
32. WRIT PETITION (CIVIL) NO. 310 OF 1996, (DATE OF JUDGMENT: 22/09/2006).
33. To ensure that the operational independence promised by the reforms does not deteriorate into a Police Raj, the court has ordered the institution of a Police Complaints Authority in each police commissionarate and revenue districts. These authorities would be headed by retired judicial officers of appropriate rank and will entertain complaints of high-handedness, misuse of powers and injustice by police officials. The Authority will instruct the police chief concerned to take such action as it feels appropriate after due inquiries. See, Julio Ribeiro, 'Marching Towards a change', One India One People, Vol. 10/6, 2007, p. 9.
34. Chamaraj, Kathyayini , 'State governments unwilling to relinquish control', available online at *http://www.indiatogether.org/2007/sep/gov-policeref.htm* [last visited on 12 August 2010].
35. According to Malimath Committee, the Federal Agency may have concurrent jurisdiction over the following categories so Crimes: Terrorist activities, war against the state, arms and drug trafficking hijacking, money laundering.
36. As law and order is under the List II (State List) on which only state can make laws.
37. Supra Note 22. At present there is no system of empanelment in the state. If now the reforms are implemented, only those officials who are empanelled for promotion will be considered for the top jobs. The D.G. of the police will be chosen among three senior most empanelled officers and this choice will be left not to one man but a body presided over by the Chief Minister or Home minister and consisting of the opposition leader, a sitting or retired High court judge and a few non-political citizens of integrity.
38. Supra note 22. (The principle thrust of the Supreme Court order on Police reforms is that the officers who are selected to head the force in each state are to be chosen for their merit and integrity and not arbitrarily as is the case at present).
39. Supra note. 22. (Once chosen, these officers should be given operational independence to run their charges professionally and without undue interference from the politicians. Since they would have two year tenure, they could be independent to a greater extent than at present. They would be accountable for the law of the land instead of the party in power).
40. In December 2008, the National Crime Records Bureau reported, India had 1.13 million police personnel — about 128 for every 1,00,000 people, just over half the United Nations-recommended norm for peaceful societies facing no major challenges. See, Pravin Swami, *'India's counter-insurgency conundrum'*, The Hindu online edition, July 23, 2010.
41. Just how poor the training of India's police personnel was graphically illustrated in June this year, when dacoit *'Ghanshayam kewat'* engaged over 400 policemen for nearly 50 hours killing four and securing his escape finally dying in chance engagement with a separate police patrol.
42. Gujarat Minister for home evades inquiry again, charge sheeted in the Sohrabuddin fake encounter case. [*The Hindu*, 23 July, 2010].

References

Criminal Procedure Code, 1973.

Committee on Reforms of Criminal Justice System (Malimath Committee Report), Vol. 1, Government of India, Ministry of Home Affairs, March 2003.

154th report 'The code of Criminal Procedure Code', 1973, Law Commission of India.

Pillai, Dr. K. N. Chandrasekharan (2001), "R.V. Kelkar's Criminal Procedure", 4th edition, Eastern Book Company, Lucknow.

Justice Y.V. Chandrachud & V.R Manohar, Ratanlal & Dhirajlal's, "The Code of Criminal Procedure", 17th edition,

Singh, M. P. (1989), 'Police Problems and Dilemmas in India', 1st edition, Mittal Publication, New Delhi.

Parekh, H. (2007), '*Law relating to Crime Investigation and Medical Science*', 1st edition, Dwivedi and Company, Allahabad.

Sharma, B. R, '*Scientific Criminal Investigation*',1st edition, Universal Law Publishing Co. Pvt. Ltd., 2006.

Sarkar, S. C. (2006), '*Commentary on the Code of Criminal Procedure*, 1973', 1st edition, Dwivedi Law Agency, Allahabad.

Chamaraj, Kathyayini (2010), '*State governments unwilling to relinquish control*', available online at *http://www.indiatogether.org/2007/sep/gov-policeref.htm* [Last visited on 12 August, 2010].

Rao, A. B. V, '*Investigation of Extremist offenses*', available online at *http://www.cidap.gov.in/documents/Investigation%20of%20Extremist%20offenses.pdf* [last visited 21 August 2010]

Mukerjee, Dr. Doel, '*Police reforms initiative in India*', available online at *http://72.14.235.132/search?q=cache:rdmOWYOjTjMJ:www.humanrightsinitiative.org/publications/police/police_reform_initiative_india.pdf+police+reforms+in+india&hl=en&ct=clnk&cd=5&gl=in [last visited on 26 December 2008]*

V. Gnagadhar (2007), '*Set up Commissions, Reforms will Follow!*' ,One India One People, Vol. 10/6.

Ribeiro, Julio (2007), '*Marching Towards a Change*', One India One People, Vol. 10/6.

Singh, Prakash, '*Ruler's Police to Peoples Police*', One India One People, Vol. 10/6, 2007.

Singh, Y. P., '*Corruption Overrules Competency*', One India One People, Vol. 10/6, 2007.

Sahney, Satish, '*Modernising the Indian Police*', One India One People, Vol. 10/6, 2007.

Soman, D. S., '*An Empty Talk*', One India One People, Vol. 10/6, 2007.

Private Law and Environmental Regulation: Between Protection and Prevention

Scott Nicholas Romaniuk*

INTRODUCTION

The impact of human activity on the environment has never been such a pressing political and legal issue as it is today. The growing body of public legislation and regulation coupled with action in the private sector to invest in new green technologies and practices attest to a world fundamentally conditioned by environmental and eco-concerns. However, beyond government as the main driver of the new environmentalism, questions have been raised concerning the role of private law in promoting environmental protection and regulation. Specifically, the capacity of the traditional systems of western civil liability, both Common Law and Civil Law, to act as a complement to the existing body of public law is of paramount interest and importance. The logic as it relates to these issues seems deceptively simple—the participation of private actions in civil liability settings would exert pressure on environmental actors, particularly large corporations, to more effectively adhere to the goals of environmental protection. In spite of this, the utility of actions in civil liability remains constrained because many cases of environmental damage do not conveniently fit into its traditional architecture. As a consequence civil liability has needed to re-conceptualize many of its base elements, such as harm, causation and the tortfeasor, in order to accommodate environmental claims.[1]

Both Common and Civil law systems impose legal liability upon persons, natural or legal, to compensate those that they have harmed from actions not arising out of contract. While both systems permit imposition of strict liability in certain situations, for example torts like defamation in Common Law or parental liability in the Civil Code of Québec, the base principle of liability remains the idea of fault.[2] The architecture of civil liability, generally in Civil law and in the Tort of Negligence, is thus constructed around the relationship

* Institute of European, Russian and Eurasian Studies (EURUS), Carleton University, 1125 Colonel By Drive, Ottawa, Canada, (E-Mail: sromaniu@connect.carleton.ca)

between an injured party, and whose harm can be causally attributed to the neglectful act of another.[3]

For environmental law, the fixation upon the relationship between two or more persons defines the initial difficulties of framing an ecological claim simply because there are often no definite human actors that can be said to have suffered direct harm. This is clearly illustrated by the case of acid rain, the diffuse effects of which cause minimal damage to individual persons, property or resources, but the resultant aggregate costs to geographic areas and ecosystems can be enormous.[4] In cases of environmental damage, the attribution of harm is problematic because the civil liability system, as noted by Peter Crane, is axiomatically concerned with reparation of specific victims.[5]

Given this concern, however, one must question cases where there is no "human victim". A fundamental yet implicit principle of contemporary civil liability systems remains that only legally recognized victims—or persons representing victims—are able to exercise a claim against a tortfeasor. In cases of environmental harm, damages are often born by collectivities or nature itself without the mediation of a human actor. Subsequently, if the civil liability system is to be conceived of as a mechanism of environmental protection then the systemic preoccupation with human victims fundamentally excludes a comprehensive range of ecological damage that is the result of human activity. This line of reasoning would suggest that without damage to property rights or the human body, a reparable harm does not exist in law as civil liability simply does not protect "things".[6] Consequently, actions in tort or civil liability for environmental damage are often incapable of acting in situations where no human actor is present, or is simply not worth the effort if damage to an individual is so minor that invoking court costs prove to be an illogical course of action.

New sources of environmental claims have had to be created within the extant structure of national civil liability systems. In Europe, a growing movement has called for the recognition of individuals to exercise a right in civil litigation to defend the "patrimoine commun" that does not belong to any particular property interest.[7] In the Untied States, different orders of government have launched, varying degrees of success, civil suits for ecological injury under *parens patriae* jurisdiction as the guardians of future generations of citizens.[8] Other jurisdictions, in particular Belgium, Brazil and the State of Illinois are currently entrenching rights to environmental protection in their own constitutions.[9] Perhaps most radically, the European Court of Justice has recognized in *Francovich v. Italy* that European Union (EU) Member States can be held liable to their citizens for failures to implement into national law directives from the European Commission (EC).[10] Although this has yet to be tested, if a Member State had not implemented into law or enforced an EU environmental directive, then consequently one of its citizens could bring an action against an EU state to force performance. In so doing, states are recognizing the environment as a social interest rather than simply an economic interest to individual citizens.

While the anthropocentric nature of civil liability has effectively excluded claims that lack a human victim, the ability of different victims to make a claim against different tortfeasors also appears to function according to the particularities of each jurisdiction. Common Law allows for a variety of claims against polluters or people with vested interests in pollution creating activities to be made. Although the tort of negligence requires the demonstration of fault, other torts such as nuisance and *Rylands v. Fletcher* have been used to impute strict liability to polluters. Civil Law systems seem by nature, more restricted in their handling of claims because they are fundamentally premised on the notion of fault. However, not all Civil Law systems are alike. Since the turn of the twentieth century, article 1384 of the French Civil code has been interpreted to engage the liability of all those who engage in a dangerous activity, including those dangerous to the environment.[11] In the Province of Québec, Canada, environmentally based actions have been grounded more in the concept of nuisance than under *fait de la chose*; however, the recent case, *Barette c. Ciment du St-Laurent*, has controversially redefined the notion of nuisance as obligations arising between "fonds voisins" rather than between individuals on those lands.[12] As commented on by doctrine, this transformation of the obligation "restrein fortement les recours possibles pour les victimes, puisque désormais celles-ci doivent être des voisins ou au moins des personnes proches, et nécessairement elles-mêmes propriétaires d'un fonds."[13] As evidenced by this section, the capacity for victims to make environmental claims relies heavily upon the particular development of a specific system of civil liability. While the fundamental principle seems to focus on human harm, the ability for victims to be able to undertake legal action against polluters by suing remains rooted as a function of particular systems of liability and nothing more.

Questions about the nature of environmental harm also have significant impact not only in the establishment of victims but also for the evaluation of reparative damages. In Civil Law, tortfeasors are responsible for compensating all "direct" damages, be they corporal, material or moral, mirrored to some extent in the Common Law's tenet of *resitutio in integrum*.[14] However, each system has extensively limited the kinds of damages that can be compensated. In France, ecological incidents such as *l'Affaire de l'Amoco-Cadiz* saw judges assess damages for "direct" damages such as cost of clean-up, land restoration and administration.[15] It should be noted, however, that such costs as loss of bio-mass or bio-diversity were not factored into the court award.[16] In *Cambridge Water Co. v Eastern Counties Leather plc.*, the House of Lords found that the defendant was not liable because the specific damages to the local aquifer were unforeseeable.[17] Such rulings on foreseeability have troubling ramifications as environmental damage tends not to function in a linear relationship with pollution. For example, Bergkamp argues that "the marginal environmental damage caused by each additional unit of pollution often increases and, above a certain level, such increases may be exponential."[18] Consequently, Court awards only compensate such damages considered "appropriate" by the judicial system. As noted by Ost, "[l]e droit traite des dommages certains et personnels; l'écologie présente des prejudices incertaines et collectives."[19] By effectively eliminating so-called "indirect" and "unforeseeable" costs, the system effectively limits the recoverable damages to a fraction of actual environmental harm.

The practice of undervaluing environmental damage has solicited responses from a range of public actors, although the efficacy of such measures is still largely disputed. Recognizing that many national civil liability systems have been reticent in awarding more than direct pecuniary costs associated with ecological damages, the Council of Europe adopted expansive language in defining recoverable damages to include "toute perte ou dommage résultant de l'altération de l'environnement."[20] However, there remains considerable tension in what can be considered part of "the environment" or what costs can be thought of as a compensable damage. The European Commission's White Paper on Environmental Liability decisively excluded from the calculation of damages "pollution with a widespread, diffuse character where it is impossible to link the negative environmental effects with the activities of certain individual actors."[21] While in principle, recognizing that environmental damage can be pervasive, actual practice has seen damages limited to the aggregate costs of acute instances of ecological destruction and its associated clean-up expenses.

Beyond the legal determination of whether and to what extent environmental damage exists, environmental claims have struggled in attempt to prove that specific damage was related to specific behaviour. Per Baoudouin, in the civil liability analysis "la nécessité d'un certain lien causal est indispensable..."[22] Although Common Law has other torts of strict liability that are available for environmental claims, for cases of negligence the Supreme Court of Canada reaffirmed the preeminent place of direct causation, including the "but-for" test, in *Hanke v. Resurfice*.[23] For environmental claims, the dominant place of fault is often a major impediment due to the claimant's inability to link specific damage with the specific actions of a potential tortfeasor. As Lee contends, "in contrast to the conventional tort cases of slipping and tripping or motor vehicle crashes, the disjunctive nature of incidents and effects [in environmental cases] complicates the imposition of liability..."[24]

In the case of acid rain, the ability to show that sustained damage was attributable to the actions of one polluter is in many cases impossible; simply put, imagine trying to pursue every driver in a major metropolitan area as potential contributor to the effects of acid rain. Consequently, the systemic inability for environmental claimants to demonstrate direct causal links has required many systems of civil liability to modify their residual principle of direct fault in order to accommodate the more diffuse nature of environmental damage. In many jurisdictions, demonstration of a causal relationship now requires a demonstration of cause-in-law rather than cause-in-fact.[25] Manifestation of cause-in-law has been achieved by different methods including a reversal in the burden of proof—whereby polluters are required to disprove that they had caused the pollution—the imposition of probabilistic causation or even perhaps the transition to new forms of "risk responsibility" like market share liability.[26] Thus, the reassessment of causation changes traditional notions of civil liability because harm is no longer directly attributed to conduct.

This major transformation of traditional fault-based liability, however, needs to be understood in light of a greater body of environmental law. Serving the particular policy goal of environmental protection is a massive corpus of public law, regulations, and tax policy, to which civil liability figures as a private-law partner. Framed as part of a greater socio-political project, environmental law permits the importing of new principles into civil liability regimes. Embodied in the 1992 Rio Declaration and supported in national and international legislation, is the polluter-payer principle.[27] While initially targeted towards public regulation, the principle has stimulated civil liability insofar as "where no effective preventative measures have been taken, the polluter-payer principle is invoked to require that the polluter compensate the environmental damage resulting from his activities."[28] In effect, the principle in its most general form stripped of nuance and context, stands for the fundamental proposition that all costs of ecologically dangerous activities must be born by those actors who engage in them. Imbued with a proactive public purpose, civil liability becomes an instrument "à prevenir à l'avenir la répétition des comportements dommageables."[29] Effectively, the adoption of polluter-payer principle dictates to environmental actors that engaging in environmentally damaging activities without assuming responsibility for the consequences is neither socially, politically nor economically acceptable.

Combining this public policy directive with the new modes of causation has essentially transformed the role and character of the tortfeasor in civil liability. Classically considered as independently acting individuals responsible for their own conduct, defendants in environmental civil liability now form part of a greater network of actors. To the extent to which actors are now responsible for others, be it through strict liability, market liability or probable causation et al., that civil liability becomes a system of risk allocation rather than holding actors responsible for their particular faulty actions. Further emulating the polluter-payer principle, the transformation from fault to no-fault liability systems reinforce the notion that environmental harm must be compensated; as Cane states "[t]he critical question is not whether the polluter should pay, but under what conditions."[30]

More precisely, the question addresses ways to best define the risk pool. How exactly will polluters be held severally responsible for their actions and how will liability be spread? In different regions of the world, a variety of liability mechanisms have been created by statute to hold polluters jointly and severally liable for damage. In the United States, liability has been tied to geographic location under the Comprehensive Environmental Response, Compensation and Liability Act (CERCLA). The Act imposes retroactive, strict, joint and several liability on owners past and present, in addition to those who deposited materials on the site and those who transported dangerous materials to a site.[31] In Germany, industry based cooperatives (*Berfugenossenschaften*) are seen as models for the creation of industrial cooperatives that will bear liability costs.[32] Japanese and German commentaries propose framing the risk not on a horizontal, industrial-wide basis, but rather in vertical relationships along production or environmental chains; as Teubner states, "[h]ere the chances for cooperative risk prevention are greater since there are preexisting contractual links that can be exploited for arrangements that define liability risks and monitor behaviour."[33] Irrespective of this approach, these various liability collectivization mechanisms demonstrate a fundamental change from the idea of individual responsibility to broadly-conceived risk networks of which compensation is the primary function.

A principle issue arising from this analysis, however, is the question of whether compensation is the *modus operandi* of the civil liability system with regards to the environment. While the polluter-payer principle provides robust justification for civil liability as corrective justice, it fails to adequately address the concern that pollution should be prevented before the devastating and, in many cases, irreversible effects are realized. While the move towards objective responsibility has provided greater certainty of compensation for victims, it has also distorted the use of civil liability as a deterrent for pollution itself. Environmental law is also animated by the maxim that, according to Ost, "mieux vaut prévenir que guérir" and so civil liability is caught between competing policy goals of prevention and compensation.[34] Economically, the cost of possible litigation and damages should serve as incentive for market actors to invest further in the formulation of prevention strategies. However, where liability is collectivized, particularly in large risk pools, the incentive for individuals to engage in preventative measures is reduced as cooperative links between pools members are missing, competitiveness prevails and selective incentives to invest do not exist.[35] In addition, the methods of collectivization, some noted above, produce risk pools whose members are in direct competition with each other as "liability law creates a collective in situations of non-cooperative behaviour."[36] Teubner emphasizes this point by stating that "individual actors are burdened with the additional responsibility for actions that other actors have committed and over whose actions they have no control", which to some extent creates disincentives to engage in proactive pollution reduction and prevention behaviours[37]

By shaping and reshaping the traditional architecture of civil liability, the policies and goals of environmental protection are exposed to a paradox insofar as a collectivization of risk allows for the fulfillment of the polluter-payer principle. At the same time, however, this undercuts the proactive goals of prevention by environmental actors. Ironically, environmental liability may have to re-appropriate some of the concepts from traditional civil liability. Teubner proposes a hybrid system whereby "collective liability makes sure the victims will be compensated in situations where no individual causation can be established; individual reapportionment [within the risk pool based on fault principles] creates incentives for individual actors to reduce ecological risk."[38] While this particular system may engage elevated administrative costs, it is promising because it holds the further advantage of addressing both functional concerns of civil liability. However, even a fusion of liability systems demonstrates that in many cases the needs of environmental claims must transcend the analytical categories of traditional fault-based liability systems, creating more complex and context specific notions of environmental responsibility.

CONCLUSION

Over the last thirty years concern with environmental degradation has come to grip the public imagination in a way previously undetected. As ecological damage presents a large yet diffuse harm caused by indeterminate social actors, it has had substantial difficulty engaging with the traditional civil liability system. Notions of injury, causation and fault simply cannot handle the many cases of environmental harm. Fundamentally, civil liability systems, both in Common Law and Civil Law jurisdictions, have had to reassess their foundational terms to provide a more flexible analysis of complex ecological problems. Furthermore, environmental liability has to be assessed in light of a greater body of public law that is animated by two fundamental propositions, those of the polluter-payer principle, and the prevention principle. In light of these two principles, civil liability faces the paradoxical charge of providing compensation to victims while encouraging ecological actors to take preventative action against pollution; whether the system has such a capacity remains to be seen.

Notes

1. Although tortfeasor is a specifically Common Law term, this essay will use it as a generic term for the individual(s) who have or are accused to have caused environmental damage.
2. Jean-Louis Baoudoin & Patrice Deslauriers, *La Responsabilité Civile.* 7e éd., (Cowansville, QB: Yvon Blais, 2007), 97. and Allen Lindin, *Canadian Tort Law.* 8th ed., (Markham, ON: LexisNexis Butterworths, 2006), 216.
3. Article 1457 CCQ.
4. Lucas Bergkamp, *Liability and Environment.* (London, UK: Kluwer Law International, 2001), 11.

5. Peter Cane, "Using Tort Law to Enforce Environmental Regulations.", *Washburn Law Journal*, No. 41, (2002), 442.
6. Robert G. Lee, "From the Individual to the Environmental: Tort Law in Turbulence", in John Lowry & Rod Edmunds, *Environmental Protection and the Common Law*. (Oxford, UK: Hart, 2000), 443.
7. Francois Ost, "La responsabilté, fil d'Ariane du driot de l'environment." *Droit et Société*, Vol. 30, No. 21, (1995), 302.
8. *Ibid.*
9. *Ibid.*, 314.
10. [1991], ECR I-5357.
11. Francois Ost, "La responsabilté, fil d'Ariane du driot de l'environment." *Droit et Société*, Vol. 30, No. 21, (1995), 285.
12. *Ciment du St-Laurent inc. c. Barrette*. (2006), QCCA 1437.
13. Jean-Louis Baoudoin & Patrice Deslauriers, *La Responsabilité Civile*. 7e éd., (Cowansville, QB: Yvon Blais, 2007), Sec. 2.
14. Article 1607 CCQ.
15. Francois Ost, "La responsabilté, fil d'Ariane du driot de l'environment." *Droit et Société*, Vol. 30, No. 21, (1995), 305.
16. *Ibid.*
17. [1994] 2, WLR 53.
18. Lucas Bergkamp, *Liability and Environment*. (London: Kluwer Law International, 2001), 11.
19. Francois Ost, "La responsabilté, fil d'Ariane du driot de l'environment." *Droit et Société*, Vol. 30, No. 21, (1995), 309.
20. *Convention on Civil Liability for Damage Resulting from Activities Dangerous to the Environment*, 21 June 1993, CETS No. 150, Article 2, Section 7.
21. EU, Commission, *White Paper on Environmental Liability*, (Luxembourg, Lux.: EU, 2000), 13.
22. Jean-Louis Baoudoin & Patrice Deslauriers, *La Responsabilité Civile*. 7e éd., (Cowansville, QB: Yvon Blais, 2007), Sec. 1-604.
23. 2007 SCC 7, [2007], 1 S.C.R. 333, Paragraphs 19 and 21.
24. Robert G. Lee, "From the Individual to the Environmental: Tort Law in Turbulence", in John Lowry & Rod Edmunds, *Environmental Protection and the Common Law*. (Oxford, UK: Hart, 2000), 81.
25. Gunther Teubner, "The Invisible Cupola: From Causal to Collective Attribution in Ecological Liability." *Cardoza L. Rev.*, No. 16, (1994), 461.
26. *Ibid.*, 461.
27. *Report of the United Nations Conference on Environment and Development*, UNEP, 1992, UN Doc. A/CONF.151/26 (Vol. I), Principle 16.
28. Lucas Bergkamp, *Liability and Environment*. (London, UK: Kluwer Law International, 2001), 16.
29. Nicolas de Sadeleer, *Les Principes du Pollueur-Payeur, de Prévention et de Précaution: Essai sur la Genèse et la Portée Juridique de Quelques Principes du Droit de l'Environnement*. (Bruxelles: Bruylant, 1999), 103.
30. Peter Cane, "Using Tort Law to Enforce Environmental Regulations.", *Washburn Law Journal*, No. 41, (2002), 442.

31. Kenneth Abraham, "The Relation Between Civil Liability and Environmental Regulation: An Analytical Overview." *Washburn Law Journal*, No. 41, (2002), 386.
32. Gunther Teubner, "The Invisible Cupola: From Causal to Collective Attribution in Ecological Liability." *Cardoza L. Rev.*, No. 16, (1994), 461.
33. *Ibid.*, 460.
34. Francois Ost, "La responsabilté, fil d'Ariane du driot de l'environment." *Droit et Société*, Vol. 30, No. 21, (1995), 287.
35. Günther Teubner, "The Invisible Cupola: From Causal to Collective Attribution in Ecological Liability." *Cardoza L. Rev.*, No. 16, (1994), 454.
36. *Ibid.*, 442.
37. *Ibid.*, 433.
38. *Ibid.*, 455.

References

Abraham, Kenneth (2002), "The Relation between Civil Liability and Environmental Regulation: An Analytical Overview." *Washburn Law Journal*, No. 41, pp. 379-398.

Article 1457 CCQ.

Article 1607 CCQ .

Baoudoin, Jean-Louis and Deslauriers, Patrice (2007), *La Responsabilité Civile*. 7e éd., Cowansville, QB: Yvon Blais.

Bergkamp, Lucas (2001), *Liability and Environment*. London, UK: Kluwer Law International.

Cane, Peter (2002), "Using Tort Law to Enforce Environmental Regulations." *Washburn Law Journal*, No. 41, pp. 427-467.

Ciment du St-Laurent inc. c. Barrette. (2006), QCCA 1437.

Convention on Civil Liability for Damage Resulting from Activities Dangerous to the *Environment*, 21 June 1993, CETS No. 150, Article 2, Section 7.

De Sadeleer, Nicolas (1999.), *Les Principes du Pollueur-Payeur, de Prévention et de Précaution: Essai sur la Genèse et la Portée Juridique de Quelques Principes du Droit de l'Environnement*. Bruxelles: Bruylant.

ECR I-5357, 1991.

EU, Commission, *White Paper on Environmental Liability*, Luxembourg, Lux.: EU, 2000.

Lee, Robert G. (2000), "From the Individual to the Environmental: Tort Law in Turbulence", in John Lowry & Rod Edmunds, *Environmental Protection and the Common Law*, Oxford, UK: Hart.

Lindin, Allen (2006), *Canadian Tort Law*. 8th ed., Markham, ON: LexisNexis Butterworths.

Ost, Francois (1995), "La Responsabilté, fil d'Ariane du driot de l'environment." *Droit et Société*, Vol. 30, No. 21, . 281-322.

Report of the United Nations Conference on Environment and Development, UNEP, 1992, UN Doc. A/CONF.151/26 (Vol. I), Principle 16.

SCC 7, 1 S. C. R. 333, 2007.

Teubner, Gunther (1994), "The Invisible Cupola: From Causal to Collective Attribution in Ecological Liability." *Cardozo L. Rev.*, No. 16, p. 429-464.

WLR (2)53, 1994.

Protecting Child Rights–
An Inevitable Agenda

Avinash Kumar*

The day will come when nations will be judged not only by their military or economic strength, nor by the splendor of their capital cities public building but by the well-being of their people;.... ...... by the provision that is made for those who are vulnerable and disadvantaged and by the protection that is afforded to the growing minds and bodies of their children **– UNICEF, Annual Report**

PROLOGUE

Children constitute over 400 million of the one billion plus population of India. It has the highest number of children in the world. More than one third of the country's population is below 18 years. Approximately 40% of the total population i.e. around 440 million is children. India shows some of the dazzling realities of children. India has the highest rate of neo-natal deaths (around 35%) in the world.[1] It constitutes 40% of child malnutrition in developing world. It has 50% of the child mortality. It has Reducing number of girls in 0-6 age group- *for every 1000 boys 927 girls.* It is reported that some 640 million children lack adequate shelter; 400 million have no access to safe drinking water; 270 million lack health care amenities and 140 million especially girls have remained outside the ambit of formal schooling.[2] It has high rate of child marriage. Its 37% of literate & 51% of illiterate girls are married below 18 years of age. Its 10% of literate and 15% of illiterate boys are married below 18. It has large number of child laborers.[3] It has large number of sexually abused children.

The word 'Child' has been used in various legislation as a term denoting relationship, as a term indicating capacity, and a term of special protection. The legal conception of a child has thus tended to vary depending upon the purpose. According to Article 1 of the United Nations

Convention on the Rights of the Child 1989, 'a child means every human being below the age of eighteen years unless, under the law applicable to the child, majority is attained earlier'.

* Fourth Year Student, 'The WB National University of Juridical Sciences', Kolkata.

Childhood is universal transcend all nationalities and know no artificial boundaries. It is indeed an important factor in shaping the future of the nation if childhood can be endowed with the minimum requisite for healthy growth and development. Recognition of the inherent dignity and of the equal and inalienable rights of all members of the human family is the foundation of freedom, justice and peace in the world.[4] These inalienable rights are guaranteed to all human beings including children. Children should be afforded the necessary protection and assistance for the harmonious development of their personality.[5]

Thus, it is imperative to have a look on the special protections offered to children.

INTERNATIONAL LEGAL FRAMEWORK PROTECTING RIGHTS OF THE CHILD

Law in the form of international conventions can contribute significantly. International instruments stress 'participation' as a core value along with survival, protection and development. Laws and legal strategies must be devised to encourage these values. Since the beginning of the twentieth century, the development of international law on the rights of the child has paralleled, in part, the development of general body of international human rights law.

The *'Declaration of the Rights of the Child, 1924'*, adopted by the fifth Assembly of the League of Nation, can be seen as the first International Instrument dealing with children's rights.[6] The Declaration establishes the claim that *'mankind owes to the child the best it has to give'*. This Declaration basically highlights the social and economic entitlements of children and establishes internationally the concept of the right of the child, and lays the foundation for setting the future international standards in the field of children's rights.

Another International instrument is *'Declaration of the Rights of the Child, 1959'*. Its preamble describes the principle as enunciating rights and freedom, which governments should observe by legislative and other measures progressively taken. Its preamble also makes reference to both the United Nation Charter and the Universal Declaration of Human Rights. This further reiterates the pledge that, 'mankind owes to the child the best it has to give'. In accordance with the Declaration, a child is entitled to a name and nationality[7], to adequate nutrition, housing, recreation, and medical services[8], special needs of physically, mentally and 'socially handicapped' children[9], children who are without family[10] etc. A noticeable departure from the principles of the 1924 Declaration is that the earlier Declaration Specified that 'Children must be the first to receive relief, whereas the 1959 Declaration lays down that children shall be 'among the first' to receive protection and relief is a good realistic approach undertaken.[11]

In 1978, on the eve of the United Nations-sponsored International Year of the Child, a draft text was proposed for the Convention on the Rights of the Child. Drawing heavily from the Universal Declaration of Human Rights; the International Covenant on Civil and Political Rights; and the International Covenant on Economic, Social and Cultural Rights, a working group within the United Nations then collaborated and revised the draft, finally agreeing what became the articles of the Convention on the Rights of the Child.[12] . The '*Convention on the Rights of the Child, 1989*',[13] brings together the children's human rights articulated in other international instruments. This Convention articulates the rights more completely and provides a set of guiding principles that fundamentally shapes the way in which we view children. The 'Convention on the Rights of the Child' was the first instrument to incorporate the complete range of international human rights– including civil, cultural, economic, political and social rights as well as aspects of humanitarian law.[14]

Article 4[15], 42[16] and 44[17] of CRC provides for General measures of implementation. This highlights the need to constantly review relevance of reservations and the importance of bringing national legislation in conformity with the convention.

Article 1 gives the definition of the age of the child. No minimum age is defined. Article 2, 3, 6 and 12 of CRC give the four general principles of the convention i.e. non-discrimination, best interest of the child, right to survival and development, and respect for the views of the child. Whereas, Articles 7, 8, 13-17 and 37(a) specify the civil rights and freedoms which include the right to name and nationality, freedom of expression and peaceful assembly, right not to be subjected to torture, etc.

There are four general principles enshrined in the convention. These are meant to ensure the interpretation of the Convention as a whole and thereby guide the national programmes of implementation. The four principles are Non-Discrimination (Article 2), Best interest of the Child (Article 3), The Right to life, and survival and development (Article 6), and The Views of the Child (Article 12).

Moreover, to deal with the growing abuse and exploitation of children worldwide, the United Nations General Assembly in year 2000 adopted two Optional Protocols to the Convention on the Child Rights to increase the protection of children from involvement in armed conflicts and from sexual exploitation.

SUBSIDIARY INTERNATIONAL INSTRUMENTS

'*Optional Protocol on the involvement of children in armed conflict*'[18] is an effort to strengthen implementation of the Convention and increase the protection of children during armed conflicts. The Protocol requires States who ratify it to "take all feasible measures" to ensure that members of their armed forces under the age of 18 do not take a direct part in hostilities. States must also raise the minimum age for voluntary recruitment into the armed forces from 15 years but does not require a minimum age of 18.

The other one is '*Optional Protocol on the sale of children, child prostitution and child pornography*'[19] The Convention's Optional Protocol on the sale of children, child prostitution and child pornography supplements the Convention by providing States with detailed requirements to end the sexual exploitation and abuse of children.[20] It also protects children from being sold for non-sexual purposes—such as other forms of forced labour,[21] illegal adoption and organ donation.

The Protocol defines the offences like 'sale of children'[22], 'child prostitution' and 'child pornography'. It also creates obligations on governments to criminalize and punish the activities related to these offences. It requires punishment not only for those offering or delivering children for the purposes of sexual exploitation, transfer of organs or children for profit or forced labour, but also for anyone accepting the child for these activities.

INTERNATIONAL INSTRUMENTS OF UNIVERSAL CHARACTER

Besides, the above stated specific international instrument, some Articles of General Global Human Rights Instruments like the '*Universal Declaration of Human Rights', 1948; 'International Covenant on Economic, Social and Cultural Rights', 1966* and *International Covenant on Civil and Political Rights (ICCPR), 1966* also deal with the Child Rights. Two Articles of UDHR expressly refer to children. Article 25(2) deal with special care and assistance and Article 26 on education.[23]

Article 10 and 12 of the 'International Covenant on Economic, Social and Cultural Rights' specifically refers to Children. Article 10 provides that states recognize the family as the 'natural and fundamental group unit of society and therefore accord the widest possible protection and assistance to the family. Article 10 (3) contains a wide ambit of protection.

Article 14 (3) (f) of ICCPR provides that criminal proceedings should take account of 'juveniles age' and their 'desirability of promoting their rehabilitation'. The Covenant prohibits the imposition of death penalty for crimes committed by persons below eighteen years of age. It also obliges states to separate accused juveniles from accused adults and bring tem as speedily as possible for adjudication and accord them treatment according to their age and legal status[24].

Furthermore, one of the Regional Instrument that is '*European Convention on Human Rights', 1950* has been used as a valuable instrument for children. Part 1 enshrines the basic principle: 'Children and young person have the right to special protection against the physical and moral hazards to which they are exposed.

ENFORCEMENT OF INTERNATIONAL INSTRUMENTS IN INDIA

On 12 November 1992, the Government of India ratified the '*Convention on the Rights of the Child*'. Article 73 of the Constitution states : 'subject to the provisions of this Constitution, the executive power of the Union shall extend to the matters with respect to which Parliament has power to make laws; and to the exercise of such rights, authority and jurisdiction as are exercisable by the Government of India by virtue of any treaty or agreement'. Article 253 of the Constitution states that 'Parliament has power to make any law for the whole or any territory or any part of the territory of India for implementing any treaty, agreement to Convention with any other country or countries or any decision made at any international conference, association or other body'.

In order to ensure child right practices and in response to India's commitment to UN declaration to this effect, the government of India set up a *National commission for Protection of Child Rights*. The Commission is a statutory body notified under an Act of the Parliament on December 29, 2006. Besides the chairperson, it will have six members from the fields of child health, education, children and development, juvenile justice, children with disabilities, elimination of child labour, child psychology or sociology and laws relating to children. The Commission has the power to inquire into complaints and take '*suo- motu*' notice of matters relating to deprivation of child's rights and non-implementation of laws providing for protection and development of children among other things. Aimed at examining and reviewing the safeguards provided by the law to protect child rights, the Commission will recommend measures for their effective implementation. It will suggest amendments, if needed, and look into complaints or take '*suo- motu*' notice of cases of violation of the constitutional and legal rights of children.

In addition to this, Convention on Rights of the Child obligate the state parties to submit periodic reports stating the measures they have taken to give effect to the provisions of the Convention.[25] Governments that ratify the Convention or one of its Optional Protocols must report to the Committee on the Rights of the Child, the body of experts charged with monitoring States' implementation of the Convention and Optional Protocols. These reports outline the situation of children in the country and explain the measures taken by the State to realize their rights. In its reviews of States reports, the Committee urges all levels of government to use the Convention as a guide in policymaking and implementation.

Also, to highlight the existence of the most egregious violations of international human rights law and encourage Governments to investigate particular cases, the United Nations Commission on Human Rights has appointed a Special Rapporteur on the sale of children, child prostitution and child pornography. The Special Rapporteur, an expert in the field, works to gather and analyze facts for the Commission.[26]

The Juvenile Justice Act is one of such attempt in consonance with the CRC, for juveniles in India. The Act provides for a special approach towards the prevention and treatment of juvenile delinquency and provides a framework for the protection, treatment and rehabilitation of children in the purview of the juvenile justice system. However, 'Juvenile Justice Act', 2000 does not either take into account lessons from law reform efforts in other parts of the world or make serious efforts to incorporate the provisions of the Child Rights Convention (CRC) that India has ratified. For instance, the Board has the power to send the child to a special home for a minimum period of not less than two years for a child who is over seventeen and less than eighteen and in case of any other juvenile till he or she ceases to be a juvenile. This provision is in clear contravention of Art. 37(b)[27] of the Convention of the Rights of the Child, which notes that arrest, detention or imprisonment of a child, shall be used only as a measure of the last resort and for the shortest appropriate period of time.[28]

The soul of the CRC is the notion that the child has the right to participate in decisions that affect her (Art 12). This fundamental principle has completely been ignored in the JJ Act 2000. If an enactment were to implement Article 12, it would mean a radical overhaul of existing ways of interacting with children. At every stage in the interface between the child and the juvenile justice system, space should be created for expression of the child's opinion. So right from the point of arrest, to adjudication before the competent authority to assessment by the authority to placement to everyday living within the institutions set up under the juvenile justice system, the child's opinion should not only be heard, but given due weight in accordance with the age and maturity of the child.

As far as Constitutional provision is concerned. Article 23 prevents trafficking in women and children for immoral purposes. Article 39(e) and (f) of the Directive Principles of State Policy states that it is the duty of the state to secure that the tender age of children are not abused and forced by economic necessity to enter vocations unsuited to their age and strength and directs the state to ensure that the children are given opportunities to develop in a healthy manner and in conditions of freedom and dignity. Furthermore, in the same line specific legislations were also enacted to deal with trafficking like *'The Suppression of Immoral Traffic in Women and Girls Act, 1956'* which was later amended in 1970 and 1986 which was result of pursuance of the UN Convention of 1950.

JUDICIAL APPROACH TO CHILD RIGHTS

One very significant structure of the legal system is represented by the courts. Courts are a body that is in authority to take decisions. In the case of *'Mayanbhai Ishwarlal Patel v. union of India'*[29] and again in the case of *'Vishaka v. State of Rajasthan'*[30] the supreme Court laid the principle that in the absence of a domestic law the contents of international conventions and norms are relevant for the purpose of interpretation of the fundamental Rights. Thus, the courts have on several occasions responded to the needs of children through public interest litigation, especially in the areas of improvement of conditions of children in institutions, prisons, illegal confinement, treatment of physically and mentally disabled children, child labor[31], adoption, Juvenile Justice, prevention of trafficking of young girls, welfare of children of prostitutes, prohibition of corporal punishment in schools and sex selection tests.

There are few judicial pronouncements which need to be mentioned here. In '*People's Union for Democratic Rights v. Union of India*'[32] the court held: but apart from the requirement of ILO Convention No. 59, we have article 24 of the Constitution of India which even if not followed up by appropriate legislation must operate '*proprio vigore*' and construction work being plainly and undoubtedly a hazardous employment, it is clear that by reason of constitutional prohibition no child below fourteen years can be allowed to be engaged in construction work.

In '*Bandhua Mukti Morcha v. Union of India and others*'[33] The court emphasized that when the allegations revealed that the workers were being held in bondage without basic amenities like shelter, drinking water, or two square meals a day, it was a violation of the fundamental rights as in this country everyone has a right to live with dignity and free form exploitation.

CONCLUSION

In spite of the several attempts at the Global and National level, Children are deprived of their fundamental and Basic Human Rights. There is need to generate a national debate on how the government and civil society can share this great responsibility which, as things now stand, seems difficult of fulfillment and achievement by the political society. The major significance of the Convention on the Rights of the Child is that it represents a commitment to improving the situation of children in India. Thus, it can be used by public advocates to force the government to take action on child issues. As the government has already agreed that these standards should be met, advocates need to bring instances of the violation of children's rights to the attention of the government and the public, and demand change. However, the efforts have not been utterly inadequate. Although law in the form of international convention or national legislation can contribute considerably towards the child rights what matters is how laws are actually implemented, what is done to reach the ideals contained in these laws. Ways must be found, therefore, to enforce the implementation and to ensure that children experience true childhood.

Notes

1. See, National Seminar on Towards a Better Pro-Child Juvenile Justice System for India *http://www.relieffoundation.org.in/Docs%20and%20Presentations Concept%20paper%20on%20Juvenile%20Justice%20in%20India%20.doc*(visited on 23 March 2010).

2. The status of children in India- Findings of UNICEF 2005 report, available online at *http://www.azadindia.org/social-issues/children-of-India.html*[last visited on 26 April, 2010]
3. Children of over 400,000 construction workers at the Commonwealth Games sites are deprived of basic rights like sanitation, schooling and healthcare (as reported by *Economic Times*, 4 Aug 2010).
4. See: Preamble to the Convention on the Rights of the Child, 1989. Adopted on 20-11-1989 and came into force in the year 1990.
5. See: Universal Declaration of Human Rights, United Nations has proclaimed that Child being Vulnerable shall be given special care and assistance.
6. See: Records of the Fifth Assembly, 1924. Supplement no. 23, *League of Nations official Journal.*
7. Principle 3 of Declaration of the Rights of the Child, 1959.
8. *Ibid*, Principle 4
9. *Ibid*, Principle 5
10. *Ibid*, Principle 6
11. Asha Bajpai, '*Child Rights in India*', 2nd edition, Oxford University Press, 2006, p. 16
12. See, *http://www.unicef.org/crc/* last visited on 14 August 2010.
13. Adopted by UN General Assembly o 20th November, 1989 and became legally binding in September 1990. Many countries ratified the Convention very soon after it was adopted and others continued to ratify or accede to it, making it the most widely ratified human rights treaty. As of December 2005, nearly all States are parties. Somalia and the United States have not yet ratified the Convention but have signed it, indicating their support.
14. Supra Note 10.
15. States Parties shall undertake all appropriate legislative, administrative, and other measures for the implementation of the rights recognized in the present Convention. With regard to economic, social and cultural rights, States Parties shall undertake such measures to the maximum extent of their available resources and, where needed, within the framework of international co-operation.
16. States Parties recognize the rights of the child to freedom of association and to freedom of peaceful assembly. No restrictions may be placed on the exercise of these rights other than those imposed in conformity with the law and which are necessary in a democratic society in the interests of national security or public safety, public order (ordre public), the protection of public health or morals or the protection of the rights and freedoms of others.
17. No child shall be subjected to arbitrary or unlawful interference with his or her privacy, family, or correspondence, nor to unlawful attacks on his or her honor and reputation. The child has the right to the protection of the law against such interference or attacks.
18. Supra Note 2.
19. After receiving the first 10 ratifications needed for its entry into force, the Optional Protocol on the sale of children, child prostitution and child pornography became legally binding on 18 January 2002.
20. It is estimated by the ILO that the number of children under 18 involved in prostitution exceeds two million, one million of whom are in Asia and 300,000 in the United States. See (United Nations Department of Public Information * DPI/1765/HR—December 1995).

21. *Ibid*, there are nearly 80 million children under 15 working as laborers.

22. *Ibid*, The Special Rapporteur said a field visit to Nepal showed that "it is primarily girls from hill-tribe groups in that country who are tricked and sold into prostitution, both local and transnational.

23. This is a non-binding resolution of the General Assembly.

24. Article 24 of ICCPR

25. Dr. S. K. Kapoor, '*International Law and Human Rights*', 16th edition, 2007, p. 893.

26. United Nations Department of Public Information * DPI/1765/HR–December 1995.

27. No child shall be deprived of his or her liberty unlawfully or arbitrarily. The arrest, detention or imprisonment of a child shall be in conformity with the law and shall be used only as a measure of last resort and for the shortest appropriate period of time.

28. Supra Note 1.

29. AIR 1969 SC 783.

30. (1997) 6 SCC 241

31. Current estimates of child labor in India vary as there is no reliable data on employment in the unorganized sectors. Regarding Child labor, India occupies the top rank among the neighbouring countries in South Asian Region. It is estimated to the 300 million all over the world. Out of this, India alone accounts for about 100 million; Non official reports estimates that there are 150 million children in the work force in our country (Avtar Singh, Child labor Problems and Prospects: Socio-Legal Measures, Social Action, Vol. 54, (2004), P. 398.

32. AIR 1982 SC 1480.

33. AIR 1984 SC 802.

References

Bajpai, Asha, *Child Rights in India: Law, Policy and Practice*, 2nd edition, Oxford University Press, New Delhi, 2006.

Kapoor, Dr. S. K, *International Law and Human Rights*, 16th edition, Central Law Agency, Allahabad, 2007.

N.S. Dr. Sreenivasulu, *Human Rights: Many sides to a Coin*, 1st edition, Regal Publication, New Delhi, 2008.

Ramcharan, B.G, *The Protection Concept of the Human Rights Council*, Manoj Kumar Sinha (Ed.), International Criminal Law and Human Rights, 1st edition, Manak Publication, New Delhi, 2010 .

Sinha, Manoj Kumar, *Implementation of Basic Human Rights*, 1st edition, Manak Publication, New Delhi, 2002.

Thukral, Enakshi Ganguly, *Children's rights in India*, Combat Law, Vol. 3, Issue 1, March 2010.

National Seminar on Towards a Better Pro-Child Juvenile Justice System for India, available online at *http://www.relieffoundation.org.in/Docs%20and%20Presentations/Concept%20paper%20on%20Juvenile%20Justice%20in%20India%20.doc [Last visited on 23 March 2010]*

United Nations Background Note, available online at *http://www.un.org/rights/dpi1765e.htm* [Last visited on 21 April 2010]

Convention on the Rights of the Child, *http://www.unicef.org/crc/* [Last visited on 26 August 2010]

Office of the United Nations High Commissioner for Human Rights, available online at *file:///D:/Human%20Right%20law/project/crc.htm* [Last visited on 21 April 2010]

The status of children in India- Findings of UNICEF 2005 report, available online at *http://www.azadindia.org/social-issues/children-of-India*

Prison Conditions and Prisoners' Rights in Punjab: A Study of the Role of Punjab State Human Rights Commission

SATNAM SINGH DEOL*

INTRODUCTION

The word 'prison', derived from French word *Prisoun* (Etymology Dictionary), is a place where people accused of infringing the law are physically confined and usually deprived of a range of personal freedoms. Regarding the meaning of prison, there is no unanimity among the writers. According to the Oxford Dictionary, "Prison is a place or building for confinement of persons accused or convicted of a crime or offence; now a public building for the detention of the persons committed by process of law. (The Oxford English Dictionary 1989) According to Encyclopedia Britannica, "Prison is an institute for the confinement of persons convicted of major crimes or felonies." (Encyclopedia Britannica 1994) The word 'jail', synonymous of prison, generally used for American prisons, was first used in England for punishment during sixteenth century. According to the prevailing usage in India, the term 'jail' or 'prison' is a generic term which applies to penal institutions, housing both prisoners, awaiting trial and prisoners committed to sentences. (Gupta 2009).

In Punjab, prison means any jail or place used permanently or temporarily under the general or special orders of Government for the detention of prisoners and includes all lands and buildings, appurtenant thereof. Central Jails, District Jails, Sub Jails, and Other jails including Female Jail, Open Air Agriculture Jail and Certified School, are the main kinds of prisons in Punjab. The prisons in Punjab are governed by the century old Prisons Act 1894 and the Prisons Act 1900 (*The Hindu* 2004) and being organized, classified and controlled according to the chapter IV, III and V of Punjab Jail Manual 1996. (Punjab Jail Manual 1996).

* *Assistant Professor, Department of Political Science, SBRS College for Women, Sadiq, Punjab, India, (E-mail: sdeol.sdeol@gmail.com)*

PRISON CONDITIONS AND PRISONERS' RIGHTS IN PUNJAB

The prisons in Punjab are the walled houses of cruelty, torture and defiled indignity. The Jail Manuals are antiquated, the architecture is primitive and the attitude of the jail authorities towards crime and criminals is not only indifferent, but unpardonably dehumanizing. There is hardly any cleanliness in the prisons. The toilet and the sanitation facilities are miserable. The prisoners are provided the unhealthy, unhygienic and even germ-infected food to eat. (Tondon 2008) The prisoners, especially women, are facing a tough time while they are being ferried to the court complex for hearings. The women prisoners face difficulties while meeting their families during the time of hearing, as they complain of eve teasing by their male counterparts. (Khanna 2009) The prisoners have to protest for the attainment of basic facilities like standardized food, clean toilets and healthy environment. (Dewan & Sharma 2009) The relatives of the prisoners, who come to meet them, are mal-treated and subjected to constant harassment at the hands of jail staff. The prisoners continue to use toilets without barracks, seek treatment from dispensaries of old designs, eat unhygienic food made in ill equipped kitchens and brave lung, skin and viral infections that are spreading faster due to neglect of basic hygiene inside prisons. (Bhatnagar 2005) The functioning of the Punjab Jails Department is in a mess. There have been scandals and embezzlements. Several cases of irregularities and malfunctioning have been highlighted by the Public Accounts Committee of the state Vidhan Sabha. (Dhaliwal 2005).

Approximately 25.2 per cent of Jail population in Punjab is beyond capacity. It is another noticeable figure that 67.66 inmates of total population are under-trials. The Central jails and the District jails are severely crammed up beyond capacity with the over capacity of 26.92 per cent and 48.07 per cent respectively. (National Human Rights Commission (NHRC) 2008) The over-crowded jail population causes several types of irregularities, incapacities and indiscipline in the jails.

The health and medical care facilities are at miserable conditions in the prisons of Punjab. The jail authorities are not providing proper medical care and health facilities to the under-trial prisoners and the convicts. It has been found that there is lack of segregation of convicts leading to psychosomatic problems among them. As a consequence the prisoners are increasingly suffering from communicable diseases due to frequent body contact. (Tondon 2005) Even the Punjab and Haryana High Court has observed that the medical facilities were lacking in the prisons of Punjab. (Malik 2008).

There are several cases of deaths in the prisons of Punjab. Especially the under-trials are the severe victims of the mysterious deaths in the jail premises. The prisons, which are now branded as the Reform Homes, are becoming the places where the inmates always have a threat of their life. At least 9 inmates had died in Central Jail Bathinda in the span of three years from 1997 to 2000. (Prakash 2000) Similarly, during the period from May 2001 to July 2001, five inmates had died in the Central Jail Ferozepore. (Prakash & Gupta 2001) Vipan, an under-trial in the Central Jail, Ferozepore, under the NDPS Act, had died at the Guru Gobind Singh Medical College and Hospital on July 11, 2001. He was brought to the hospital from the Central Jail of Ferozepore in a critical condition and after the staff of Civil Hospital of Ferozepore had referred him to Guru Gobind Singh Medical College and Hospital, Faridkot. (*The Tribune* 2001) Similarly, Amit Savio an under-trial in the Pathankot Jail had died an unnatural death in the Jail on May 10, 2003. (*The Tribune* 2003)

ROLE OF PSHRC REGARDING PRISON CONDITIONS AND PRISONERS' RIGHTS

The PSHRC was set up by the Government of Punjab through Notification dated 17 of March 1997 under the provisions of Section 21 of the Protection of Human Rights Act (PHRA), 1993. (Arora 2007) The prerequisite purpose behind the constitution of the PSHRC, as described in its debut annual report of 1997-1998, among others, is to review the existing laws and procedures and the system of administration with a view of bringing about greater efficiency and transparency. Besides that, other prior and paramount aims of the PSHRC are to inquire human rights violations and to promote respect and awareness for human rights, to improve jail conditions, promote human rights literacy, promote awareness about human rights and to encourage the efforts of non-governmental organizations and institutions, working in the field of human rights. (PSHRC 1997-98) The PSHRC, during its functioning of 13 years since 1997 till 2010, has performed a remarkable job to alleviate the violation of human rights in Punjab. The victims of human rights violations in Punjab assume the PSHRC as the most reliable resort to their complaints. The statistical data containing the total number of complaints reveals that the PSHRC, from March 31, 1997, till November 30, 2009, has instituted as many as 131307 complaints relating to different forms of human rights violations. (PSHRC 2009) Besides other major fields of human rights violations, the PSHRC has received, registered and adjudicated a huge influx of complains regarding prisoners' rights and prison conditions.

The PSHRC instituted 11 cases regarding Jails in 1997. It was only in the first year of its functioning that the number of cases was quite less. A rapid and sudden flow of the cases related with Jails was noticed in 1998 and the PSHRC instituted 58 cases. That increases continued in the successive years also and the PSHRC instituted as many as 121 cases in 1999, 287 cases in 2000 and 327 cases in 2001 related with prisons. The number of cases had declined a little in 2002 when 278 cases regarding the Jails were instituted by the PSHRC. But again, in the year 2003, the number of cases has increased to 306. In 2004 the PSHRC had instituted 297 cases, in 2005, 232 cases and in 2006, the number of cases regarding the Jails was decreased a little to 131. In 2007 and 2008, the Commission had instituted 268 and 243 cases respectively. In the year 2009, the PSHRC registered total 290 cases.

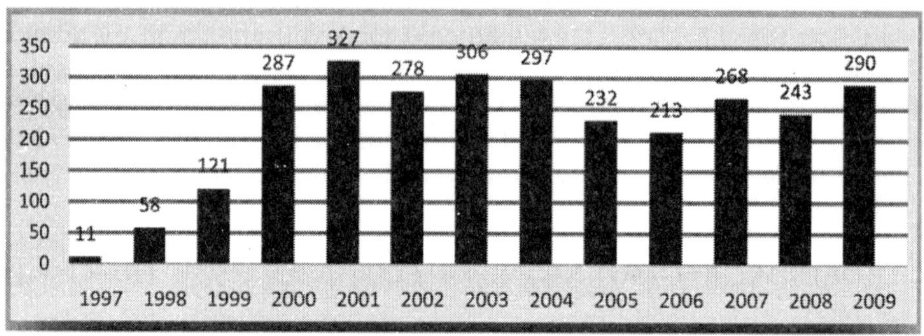

Diagram 1: Cases Instituted by PSHRC Regarding Prison Conditions and Prisoners' Rights

Source: Year-Wise Statistical Data of Complaints Instituted by PSHRC.

The table shows that the PSHRC has instituted total 2931 complaints regarding prisons conditions and prisoners' rights in ten years of its functioning from 1997 to November 30, 2009. It constitutes 2.23 per cent of the total complaints (131307) instituted by the PSHRC till November 2009. It means that the PSHRC has admitted approximate 4 cases in a week regarding prison conditions and the rights of prisoners. The data reveals that during first three years of its functioning (from 1997 to 1999), the Commission had registered only 190 complaints which constitute only 6.93 per cent of the total number of complaints (2931) regarding prison conditions and prisoners' rights. Firstly, due to the unawareness of common masses regarding the constitution and functioning of the PSHRC; and secondly, the victims, in these years had been still feeling the panic created by the police during counter-terrorism era in Punjab. But since 2000 to 2001, only in two years, the number of complaints has grown in a distressing manner (21 per cent). Furthermore 30.5 per cent of the total number of complaints was registered by the PSHRC in consecutive three years (2002 to 2004). The in-depth analysis of the data confirms that in 13 years of its functioning, 51.5 per cent of the total number of complaints (2931) were instituted by the PSHRC in the time span of 5 years (since 2000 to 2004). Above all, the registration of hundreds of complaints by the PSHRC every year has explored the miserable conditions of prisons in Punjab and the poor functioning of the PSHRC in controlling the violation of prisoners' rights.

The PSHRC has classified the complaints regarding prison conditions and prisoners' rights into 15 main categories. The statistical data of all these fifteen categories has been mentioned in the table given below.

Table 1
Categorization of the Cases Instituted by PSHRC Regarding Prison Conditions and Prisoners' Rights (1997-2009)

Categories of Cases	*Number of Cases*	*Percentage*
Jail Conditions	792	27.02%
Deaths in Judicial Custody	765	26.10%
Rape in Judicial Custody	20	0.68%
Exploitation of Child Prisoners	11	0.37%
Debarment of Legal Aid	52	1.77%
Harassment of Prisoners	669	22.82%
Inequalities in Prisons	31	1.05%
Irregularities in Jails	330	11.25%
Unlawful Confinement of Prisoners	32	1.09%
Lack of Medical Facilities	118	4.02%
Lack of Proper Food	4	0.13%
Indians in Jails in the Other Countries	6	0.20%
Delay to Produce Under-Trials in Court	5	0.17%
Sexual Harassment in Jails	4	0.13%
Premature Release	93	3.17%

Source: Year-Wise Statistical Data of Complaints Instituted by PSHRC.

The Table asserts that out of total 2932 complaints related with prison conditions and prisoners, there are only a minimal number of complaints (12.80%) regarding 10 categories of cases including custodial rapes, exploitation of child prisoners, debarment of legal aid, inequalities in prisons, unlawful solitary confinement of prisoners, lack of medical facilities, lack of proper food, Indians in the jails in the other countries, delay in producing under-trials in the courts and sexual harassment in the jails. On the other side, an enormous majority of the complaints (87.20%) are concerning 4 major categories which include the cases of general jail conditions, custodial deaths in the Jails during judicial custody, harassment of the prisoners, and Jail irregularities.

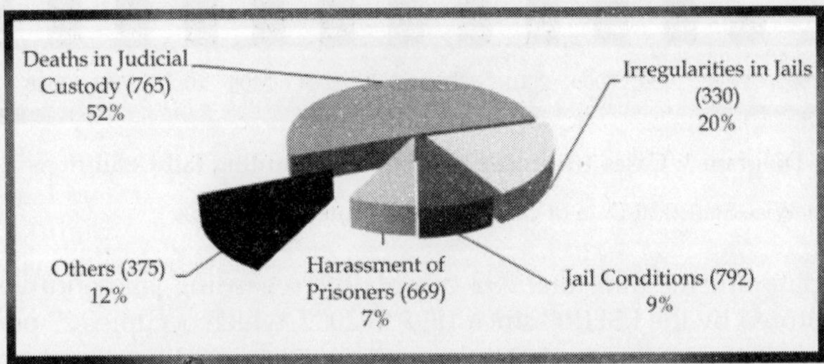

Diagram 2: Categories of Majority Number of Cases Instituted by PSHRC Regarding Prison Conditions and Prisoners' Rights

Source: Year-Wise Statistical Data of Complaints Instituted by PSHRC

The analysis makes it worthwhile to study those categories as foremost attention in which majority of the complaints have been documented by the PSHRC. Hence, while observing and critically analyzing the role of PSHRC regarding improving prison conditions and protecting the rights of prisoners, the prime focus of the present study is on the 4 major categories of cases including Jail Conditions (general), Custodial Deaths in the Jails during Judicial Custody, Harassment of the Prisoners, and Jail irregularities.

PSHRC and Cases regarding Jail Conditions

The PSHRC, in 1997, the first year of its functioning, had instituted 4 complaints regarding jail conditions. The number increased to 18 in 1998 and 44 in 1999. The number again increased to more than the double and the Commission instituted 100 complaints in 2000. The steep increase kept on rising with 125 complaints in 2001. In 2002, however, there was a noticeable decrease in the number of complaints during the successive years and the PSHRC had instituted 67 complaints in 2002, 59 complaints in 2003 and 46 complaints in 2004. The decrease in the number was still there in the following years with the institution of 44 complaints in 2005 and 34 complaints in 2006. Contrarily, since the year 2007 onwards, there was again an increase in the number of complaints instituted by the PSHRC and it had instituted 49 complaints in 2007, 54 complaints in 2008 and most number of as many as 148 complaints in 2009.

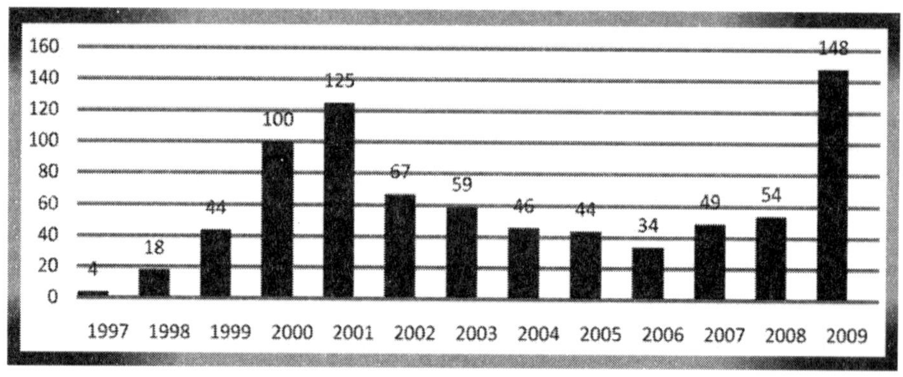

Diagram 3: Cases Instituted by PSHRC Regarding Jail Conditions

Source: Year-Wise Statistical Data of Complaints Instituted by PSHRC.

The data affirms that total 792 complaints regarding jail conditions have been instituted by the PSHRC since 1997 to 2009, which occupies 27 per cent of total number of complaints (2931) regarding prison conditions and prisoners' rights. The data corroborates that average 61 cases regarding miserable jail conditions have been instituted by the PSHRC. It further validates that average 1 case of such category has been instituted by the Commission after every 6 days. In first two years of its functioning, the number of complaints received by the PSHRC was quite bearable. It has been reasonably understandable because, in first two years of its functioning, the PSHRC was not yet able to establish itself as a reliable resort of human rights violations; hence there were less number of complaints received by it. But in 1999 the number started increasing which went to a worrying scale in two years. The number of complaints instituted by the Commission in 2000 (100) and 2001 (125) constitutes 17.04 per cent of the total number of complaints. After that there was a continuous descend in the number since 2006. The number again started ascending in 2007 and 2008, which reached, in 2009, at the maximum number of complaints (148) in 2009. The complaints instituted by the PSHRC during 2009 constitute 18.68 per cent of the total number of complaints regarding prison conditions. The registration of 148 complaints by PSHRC concerning jail conditions, after 13 years of its functioning, proves that PSHRC has so far got failed to improve the jail conditions.

The PSHRC, in June 2003, directed the State of Punjab and ADGP (Prisons) to inquire into the matter and submit its report by September 4, 2003 regarding some prisoners lodged in Punjab jails despite completion of their sentence, insanitary conditions and lack of basic amenities in the prisons. The PSHRC had also sought an inquiry from the State of Punjab and the ADGP (Prisons) about the sanitary conditions in various jails and sub-jails in Punjab, the approved capacity of inmates and the number of inmates lodged in each jail, besides the plan of the state government for the improvement of poor sanitary conditions of the barracks and workshops being held in the jails. (*The Tribune* 2003).

PSHRC and Deaths of Prisoners during Judicial Custody

In 1997, the PSHRC had instituted only 2 cases of custodial deaths of under-trials during their judicial custody. In 1998, however, the number of cases instituted regarding custodial deaths in the Jails during judicial custody reached to 13 and it was 14 in 1999. Since the year 2000, there was a noticeable increase in the cases regarding the custodial deaths in Jails and the number had reached to 61. That continuous increase was followed by the successive years and the PSHRC had instituted 70 cases in 2001, 79 in 2002 and 90 in the year 2003. In the year 2004 the PSHRC had instituted 79 cases regarding custodial deaths of under-trials in judicial custody. The number was followed by 63 in the year 2005 and 70 in 2006. As many as 65 cases in 2007 and 83 cases in 2008 were instituted by the Commission. In 2009 the PSHRC had instituted 64 cases of custodial deaths of under-trials in the Jail premises during judicial custody.

The PSHRC has received total 753 cases of custodial deaths (judicial) from 1997 to 2009. It constitutes 25.69 per cent of total cases admitted by the PSHRC

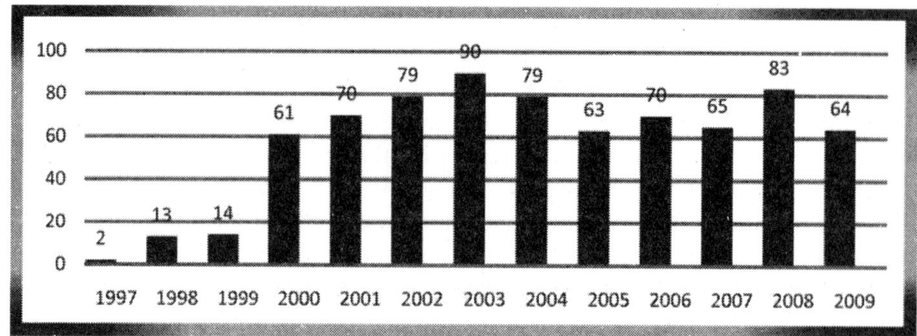

Diagram 4: Cases Instituted by PSHRC Regarding Deaths in Judicial Custody

Source: Year-Wise Statistical Data of Complaints Instituted by PSHRC.

regarding prisoners' rights and the prison conditions. The data confirms that average 58 cases are registered by the PSHRC every year. It further establishes that average 1 case regarding death in judicial custody has been registered by the PSHRC after every 6 days. The table shows the tragedy of prisoners that there is not even single year in which the PSHRC has not received and admitted the complaint of death of under-trials under judicial custody.

Custodial Death of Natha Singh in District Jail Sangrur (PSHRC 1997-98)

The PSHRC received the information from the SSP Sangrur district about the custodial death of Natha Singh son of Arjun Singh in the district jail in 1998. After considering all facts, including the Magistrial inquiry of the Sub-Divisional Magistrate, the PSHRC reached to the conclusion that Natha Singh had committed suicide due to the negligence of the Jail authorities in performance of their statutory duties. The PSHRC reached to the conclusion that it would be in the interest of justice and would be fair to award Rs 30,000 as interim compensation to the three sisters of the deceased. Arjun Singh, the father of the deceased was interviewed to know his views and opinion regarding the role played by the PSHRC in adjudicating the case of the custodial death of his son Natha Singh. Arjun Singh expressed his anger against the PSHRC manifestly by saying that the amount of Rs 30,000 was very less which the Commission directed the government to pay to the three sisters of the deceased. Moreover, the old aged Arjun Singh revealed that he wanted the guilty police officials to be severely punished as per law and uttered his resentment that the PSHRC had not recommended any severe punishments against the accused.

Custodial Death of Under-Trial Bhikham Shah, in Central Jail of Jallandhar (The Tribune 2008)

On July 17, 2006, the PSHRC received a communication from the Superintendent of Jallandhar Jail regarding the custodial death of under-trial prisoner Bhikham Shah, in Central Jail of Jallandhar. The PSHRC observed that on the basis of the postmortem report, the death of under-trial took place due to the consumption of Oregano Phosphorus compound and was not a case of natural death as was being insisted by the Superintendent of the Central Jail, Jallandhar and the DGP (Jails) Punjab. The PSHRC recommended the payment of Rs. 1 lakh as compensation to the victim's family by the State Government. The PSHRC further directed that the government would be at the liberty to fix responsibility on one or more than one officers in the department to get that money from them.

PSHRC AND CASES REGARDING HARASSMENT OF JAIL INMATES

In 1997, the PSHRC had instituted only 3 cases, but soon after one year, in 1998, it instituted 10 cases regarding the harassment of inmates in the Jails. There were total 31 cases in 1999 and 52 in 2000, which were related with harassment of inmates and were instituted by the PSHRC. In the successive years the number was quite closer to the previous one and the PSHRC had instituted 49, 44 and 54 cases in the years 2001, 2002 and 2003 respectively. There was a slight increase in the number of cases regarding harassment of the inmates in the prisons and the PSHRC had instituted 75 cases in the year 2004. In 2005, the number of cases was 61, which was followed by 75 in 2006. Further the PSHRC had instituted 92 cases in 2007, total 73 cases in 2008 and 50 cases in 2009 related with the harassment of inmates in the prisons.

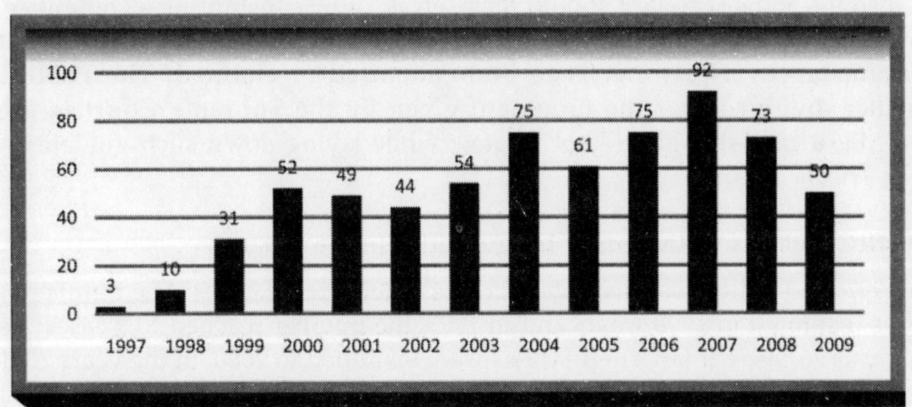

Diagram 5: Cases Instituted by PSHRC Regarding Harassment of Prisoners

Source: Year-Wise Statistical Data of Complaints Instituted by PSHRC.

The PSHRC has instituted as many as 669 cases regarding the harassment of inmates in the prisons from 1997 to 2009. It constitutes 22.82 per cent of total cases admitted by the PSHRC regarding prisoners' rights and the prison conditions. The data further confirms that average 51 concerning the harassment of the prisoners are registered by the PSHRC every year; while average 1 case of such violation has been instituted in a week. There is a continuous increase in the number of cases which reveals the continuous harassment of jail inmates and the failure of the PSHRC in performing its duties efficiently.

Harassment of Three Inmates at Central Jail Ferozepore (*The Tribune* 2001)

In July 2001, a complaint was filed by a human rights organization Lawyers for Social Reform (LSR) to the PSHRC regarding mental and physical harassment of three inmate named Balwinder Singh, Sukhwinder Singh and Mandeep Singh of the Central Jail Ferozepore by the Jail authorities. The PSHRC had immediately taken the cognizance of the complaint. It directed the Principal Secretary of the Punjab Government to visit the Central Jail of Ferozepore and hold an inquiry into the whole incident of harassment of the inmates. After getting the details of whole investigation, the Commission directed the State Jail Department to take a needed lawful action against the officials guilty of harassing and humiliating the inmates.

The Punjab State Human Rights Commission, In April 2010, asked the Punjab police and the jail authorities in the state to lay down guidelines regarding the handcuffing of prisoners while they are being moved outside the jail. Taking up the case of an under-trial, Dr. Ravinder Verma, who was handcuffed when he was taken from the jail to a hospital, the full bench of the commission ordered that the DGP, prisons, and the DGP, as also the home secretary should themselves, or by constituting a committee, lay down guidelines for the authorities concerned as to under what circumstances a prisoner is to be handcuffed or chained. The PSHRC further divulged that the judgment given by the Supreme Court in the D.K. Basu case should be kept in view while laying down such guidelines. (*The Tribune* 2010).

PSHRC and Cases Regarding Irregularities in the Prisons

In 1997 the PSHRC had instituted 2 cases of Jail irregularities. The number of cases instituted in 1998 was 5 and in 1999, the number reached to 9 cases. As many as 26 cases of Jail irregularities were instituted in 2000. In the years 2001 and 2002, 36 cases were instituted in each year. In 2003, 58 cases, highest in a year till March 31, 2007, were instituted. The PSHRC had instituted 45 cases in 2004 and 37 cases in 2005 regarding the Jail irregularities. In the year 2006, there was again decrease in the number of cases and the PSHRC had instituted 21 cases in that year. Total 30 cases were instituted by the PSHRC regarding Jail irregularities in 2007. The number was followed by 14 cases in 2008 and 11 cases in 2009.

PSHRC has instituted total 330 cases of Jail irregularities since March 1997 till 2009. It constitutes 11.25 per cent of total cases admitted by the PSHRC regarding prisoners' rights and the prison conditions. The data further

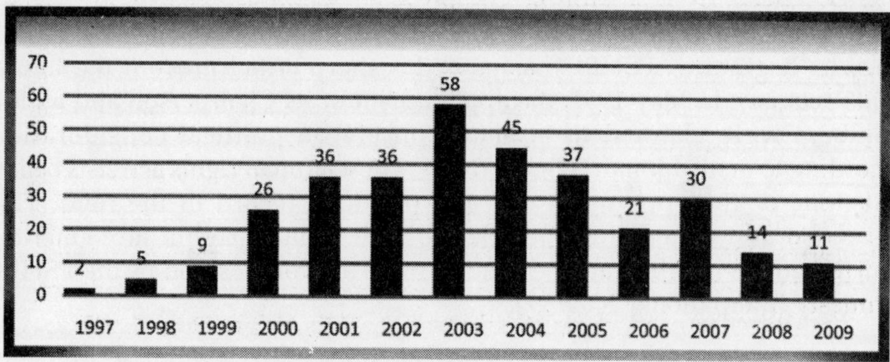

Diagram 6: Cases Instituted by PSHRC Regarding Irregularies in Jails

Source: Year-wise Statistical Data of Complaints Instituted by PSHRC

establishes that average 25 cases of irregularities in the jails are instituted by the PSHRC in a year. The table depicts that there is a continuous increase in the number of cases till 2003. But from 2004 onwards an evident decrease has been noticed. The decrease in the number of complaints implies that PSHRC, after seven years of its functioning, had been however, able to curb and control the irregularities in the prisons.

Visit at Central Jail and Borstal Jail of Ludhiana (PSHRC 1997-98: 33)

Justice J.S. Sekhon, honourable member of the PSHRC, inspected Central Jail of Ludhiana on August 22, 1997. While inspecting the Jail, he found fungus in wheat flour and directed that it must be got tested from the concerned authority to find out if it was fit for human consumption. He found that a convict named Raghbir Singh, needed By-Pass surgery. With the efforts of PSHRC, later, he was sanctioned Rs 65,000 by the State Government to bear the charges of his by-pass surgery.

A CRITICAL ANALYSIS

Thus, is has been established as a fact that the PSHRC has been performing its mandatory obligations to protect the prisoners rights quite reasonably. It has been a reality that even the victims have been showing more and more faith in PSHRC as a resort to their complaints, which is evident from the increase of the number of complaints it institutes every year. The PSHRC, which had admitted only 11 complaints in 1997, had instituted 290 complaints in 2009. But still a question arises that whether PSHRC has played a role to get even 'satisfactory' remarks from the victims as well as the observers of prisoners' rights and prison conditions in the State? Unfortunately, answer of question does not favour the PSHRC at all. The reason is that the PSHRC possesses a lot of limitations, shortcomings and even inefficiencies, which hinder its way to reach the mark of excellence.

Biased Appointments

Since its beginning, PSHRC has gained a sharp criticism from the human rights activists. In May 1997, the appointment of its Chairperson and all four members were claimed to be made purely on political considerations according to many human rights activists. These human rights activists believe that none of the appointees had any previous record in the field. They were also concerned that members of the human rights movement in Punjab had been deliberately excluded from the composition of the PSHRC. (Amnesty International 2002: 27).

Non-Publications of Annual Reports

It is very difficult to assess the role of PSHRC in improving prison conditions and protecting prisoners' rights, as it has not published any of its annual reports disclosing the way of functioning of the PSHRC, major areas of its concerns and different patterns of human rights violations in the state. Under the Protection of Human Rights Act (Section 28), every State Human Rights Commission should produce an annual report and present it for discussion to the State Legislative Assembly before publication. But the PSHRC has produced and placed before the Punjab Legislative Assembly the annual report only for 1997-98, but even that report has reportedly not been published. (Walia 2001: 144).

Only a Recommendatory Status

The PSHRC does not have any authority or power to make any order to the State government, Department of Prisons or the jail officials. At the most, it could simply make a recommendation to the State government or Jail Department but such recommendations are not binding on them. (PSHRC 1997-98: 8-14) It has been observed that the position of the PSHRC becomes very miserable when its directions are completely ignored by the State Government.

Non-Registration of all Complaints

As far as the powers of PSHRC to investigate individual cases of human rights violations are concerned, they are limited by the protection of Human Rights Act itself. Under Section 36 (2) of the PHRA, 1993, while reading with Section 29, the PSHRC may not investigate cases of human rights violations after one year of these violations occurred. It means the complaints of miserable prison conditions and other violations of prisoners' rights are registered only within a time period of one year since the occurrence of violation.

Limitations Regarding Visits in Jails

As per provisions of PHRA, 1993, The PSHRC deputes its members to visit different jails in the state to have first hand account of the conditions of inmates lodged therein. (PHRA 1993) But interestingly, the Commission lacks jurisdiction to enter a jail without intimation to the State government. According to the provisions of Protection of Human Rights Act, the Commission gives a one week's prior notice to the jail Superintendent and the District Magistrate concerned and on the day of inspection members visit the jail along with the Jail Superintendent or the District Magistrate concerned. Hence, it is clear that the inspection to the Jail proves to be more of a show-off than achieving any fruitful result.

RECOMMENDATIONS AND SUGGESTIONS

Undoubtedly, the prison conditions and prisoners' rights in Punjab are at the state of denial. The unenthusiastic approach of governmental authorities, lackadaisical attitude of prison administration and the shortcomings within the PSHRC hinder the attainment of satisfactory prison conditions and prisoners rights in Punjab. There are some suggestions and recommendations for the state government, prison authorities and the PSHRC, which if acknowledged, can prove to be productive in improving prison conditions and protecting the rights of the prisoners.

- The Government of Punjab should publicly accept its commitment to protect human rights. In that regard it should give its full support to the PSHRC while providing all necessary manual, mechanical and financial resources to the PSHRC and while implementing its recommendations.
- Provisions contained in the PHRA 1993 regarding the appointment of members of the PSHRC should be strictly followed. In particular, those eminent and dedicated persons should be appointed as the members of the NHRC as well as PSHRC, who have real "knowledge of, or practical experience in, matters relating to human rights" as assumed by the PHRA 1993.
- The PSHRC should look beyond monetary compensation and ensure that its recommendations include means to ensure restitution, satisfaction and guarantees of non-repetition. The PSHRC should recommend, when feels it appropriate, the prosecution of all person who are found guilty of violating the rights of prisoners as a means to provide redress to the victims, in addition to the granting of a monetary compensation.
- The PSHRC should be given the power to visit all prison, confinement cells and other custodial institutions without prior informing the state officials.
- The PSHRC should monitor, record and publish the numbers of complaints concerning prisoners' rights and prison conditions which are brought to them, including a separate category for the number of

complaints of deaths in judicial custody, lack of medical facilities and harassment of prisoners etc.

- The PSHRC should establish a mechanism for reviewing its recommendations on a periodic basis as a means of checking whether their recommendations have been implemented and followed up by the concerned authorities.

The graph of the complaints of human rights violations has been increasing day by day. It has been established as an evident fact that PSHRC has not been able to protect the rights of the prisoners in Punjab as per expectations. The reason is that PSHRC enjoys only a recommendatory status and its directions are not mandatory for the concerned authorities. Furthermore, the PSHRC totally overlook the follow up procedure and concentrate only on providing monetary reliefs to the victims in shape of the interim compensations. It seldom recommends any punitive measures against the guilty prison officials. The trauma faced by the victims due to the breach of their basic rights can never be paid off by providing them monitory relief. Secondly, it gives an expression to the society that the governmental set up shields the unlawful activities of the jail officials and thus encourages them to commit more crimes against prisoners. Thus, there is huge need to amend the PHRA 1993, and improve the functioning of the PSHRC, if the missions of improving prison conditions and the protection of prisoners' rights are to be achieved.

References

Amnesty International (2002), India: Break the Cycle of Impunity and Torture in Punjab. Amnesty International Publications, 27.

Arora, Krishna (ed.) (2007), The Protection of Human Rights Act 1993. BARE ACT, 2007, 16.

Asian Centre for Human Rights (ACHR) (2008), India, Human Rights Report- Punjab. ACHR Publications, New Delhi, 254.

Bhatnagar, A.P. (2005), Report on Prison Reforms in Punjab. Prisons Department, Punjab, Chandigarh, 17-18.

Chapter III, IV and V of the Punjab Jail Manual 1996 Provide Explicit and Detailed Directions Regarding the Constitution, Classification, Administration, Functioning of the Prisons in Punjab.

Dewan, Umesh, Rajneesh Sharma (December 9, 2009), Nabha Jail Inmates go on Strike- Say Food Substandard. *The Tribune. The Tribune News Services,* Chandigarh.

Dhaliwal, Sarbjit (April 23, 2005), Accounts Panel Focuses on Jail Irregularities. *The Tribune. The Tribune News Services,* Chandigarh.

Encyclopedia Britannica (1994), Vol. 9 (Micropedia). Encyclopedia Britannica Inc. Chicago: 710-2B.

Gupta, Sarju (2009), Status of Jails in Punjab. Legal Service India-Articles. Retrieved from *http://www.legalserviceindia.com.../l355-Status-Of-Jails-In-Punjab.html*

Khanna, Mohit (March 17, 2009), Woman Prisoners a Harassed Lot- Have to 'Bribe' Cops to Meet Kids. *The Tribune. The Tribune News Services,* Chandigarh.

Malik, Saurabh (May 24, 2008), Punjab to Hire Docs in Jails. *The Tribune. The Tribune News Services,* Chandigarh.

National Human Rights Commission (NHRC) (2008), Prison Statistics - 2008, Custodial Justice Cell, New Delhi. retrieved from *http.//www.nhrc.nic.in/PRISONS_STATS_JUN_08_FOR_NIC.xls*

Parkash, Chander & Gupta, Anirudh (July 19, 2001), Rights Secretary Finds Jail Overcrowded-Probe Held in Custodial Deaths. *The Tribune. The Tribune New Services,* Chandigarh.

Parkash, Chander (May 16, 2000), Under-trials Beaten in Jail. *The Tribune. The Tribune News Services,* Chandigarh.

Protection of Human Rights Act, 1993, (2007), Section 12 (C), [As amended by the Protection of Human Rights (Amendment) Act, 2006–No. 43 of 2006].

PSHRC (1998), Annual Report, 1997-1998: 8-14.

PSHRC (1998), Complaint No. 1 of 1998. Annual Report-1997-1998, 17. Also Personal Interview of Arjun Singh (Father of the Deceased).

PSHRC (1998), Complaint No. 38 of 1997. Annual Report, 1997-1998, 33.

PSHRC (1998), Annual Report, 1997-1998, 1.

Sethi, Chitleen K. (May 6, 2009), Improve Medical Facilities in Jails-Panel Tells Govt. *The Tribune. The Tribune News Services,* Chandigarh.

Tandon, Aditi (January 8, 2008), In this Jail Life drags its Feet- 1391 Prisoners Lodged against Capacity of 500. *The Tribune. The Tribune News Services,* Chandigarh.

The Hindu, (April 20, 2004), Indian Prisons-Rhetoric and Reality. The Hindu News Agency, Chennai.

The Online Etymology Dictionary. Retrieved on July 07, 2010, from *http://www.etymonline.com/index.php?search=prison&searchmode=none*

The Oxford Dictionary (1989), 2nd Edition, Vol. VIII. Oxford Clarendon Press, Oxford: 180.

The Tribune (April 20, 2010), Lay Down Guidelines on Handcuffing: Rights Panel. *The Tribune News Services,* Chandigarh.

The Tribune (December 7, 2008), Toll of Custodial Deaths on Increase-Another Under-trial Dies. *The Tribune News Services,* Chandigarh.

The Tribune (July 18, 2001), Inmates Harassed of Ferozepore Jail. *The Tribune News Services,* Chandigarh.

The Tribune (July 4, 2001), One More Under-Trial Dies. *The Tribune News Services,* Chandigarh.

The Tribune (June 7, 2003), PSHRC Seeks Report on Jail Conditions. *The Tribune News Services,* Chandigarh.

The Tribune (May 11, 2003), Under-Trial Dies in Judicial Lock-up. The Tribune News Services, Chandigarh.

Tondon, Aditi (July 20, 2005), Better Health Care for Punjab Prisoners in Offing. *The Tribune. The Tribune News Services,* Chandigarh.

Walia, Arunjeev Singh and Sudan, Tejinder Singh (2001), Genesis of State Terrorism in Punjab. Published by Lawyers For Human Rights International, Chandigarh: 144.

Year-Wise Statistical Data of Complaints Instituted by the PSHRC, *http://www.pshrc.net/html/statistics%20of%20Complaints%20nov2009.htm*

Sexual Harassment of Women at Workplace

R. N. Mangoli*

INTRODUCTION

The various cases of seeking the sexual favor have come to the light, which advances in exchange for benefits, such as promises of promotion, higher pay, academic advancements, etc. Where as in some of the sexual assaults incidents it is noticed that unwelcome sexual harassment occurs simply because she is woman (Paranjape 2008). Data also shows that how the magnitude of sexual harassment against women has greatly increased in the last twenty years (Crime in India 2008).

As today, women play a crucial role in the socio-economic development of a country; she is working hard with shoulder to shoulder of her male folk in the different shifts even in late nights in the same premises, and thus easily become target to their counter part male colleagues, bosses or whoever in authority in work place (Srivastav 2007).

Sexual harassment affects all women in some form or other particularly at work place, even intentionally touching to a woman becomes the kind of sexual harassment (Dasgupta 2001). Sexual harassment at workplace is an extension of violence in every day life and is discriminatory, exploitative, thriving in atmosphere of threat, terror and reprisal.

OBJECTIVES OF THE STUDIES

- To understand the real problems of Sexual Harassment in Indian society.
- To know the causes of increasing sexual harassment in the society.
- To know the remedial measures taken againsr sexual harassment of women at workplace.
- To know the existing laws combating against sexual harassment.

* *Assistant Professor, P.G. Dept. of Studies in Criminology and Forensic Science, Karnatak University, Dharwad-580 003, (E-mail: drmangoli.rn@gmail.com)*

METHODS AND MATERIALS

What is Sexual Harassment?

The broader definition given by Supreme Court of India gave judgment in the case of Vishaka vs Rajastan i.e. Sexual Harassment includes such unwelcome sexually determined behavior (Whether directly or by implications) as:

(a) Physical contact and advances;

(b) A demand or request for sexual favours;

(c) Sexually coloured remarks;

(d) Showing pornography;

(e) Any other unwelcome physical, verbal or non-verbal conduct of sexual nature.

Facilitating Factors

(a) *Social Norms* - is the most important contributing factor that leads to sexual harassment. As the subordinate position of women in society is considered both the determined and maintained by constricting set of norms and customs which work against their liberty.

(b) *Evolving Social Reality* - In increasing numbers, women now are seeking more and more employment in the traditional male sphere of work. As a result, men and women have to learn new ways of relating to one another, as equal co-workers, this process of change created tension that can take the form sexual harassment.

(c) *Lack of Communication* - Women of sexually harassed or any kind of threat received at work place either by co-worker or a superior officer or authority in power, clearly does not communicate the incident to their colleagues or with their family and also due to the diverse attitude of society towards victims.

(d) *Non-Reporting of Cases* - usually Indian Women in cases of sexual harassment, hesitate to register their complaint or complaining any committee or authority due to fear of stigma, fear of reprisal by losing of jobs or adverse effect on career and fact of non co-operations and support form colleagues.

That all the above, factors which will lead to strengthen the position of culprit and hence increase in the number of incidents.

MAGNITUDE AND EXTENT OF THE PROBLEM

In different parts of the world, between 16% and 52% of women suffer physical violence from their male partners and at least one in five women suffer sexual harassment, rape or attempted to rape in there life times. It is also well known that sexual harassment are systematically used to weapons of war. Violence negates women's autonomy and undermines their potential as individuals and members of society (statement of WHO Director-General) 1997.

It was only in August, 1997 that a landmark Supreme Court Judgment in Vishakha.V. State of Rajastan (1997 VIII AD SC 53) recognized sexual harassment of women at the work place as a human rights violation, keeping in view India's obligation under CEDAW and other human rights instruments.

This judgment laid down detailed guidelines and norms keeping in the mind of defamation of "human rights" in Section 2(d) of the protection of Human Rights Act, 1993. It further paved the way of setting up a complaints mechanism system, which makes it mandatory for every organization, irrespective of Government, Private, industrial or education institution to have asexual harassment complaints committee.

The data also shows that the magnitude of sexual harassment against women has greatly increased in the last twenty years–

(a) A survey conducted by SAKSHI in 1993 showed that 54% to 67 women from a cross-section of industries have experienced some from of sexual harassment, studies also shows that the problem is more sever among lower caste women.

(b) In 1991, report on atrocities against Dalits reported 21,362 cases, out of that 1061 of these were sexual harassment.

(c) According to TAPASYA during its campaign for the self-sufficient awareness program, it was noticed that sexual harassment affects the lives of more that 40% to 60% of working woman. Nearly 68.26% faced mental harassments due to whistling, winking, passed lewd remarks and sexual gestures. Nearly 25.17% of the victims of Sexual Violence suffered some kind of physical harassment. Nearly 32% complained of discrimination vis a vis employment matters like leave, salary, promotions, working hours and work distribution. However, the actual figure could be much higher.

(d) National Commission for women, conducted a survey revealed that the Supreme Court much lauded directories in the year 1997, which aims at restoring respectability to women at their working places seems to have little affect on the sensibility of male dominated establishments. Nearly 50% of the women, surveyed by the team complained of gender discrimination, physical and mental harassment at work places. Out of 1200 women contacted across the country, including both in urban and rural areas and at various levels in the organized and unorganized sectors, speak of no different situations even after the verdict was pronounced. While 40% of the women said that they "usually ignored" such provocations, 3.54% said that they reported these to their superiors, 78% said they reported to their colleagues and 1.24% to the police. About 10% said they protested against such behaviour while 9% said they warned the offender. At least 20.17% of the respondent said that the accused was punished but the other 17.25% said that the offender went Scot-free. About 4% said that no investigation was done against their complaints, while 1.5% said that police harassed them again instead of making the enquiries. Where as the majority of the respondents (84.92%) even not aware of the Supreme Court judgment given in 1997 for specific protections of women from sexual harassment at work place.

Table 1
Crime Head -wise Incidents of Crime Against Women during 2003-2007 and Percentage Variation in 2007 over 2006

Crime Head	*Year*					*Percentage variation in 2007 over 2006*
	2003	*2004*	*2005*	*2006*	*2007*	
Sexual Harassment (Sec. 509 IPC)	12325	10001	9984	9966	10950	9.9%

Source: Crime in India, 2007, National Crime Record Bureau.

It is obvious from above mentioned data table No 1 that Sexual Harassment (Eve teasing) under (Sec. 509 IPC) total (Incidence 10,950) occurred during 2007 shows sharp increase. The number of such cases has increased by (9.9%) over the previous year (10,950). Andhra Pradesh has reported (30.3%) of highest cases (3,316) followed by Uttar Pradesh (26.3%) (2,882). Andhra Pradesh has reported the highest crime rate (4.1%) as compared to the National average of (1.0%).

All these statistical data make it apparent that sexual harassment is a very big and real problem, affecting and victimizing a large proportion of Indian women population and became a menace in Indian society. The problem of sexual harassment at work place does not only affect and victimize women of low socio-economic background but also it equally affect, victimize women of all sectors and strata of society irrespective of cast, creed, colour and religion. Also it is not only committed by uneducated and ignorant men but men of various grounds. It also indicates a wide gap between the constitutional rights and the social reality. Women's right to personal liberty is seriously limited by their fear for their personal safety in the workplace; the threat often comes from there in authority, leaving them with no one to turn for support (Dasgupta Rajashri 2001).

Out of the various problems, the problem is the veil of silence that is maintained around the issue. Society's attitude towards the victim of sexual harassment ensure that women are hesitant to speak out against their for mentors. To do so, would be risk, ridicule and humiliation (Chaudhari Swati

1998). A woman who speaks of their experiences is more likely to blame for the incidents than supported and thus so many are reluctant to take that bold step.

Some Cases of Sexual Harassment

The following cases has been registered and published by National Human rights Commission, New Delhi in its Annual Repot 2005, are few examples demonstrate that any one can become a victim of sexual harassment and any one can perpetrate or facilitate this behavior:

1. Sexual harassment on Ms.Asha Rajora, a Technical Assistant in the Herbal Research and Development Institute. Gopeshwar, Uttaranchal by the Director of the Institute, allegation of further harassment by way of non-renewal of her job contract were leveled on dated; 12-03-2004, the Human Right Commission took the cognizance of a complaint. After the detail enquiry conducted by the Vigilance Committee constituted NHRC on the recommendation of the committed the services of Dr.J.S.Rawat the Director HRDI, Gopeshwar were terminated w.e.lf.04-10-2004.
2. Former Director General of Police of Punjab, K.P.S.Gill has been convicted of sexually harassing Mrs. Rupan Deol Bajaj, a senior IAS Officer of the Punjab Cadre on July 18, 1988 at an official dinner party. Although his outstanding contribution to the elimination of terrorism in the Punjab especially in operation black thunder, the Supreme Court finally on October, 12, 1995 directed the Chief Judicial Magistrate, Darshan Singh announced that Gill is convicted under the Section 354 & Section 509 of IPC & sentenced 3 months rigorous imprisonment.
3. On December 21, 1999, Nalini Netto, a senior IAS Officer, was called the Kerala Transport & Forest Minister's Office in the assemble complex to discuss official matters but faced harassment. She then lodged a formal complaint a letter dated, February 1, 2000 giving details of how the Minister had misbehaved with her in his chamber, three day after Nalini Netto filed a complaint, another young woman, Prakriti Srivastava, a Divisional Forest Officer, Nilambur North Division, Kelrala, alleged that the same Minister had sexually harassed her, then finally in December, 2000, Nalini won the first round of her battle against the Minister, then crime branch filed a charge sheet against the minister for physically assaulting Nalini Netto.
4. In the year 1999-2000, NHRC in its annual report, received the number or complaints form villagers and tribals, through NGOs that the harassment by Joint Special Task Force(JSTF) of the State of Tamil Nadu and Karnataka in the area of operation against Veerappan and his associates.

All these cases demonstrate that sexual harassment affects women of all sectors and strata of society and any one can commit such crime. Due to the silence surrounding the issue, it is often not discussed but it lies beneath the surface of gender relations in workplaces across indices.

RESULT AND DISCUSSION

Impact of the Offence

Sexual harassment at work place has a variety of negative consequences for women workers. In addition to the discomfort associated with the sexually harassing experience and violation of physical privacy, women often find that their careers are interrupted. Either they are forced to resign or fired by the company just because the "man" who harassed her happens to be a higher official with lots of influence and value[5]. However, most women ignore sexual harassment, hoping that it would be a one-time incident or avoid the harasser or avoid going to places where the harasser would be. Thus, harassment constraints the potential for forming friendships or work alliances with male worker. Further more, women are likely to go through the feelings of anger and resentment and even exhibit self-blame which leads to additional stress.

Hence, the emotional effects can vary from anxiety, low self-esteem, confusion and embarrassment to fear, depression, humiliation, shame etc., and can finally leads to suicide also[6]. Out of the various problems, the problem is the veil of silence that is maintained around the issue[11]. Society's attitude towards the victim of sexual harassment ensure that women are hesitant to speak out against their for mentors This problem becomes more and more acute because there is very little sympathy given to them by society and they are often accused of having invited the attention through behavior and dressing (Silverman 1977). This creates mental disturbances, which manifest as psychosomatic disorders. Women develop blood pressure, headache, backache, insomnia etc.

In Toto, as a whole, sexual harassment at work place serve as a hidden acceptional hazard and it also affects women's personal lives in the form of physical and emotional illness and disruption of marriage or other relationships with men and disrespect in the Society at large. A woman ultimately stated that due to her powerlessness in dealing with harassment made her regret being born a woman.

Existing Laws against Sexual Harassment in India

Sexual Harassment and Indian Constitution

Sexual harassment of any women at the work place is a gross violation of Fundamental Rights guaranteed under Part-III of the constitution of India.

Each such incident results in violation of the fundamental rights "Gender Equality" and the "Right to life and liberty", it is a clear violation of the rights under Articles 14, 15, 21 of the constitution.

One of the logical consequences of such an incident is also the violation of the victim's fundamental right under Article 19(1)(9) "to practice any profession or carry out any occupation, trade or business" such violations therefore attracts the remedy under Article 32 for the enforcement of these fundamental rights of women[14]. The fundamental right to carry out any occupation, trade or profession depends on the availability of "safe" working environment. Various Supreme Court judgments have also at time and again emphasized that right to life means right to life with dignity. Apart from the above, Article 42 also provides for just and human conditions of work and maternity relief.

Ultimately, India is also become a part to various international conventions and human rights instruments aimed at securing the "Rights of Women". Key amongst them is CEDAW adopted by the United Nations in 1979 which was ratified by the Govt. of India in the year 1993 with some reservation. Further at the Fourth World Conference on women in Beijing, the Govt. of India has also made an official commitment to formulate and operationalise a national policy on women which will continuously guide and inform action at every level and in every sector; to set up a Commissions of Women's Rights to act as a public defender of Women's Rights and to institutionalize a national level mechanism to monitor the implementation of the Platform for Action. Therefore, now it becomes mandatory on the part of the state to protect women who are subjected to sexual harassment.

Sexual Harassment and Domestic Law

The Indian Penal Code (1860) which contains laws for punishment of offences committed within India, but lacks specific provisions to deal with instances of sexual harassment of women at the work place. However, except for certain section in the IPC (1860), such as Section 294 (obscene acts and songs), Section 354 (assault or criminal force to women with intent to outrage her modestly). Section 375(Rape), Section 509 (World, gesture or act intended to insult the modestly of women), etc.

In respect to other Acts in Indian the Industrial Dispute Act, 1947, under ruke 5, schedule 5, sexual harassment cases can be argued on the bases of unfair labour practices listed in the schedule. In Indecent Representation of Women (Prohibition) Act 1997, deals if an individual harasses another with books, pronograhs, paintings, films, pamphlets, packages etc, containing indecent representation of women, in such cases women can lodge a complaint against the harasser.

However, in the other remaining domestic Act like Factories Act, 1948, Plantation Labour Act, 1951, Mines Act, 1952, Maternity Benefit Act, 1961, Beedi

& Cigar Workers (Conduction of Employment)Act, 1966, Equal Remuneration Act, 1976. Indecent Representations of Women (Prohibition)Act, 1987 of Eve Teasing Act, 1988 etc., there does not exist any specific complain mechanism system to deal with cases of sexual harassment of women at the work place under the circumstances if any women who is victimized has no recourse but to take shelter under the Indian Penal Code.

The Working Women (Prevention of Sexual Harassment at Workplace) Bill 2006

Now recently a bill has been introduced in the Rajya Sabha on 3rd March, 2006 (Bill No.VIII of 2006) named, "The working women (Prevention of Sexual harassment at work places) Bill, 2006. The Bill defines, "Sexual Harassment or Sexual Exploitation" as "any unwanted or unwarranted gestures or verbal sexual advances, sexuality explicit and derogatory statement or remarks, avoidable or unwarranted physical contacts, willfully touching or patting, suggestive sexual remarks, sexuality slanted and obscene jokes, vulgar comments about physical appearance, indecent invitations, use of pornographic materials, demand of sexual favours, demanding sexual favours by telephonic calls or sending SMS, threats of physical assaults or molestation on refusal by women workers by their male supervisors, colleagues or any one, who for the time being, is in a position to sexually exploit or harass the working women at any work place".

Like that, the Supreme Court Guidelines as well as Bill, 2006 describe in concrete terms what constitute sexual harassment and state that this behavior is totally unacceptable. However, even so, the social reality is slow to change, the problem of sexual harassment still affects women of all classes, strata and communities and the problem is growing more and more with the increase in the number of working women

United Nations Conventions on Sexual Harassment

The following are the few United Nation's Convention and declarations which address the core issue of victims of sexual harassment in order to prevent and eradicate such heinous activities from the very Society.

(a) The untied nations Conventions on the elimination of all forms of Discrimination against Women (CEDAW) 1979. Prohibit discrimination against women in employment as per Article 11 of CEDAW. Article 17 denotes that "equality in employment can be seriously impaired when women are subjected to gender specific violence such as sexual harassment in the work place" (Para 17).

(b) The NAIROBE forward looking strategies for the advancement of women July 1985 was the first United Nations document to directly address the issue of sexual harassment.

(c) Organization of the European Union 1990 has been the most active international organization in defining the specific obligations of its member countries to provide legal protection against sexual harassment. The council of Ministers adopted the Resolution on the protection of the Dignity of Women and men at work, the Resolution affirms that sexual harassment is unacceptable and violates the protection of the dignity of the women and men at work.

(d) The VIENNA declaration and programme of action 1993, recognizes that sexual harassment is a practice incompatible with human dignity. It stresses the importance of working towards the elimination of violence against women in "public and private life".

(e) Declarations on the elimination of violence against women (DEVAW) 1994, condemns sexual harassment as a violence of the fundamental human rights of women (Article3). Article 2 of DEVAW states that violence against women encompasses- " Physical, sexual and psychological violence occurring within the general community including rape, sexual abuse, sexual harassment and intimidation at work in educations and elsewhere trafficking in women and forced prostitution".

(f) Beijing declaration and platform for action 1995, at the United Nations Fourth World Conference on Women, also condemns sexual harassment of women. It defines violence against women in a language similar at the DEVAW.

(g) Organization of American States 1994, adopted the Inter-American Convention on the Prevention, Punishment and Eradication of violence against women.

The convention also particularly states the need for public education, research and specific programme to eliminate the problem of sexual harassment.

SUGGESTIONS

- A woman has to shed her mentality of tolerance and has to stop telling herself that this kind of behavior on the part of a man is inevitable and unavoidable and has to fight back for self-respect.
- A woman has to show resistance as at the very first time it occurs; if the action is not strongly resisted then the offender will assume that he has the consent.
- A woman has to maintain self-respect at your level best by not encourage man to behave unevenly with any kind of undue attention with you.
- Dressing of a woman plays a very important role, so dress yourself in a manner that befits a work environment.

- If someone's behavior is objectionable and uncomfortable, woman has to protest loudly at once. Let others know that such conduct has been meted out to you.
- A woman has to keep safe distance from the offending party.
- A woman has to first register a First Information Report with the police station as soon as the incident occurred.
- A woman has to be aware of their rights and all the laws so that they can protect themselves through legal measures.
- It should be mandatory for the Management to take active part in the implementation of the guidelines and formation of the committee to create forum for discussing the issue.
- NGO's should take the responsibility to generate public awareness about the issue and support the victim on the same.
- Workshops should be designed to empower women to speak out about their experiences and learn to protect themselves from sexual harassment in the work place. Often simply making a verbal objection to inappropriate behavior is enough to improve a situation. Non-communication only exacerbates the situation.

There is also a badly need of a People's Friendly Police Station as a model is to be created and to be trained Police Personnel in this directions. Particularly, towards their structures, procedures, attitudes, resources and most importantly community connections in order to check such sexual harassment in the society.

CONCLUSION

It is clear from the on going discussion that the problem of sexual harassment of women at workplace is rampant. It affects women of all sector and strata irrespective of caste, creed, colour and religion. Either she may be a daily wage worker in building construction work or having good position in Government, Semi-Government, Private and Public Sector companies, she is equally harassed by their male counterpart. Its proved that increase in the job of women equally increases the problem of sexual harassment in the male dominated establishment. Also it is seen that women tolerating against such incidents encourage their counter part to commit sexual harassment. Further, the constitution of India provides equal opportunities for both men and women workers. However, in reality women in India often subject to severe discrimination at the work place. Cases of sexual harassment at the work place are on a rise in India.

On earlier times, there were very few men who willingly accepted that women had any right to be in the work place at all. But, now a day many will consider that women have an equal right to work and that too a healthy work environment. In this respect, we can say that the situation is improving but with that the problem of sexual harassment is also increasing. Its also due to modernization of women with indecent dressing pattern, also due to day by day rapidly diminishing the religious teachings, morals and ethics in both men and women equally, which gives room to the immoral and unethical activities in the very web of society which ultimately disturbs the smooth functioning. Resultantly, increase in the cases of victimilization of sexual harassment at work places have became the menace in society. Either, the only way, ought to change these habits is through a better understanding of sexual harassment and the attitudes that underlie it and through proper moral, ethical and religious education and awareness of generation on this issue among men and women.

We must also ensure that they are to be treated with dignity on the basis of gender equality. They should not be discriminated on any account of their sex. If any one discriminate and harass them sexually then culprit should be immediately booked under section 509 of Indian Penal Code 1860. Women can play a crucial role in the architect of a good and prosperous society.

Notes & References

1. Canbell, J. C., Soeken, K. (1999), *Forced Sex and Intimate Partner Violence; Effects on Women's Health;* Violence Against Women.
2. Dasgupta Rajashris (2001*), The Politics of Silence, Sexual Harassment at Worlplace*; Kolkata.
3. EEOC (1982), Policy Guidelines on Sexual Harassment. Mullen, P.E, et.al.1988. *Impact of Sexual and Physical abuse on Women's Mental Health,* Lances.
4. Miyan, D.S. (2005), *Implementation of Supreme Court Guidelines on Sexual Harassment at Work place & Evolving Strategies to cover Women in Unorganized Sector and Need for a Bill National Commission of Women.*
5. NHRC (2004-2005), Publication on "*Sexual Harassment of Women at the Work Place*", New Delhi.
6. National Crime Record Board (2005), New Delhi National Crime Record Board. 2007, New Delhi
7. Srivastava, S. S. (2007), *Criminology Criminal Administration.* Allahabad: Central Law Agency.
8. UNIFEM (1995), *Fourth World Conference Report on Women in Beijing,* New Delhi.
9. The Supreme Court *12 point Guidelines on Sexual Harassment.* 2005. New Delhi.
10. The Working Women *(Prevention of Sexual Harassment at Workplace)* Bill. 2006.
11. The Constitution of Law of India, 949.
12. The Indian Penal Code. 1860. An Act.
13. Watt, C. Zimmerman, C. 2002. *Violence agains*ι *Women; Global Scope and its Magnitude.* Lances.
14. *www.sextualharrashmet.com*

Taking Risks Ethically

JOHN D. HASKELL*

INTRODUCTION: APOLOGY AND UTOPIA

In his *Grotius Series Lectures* at Cambridge University, the legal theorist Nathaniel Berman noted that the international legal order is plagued by two warring tensions.[1] On the one hand, we have the tendency to look at the horrors in places like Sudan or the Congo and say something must be done. We cannot just allow aggression to go unchecked. Remember Rwanda. We see intervention in Kosovo if not legal at least legitimate. There may be dark sides to our virtue-human rights the language of aircraft carriers not peace protesters - but even so, what is the point of our military resources if we do not use them for good? Isn't that, at least partly, what we have them for?[2]

On the other hand, the professional policy makers and bureaucracies of global governance remain, or have become skeptical, of things like humanitarian intervention or normative projects for civil society. These misgivings come from all sides of the aisle, ranging from arguments concerning territorial sovereignty to accusations that, as in the case of the former Soviet Union, humanitarians' best intentions often do more harm than good for the people they are trying to help (e.g., eradicating their cultural traditions, destabilizing populations, etcetera).[3] A liberal democratic model seems increasingly unable to meet the technological and cultural transformations of the international community.

Indeed, things seem to have somehow gotten away from the normative aspirations of post-60s humanitarians: the war on terrorism, the widening gap between rich and poor, unresponsive and over-reaching governments, as well as cultural tensions both at home and abroad concerning issues of religion, traditions and politics.[4] Polemics for democratic institutions harbor deep cynicisms toward domestic administrations, and the possibility of meaningful adaptation to slipping hegemony. Just as words like 'civilization' and 'colonialism' became unpopular in the years following the First World War in Europe, many today have become skeptical towards the sincerity and feasibility

* *Visiting Researcher, Institute for Global Law and Policy (IGLP), Harvard Law School.*

of a humanitarian rule of law and liberal democratic values. The world feels more than ever outside of our own making. In the words of the American poet, Robinson Jeffers, modern man dances to a "dreamled ... Disastrous rhythm," somehow both intimate and irreversible.[5]

Within the liberal cosmopolitan sentiment today, it has become almost a rite of authority to admit personal ambivalence or misgiving towards the nature and momentum of not only our institutions, but our very language and roles. Practicing lawyers are viewed as national diplomats; academic discourse has come to be distrusted or seen as unapproachable.[6] Law and politics are flip sides of the same coin, ideals serving the agendas of powerful political actors who cannot be clearly identified. There is a general feeling that the international community is poised at the edge of some emerging epoch, though exactly what this may bring is up in the air.[7] We perceive ourselves in a world without historical context – the post Cold War becomes the post 9/11 world as we wait for the next danger to arise, whether it come in the form of ecology, economics, or some new military conflict.

It is within this moment without foundation or certainty that we come searching for a post-foundational posture that might lead us forward.[8] This challenge is complicated because as the world becomes increasingly interlinked, any set of normative values must somehow be international in scope, sufficiently able to derive consensus, while also meeting the particular needs and agendas of disparate social hierarchies and cultures. On the one hand, abstract principles will lead, at best, to an abstract consensus, and tends to ignore the historically contingent character of values. On the other hand, to rigidly define liberty would ironically only result in liberty denied.[9] In the current economic crisis that has descended around the globe, these challenges feel all the more radically present, demanding some new way forward.

In this paper, I have adopted a two-fold approach to these challenges. First, I want to briefly think about some common 'illusions' that may restrict our ability to cope with the violence and paranoia that haunts our horizons. My suspicion is that too often we see ourselves in the role of architects, embroiled in debates over the structural aspects of civil society at home and global governance abroad. In this sense, I want to suggest that it is not our institutions or ideological underpinnings that stifle our efforts, but something more intimate, something about our most cherished conceptions of our past, those illusions about our own personality and the projects we sign up to. This might be seen as the search less for a set of concrete virtues, and more for a posture or sensibility to guide us forward. Second, I want to turn and think about how this sensibility might be applied in practice, and specifically to think about this in relation to the looming financial crisis. My hope in this work is not to provide an in-depth analysis of any of the current challenges that face global law and policy, but to focus on the sensibility that experts more often than not bring to the table, and to inject into this ongoing conversation the more recent advances within Continental European philosophy[10] and critical theory in international law and development studies.[11] The question here, in other words, is to propose an initial step into thinking how we might move more boldly beyond the politics of knowledge, of self-reflection and ambivalence, to a politics of truth, what we might see as an experience of the freedom, or perhaps the thrill, of taking risks ethically?

A GENTLE CIVILIZING SPIRIT?

We tend to share the sentiment that our professional traditions and liberal humanitarian rigor stand against the violence of empire, and that we are the natural or deserving descendents of those great dead white men of the Enlightenment who first began to dispel the superstitions and irrationalities of our past with reason and genuine, if at times flawed, good will. As John Gray, the British economist and philosopher at LSE, states: "we are all modernizers today."[12] History may be uncertain, but we all approach it with our technocratic toolboxes, informed by scientific fact and weathered experience.[13] If anything, while we may be suspicious about some of our colleagues' abilities or views, we count ourselves among that number emancipated from the past and committed to a better tomorrow.

This attitude though ignores that colonial empires have always been controlled by a technology of knowledge, rulership dressed up, consciously or unconsciously, in philanthropic and 'lawful' motives to further understanding and order. As the legal theorist Scott Newton points out, we need look no further than the British Museum to see that part of the imperial project was to collect objects from around the world and classify them. I do not imagine that the colonial experts then saw themselves as bad people or acted on bad intentions any more than we understand our roles today. They also held conferences to share their experiences in far off lands about methods of good governance. The Berlin Conference of 1885 dividing Africa into a series of straight lines and right angles was done in the name of the moral and material well being of the African people - carried out by humanitarians, priests, government officers and soldiers. They too were concerned with humanity and armed with the cutting-edge tricks of the day.

In this sense, to some degree the various opinions and debates currently at play are more likely rhetoric and polemics, an intellectual excursion or opportunity for professional networking and entertainment than they actually provide any hope of something new. To draw from Edward Said, we may be merely telling ourselves as every nation does that "[our] mission is not to plunder and control, but to educate and liberate."[14] That behind our clever arguments and compassionate sensibilities lay the fact that perhaps things have not changed except for the technology of our warfare - how the impulse is organized and its targets defined. And if this is so, the question falls upon us, how can we address such concerns without slipping into self-induced, post-modern atrophy?

For many within the United States, often identifying themselves as progressive or liberal, inspiration may be found in a more fraternal universalism- what is in fact a federalist, and predominantly European, conception of social organization. Nations here are obliged to defer domestic legislative authority to ratified international agreements, the generalized interests of "civilized" nations trumping particular political interests, especially when they violate some long-standing, recognized norm of law governing state behavior. Appeals to a universal legal order, however, does nothing to settle suspicions that these appeals actual reflect the agendas of powerful political actors - legal instruments advancing particular actors the same way a papal decree served the Holy Roman Catholic Church. In the words of Martti Koskenniemi, institutions (such as democracy or human rights) do not end politics - they merely enact them. Powerful nation states have typically upheld their sovereign will above the reach of any international judiciary that would claim universal or permanent jurisdiction. In practice, the majority of states share at best an uneasy allegiance, more in spirit and diplomatic rhetoric than a sincere appreciation of common interests. One might indeed question how international law may promote national self-determination projects as the authentic expression of a people, and at the same moment submit the emerging sovereignty to a rigid set of expectations and responsibilities completely foreign to it.

In a world increasingly brought together by technological innovation and invisible forces of capital, it seems inevitable that we look to a future of escalating conflict over resources. Blood is thicker than water; the contingencies of the moment triumph over idealism. The future will be marked by more, not less conflict and catastrophe. It is foolish to dream otherwise. To this extent, the tendency to blame American diplomacy or to seek inspiration from Europe or the United Nations' framework of process, sanctions and rights seem misguided at best. However, policy makers might be equally cautious of looking back to our own government bureaucracies and national traditions for a more authentic or sincere answer to governance. The litany of reoccurring political scheming and scandals (i.e., treatment of American Indians, Iran Contra Affair, Monica Lewinski investigation, officially sanctioned torture, the lobby interests involved in the ongoing health care debate, and so on) have produced a visible attitude within the American mainstream that anything our government leaders say, Democrat or Republican, must be taken with a pound of salt. The good life has become a semantic battle of pundits, government officials and scholars, while Americans uncomfortably confront a future of economic hardship and greater surveillance by a government where public opinion only counts as far as it can be charted and manipulated for political profit and politicians limit their commitments to talking points and carefully staged photo ops.[15]

Intellectual criteria today require a certain internationalist perspective in politics, just as it requires a multi-disciplinary approach in academia. In reality, however, the international community remains both physically and metaphorically set in its own backyard. We speak of the Rwandan genocide in Borders Book Store over Starbucks fair trade coffee. We plan humanitarian projects for places where we do not speak the language and have never been ourselves. We may speak for the dispossessed, but it is we speaking - heroic protagonists in a world drama. We travel on large commercial aircrafts to speak at conferences concerning environment woes. We claim allegiance with the American working class while we wear clothes from overseas sweatshops.

In the international legal community, we have taken words like human rights and the rule of law to stand in as the answers and rationalizations for our future projects. Indeed, if the 19th century was the era of nations, we live today in an era of law. The drive for progress through a world ruled by law has become an unimpeachable fact in the existence of humankind's struggle against chaos as Western scholars and practitioners carry on the colonial mentality - the white man's academic burden to write histories not his own, to perform humanitarian experiments in strange lands, to continually act as chief architect of humanity, justifying global rulership upon hazy acknowledgements of responsibility or technocratic knowledge and skill.

It may then be time that we come to terms with the fact that progress itself is, in the words of Karl Kraus, merely a "pyrrhic victory over nature" - our best laid plans meet the "sudden surprises ... and decay" inherit to our human frailty. A more celebratory attitude only marks the bravery of being momentarily out of range. We should not put too much faith in finding solutions in a professional attitude of enlightened self-interest any more than we can hope to nurture some sort of 'gentle civilizing spirit'. As part of a cultural elite with cosmopolitan backgrounds, we may have to put aside our architectural inclinations and grand ideological differences, and begin to look at our every-day lives and how our experiences are so far removed from the realities that we speak about in our writing, in the classroom, at conferences, or even in conversation. If Gandhi is right that change in the world must start with oneself then the commitment to help Africa or Iraq, for instance, must begin with a rigorous examination of our own habits and customs rather than continually look for inspiration in refashioning the world over our borders.[16] We must begin to historicize our assumptions in order to denaturalize those judgments that keep us tied to pre-written scripts;[17] to explore the limits of our own responsibility, of our ability to take responsibility, and not venture further than where we are actually willing to remain after the cards have been played.

THE END OF AMBIVALENCE?

Here, I want to turn to think about how these notions of ethical responsibility might meet the challenge and propose concrete virtues to the ongoing global economic crisis. For in the wake of the financial meltdown, where we only recently would speak of uncertainty and approach even the most virtuous projects with ambivalence, action now seems the name of the game. Everything is immanent, only bold proposals are open to consideration. In philosophical terms, we speak within the wake of what Alain Badiou called the "incalculable event", that moment that compels some sort of "tenacious militant determinism."[18] Or as the Austrian and Chicago economists put it more crassly, "only a crisis, actual or perceived, produces real change."[19] In my own country, even President Bush appeared to be marching to the same tune. "I'm a market oriented guy," he said at a speech from November 2008, "but not when I'm faced with the prospect of a global meltdown."[20]

Of course, what caused the financial crisis or our vision and goals of engagement are up for fierce debate. Is the crisis just one of those things that happen in cyclical fashion – an almost natural event, an economic hurricane, something that can only be engaged with at the last minute, weathered out and dealt with largely after the fact? Or was it due to those mysterious formulas and investment instruments concocted by those nerdy economists from Chicago that came to dominance in the 70s/80s?[21] Likewise, even if the blame ultimately resides with the simple corruption and greed of Wall Street and a coked up capitalist ideology, how do we move forward?[22] At the end of the day, after all our proposals and criticisms are out of the way, De Soto observes that in one form or another "capitalism [still] stands alone as the only feasible way rationally to organize a modern economy," at least in the immediate term.[23]

But maybe this is wrong. Perhaps this is exactly the problem, that we have forgotten the exhilaration of thinking outside the box, to regain what it would mean to be caught up in the throes of some "new militant apparatus of truth".[24] After all, nothing is absolute; everything is ultimately contingent.[25] Who could have predicted the rise of the Internet or the fall of the Soviet Union 50 years ago? We find causes after the effects, but even effects more often than not come to us as black swans. There is no reason that the current capitalist order is any more inescapable – it merely reflects the lack of our will to power and imagination.

Whatever the case, the New American Century appears to already have run out of steam. The specter of univocal global order feels increasingly remote. Iraq continues to drain American will and resources; the American military woefully underprepared for urban combat warfare and long-term occupation and reconstruction efforts. The United States' share of global imports is down to 15%, its currency weakened without any foreseeable reversals, all while alternative stock exchanges and sovereign wealth funds transfer capital to new centers of national power. And with the demise of American hegemony and contagious financial instability have simultaneously spread predictions that the free-market economy itself, whatever that means, teeters on the verge of collapse. If the neo-conservative agenda has proven itself ideologically and practically bankrupt, the hope seems to be that some more equitable order can fill the gap – whether that is expressed in some call for a more democratic balance of powers among nations, or alternatively for the nation-state as a more active stakeholder and regulatory agent in the market. In my mind, both programs are misguided if our goal is to achieve a more progressive, realizable future.

All roads no longer lead to Washington, but they do not alternatively lead to any necessarily stable sharing of influence among great powers. Not only does the fate of the global order seem to rely increasingly on those next tier of 'tipping point states', but with the diffusion of power now among dozens of actors: media conglomerates, drug cartels, militia, global corporations, regional organizations, and so on. In the world to come, diplomacy and collective action will most likely become more, not less, tricky and precarious. Moreover, unlike the Soviet Union that posed an ideological/political alternative for decolonized states, the ascending national powers today seem all too eager to leverage their positions in the existing economic regime. Indeed, it may be that what Western capitalism could not achieve through economic, political, or cultural coercion, it may succeed through importing crisis. Chaos brings its own temptations and opportunities as nations scramble to shore up their declining sovereignty through massive government commitment to the global economic order. If anything, we may very well be moving from a North-South to an East-West axel-ity reminiscent of the late 19th century colonial experience - nations like Russia and China and the United States and within Western Europe simultaneously competing with one another for territory and resources while disavowing any responsibility to act as a buffer for the social costs to their national populations.

What we are experiencing in the West, then, is a more immanent, internalized return of colonialism: the development and law policies carried out in Latin America in the 70s and in Central and Eastern Europe in the late 80s and early 90s now visited in full force upon North Atlantic populations. As journalist and freelance author, Naomi Klein, points out, "Under the cover of emergency... the [US] administration's approach to the financial crisis and its approach the Iraq war... [bear] moving parallels", the state hollowed out as a cash source for corporations that in turn don't deliver the goods and end up ratcheting the burden upon an increasingly paralyzed citizenry. For Klein, it is not the banks and corporations being nationalized, but the nation-state being privatized one emergency, or shock, at a time.[26]

In this light, the call for stricter legal regulation to fix the inherited chaos of economic over-speculation and political corruption appears doomed to failure. Capitalism is, after all, made of nothing but law - it is juridical, the very stuff of commercial markets. Far from a space of utter lawlessness, the free market crisis we have inherited is a space already brimming with expertise, procedure, scrutiny and analysis.[27] Likewise, we should not imagine that any mere nationalization scheme is somehow anathema to capitalism; the social state is as old as industrial capitalism. Here, to treat any set of regulatory law in and of itself as some sort of redemptive force if only properly responsible and enforced obscures not only the fact that these very norms may have contributed to creating and sustaining the problems, but also empty the situation of its 'scandalous political content'.[28] Heated discussions how the agendas of particular subcultures and agents prime and manipulate the system become whitewashed into civilized conversations about the structure and limits of fair and efficient administration – what turns into 'politics without politics'.

The reliance upon ever more dramatic techniques by the corporatist crusade to remake the world in the image of homoeconomics does not necessarily mean it has won the day – we could as easily be witnessing a system unraveling by its own schemes. Or alternatively, perhaps this is just capitalism going through growing pains, reinventing and disciplining itself as new actors force their way into the game.[29] Perhaps we just too easily forget the emotions of crisis, and imagine each time around some apocalyptic scenario, some hope that we have suffered towards something monumental, of long-lasting significance - as Barack Obama's world-wide appeal demonstrates, populations want to believe in change.

But if everything is contingent, there is always room for strategy and reversals of fortune. In my mind, however, this can only happen if we move from a strictly critical to a more programmatic attitude that looks beyond law or the nation-state or any romantic notions of an international collective responsibility. While we may find fatherly comfort in law and regulation, it ultimately "entail[s] inevitable ideological and distributional choices ... [that can] only be resolved by resort to values and policies which are external to the law."[30] We must come to accept that law does not provide "closure to ideological disputes and political conflicts" but merely enacts and naturalizes them. Law always leads us elsewhere, to somewhere outside its own reference points and logic. Moreover, the debate over the extent of state 'intrusion' into the market is misguided, a myth of liberalism. Private economic power "operates necessarily through and with the exercise of public power."[31] What might be more interesting to ask ourselves, is what exactly do we want the state doing. If we are truly experiencing development strategies now being played out again upon Western populations, perhaps we should look to the East Asian examples of export-production focused growth as opposed to the more traditional market-based approaches taken in places like Egypt or Argentina. Likewise, while there has been no shortage of rejections of global inequality, there have been little hard institutional thinking putting forward meaningful alternative projects. How could we escape industrial-led growth and everything that seems to come with it, even if we wanted to?

CONCLUSION: TAKING RISKS ETHICALLY

Too often our passion for justice in the past has taken on an international character, resigned to some abstract universalism. We condemn coercion on the global sphere while tolerating it within our national boundaries, always choosing battles that we have the privilege to disengage from at any time if the stakes get too high. The crisis, however, has brought home the uncomfortable fact that colonialism and violence occur in a more broad and intimate field of inquiry than we often assume – within the landscape of London and Los Angeles as much as Namibia and Sierra Leone. In this light, as George Kennan said many years ago, perhaps "the first thing we [Americans] need to learn to contain is, in some ways, ourselves... [and] that a large proportion of the sources of our troubles and dangers lie... within ourselves."[32] Revolutions happen through people like Luther and Lenin, not Derrida and Foucault. In short, we must take risks and put our own houses in order. If this means that we check our wishes, that we cannot escape the limits and boredom of our everyday world, then perhaps that is the price. But if so, it might also allow for a full wager, some politics of truth, which could function as the very opening to the concrete realization of the impossible.

Notes

1. *See* Nathaniel Berman, *In the Wake of Empire*, 14 Am. U. Int. L. Rev. 1515, 1554 (1999).
2. *See* David Kennedy, The International Human Rights Movement: Part of the Problem?, 15 *Harvard Human Rights Journal*, 99 (2001).
3. *See* John Haskell and Boris Mamlyuk, *Capitalism, Communism... and Colonialism?: Revisiting Transitology as the Ideology of Informal Empire*, Vol. 9, Iss. 2, Art. 7 (2009).
4. *See* Jose Casanova, *Religion, European Secular Identities and European Integration*, Eurozine (July 27, 2004).
5. *See* Robinson Jeffers, *Rearmament* (1935). Disillusioned with politics by the "high level betrayals like Versailles," Robinson draws the title of the poem from Stalin's 1934 announcement of Russian rearmament, and sees in it the "first signs of the drift toward war in Europe."
6. Kae Matundu-Tjiparuro, an Ovambandero – Ovaherero activist and journalist, expresses this distrust poignantly. In *An Open Letter to Professor Hinz and Fellow "verkampte" Academics* (on file with author), he writes, "It is time to speak to the pseudo good intentions of some German siblings masquerading as academia. It's a suspicion I've been harboring for some time. And suspicion is putting it very mildly." In particular, he is skeptical of academics' "self-proclaimed liberalism, humanitarianism, and critical thinking." For Matundu-Tjiparuro, these academics are "daily, and at a cruising speed, revealing their true colors. At the end of the day, blood is thicker than water."
7. In reviewing the findings of their polling, for example, Balz and Brownstein observed that "large numbers feel themselves uprooted by developments that they cannot understand or control ... that they can no longer shape their own future." *See* Martin Castells, THE POWER OF IDENTITY 173 (2004).
8. The post-foundational tradition in political philosophy dates at least back to interwar German philosophers and jurists, such as Heidegger and Schmitt, and has recently re-entered international legal theory through authors such as David Kennedy and Martti Koskenniemi. For a concise but useful overview of post-foundational thought, *see* Oliver Marchart, *Post-foundational Political Thought: Political Difference in Nancy, Lefort, Badiou, And Laclau* (2007).

9. *See* R. Shea & R. A. Wilson, *The Illuminatus Trilogy* 452-454 (1975) (stating and expanding on the line, "[f]reedom defined is freedom denied").

10. In particular, I am thinking about the political philosophy of authors such as Alain Badiou in response to the anti-Marxist left within French intellectual circles.

11. *See e.g.*, David M. Trubek and Alvaro Santos, eds, The New Law and Economic Development: A Critical Appraisal (2006).

12. *See* John Gray, STRAW DOGS 173 (2003).

13. *See* Martti Koskenniemi, *'The Lady Doth Protest Too Much' Kosovo, and the Turn to Ethics in International Law*, 65 Modern Law Review 159 (2002).

14. *See* Edward Said, Imperial Perspectives, *available at http://www.zmag.org/content/showarticle.cfm?SectionID=22&ItemID=3949* (last visited Dec. 1, 2009).

15. *See generally* David Kennedy, OF WAR AND LAW (2006)(discussing the modern limitations of political responsibility and the 'shaming' of Political actors).

16. *See* Slavoj Zizek, IN DEFENSE OF LOST CAUSES 161 (2009)(discussing the source of Robespierre's 'pacificism' in his speech, 'On War', not in any 'humanitarian sensitivity', but because war between nations seves as 'the means to obfuscate revolutionary struggle within each nation').

17. *See generally* Harold Bloom, *The Anxiety of Influence: A Theory of Poetry* (1973).

18. This theme runs through Alain Badiou's work. *See Being and Event* (1988); ST. PAUL: *The Foundation of Universalism* (1997) (hereafter ST. PAUL), and *Ethics: An Essay on the Understanding of Evil* (2001). For Badiou, Paul's conversion to Christianity on the road to Damascus is a clear example of this militancy. "Just as the Resurrection remains totally incalculable ... nothing leads up to... Paul's faith... The event – 'it happened', purely and simply, in the anonymity of a road – is the subjective sign of the event proper that is the Resurrection of Christ." In Badiou's thinking, the truth, coming as an act of grace, transcending particularity and subjectivity, is ultimately the only stable source of "effective declaration", for the "possible power of thought". *See* ST. PAUL at 17, 88.

19. *See generally* Milton Friedman, *Capitalism and Freedom* (1962)

20. The United States White House claims that its actions are "unprecedented", "aggressive" and "extraordinary". *See* the White House official webpage, *available at www.whitehouse.gov* (last visited December 7, 2008).

21. *See* Yves Dezalay and Bryant Garth, *The Internationalization of Palace Wars: Lawyers, Economists, and the Contest to Transform Latin American States*, 73-94, (2002).

22. The recent letter from the President of the United Steelworkers, Leo Gerard, to US Treasury Secretary Henry Paulson criticizes the "unbridled pursuit of greed that you and your friends on Wall Street have celebrated as a national religion", but continues on to call for a re-investment in "the American dream" – itself perhaps, in many ways, part and parcel of the very same problems that have buffered the "philosophy that worships only business, deregulation and free trade". For a copy of the letter in the context of neo-colonial 'plunder', *see* Ugo Mattei's Red Room blog, *available at http://www.redroom.com/blog/ugo-mattei/plunder-blog-mr-paulson-plunders-taxpayers-sake-his-own-firm* (last visited Dec. 20, 2009).

23. *See* Hernando De Soto, *The Mystery of Capital: Why Capitalism Triumphs in the West and Fails Everywhere Else*, (2001).

24. This phrase comes from Alain Badiou. For an in-depth analysis of this idea, *see* Peter Hallward and Slavoj Zizek, BADIOU 108-110 (2003). Of course, as Zizek has pointed out, there seems to be an irresolvable tension that often rises between meaningful action and taking responsibility. While we may abstractly favor the right of political agents to posit themselves outside the conventional social edifice, we might be "afraid of the potential totalitarian terrorist consequences of asserting actual freedom as the direct inscription of the Event into the order of Being." *See* Slavoj Zizek, ON BELIEF 125 (2001).

25. For a philosophical polemic of this idea, *see* Quentin Meillassoux, *After Finitude: An Essay on the Necessity of Contingency* (2006); *see also* Nassim Nicholas Taleb, *The Black Swan: The Impact of the Highly Improbable)* (2007).

26. *See* Naomi Klein, *The New Trough, available at http://www.rollingstone.com/politics/story/ 24012700/ the_new_trough,* Rolling Stone Magazine Online, Nov. 13, 2008 (last visited Dec. 20, 2009).

27. I have drawn this idea and the general language from Fleur Johns' article, *Guantanamo Bay and the Annihilation of the Exception*, 16(4) European Journal of International Law 613-635 (2005).

28. I have drawn this general idea and language from Susan Marks, *State-Centrism, International Law, and the Anxieties of Influence*, 19 *Leiden Journal of International Law*, (2006).

29. "Constant revolutionizing of production, uninterrupted disturbance of all social conditions, everlasting uncertainty and agitation distinguish the bourgeois epoch from all earlier ones. All fixed, fast frozen relations, with their train of ancient and venerable prejudices and opinions, are swept away, all new-formed ones become antiquated before they can ossify. All that is solid melts into air." *See* Marx and Engels, *The Communist Manifesto* (1848).

30. *See* Kerry Rittich, *Recharacterizing Restructuring: Law, Distribution and Gender in Market Reform* 133 (2002). *See also* Duncan Kennedy, *The Stakes of Law, or Hale and Foucault!*, 15 Legal Studies Forum 327 (1991)

31. *Id.*, at 135.

32. *See* George Kennan, *Containment: 40 Years Later: Containment Then and Now*, Foreign Affairs (Spring 1987).

Sex Work, HIV/AIDs and Sexual Rights in Africa: The Nigerian Experience

EBENEZER DUROJAYE*, OLUBAYO OLUDURO** & UJU OKEKE***

INTRODUCTION

Sex work flourishes in the world, despite the negative perception held by the public of it. In fact, sex work is regarded as one of the oldest professions in the world. It is believed that it was first practiced as far back as the middle ages where it boomed greatly and was a huge source of revenue to municipalities.[1] It is a truism that African society is generally a conservative one, which lays heavy emphasis on issues of morality and religion. Thus issues such as sex work and same sex relationships are seen generally as 'unAfrican' and a contamination of the moral value of the African society. Yet, in many African countries sex work has continued to thrive and same sex relationships have continued to surface especially in the wake of HIV/AIDS pandemic in the region. In Nigeria, sex work has been in existence since the colonial period. Although at that time it was carried out on a low scale, it soon gained momentum after independence around 1960. Sex work related activities for a long time have been criminalised in Nigeria but this has not by any means stopped people from engaging in sex work. Rather than curbing the practice of sex work, criminalisation seems to have fuelled an increase in the number of people engaging in sex work in the country.

Thus, the question is being asked if there is any logical reason for the continued criminalisation of sex work associated activities in the country. This question has even become more germane when the socio-economic situation in Nigeria is taken into consideration. Here is a country where the majority of the population is said to be living below poverty level. Unemployment is rife and inflation is at its peak. Furthermore, the HIV/AIDS pandemic is taking its

* *Research Assistant Department of Constitutional Law and Philosophy of Law University of the Free State South Africa , (durojayeet.rd@ufs.ac.za)*

** *LLB, LLM Lagos. Senior Lecturer and Acting Dean of Law Adekunle Ajasin University Ondo State.*

*** *LLB (OAU,)LLM (Specialising in Sexual and Reproductive Rights) University of the Free State South Africa portablecute@yahoo.com* toll on the country. Current statistic shows that about 4.4 per cent of the population is infected with HIV.[2] In view of this predicament, it is being suggested in many quarters that legalisation or decriminalisation of sex work is a serious option, which Nigerian government should begin to consider.

This article will examine the meaning of sex work and its types as practiced in Nigeria. It will then consider the diverging views often expressed by feminist scholars with regard to sex work. It will similarly examine the various approaches such as criminalisation, legalisation and decriminalisation, which have been adopted to sex work worldwide and in particular the approach in Nigeria. The article then suggests that based on the high prevalence of HIV/AIDS in Nigeria and the fact that restrictive laws on sex work have often exposed sex workers to danger and human rights violations, Nigerian government should begin to consider liberal approach towards sex work. Such an approach should take into cognizance the well being and respect for the dignity of sex workers. More importantly, the article will consider the human rights issue -using the sexual rights lens-raised by sex work. This article will draw examples from other jurisdictions where attempts are being made to legalise or decriminalise sex work. It will then suggest the best approach Nigerian government should adopt in addressing this controversial issue.

MEANING OF SEX WORK

The term 'sex work' may be described as a situation where a person exchanges sexual pleasure for monetary or material reward.[3] The English court in *R v Munck*[4] described sex work as the offering of a girl of her body for purposes amounting to lewdness for payment. A similar definition was adopted in *Webb* case.[5] A person who engages in this act is called a sex worker. This definition may however, not adequately reflect the variety of services sex workers offer or the circumstances under which they operate. In many societies, sex work is often associated with females; however, recent developments have shown that men also engage in sex work. Nowadays sex workers may be women, men or transgendered persons spanning a wide range of ages, backgrounds and sexual orientations. Some are self-employed; some work for others. Sex work may be open and—in rare cases—legal, but it is more often covert and illegal.[6]

Throughout this article, any reference to sex workers should be taken to mean female sex workers. In more popular parlance sex work is often regarded to as 'prostitution'. This term is said to be derogatory and demeaning to those who engage in this business. Moreover, many activists working in this area find it judgmental and unacceptable. Thus, the term sex work is often preferred as this is more glorifying and acceptable. Besides, it is said to be value neutral and non-judgmental.[7]

Feminists' Perspective of Sex Work

It must be mentioned here that feminist scholars have expressed diverging views on the issue of sex work. Feminists have hotly debated the propriety or otherwise of sex work without a uniform opinion emerging. The debate has been so furious that it was tagged 'sex wars'[8] Leading feminist opinions on this issue are that of radical and liberal feminists. The former are of the view that sex work is demeaning to women and further perpetuates male domination over women's bodies.[9] They further argue for intervention insisting that women will be far from attaining equality for as long as their sexuality is commercialised and as long as economic domination is conflated with sexual pleasure.[10] Therefore, radical feminists condemn sex work in its totality. A notable radical feminist who has expressed great abhorrence for sex work is Dworkin. She argues that sex work is dirty and merely demeans a woman as human being. Her repugnance for sex work is captured in the following words:

> I think that prostitutes experience a specific inferiority. Women in general are considered to be dirty. Most of us experience this as a metaphor…but a prostitute lives the reality of being the dirty woman….She is perceived as, treated as…..vaginal slime. She is dirty, a lot of men have been there….all women are considered dirty because of menstrual blood but she bleeds other times, other places…..When men use women in prostitution, they are expressing a pure hatred of the female body…it is a contempt so deep, that a whole human life is reduced to a few sexual orifices he can do anything he wants…..[11]

This comment no doubt appears harsh and yet it represents radical feminists' perception of sex work as inherently dehumanizing to women - and the ultimate objectification of a person. It is also to be noted that this statement summarizes the public's view of sex work.

On the other hand, liberal feminists hold the view that sex work is an expression of women's freedom and right over their bodies. Thus, they argue that there is nothing wrong for women to enter into an agreement over their bodies.[12] According to this group of feminists sex work is nothing but a contract between consenting people to provide sex in exchange for payment. For instance Vance has argued that an attempt to censor sexual behavior between consenting adults will only resort in danger for sexual minorities and women.[13]

SEX WORK IN NIGERIA

The history of sex work in Nigeria dates back to colonial era and sexual habits of the colonists.[14] It is believed that colonialism in the country precipitated a monetary economy where sex could easily be bought just like any other commodity.[15] In the past it used to be thought that majority of those who engaged in sex work in the country were women who had lost their husbands and had no means of livelihood. But recent developments have shown that more female adolescents are increasingly engaged in sex work in the country. It has been estimated that about 43 per cent of sex workers in Nigeria are female adolescents.[16] As observed by Bamgbose sex work is no longer a strange business in Nigeria rather it is now a thriving business in most Nigerian cities.[17] She stated further that the reason for this is that the cultural values in Nigeria have broken down and little or no attention is being paid to the rights to life and to proper development of adolescents.[18]

Several factors have been attributed to the sudden upsurge of sex wok in Nigeria. These factors can be classified under two broad headings-economic and social factors. Many sociologists will agree that societal effects play a prominent role in human behaviour in every society. It has been identified that factors such as rapid urbanization, increased rural migration and high unemployment rate are key drivers of adolescent sex work in Nigeria.[19] Some studies conducted in the country have shown that the wide gap between the rich and the poor and the need of female students to meet educational expenses have fuelled sex work in the country.[20] It is also to be noted that many of the sex workers make an averagely reasonable amount of income daily comparable to that of civil servants in the country. Thus, sex workers may find it very lucrative and not think of leaving for any other work.[21]

There is no gain saying the fact that one of the driving forces for sex work is the financial benefits which accrue to sex workers. This is more so in an environment such as Nigeria where unemployment is on the increase and poverty is becoming the order of the day for majority of the population. It is believed that majority of Nigerians live on less than one dollar per day. One of the survival strategies and coping mechanisms, which young girls have adopted in reaction to the harsh economic condition, is the offering of their bodies for the purpose of material reward. This is nothing short of engaging in sex work.

Sociological factors, which have fuelled increase in sex work, include high rate of migration of young girls from rural areas to urban areas in search of jobs, which in most cases are non-existence. In addition, the craze for materialist wealth, peer influence and changing social values make young girls easy prey for sex work.[22] While it is noted that the economic and social factors mentioned above affect every member of the society young girls are worst affected. This is because the stage of adolescence is a transitional one in an individual's life, therefore, making adolescents vulnerable to the harsh realities of life. They are easily susceptible to pressure from peers, parents or guardians and many of the older men that patronize sex workers often prefer young girls, thus making female adolescents easy target for sex work. [23]

Forms and nature of Sex work in Nigeria

The fact that sex workers operate under clandestine condition in Nigeria makes it more tasking in determining forms and trends of sex work in the country. However, one noticeable trend as earlier pointed out is that more and more young girls than ever, are becoming visible in the business. The business of sex work used to be the exclusive preserve of older women in the country but this is changing fast. Presently, older women who remain in sex work do so either as practitioners with fewer clients or, commonly as pimps or 'madams' who procure and train the younger ones for the business.[24]

The common forms of sex work operating in Nigeria include operation of brothels, streetwalkers, call girls, and causal, part- time or floating sex workers.[25] Many of the young girls now engaged in sex work begin their career in sex work in more comfortable hotel rooms or sophisticated surroundings. Thus, this has given rise to the popular 'sugar daddy' syndrome. This is a situation where young girls patronize older men for sexual pleasure in return for gifts, favor or financial reward. These older men who are often very rich are referred to as 'sugar daddies'. It is very controversial classifying this act as sex work as the relationship is often for a longer period and in most cases with a particular man. Young girls who engage in this type of relationship do not see themselves as being involved in sex work. Moreover, in some situation the relationship with the older men has some emotional attachments and goes beyond mere sex worker-client relationship.

A common form of sex work in Nigeria is known as the 'night brides'. These are young girls who adorn the major streets and junctions of cities in the country, usually during the nights, waiting for their customers. These young girls are willing to take any one who is willing to pay for their services. In most cases, preference is given to foreigners who are willing to pay in foreign currency. [26] It is to be observed that while some people engage in sex work on a part time basis others do it as a full time job. Among those who engage in part time sex work, include secondary school students, usually in need of money to pay for their school fees or for other material needs.[27]

Another form of sex workers in the country are the 'floating sex workers' These are young girls usually found loitering or hawking goods around motor parks and markets in day time. Many of these girls engage in regular sexual intercourse with older men in return for a small amount of money or gifts, which they hand over to their families.[28]

A peculiar form of well-organised sex work, which goes on in Nigerian higher institutions, is referred to as 'call girls'. In this type of situation, male and female pimps get in contact with already known and available females whenever there is a demand for them. The male clients in this form of sex work are usually rich and influential men in the society. This fact suggests the oppressive nature of sex work. The pimps live on the commission for making the contact.[29]

Also a recent form of sex work, which is becoming very prevalent in the country, is trafficking of young girls across Nigerian borders to Europe. In this form of sex work, young girls are lured to leave the country with a promise of better jobs abroad. Many of these girls only get to know that they have been tricked into sex work when they reach their destination abroad. Such girls are expected to work for a period of time to raise money to cover the traveling expenses and to show appreciation to the 'agent' who facilitated the journey abroad. This has been described as modern form of slavery. It is often highly organized by syndicates who are very rich and well connected. Trafficking of girls for sex work abroad has brought negative publicity to the Nigerian government in recent times. In reaction to this, the government has enacted a law and set up a body to specifically address this issue and to punish any one found engage in this business.[30] This form of sex work will not be examined in detail in this article.

HIV/AIDS and Sex Work in Nigeria

The first two diagnosed cases of AIDS in Nigeria occurred in 1985; however, it was officially reported in 1986.[31] Since that time the infection rate in the country has risen from 1.8 per cent in 1991 to 4.5 per cent in 1996 and then 5.4 per cent in 1999. By 2001 the prevalence rate has jumped to 5.8 per cent. However, by 2003 the national prevalence rate dropped to 5.0 per cent although some states such as Cross Rivers (12.0 per cent), Benue (9.3 per cent) and Taraba (7.3 per cent) have higher prevalence rates.[32] The current figure stands at 4.4 per cent of the population.[33] The major mode of HIV transmission in Nigeria is through unsafe sexual intercourse-heterosexual. Of recent, however, there seem to have been an increase in infection rate through homosexual activities.[34] Other modes of transmission include blood transfusions; unsafe injection and mother-to-child-transmission.

As in other society sex workers in Nigeria are often regarded as vectors of HIV/AIDS. While this assumption cannot be said to be totally correct, studies have revealed increase in infection rates among sex workers from 17.5 per cent in 1991 to 22.5 per cent in 1993 and 36.5 per cent in 1995.[35] It is believed that sex workers, long distance truck drivers, commercial motorcyclists, military personnel, migrant and mobile population etc. are high risk groups in Nigeria because they engage in risky behaviors such as unsafe sex, commercial sex, injection drug use with contaminated needles.[36] Nigerian government has taken a number of steps to combat the spread of the epidemic in the country. Upon return of the country to democratic rule in 1999 the Obasanjo's administration set up the Presidential Committee on AIDS and the multi sectoral body National Action Committee on AIDS (NACA).[37] This body has been mainly responsible for implementing government programs to address the spread of the HIV/ AIDS epidemic in the country.

One of the reasons while sex workers are classified as high risk groups is the fact that many of them are poor, lack formal education, marginalized and stigmatized. Moreover, sex workers have frequent sex with multiple partners, often unprotected and also bear high burden of sexually transmitted infections Surveys carried out in parts of the country have consistently shown an astronomical rise in infection rates among sex workers. For instance, in Lagos, infection rates among sex workers increased from a mere two per cent in 1988-1989 to about 12 per cent in 1990-1991 and then a staggering 70 per cent by 1995-1996.[38] Also a study in Jos, Plateau State has shown that about 52 per cent infections rate of HIV has been recorded among brothel based sex workers.[39]

Prevention of HIV/AIDS among sex workers is significantly low. Another study conducted in 2000 revealed that knowledge of HIV prevention among female sex workers was low and consistent use of condom varied from 24 per cent in one state to 89 per cent in Lagos.[40] This study further revealed that there was low level of HIV testing uptake among female sex workers as only about 24 per cent of those surveyed reported having had HIV testing and even learnt of the result.[41] A number of socio-economic factors predispose sex workers to HIV infection in the country. Some of these include low economic status of female sex workers, constant susceptibility to violence, coerced sex or rape leading to abrasion and bleeding thus increasing risk of infection.[42] Also, lack of self esteem coupled with poor negotiating skills and illegal status of sex work all compromise their ability to manage the situation and even seek legal redress.[43]

It is noted with concern that despite high infection rates of HIV among sex workers, little effort is being made by the government to incorporate sex workers into HIV/AIDS prevention programme in the country. Most of the prevention programmes have been initiated by few non-governmental organizations (NGOs) working with sex workers. But the challenge for these organizations is lack of funds. Although, Nigeria is one of the beneficiaries of the United States government's President Emergency Plan Fund for AIDS Relief (PEPFAR), a provision requiring all recipients of U.S. global HIV/AIDS funding to adopt an explicit policy 'opposing' sex work, has made it more difficult for these NGOs to effectively reach out to sex workers.[44] Unlike in other jurisdictions as in India where sex workers have been able to come together as a formidable pressure group or organization, there is no yet in Nigeria an organization that is entirely made of sex workers to champion their cause. This has further worsened the situation of sex workers in the country.

APPROACHES TOWARDS SEX WORK

There are different approaches towards sex work, which countries over the world have adopted. These include criminalisation, abolitionism, legalisation and decriminalisation. Of these approaches, criminalisation is the commonest and is the one adopted by Nigeria.

Move Towards Criminalisation

As in other countries of the world, the Nigerian society expresses negative attitudes towards sex work. Busia has observed that during colonialism family members of the sex workers saw sex work in Nigeria as being disgraceful and highly condemnable.[45] Many of the sex workers are treated with great disdain and even barred from attending social functions in the community.[46] This situation is neither peculiar to colonial era only nor to Nigeria alone similar attitudes are meted out to sex workers in other countries as well. In a country like United Kingdom, it has been reported that migrant sex workers have been made subject of deportation after a raid of brothels in London. [47] This aversion for sex work led the Nigerian government to criminalize any activity related to the business during the colonial period. The Criminal code[48] applicable to Southern Nigeria contains important provisions criminalizing sex work related activities in the country. Section 225A of the code provides thus:

(1) Every male person who-

(a) Knowingly lives wholly or in part on the earnings of prostitution; or

(b) In any public place persistently solicits or importunes for immoral purposes, shall be liable to imprisonment for two years, and in the case of a second or subsequent conviction, shall, in addition to any term of imprisonment awarded, be liable to caning.

(2) Any magistrate who is satisfied, by evidence upon oath, that there is reason to suspect that any premises or any part of any premises are or is used by a female for, Purposes of prostitution, and that any male person residing in or frequenting the premises is living wholly or in part on the earnings of the prostitute, may issue a warrant under his hand authorizing any constable to enter and search the premises and to arrest that male person.

(3) Where a male person is proved to live with or to be habitually in the company of a prostitute or is proved to have exercised control, direction, or influence over the movements of a prostitute in such a manner as to show that he is aiding, abetting or compelling her prostitution with any other person or generally, he shall, unless he can satisfy the court to the contrary, be deemed to be knowingly living on the earnings of the prostitution.

(4) Every female who is proved to have, for the purposes of gain, exercised control, direction or influence over the movements of a prostitute in such a manner as to show that she is aiding, abetting or compelling her prostitution with any person or generally shall be liable to imprisonment for two years.

It is further provided in section 225B of the code that whoever;

Keeps or manages or assists in the management of a brothel; or

Being the tenant, lessee, or occupier or person in charge of any premises, knowingly permits such premises or any part thereof to be used as a brothel or for the purposes of habitual prostitution; or

Being the lessor or landlord of any premises, or the agent of such lessor or landlord, lets the same or any part thereof with the knowledge that such premises or some part thereof are or is to be used as a brothel, or is willfully a party to the continued use of such premises or any part thereof as a brothel, shall be liable-

To a fine of one hundred naira or to imprisonment for six months, and

On a second or subsequent conviction, to a fine of three hundred naira or to imprisonment for one year; or in either case, to both fine and imprisonment.

From these provisions, two underlying aims of the criminal code can be deduced. First, the law intends to protect sex workers from exploitation by third parties, and second, it seeks to protect the society from the menace of sex work. It is interesting to observe that these provisions of the law seek to prohibit both male and female sex works related activities in the country. However, in reality the enforcement of this law has targeted female rather than male sex workers. Many of the arrests made by government security agents have only involved female sex workers.

Many reasons often cited for criminalizing sex works include need to prevent spread of sexually transmitted infections(including HVI/ AIDS) among the population, fear of breeding criminality, need to protect sex workers from exploitation and need to preserve moral sanctity of the society. But rather than protecting sex workers from exploitation, criminalisation of sex works has tended to render sex workers vulnerable to attack and violence from security agents or other persons. This has further worsened the working conditions of sex workers. An example of nature of violence experienced by sex workers is captured in this narrative

> A street prostitute was beaten, choked with a rope and left unconscious in an alley. She had severe bruising on her neck and face the next day when she approached two female police officers to report the incident. They asked her what she expected in her line of work and refused to take a report.[49]

This type of negative attitude towards sex work often force sex workers to operate under ground and unable to have control over their customers. This similarly has the implication that in most cases sex workers will not be able to negotiate condom use with their clients.

On the reason that sex work leads to urban crime, drugs use and general decay of urban areas, studies around the world have shown no direct link between sex work and these concerns. For instance, a 1977 study conducted in Boston, United States showed that the connection between urban decay, crime and sex work resulted because sex work was only allowed to exist in areas the city had already written off.[50] By way of proof, the study noted the effects of regulation in Boston, which quickly transformed an already borderline area into the 'Combat Zone'. The study further found that the 'anything goes' attitude of the police, rather than sex work, allowed crime to get out of hand.[51]

Similarly, justifying criminalisation of sex work based on the belief that sex workers are vectors of sexually transmitted infections including HIV/ AIDS, has been found to be highly contentious. A study has shown that sex workers are potentially at risk of HIV infection because they routinely have sex with paying customers and individuals –usually boyfriends, husbands, casual friends or acquaintances -who do not pay.[52] Implicit in this fact is that sex workers are less likely to use condom with the non paying individuals thus increasing the risk of HIV transmission to and from non paying individual customers.

To the contrary, studies in countries where sex work is also criminalised have shown that sex workers are at lower risks of transmitting HIV/AIDS than their customers.[53] Studies in some of these countries further reveal that in general, needle use, not sex work is the main source of AIDS transmission.[54] This seems to corroborate an earlier study conducted, which showed sex workers to be at very low risks of transmission of venereal infections.[55] Indeed Mackinnon has argued that criminalisation of sex work often perpetuates discrimination against women and makes women criminals even for being victimized.[56]

Though sex work related activities are criminalised in Nigeria, there is low rate of prosecution or conviction on this issue in the country. In fact it is doubtful if there is a reported case where any one has been tried and found guilty under provision of section 225 of the criminal code. Sex work has continued to thrive in the country as if it was a legal business. This may be an indication of the unwillingness of government to prosecute offenders or may suggest a change in attitudes by the public about sex work. It has been observed that more liberal outlook towards sex work now exists in Nigeria.[57] Although sex work is still not morally acceptable, the biting economic situation seems to have triggered moral adjustment on this issue. Besides sex workers that give financial support to family members are now tolerated.

Undoubtedly the failure of criminal law to stop sex work in Nigeria is an indication that criminal law may not always be the best option in addressing public health issues as sex work. Whilst it is admitted that drastic measures may be taken in certain circumstances to protect the public, such measures must respect individuals' rights and be reasonable and just. There is little evidence to support the assertion that criminalisation of sex work has served the purpose for which it was intended in the country.

Abolitionism

Aside from those who believe in criminalisation of sex work other arguments in relation to sex work include the abolitionists and legalisation or decriminalisation theories. Abolitionism has been described as the final stop on the legal spectrum between complete criminalisation and total decriminalisation of sex work.[58] Abolitionism criminalises the activities of those seen as exploiting or coercing prostitutes (so-called 'pimping' and 'procuring' laws) while leaving prostitutes themselves free from regulation. It is being regarded as a compromise between criminalisation and total decriminalisation of sex work. This form of approach towards sex work has been endorsed by the UN Convention for the Suppression of the Traffic in Persons and the Exploitation of the Prostitution of Others.[59]

The logic behind this approach is that sex workers are seen as victims rather than target of criminal law. Thus, this approach does not in itself endorse sex work. Rather, it seeks to protect sex workers from exploitation by pimps and brothel owners while aiming towards abolition of sex work completely.[60] The UN has recommended that this approach should be accompanied by efforts from governments to 'reintegrate' sex workers back into 'legitimate' society.[61] No country presently has adopted strictly this approach.[62] Although abolitionism seems to receive the support of some feminists, it has been criticized for adopting a hypocritical approach towards sex work. In that, while it purports to protect sex workers from third parties, it indirectly stigmatises sex worker and makes society to treat them separately and unequally.[63]

Legalisation and Decriminalisation

As seen from above both criminalisation and abolitionism methods towards sex work have failed and not yielded desired effects. Therefore, organizations working in the area of sex work and other feminists have suggested decriminalisation as the way out. Decriminalisation is the complete removal of sex work and sex work related offenses from the criminal code, including those offenses dealing with the exploitation or coercion of sex workers.[64] It is important to note here the difference between decriminalisation and legalisation. The former not only legalises sex work but also removes all regulation, save those to which any business might be subjected, from criminal codes and allows sex workers to work as they deem fit. It, thus, removes the opportunity for abuse of sex workers by the authorities.[65] This is the system most recommended by sex workers' organizations.[66] Legalisation, on the other hand, is often attended by regulations and licensing, usually with mandatory health inspections and health cards.[67] This operates in places such as Germany, part of Australia and Netherlands. In Netherlands for instance, ban on brothels and sex work has been lifted since year 2000. Sex work is recognized like other professions. Moreover, sex workers now pay taxes like every other employee in the country. However, operation of sex work is restricted to certain areas and law on nuisance is still retained.[68] This approach guarantees sex workers their right to work, dignity and freedom from discrimination and violence.

Those who favor the approach of decriminalisation argue that specialised treatment for sex workers merely reinforces prejudice and stigmatisation of sex work which, rather than increasing, has decreased the quality of life of sex workers and their chances of leaving the profession. It must be noted here that the effectiveness of decriminalisation is dependent on two key factors. One, it is necessary that all the parties including sex workers be in consensus about its implementation. Second, there is need to strengthen sex workers representation and sex workers rights groups in the society. It is believed that decriminalisation will make sex workers visible in the society and therefore be easily integrated into HIV/AIDS prevention programmes. At present most prevention programmes on HIV/AIDS hardly involve sex workers as they are difficult to reach due to criminalisation of the profession. Decriminalisation has the potential to overcome this problem. It will also promote the sexual health of sex workers as they are able to negotiate safer sex and seek medical attention for sexually transmitted infections without fear of stigmatisation or harassment.

There are however, some concerns raised with regard to decriminalisation. Many people are of the view that it will be difficult to implement since Nigerian society is already used to criminalisation of sex work. This will require a change of attitudes which may not be easy to achieve as great resistance is expected from different quarters. This can be true of a conservative and religiously polarised society such as Nigeria. It has similarly been argued that decriminalisation of sex work will not necessarily translate to protection of sex worker's rights.[69] On the contrary it is argued that decriminalisation will further endorse violence and stigma associated with sex work since it may not be able to effectively address the power imbalance between sex workers and pimps.[70] Others have said that decriminalisation will suggest that government endorses exploitation of sex workers in the society.[71]

In response to some of these fears it has been argued that merely decriminalising sex work does not imply sanctioning of sex work by government. This is because in some societies abortion, adultery and attempted murder are all excluded from criminal law and yet governments have not been accused of endorsing these practices.[72] Exclusion of adultery and attempted suicide from criminal punishment is an indication of recent trends that such matters are not appropriate for criminal law. Developments around the world in the past half-century seem to confirm attempts to move away from legislating morality. A good example exists in United Kingdom via Lord Wolfenden Committee, whose report in 1963 formed the basis for British law reform on sex work.[73] In addressing this issue the Committee submitted in this way:

> [the function of the criminal law is] to preserve public order and decency, to protect the citizen from what is injurious or offensive and to provide safeguards against the exploitation and corruption of others, ... It is not, in our view, the function of the law to intervene in the private lives of citizens, or to seek to enforce any particular code of behavior, further than is necessary to carry out the purposes of what we have outlined.[74]

This statement no doubt provides the necessary impetus to challenge government's intervention in private acts as in case of consensual sexual intercourse between or among adults. It further brings into focus the futility of criminalising what the society has tagged 'immorality'

SEX WORK AND HUMAN RIGHTS

In many countries including Nigeria, where sex work related activities are criminalised, security agents have constantly made sex workers the subject of abuse. Many a time sex workers suffer violence and extortion from overzealous police officers. This has raised concerns among human rights activists who tend to condemn these acts as gross violations of fundamental rights of sex workers. In particular, it is being argued that violence against sex workers amounts to an infringement of their sexual rights. It is interesting to note that there is no specific human rights instrument that explicitly addresses the issue of sex work as a human rights concern. Equally of note is the fact no UN Declaration has yet specifically addressed the issue of sex work. However, one is quick to mention here that, the various fundamental human rights provisions such as right to life, privacy, dignity, freedom from torture, highest attainable state of health, freedom from discrimination etc contained in numerous human rights instruments can be invoked directly or indirectly to apply to sex work.

Understanding Human Sexuality

In attempting to attach a human rights approach to sexuality related issues as sex work an understanding of human sexuality is imperative Human sexuality has remained one controversial and complex subject, which is often avoided by many. The discipline of human sexuality has often appeared to share a prevailing cultural view that sexuality is not an entirely legitimate study and that such study often cast doubt not only on the research but also on the motive and character of the researcher. Yet, sexuality has been described as an intrinsic part of human existence.[75] It has always been with man from time immemorial. According to Goldenweiser 'In the beginning was sex and sex will be in the end… I maintain -and this is my thesis- that sex as a feature of man and society was always central and remain such. …'[76]

Perhaps the reason why sexuality has often been misconceived is because of its equation with sex. However, human sexuality is much more than sex. In Fonseca's view, it is 'the quality of being human all that we are as men and women'.[77] Unlike sex, which represents a physiologic act, human sexuality connotes the totality of human being. According to the World Health Organization, human sexuality includes the following:

> A central aspect of being human throughout life and encompasses sex, gender identities and roles, sexual orientation eroticism, pleasure, intimacy and reproduction. Sexuality is experienced in thought, fantasies desires, beliefs, attitudes, values, behavior, practices, roles and relationships. While sexuality can include all of these dimensions, not all of them are always experienced or expressed. Sexuality is influenced by interaction biological, psychological, social, economic, political, cultural, ethical, historical, religious and spiritual factors. [78]

It is clear from this broad explanation, that human sexuality comprises the biologic, physiologic, socio-cultural and ethical component of sexual behaviour.[79]

The Evolution of Sexual Right as Human Rights

The notion of sexual rights first gained the attention of the world during the World Conference on Human Rights in Vienna 1993.[80] There, it was agreed that act of violence against women 'impairs and nullifies' the enjoyment of their fundamental rights and freedom. Prior to this time, there had been no international or national instruments on human rights that specifically mentioned sexuality or sexual right. This is apparently due to universal tendency to shy away from discussion relating to sexuality. The notion of sexual rights was popularised by the activities of gay and lesbian movement, advocacy surrounding women's reproductive health, population control, health as a human right unwanted pregnancy, sexual violence Female Genital Cutting (FGC), HIV/AIDS etc. All of these acted as a catalyst for emergency formulation of sexual rights as a human rights concept.[81] The United Nations Declaration on Elimination of Violence against Women of 1993, which specifically focused on the elimination of physical, sexual and psychological violence against women, further consolidated this development. Both the Vienna Declaration of Action and the UN Declaration on Violence Against women brought to the fore the implicit recognition of sexual violence as a violation of human rights.

Perhaps the turning point in raising the profile of sexual rights as part of human rights occurred during the International Conference on Population and Development (ICPD) 1994[82] and the Fourth World Conference on Women (FWCW) Beijing 1995.[83] The ICPD urges state members to 'Take all measures to eliminate all forms of exploitation, sexual abuse, harassment and violence against women, adolescent and children'.[84] Indeed Parker[85] has asserted that this conference was the first of its kind where issues relating to sex, sexuality and sexual health were openly debated as a central point to the agenda. He further argues that these issues were considered not only as a form of violence against women, but as a violation of human rights, which deserve the utmost protection. At the Beijing Conference it was agreed that sexual rights include the rights of women to have control over and decide freely and responsibly on matters related to their sexuality, including sexual and reproductive health, free of coercion, discrimination and violence.[86] It has been observed, though, that the languages adopted at these two Conferences seem to subsume sexual rights under reproductive rights.[87] Notwithstanding, it is not debatable that these conferences added voices to the recognition of sexual rights as human rights. Whilst it is noted that decisions reached at these conferences are not binding on states they constitute consensus statements and willingness on part of states to implement them.

In addition to the above-mentioned conferences, provisions of international and regional human rights instruments such as the International Covenant on Civil and Political Rights (ICCPR)[88], the International Covenant on Economic, Social and Cultural Rights(ICESCR)[89], the Convention on the Elimination of All Forms of Discrimination Against Women (CEDAW)[90], the African Charter on Human and Peoples' Rights[91] and the Protocol to the African Charter on the Rights of Women(Women Protocol)[92] are useful in promoting sexual rights of an individual. Although none of these instruments specifically explains sexual rights, the World Health Organization has described sexual rights as:

> The right of all people free of coercion, discrimination and violence: To the highest attainable standard of sexual health, and to access to sexual and reproductive healthcare services; to seek, receive and impart information related to sexuality; to sexuality education; to respect for bodily integrity; to choose their partners; to decide to be sexually active or not; to consensual sexual relation; to consensual marriage to decide whether or not and when, to have children; and to pursue a satisfying safe and pleasurable sex life

It further reasons that sexual rights 'embrace human rights that are already recognized in national laws, international human rights documents and other consensus statements.' It must also be noted that the World Charter For Prostitutes 'Rights (WCPR)[93] agreed upon at the International Committee for Prostitutes Rights held in Amsterdam 1985 similarly advocates amongst other things for the eradication of laws that are capable of denying freedom of association or freedom to travel to prostitutes between countries.

Ngwena[94] has rightly observed that the notion of sexual rights should not be construed narrowly but rather should be expansively interpreted to embrace different categories of activities. His observation finds supports in Millers' universality approach to sexuality rights. She opines as follows:

> The language of sexuality rights as human rights must be by definition engage with the concept of sexuality as a characteristics of all human beings -straight and gay, female and male, old and young across all countries, culture, and religion.[95]

It is to be noted that human rights advocates often use the term 'sexual rights' in argument that existing rights such as right to life, liberty and security of persons to equality and discrimination would, if applied properly, protect certain forms of sexual activity and expression.[96] One may safely argue therefore, from the above observations, that those who engage in sex work are merely expressing their sexuality rights and therefore deserve protection of the law. In buttressing this view, the Committee on Convention of All Forms of Elimination against Women (CEDAW) in its General Recommendation 19 has observed that states should take adequate measures to prevent violence against women in general and in particular vulnerable groups such as sex workers.[97] The Committee further calls on states to take measures to combat gender -based violence which may impair or nullify the ability of women to enjoy their human rights and fundamental freedoms such as the right to life, the right not to be subject to torture or cruel, inhuman and degrading treatment, the right to security of persons and the right to equal protection under the law. In one of its Concluding Observations regarding China the Committee expressed grave concern on criminalisation of sex work in the country and advised that in the interest of women sex workers, sex work should be decriminalised in China.[98]

It is imperative to point out here that even though the constitutions of many African countries including Nigeria, contain provisions on equality, non-discrimination and privacy many of these countries have criminalised consensual sexual acts between adults. This is due to the fact that these provisions of the laws were inherited from their colonial masters. African countries in general, perhaps with the exception of South Africa, have exhibited great aversion to issues relating to same sex and sex work For instance, the Zimbabwean Supreme Court has held in *Banana* case[99]- despite the provision of section 23 of the Constitution which guarantees a right not to be unfairly discriminated against- that the provision relating to sodomy in the country's criminal code is not in contravention of section 23 of the Constitution. In arriving at its decision the court, in what appears to be a reinforcement of public perception about sexuality, reasons as follows:

> In the particular circumstances of this case, I do not believe that the 'social norms and values' of Zimbabwe are pushing us to decriminalize consensual sodomy. Zimbabwe is, broadly speaking, a conservative society in matters of sexual behavior. More conservative, say, than France or Sweden; less conservative than, Saudi Arabia. But generally, more conservative than liberal. I take that to be a relevant consideration in interpreting the Constitution in relation to matters of sexual freedom. Put differently, I do not believe that this court, lacking the democratic credentials of a properly elected parliament, should strain to place a sexually liberal interpretation on the Constitution of a country whose social norms and values in such matters should be conservative

This decision clearly captures the negative attitudes often displayed by Africans to issues of sexuality. It is noted that the issue of sex work raises concerns about non-respect for privacy, human dignity and equality of person, health care and economic activity. The implications of these rights for sex workers are considered below.

Right to Privacy

The right to privacy, guaranteed in notable human rights instruments such as article 12 of Universal Declaration of Human Rights[100] and article 17 of the International Covenant of Civil and Political Rights (ICCPR),[101] has been described to mean the right to be left alone in peace. Article 17 of the ICCPR in relation to right[102] to Privacy states that 'No one shall be subjected, to arbitrary or unlawful interference with his privacy; family, home or correspondence, nor to unlawful attacks on his honour and reputation'. It similarly states that everyone has the right to the protection of the law against such interference or attacks. This simply connotes that an individual has a right to the use of his/her body without any form of interference from another person. Privacy has also been defined as the desire of individuals for solitude, intimacy, anonymity and reserve.[103]

Nigeria has ratified the ICCPR and also guarantees the right to privacy under section 37 of its Constitution 1999. The language of section 37 of the Nigerian Constitution is very similar to that of article 17 of the ICCPR. The right to privacy includes 'freedom from unwarranted and unreasonable intrusions into activities that society recognizes as belonging to the realm of individual autonomy.[104] A state can only interfere with the enjoyment of this right on the basis of law 'which itself must comply with the provisions, aims and objectives of the ICCPR'[105]

It should be noted that article 17 of the ICCPR does not expressly protect privacy in respect of sexuality or sexual life, however, recent trends in the international community has tended to give a wider meaning to the right to privacy. For instance, the European Court of Human Rights has interpreted broadly right to respect for private life under Article 8 of the European Convention on Human Rights to include 'to a certain degree, the right to establish and to develop relationships with other human beings, especially in the emotional field for the development and fulfillment of one's own personality'.[106] The Human Rights Committee in the case of *Toonen v Australia* explained that the rights to privacy and sexual non-discrimination are violated where the state prohibited consensual sexual conduct between homosexual male adults.[107] Such prohibition was described as unwarranted interference by the state in the privacy of individuals. In addition, it has been observed that article 17 of the ICCPR protects the right to be different and live accordingly.[108] The European Court of Human Rights has arrived at a decision similar to that of the Human Rights Committee in the case of *Norris v Ireland* where the court found as a violation of right to private life, legislation in Ireland criminalising homosexual conduct between consenting male adults.[109]

Ackermann J in *National Coalition of Gay and Lesbian Equality v The Minister of Justice*[110] describes the right to privacy in this manner:

> Privacy recognizes that we all have a right to a sphere of private intimacy and autonomy, which allows us to establish and nurture human relationships without interference from the outside community. The way in which we give expression to our sexuality is at the core of this area of private intimacy. If, in expressing our sexuality, we act consensually and without harming one another, invasion of that precinct will be a breach of our privacy.

In the US case of *Bowers v Hardwick*[111] the respondent brought an action against the State of Georgia challenging the constitutionality of the statute insofar as it criminalised consensual sodomy. The respondent had alleged that since the consensual sexual act with male partner took place in his bedroom his fundamental right to privacy was violated by the offence of sodomy. The court of first instance granted the defendants' motion to dismiss the case for failure to state a claim. The Court of Appeals reversed and remanded, holding that the Georgia statute violated respondent's fundamental rights. In overturning this decision the US Supreme Court held that the US Constitution never confers on homosexuals fundamental rights to commit sodomy. It further held that to claim that any form of private sexual conduct between consenting adults is constitutionally insulated from state proscription is unsupportable. Delivering the opinion of the court White J, in what seems to be a conservative approach to the issue, reasons as follows:

> Even if the conduct at issue here is not a fundamental right, respondent asserts that there must be a rational basis for the law and that there is none in this case other than the presumed belief of a majority of the electorate in Georgia that homosexual sodomy is immoral and unacceptable. This is said to be an inadequate rationale to support the law. The law, however, is constantly based on notions of morality, and if all laws representing essentially moral choices are to be invalidated under the Due Process Clause, the courts will be very busy indeed. Even respondent makes no such claim, but insists that majority sentiments about the morality of homosexuality should be declared inadequate. We do not agree, and are unpersuaded that the sodomy laws of some 25 States should be invalidated on this basis.[112]

This clearly represents a puritanical approach, to the discussion of sexuality, which obviates respect for individual rights and freedom. Such an approach must be viewed with caution. However, the dissenting view of the minority in this case seems to be more persuasive albeit convincing. Blackmun J leading the minority holds the view that the constitutional right to privacy of the respondent should not be compromised based merely on morality or religious belief. He explicitly explains this as follows:

> I believe we must analyze respondent Hardwick's claim in the light of the values that underlie the constitutional right to privacy. If that right means anything, it means that, before Georgia can prosecute its citizens for making choices about the most intimate aspects of their lives, it must do more than assert that the choice they have made is an 'abominable crime not fit to be named among Christians.'[113]

Explaining further, the minority opinion reasons that sexual relationship constitutes an integral part of human privacy and only the most willful blindness could obscure the fact that sexual intimacy is "a sensitive, key relationship of human existence, central to family life, community welfare, and the development of human personality'[114] It is instructive to state here that the decision in Bowers case was overruled by a subsequent decision of the US Supreme court in *Lawrence v Texas* [115]In that case the Court found that laws that criminalize consensual sexual activities between male adults violated the right to liberty guaranteed in American Constitution. In arriving at this decision the court explained as follows:

> Liberty protects the person from unwarranted government intrusions into a dwelling or other private places. In our tradition the State is not omnipresent in the home. And there are other spheres of our lives and existence, outside the home, where the State should not be a dominant presence. Freedom extends beyond spatial bounds. Liberty presumes an autonomy of self that includes

> freedom of thought, belief, expression, and certain intimate conduct. The instant case "the essence of a Fourth Amendment violation is `not the breaking of [a person's] doors, and the rummaging of his drawers,' but rather is `the invasion of his indefensible right of personal liberty of the person both in its spatial and more transcendent dimensions.

This decision clearly indicates that the state should not turn itself to a busy body bothering itself with two adults in a consensual sexual act in private. It may be argued that the right to privacy indeed, gives an individual the liberty to act differently from others Thus, one may say that those who engage in sex work are expressing their liberty to do what they like even though it may not be acceptable to some members of the public. As it was succinctly put in *West Virginia Board of Education v. Barnette*[116], '[F]reedom to differ is not limited to things that do not matter much. That would be a mere shadow of freedom. The test of its substance is the right to differ as to things that touch the heart of the existing order'. The European Court of Human Rights has also reiterated that issue as gender identification name and sexual orientation and sexual life all fall within the personal sphere protected under article 8 of the European Convention.[117] From these comments one may conclude that criminalisation of sex work violates the right to privacy of sex workers.

It should be recognised, however, that the right to sexual privacy like any other rights is never absolute. Thus, there may be situations warranting state to lift the veil of private life and interfere in sexual expression in the over all interest of the public. For instance, explicit sexual act between two adults in the public may likely cause serious affront and distress to others, and may therefore be properly regarded as harm.[118] Also, circumstances may arise where the state may control the age of sexual intercourse for the benefit of the society. But as argued above it does seem that criminalisation of sex work -which is a consensual act between persons in private-will amount to arbitrary interference into the right of those who engage in this act.

Right to Dignity

The right to dignity is an important human right which indeed embodies the totality of rights enjoyed by human beings. The Universal Declaration on Human Rights in its preamble declares that 'Whereas recognition of the *inherent dignity* and of the *equal and inalienable rights* of all members of the human family is the foundation of freedom, justice and peace in the world…'[119] It states further in its article 1 that 'All human beings are born free and equal in dignity and rights. They are endowed with reason and conscience and should act towards one another in a spirit of brotherhood'.[120]

Virtually all the other human rights instruments guarantee the right to dignity. Article 5 of the African Charter protects the right to dignity of all persons. Whereas the Women's Protocol in its article 3 does provide that State parties to the treaty shall take necessary measure for the protection of women's right to respect her dignity and be free from every form of violence. In a more radical and progressive manner the Women's Protocol provides that every woman shall have the right to dignity inherent in a human being and to the recognition and protection of her human and legal rights. It similarly declares that 'Every woman shall have the right to respect as a person and to the free development of her personality'. It enjoins states parties to implement appropriate measures to prohibit exploitation or degradation of women.[121] In addition section 34 of the Nigerian Constitution guarantees the right to human dignity. It provides that 'Every individual is entitled to respect for the dignity of his person'. It states further in paragraph (a) of subsection 1 that no person shall be subjected to torture or to inhuman or degrading treatment.

Every human being by reason of being human is entitled to be treated with dignity, or with a minimum of respect and decency. According to Margalit dignity unlike honour, is not a positional good. It is supposed to be accorded to everybody, by virtue of the most universal common denominator of being human.[122] In Donelly's words[123]:

> Human rights are "needed" not for life but for a life of dignity...violations of human rights deny one's humanity; they do not necessarily keep one from satisfying one's needs. We have human rights not to the requisites for health but to those things "needed" for a life of dignity, for a life worthy of a human being, a life that cannot be enjoyed without these rights.

Considering the importance of the right to dignity to the enjoyment of other human rights this right has been described to be a 'mother right' in two senses- first, the majority of fundamental rights can be derived from it, secondly, a series of rights not emphasized in a constitution can be drawn from it.[124] Inability of sex workers to express their sexual desire without coercion or discrimination amounts to a violation of their right to human dignity.

General acts of aversion, condemnation and violence often meted out to sex workers can be said to impugn on their right to human dignity. As stated by the South African court in *National Coalition of Lesbians and Gay* case 'Dignity is a difficult concept to capture in precise terms. At its least, it is clear that the constitutional protection of dignity requires us to acknowledge the value and worth of all individuals as members of our society'[125] When a woman is labeled as 'unclean', 'immoral' and 'loose' simply for exercising her sexual autonomy, her humanity is debased and her dignity as a human being is eroded.

This right as defined under article 3 of the Women's Protocol presupposes that criminalisation of female sex works infringes on a woman's right to security of person and may likely breed violence against such a woman Indeed the language of the Protocol intends to protect women from any act that may result in violence against them. Experience has shown that female sex workers are often made subject of violent attacks by state security agents. The Africa Commission has held that exposing a person to 'suffering and indignity' will amount to a violation of the right to dignity guaranteed under article 5 of the Charter.[126]

Right to Equality

Equality as a legal term is imprecise of a generally acceptable definition. However, it has been recognized that equality is tantamount to non-discrimination hence; an act of discrimination will lead to the violation of rights to equality.[127] The principle of non- discrimination has been well recognized in virtually all human rights instruments. For instance, article 2 of the African Charter provides that all human beings be treated with respect for their rights without distinction as to race, sex, political belief, religious belief and other status.[128] A distinction is often made between formal and substantive equality. Formal equality -often referred to as mathematical, absolute or numerical equality- merely treats every member of the society in the same way without taking into cognizance their specific differences. This type of approach is said to be blind to socio- economic disparities that exist in every society. Adherence to formal equality in the real sense does not guarantee true equality but disparity. Dworking warning Americans that sameness of treatment does not ensure true equality opines that 'We must take care not to use the Equal Protection Clause [of the 14th Amendment of the American Constitution] to cheat ourselves of equality'.[129]

On the other hand the notion of substantive equality implies that every individual is treated in the same manner taking into consideration each one's peculiar circumstances. In other words, substantive equality as different from formal equality aims at promoting social justice and egalitarianism in a society particularly for the marginalised or vulnerable groups.[130] The non-discrimination provisions in the CEDAW and the Protocol to the African Charter on the Rights of Women are an affirmation of the principle of substantive equality. According to article 1 of CEDAW discrimination is widely defined to embrace any distinction, exclusion or restriction made on the basis of sex which has the effect or purpose of impairing or nullifying the recognition, enjoyment or exercise by women on equal basis with their male counterpart. In a more radical and progressive language the Women's Protocol defines discrimination against women as 'any distinction, exclusion or restriction or any differential treatment based on sex and whose objectives or effects compromise or destroy the recognition, enjoyment or the exercise by women, regardless of their mental status, of human rights and fundamental freedoms in all spheres of life'

This definition covers virtually every area of human endeavor including women that engage in sex work. Therefore, criminalisation of sex work will no doubt violate the right to equality of person.[131] The Human Rights Committee in its General Comment 28 has observed that Article 3 of the ICCPR implies that all human beings should enjoy the rights provided for in the covenant, on an equal basis and in their totality. The full effect of this provision is impaired whenever any person is denied the full and equal enjoyment of any right.[132] The Committee states further in paragraph 4 that states parties are responsible for ensuring the equal enjoyment of rights without any discrimination. Articles 2 and 3 of ICCPR mandate States parties to take all steps necessary, including the prohibition of discrimination on the ground of sex, to put an end to discriminatory actions both in the public and the private sector which impair the equal enjoyment of rights.

The essence of equality of persons is to safeguard human dignity. This right together with other rights was (as it relates to sex work) put to test in the South African Constitutional Court decision in *Jordan* case.[133] In that case, the appellants were challenging the provision of section 20(1) (aA) of the Sexual Offences Act 23 of 1957 which forbids sex work as being contrary to the provision of South African interim Constitution. In the majority judgment read by Ngcobo J the Court held that section 20(1) (aA) of the Act was not unconstitutional as its retention was reasonably justifiable to control the ills of sex work. This control is necessary since sex work has a propensity towards precipitating criminality in the society. The Court, surprisingly, further reasoned that this provision of the Act was not in violation of equality, dignity or privacy of sex workers. According to the Court, sex workers who engage in sex work have already mortgaged away their dignity and therefore they have no dignity to be protected.[134] This seems to have been captured in these words.

Once it is accepted that section 20(1)(aA) is gender neutral and that by engaging in commercial sex work prostitutes knowingly attract the stigma associated with prostitution, it can hardly be contended that female prostitutes are discriminated against on the basis of gender. I am not persuaded by the argument that gender discrimination exists simply because there are more female prostitutes than male prostitutes just as I would not be persuaded if the same argument were to be advanced by males accused of certain crimes, the great majority of which are committed by men.[135]

The minority judgment in that case did observe that the provision of the Sexual Offences Act contravened the equality provision of the Constitution. This is a better approach and more persuasive conclusion than that of the majority. However, the minority, fell into the same pit as the majority, by coming to the same conclusion as to whether the Sexual Offences Act violated right to dignity and privacy of sex workers. The minority declined to hold that the Sexual Offences Act violated the right to dignity and privacy of sex workers. Clearly, this decision merely reflects the general bias by the public on sex work. As noted by Kruger, this decision is not only moralistic in nature but also judgmental of sex workers.[136] It is more or less an explicit attempt by the court to enforce morality-.an attitude which a court of law should always avoid. It was as if the Court in this case had a premeditated mind on the issue of sex work and therefore, nothing could be said or done to swerve the mind of the court from its belief. In the English case of *Smeaton v Secretary of State* the judge, cautioning about this type of attitude, says 'the days are past when the business of judges was the enforcement of morals or religious belief'[137].

This decision falls short of expectation of a caliber of a court as the Constitutional Court. It is at variance with the reasoning of the same Court in *Harksen*[138] case and other notable decisions where the court laid down the steps to follow in finding violation of the equality clause of the Constitution. More importantly in *National Coalition of Gay and Lesbians v Minister of Justice*[139] the Constitutional Court demonstrated an ability to give life to the provision of the South African Constitution when it held that a law criminalizing sodomy violated right to equality, dignity and privacy of homosexuals. The same progressive approach should have been applied in *Jordan* case.

The Right to Engage in Economic Activity

The right of an individual to engage in any work of his or her choice has received recognition in so many human rights instruments. For instance article 23 of the Universal Declaration provides that 'Everyone has the right to work, to free choice of employment, to just and favorable conditions of work and to protection against unemployment.' In a similar manner article 6 (1) of the ICSCER recognizes the right of every one to the opportunity to gain a living by work which he/she freely chooses, accepts and will take appropriate steps to safeguard this right. Interestingly there is yet to be a General Comment clarifying the nature of the obligations imposed on states by article 6. Under article 11 of CEDAW the right to work in a safe and conducive environment for women is guaranteed. At the regional level the African Charter in its article 15 guarantees the right to work under equitable and satisfactory condition. However, the most comprehensive and radical provisions on this right as it concerns women is found in article 13 of the Women's Protocol. It provides thus;

States Parties shall adopt and enforce legislative and other measures to guarantee women equal opportunities in work and career advancement and other economic opportunities.

In this respect, they shall:

(a) promote equality of access to employment;

(b) promote the right to equal remuneration for jobs of equal value for women and men;

(c) ensure transparency in recruitment, promotion and dismissal of women and combat and punish sexual harassment in the workplace,

(d) guarantee women the freedom to choose their occupation, and protect them from exploitation by their employers violating and exploiting their fundamental rights as recognised and guaranteed by conventions, laws and regulations in force;

(e) create conditions to promote and support the occupations and economic activities of women, in particular, within the informal sector; ...

(h) take the necessary measures to recognise the economic value of the work of women in the home...

No doubt, this is about one of the few human rights instruments that have elaborately protected women's rights in relation to work. This is born out of the high disparity in income earning that exists between men and women working across the African continent. Besides there are certain forms of work which are peculiar to women and are often not remunerated or recognized thereby further deepening the gap that exists between men and women in the region. One such work is 'house wife' which the Women's Protocol now provides must be given economic value. More importantly, the Protocol guarantees women's rights to choose the occupation of their choice and protect women working in the informal sector. These provisions are germane to our discussion on sex work. Undoubtedly a purposive reading of these provisions will mean that women who have chosen sex work as an occupation, rather than be condemned and disparaged, should have their choice of work protected. This reasoning tallies with the view of the liberal feminists mentioned earlier on.

The Nigerian Constitution does not guarantee the right to work. Instead, social and economic rights such as right to education, health and work are found in Chapter 2 of the Constitution-Directive Principle of Government Policy[140]- which are usually unjusticiable. However, Nigeria has ratified the various human instruments including the Women's Protocol guaranteeing this right. In particular the African Charter has been incorporated into Nigeria domestic law. From the foregoing, if it is agreed, as implied by the Women's Protocol that sex work is a form of work, then it becomes very important that government should provide necessary protection and support for women who engage in this work. In short, women in sex work should have their rights equally protected like other workers in other fields of work.[141]

Sex work is regarded as a legitimate occupation just like every other occupation and as such those who freely choose to be in this occupation deserve the protection of the law like others. It is important that a clear distinction has to be made between those who are forced or coerced into sex work by a third party in the form of deception, violence of debt bondage and those who of their own choice make up their mind to engage in sex work as a way of expressing their sexual liberation. While the former may be condemned as being exploitative of women the latter cannot be said in any way to be injurious to the dignity of women.

Those who support sex work as an occupation have argued that the seeming exploitation and hazards sex workers face are not limited to this kind of work alone. There are some other women who engage in low status work such as domestic work, work in the factories or work on the land and similarly face grave exploitation and danger in their work.[142]

The concern of the society is to ensure that appropriate laws and regulations are developed that will curtail some of the abuses faced by sex workers as in other informal sector. The challenge however, is that because sex work is illegal in many societies, sex workers continue to be marginalised and are often excluded from international and national protection afforded to other workers. This kind of attitude merely reinforces stigmatisation and vulnerability of sex workers in the society. As observed by Bindman 'Sex workers without rights in their place of work are uniquely vulnerable to infection with HIV and other sexually transmitted disease, as they routinely lack the information, materials or authority to protect themselves and their clients'[143].

While it is admitted that existing labor standard and rules in many Africa countries including Nigeria, may not have adequately protected right to security of persons of sex workers, this is not enough to entirely dismiss sex work as abusive. Doing this is to obscure the peculiar problems and violations of international norms within the industry which are of concern to sex workers.[144]

In one of its reports based on studies conducted on sex work in four countries in Southeast Asia, the International Labor Organization (ILO)[145] has called for economic recognition of sex work. While noting the huge economic contribution of sex work to economies of these countries- Indonesia, Malaysia, the Philippines and Thailand- the ILO further calls for better working condition for those who engage in sex work. In the said report it is estimated that sex work accounts for between 2 to 14 per cent of the Gross Domestic Products.(GDP) of these countries and the revenue it has generated has been very crucial to livelihoods and earnings of million of people who are not even directly involved in sex work. The ILO has further noted that 'For those adult individuals who freely choose sex work, the policy concerns should focus on improving their working conditions and social protection, and on ensuring that they are entitled to the same labòur rights and benefits as other workers.'[146]

This report clearly exemplifies the need to accord sex work equal status with other occupation. Therefore, there is an obligation on Nigerian government to take adequate measures in removing barriers militating against women who engage in sex work and give recognition to sex work within its territory.

The Right to Health and Sexual and Reproductive Health Care

The right to health is guaranteed in numerous international and regional human rights instruments. However, the most authoritative provision on this is article 12 of the International Covenant on Economic, Social and Cultural Rights (ICESCR).[147] It provides that state parties to the Covenant shall recognize the right of every one to the enjoyment of the highest attainable standard of physical and mental health .It further stipulates the determinants essential for the enjoyment of the right to health. The Committee responsible for the implementation of the Covenant in its General Comment 14 has noted that the right to health is linked with other rights such as right to life, non-discrimination, dignity, equality liberty etc.[148] It further observes that the health care services should be guaranteed for all on a non-discriminatory basis taking into cognisance the situation of vulnerable and marginalized members of the society such as women and people living with HIV/AIDS.[149] According to the Committee health care services should be made available, accessible, acceptable and of good quality to all. It states further 'The right to health must be understood as the right to the enjoyment of a variety of facilities, goods, services and conditions necessary for the realisation of the highest attainable standard of health'.[150]

Apart from the provision in the ICESCR aarticle 12 of the Convention on Elimination of All Forms of Discrimination against Women (CEDAW)[151] similarly guarantees the right to access to health care for women on equal basis with men. The Convention additionally guarantees women's right to 'appropriate services in connection with pregnancy'[152] The Committee on CEDAW in its General Recommendation 24 on Women and Health[153] has noted that states are under obligations to ensure that policies and laws facilitate equal access to health care for women in a non-discriminatory manner. More particularly the Committee urges states to ensure that health care facilities are guaranteed to marginalised and vulnerable women such as migrant workers and sex workers.

At the regional level article 16 of the African Charter on Human and People's Rights (African Charter) guarantees the right to health.[154] Article 16 states that everyone has the right to enjoy the best attainable state of physical and mental health. The African Commission on Human and Peoples' Rights in one of its decisions involving *Purohit and Moore v The Gambia*[155] has held that 'Enjoyment of the human right to health as it is widely known is vital to all aspects of a person's life and well-being, and is crucial to the realization of all the other fundamental human rights and freedoms.' It states further that the right includes the right to health facilities, access to goods and services to be guaranteed to all without discrimination of any kind. In addition, the Protocol [156] in its article 14 contains important provisions relevant in advancing sexual and reproductive health of women. This article is very instructive on this issue.Under article 14; states are required to "ensure that the right to health of women, including sexual and reproductive health of women, is respected and promoted'. This important article further provides that states should respect and promote women's right to , control her fertility, decide whether or not to have children ,the number of children and the spacing of children, choose any method of contraception, self protection from sexually transmitted infections, to be informed of her health status and the health status of her partner especially if affected by sexually transmitted infections including HIV/AIDS in accordance with internationally recognized standards and family planning. Similarly the provision enjoins states parties to take appropriate measures to 'provide adequate, affordable and accessible health services, including information, education and communication programmes to women especially those in rural areas'.

These unique and radical provisions become one of the very few international human rights instruments that clearly recognize women's reproductive health as human rights and contain specific provisions on women's protection in the context of HIV/AIDS.

As earlier mentioned the right to health like other social and economic rights is not guaranteed as an enforceable right under Nigerian Constitution. However, Nigeria has ratified most of these instruments mentioned above guaranteeing this right. This is in addition to the fact that the African Charter has been incorporated into the domestic law. A court has invoked article 16 of the African Charter to hold that Nigerian government was in violation of the right to health of four HIV positive prisoners that were denied medical treatment when they fell ill in prison. [157]

Despite these entire provisions one is quick to point out here that the right to health has remained subject of criticisms for being too vague and intersecting with so many other rights.[158] More importantly, like other social and economic rights, the right to health has been relegated to the background as second-generation rights of lesser value as compared to civil and political rights.[159] Many commonwealth countries including Nigeria do not guarantee the right to health as justiciable right in their constitutions but merely include it under the Directive Principles of Government Policy.[160]

As part of women's right to health and reproductive care on a non-discriminatory basis, female sex workers infected or affected by sexually transmitted infections including HIV deserve access to care and treatment .Because of fear of violence or stigma most sex workers fear to seek medical attention in health care institutions or even test for HIV. The ability of sex workers to gain access to HIV services is impeded by widespread violence, discrimination, and punitive approaches to sex work. Moreover, as earlier mentioned sex workers in most cases are excluded from most of government's intervention programmes on HIV/AIDS. This is often based on morality and religious sentiment. Such acts undoubtedly contradict Nigerian's obligations under international human rights law with regard to respecting, protecting and fulfilling rights to health of sex workers. Cook and Ngwena have rightly advised that governmental polices and laws on sensitive health issues -such as pertaining to health care of sex workers- should not be based on sentiment or morality but rather on evidence based reports.[161]

The Special Rapporteur on the right to health, in his report on Romania, has observed that stigma associated with sex work can affect how health providers react to sex workers and may cause them to be denied health care services including treatment for sexually transmitted infections.[162] He therefore, urges governments to take steps to combat stigma and discrimination against sex workers. Similarly the Committee on CEDAW in one of its concluding observation regarding Cameroun has called for the protection of sex workers rights to health through access to a comprehensive reproductive health services.[163] As part of government's obligations to guarantee right health to all on a non-discriminatory basis government must ensure that health care facilities such as condoms and drugs including antiretroviral drugs are available and accessible to sex workers.

CONCLUSION

It is obvious from the above that criminalization of sex work in Nigeria has not been fruitful. It has merely led to stigmatization of sex workers and further renders them vulnerable to abuse and sexually transmitted infections including HIV/ AIDS. If sex workers must be allowed to live a worthy life where their reproductive and sexual rights are respected then criminalization of sex work must be done away with. The National Policy on HIV/AIDS launched in 2003 does recognize this fact when it aims at incorporating sex workers into HIV/ AIDS programs in the country.[164] This is a welcome development and it is in line with the suggestion of Committee on CEDAW that criminalization of sex work should be avoided. However, in reality government's measures taken in combating HIV/AIDS in the country have hardly incorporate sex workers in to them. This is a clarion call to Nigerian government that it should pay more attention to the plight of sex workers by ensuring that programs aimed at combating HIV/AIDS and other sexually transmitted infections in the country target sex workers as beneficiaries. The reality on ground is that as long as government continues to pretend on the issue of sex work, through exclusion of sex workers from intervention programs on HIV/AIDS and sexually transmitted infections, so long will vulnerability of the society to the epidemic increase.

Removing sex work from criminal code supplemented by awareness programs on this issue ensures that government is able to easily monitor activities of sex workers and be able to protect sex workers from human rights abuses. Moreover, they will be able to freely negotiate safer sex with their clients thereby protecting themselves and others from contacting sexually transmitted infections. On the long run the ultimate beneficiary of this change will be the entire society. This is not going to be an easy task, but with awareness programme and commitment on the part of the government and civil society it is achievable.

Notes

1. 'Early history of Prostitution' available at *http://www.infoplease.com/ce6/society/A0860556.html*. Accessed on 21 October, 2005.
2. Federal Ministry of Health *Surveillance Report on HIV/AIDS and STIs in Nigeria*, (Abuja: FMOH, 2005).

3. Ditmore, 'Reaching out to Sex Workers', in Murphy and Hendrix-Jenkins (eds), *Reproductive Health and Rights – Reaching the Hardly Reached* , (Washington: PATH 2002) 16.

4. [1918] 82 JP 160 (CCA).

5. R V Webb [1964] 1 QB 357. The Court reasoned in that case that sex work is established where a woman offers herself as a participant in physical acts of indecency for the sexual gratification of men, for payment.

6. Ditmore supra note 3 at 17

7. Kruger 'Sex Work from a Feminist Perspective: A Visit to the *Jordan* Case' (2004) 20 *South Afrcan Human Rights Law Journal*, 138 at 139

8. See Heise 'Violence, Sexuality and Women's Lives', in *Conceiving Sexuality* in Parker & Gagnon (eds) (New York: Routledge, 1995) 119.

9. Satz 'Markets in Women's Sexual Labour '(1995) 106 *Ethics* 78, See also Mackinnon 'Prostitution and Civil Rights' (1993) 1 *Michigan Journal of Gender and Law* 13 at16 where she argues that sex work in most cases is coercive in nature and thus 'subordinates and exploits and disadvantages women as women in social life'.

10. Heise supra note 8 at 111

11. Dworkin 'Prostitution and Male Supremancy' in Dworkin (ed) *Life and Death: Un apologetic Writings on the Conituining War Against Women*, (New York: Free Press, 1997) 144.

12. Bromberg 'Feminist Issues in Prostitution' in *On Whores, Hustlers and Johns* available at *http://www.hutch.demon.co.uk/prom/prostitu.htm.* Accessed on 3 June, 2007.

13. Vance 'Pleasure and Dange Towards a Politic of Sexuality' in Vance (ed*) Pleasure and Danger: Exploring Female Sexuality* (Boston and London: Routedlege and Kegan Paul, 1984) 1-27.

14. Naanem 'Itinerant Gold Mines; Prostitution in the Cross River Basin of Nigeria 1930-1950' (1991) 34 *African Studies Review*, 57.

15. *Ibid.*

16. Osirike 'Perception of AIDS Risks and Severity amongst Youths in Nigeria : Implications for Policy' (1998) 13 *African Studies Review*, 71.

17. Bamgbose , 'Teenage Prostitution in Nigeria', (2002) 42 *International Journal of Offender Therapy and Comparative Criminology* 569 at 570

18. *Ibid.*

19. *Ibid*, 575.

20. Orubuloye *et al* 'Commercial Sex Workers in Nigeria in the Shadow of AIDS', in Orubuloye et al (eds) Networking STDs and AIDS in sub-Sahara Africa Behaviour Research and the Social Context Series no 4 (Caberra: Australian National University, 1994) 101-116.

21. Odiagbe '*The Social life of Truck Drivers and Prostitutes and its Implications of the Spread of HIV/AIDS: A Study of Truck Drivers and Prostitutes in Aviele and Oluku in Edo State , Nigeria* . (An unpublished thesis submitted to the Department of Sociology University of Ibadan 1994).

22. *Ibid.*

23. Bamgbose *supra note* 17 at 576
24. *Ibid.*
25. Adisa 'Lagos: Street Culture and Families in the Street 'in G Hercuilt et al (eds) *Youth, Street Culture and Urban Violence in Africa* . Proceedings of the International Symposium held in Abidjan 5-7 May (1997).
26. *Bid..*
27. Bamgbose supra note 17 at 572.
28. Adisa supra note 25.
29. Bamgbose supra note 17 at 573.
30. The Trafficking in Persons (Prohibition) Law Enforcement and Administration Act 2003 which set up the National Agency for the Prohibition of Trafficking I Persons (NATIP).
31. Nasidi and Harry 'The Epidemiology of HIV/AIDS in Nigeria' in Adeyi *et al* (eds) *AIDS in Nigeria: A nation in Threshold* (Harvard: Harvard University Press, 2006) 14.
32. *Ibid.*
33. Federal Ministry of Health supra note, 2.
34. Owuliri and Jolayemi 'Reaching Vulnerable and High Risk Groups in Nigeria' in Adeyi *et al* (eds) *AIDS in Nigeria: A nation in Threshold* (Harvard: Harvard University Press, 2006) 309 at 310.
35. Society for Family Health(SFH) , National Behavioural Survey 1: Brothel based Sex work in Nigeria (Lagos: SFH, 2001)
36. Owuliri and Jolayemi supra note 34 at 310.
37. This body by virtue of a law recently enacted is now known as National Agency for Control of AIDS in Nigeria (NACA)
38. USAIDS, HIV/AIDS in Nigeria: A USAID Brief (2002).
39. Zetal 'Trends of HIV among Sex Workers in Jos, Nigeria; Seven years review' .An abstract submitted for the XIII International Conference on AIDS and STDs in Africa Nairobi , Kenya September, 21-26 (2003).
40. Family Health International(FHI) , *Behavioural Surveillance Survey: Nigeria* (Lagos: FHI, 2000) 4
41. *Ibid.*
42. *Ibid.*
43. See for example Viola et al, Educating Sex Workers in Nigeria in a compilation by Nigerian Institute of Medical Research (NIMR) *Nigeria's Contribution to Regional and Global meetings on HIV/AIDS/STIs 1986-2000,* (Lagos: Nigerian Institute of Medical Research (2003).
44. In the case of *Alliance for Open Society Intern., Inc. v. U.S. Agency for Development* 430 F. Supp. 2d 222.a Federal judge in the Southern District of New York ruled that this law violated Constitution's guarantee of freedom of speech contained in the First Amendment of the US Constitution.
45. Busia *Report on a Social Survey of Secondi Takoradi* (Accra: Government of the Gold Coast Printing Press, 1950).
46. Little, Africa women in Towns: An Aspect of Africa's Social Revolution (Cambridge: Cambridge University Press, 1973).73.

47. Ditmore supra note 3 at 17.
48. Criminal Code Act, Cap 77 Laws of the Federation of Nigeria (1990).
49. From the "Police Response to Reports of Violence Against Prostitutes", (A Submission by Maggie's to the Canadian Metro Committee on the Status of Women) 3.
50. Millman, 'New Rules for the Oldest Profession: Should We Change Our Prostitution Laws?', (1980) 3 *Harvard Women's Law Journal*, 1 at 35.
51. Ibid 54-57.
52. Sarang and Hoover , *Sex Work, HIV/AIDS and Human Rights in Central and Eastern Asia* (Lithuania: Central and Eastern European HARM Reduction Network, 2005), 55.
53. Jolin, 'Germany', in Davis (ed*) Prostitution: An International Hand book on Trends, Problems and Policies* ((London: Greenwood Press, 1993). 129 at 143
54. Alexander, 'Prostitutes Are Being Scapegoated for Heterosexual AIDS' in Delacosta and Alexander(eds) Sex work; Writings by Women in the Sex Industry, (Pittsburg: Cleis Press,1987) 248.
55. See Scibelli, 'Empowering Prostitutes: A Proposal for International Legal Reform', (1987) 10 *Harvard Women's Law Journal* 117 at 118.
56. Mackinnon 'Prostitution and Civil Rights' (1993)1 *Michigan Journal of Gender and Law*, 13 at 16
57. Bamgbose supra note 17 at 576.
58. Davis and Shaffer 'Prostitution in Canada: The Invisible Menace or the Menace of Invisibility?' available at *http://www.walnet.org/csis/papers/index.html*. Accessed on 2 June 2007.
59. Convention on Suppression of the Traffic in Persons and of the Exploitation of the Prostitution of Others U.N. Department of Economic and Social Affairs, U.N. Doc. St./ SOA/ SD/8 (1959).
60. In 1987, the International Abolitionist Federation entitled their 29th congress 'Prostitution: A World Problem, A Threat to Humanity' — see Pheterson, 'Not Repeating History' in Pheterson (ed) *A Vindication of the Rights of Whores* (Seattle: The Seal Press, 1989). 3 at 14
61. Bullough and Bullough, *Women and Prostitution: A Social History* (Buffalo: Prometheus Books , 1987) 287.
62. There are several examples of jurisdictions where abolitionism is theoretically in place, such as France and New South Wales, Australia. However, in practice general nuisance laws are used to criminalise independent prostitution. See. Scibelli supra note 54
63. Davis:& Shaffer supra note 56
64. *Ibid.*
65. Ditmore supra note 3 at 18.
66. New Zealand in 2003 enacted a new law decriminalizing sex work in that country.
67. Ditmore supra note 3 at 18
68. Netherlands Ministry of Foreign Affairs *Dutch Policy on Prostitution: Questions and Answer*, (Amsterdam: Ministry of Foreign Affairs Publication, 2005)1.
69. Farley 'Bad for the Body Bad for the Heart'? Prostitution Harms Women Even if Legalized or Decriminalized (2004) 10 *Violence Against Women* 1087 at 1125

70. *Ibid.*, 1194
71. See Special Committee on Pornography and Prostitution (The Fraser Committee)' Pornography and Prostitution in Canada' Ottawa: Department of Supply and Services (1985).
72. Davis:& Shaffer supra note 56.
73. The Wolfenden Report: Report of the Committee on Homosexual Offenses and Prostitution (1963) (Chair: Lord Wolfenden) cited in Quigley, 'The Dilemma of Prostitution Law Reform: Lessons From the Soviet Russian Experiment', (1992) 29 *American Criminal Law Review* 1197 at 1229.
74. Lord Wolfenden (1958) as quoted in Soliciting for Change, Josephine Butler Trust 10 (1993).
75. Hogan *Human Sexuality: A Nursing Perspectives* (Appleton: Century Croft, 1985) 20.
76. Goldenweiser 'Sex and Primitive Society' in Calverton and Schmalhausen (eds*) Sex and Civilization* , (1929) 53 -66.
77. Fonseca, 'Sexuality a Quality of being Human', (1970) *Nursing Outlook*, 18
78. World Health Organization (WHO), Defining Sexual Health: Report of a Technical Consultation of Sexual Health (Geneva: WHO, 2005) 5.
79. Hogan supra note, 73.
80. Vienna Declaration and Programme of Action, World Conference on Human Rights, Vienna, June 1993, UN Doc. A/CONF.157/24.
81. Ngwena 'Sexuality Rights as Human Rights in Southern Africa with Particular Reference to South Africa, (2002) 17 *South African Public Law*, 1.
82. Programme of Action of the International Conference on Population and Development (ICPD). Adopted in Cairo 5-13 September 1994, UN Doc. A/CONF. 171/13 1994.
83. Beijing Declaration Platform for Action, Fourth World Conference on Women, 15 September 1995, A/CONF.177/20 (1995) and A/CONF.177/20/Add.1(1995).
84. ICPD supra note 80.
85. Parker 'Sexual Rights :Concepts and Action' (1997) 2(3) *Health and Human Rights* 31
86. Forth World Conference on Women supra note 81
87. See Report of Paul Hunt the Special Rapporteur on the right of every one to the enjoyment of the highest attainable standard of physical and mental health E/CN.4/2004/4916 February, 2004.
88. International Covenant on Civil and Political Rights, G.A. Res. 2200, U.N GAOR, Supp. NO. 16 at 52, U.N DOC. A/6316 (1966), 999 U.N.T.S. 171, 174 (entered into force on March 23, 1976). (Herein after ICCPR).
89. International Covenant on Economic, Social and Cultural Rights, adopted 16 December 1966; GA Res 2200 (XXI), UN Doc A/6316 (1966) 993 UNTS 3 (entered into force 3 January 1976).
90. Convention on the Elimination of All Forms of Discrimination Against Women GA Res 54/180 UN GAOR 34th Session Supp No 46 UN Doc A/34/46 1980.
91. African Charter on Human and Peoples' Rights OAU Doc CAB/LEG/67/3/Rev 5, adopted by the Organisation of African Unity, 27 June 1981, entered into force 21 October 1986.

92. The Protocol of African Charter on Human and People's Rights on the Rights of Women in Africa Adopted by the 2nd Ordinary Session of the African Union General Assembly in 2003 in Maputo CAB/LEG/66.6 (2003) entered into force 25 November, 2005.

93. Written at the First World Whores Congress held in February 1985 in Amsterdam organized by the defunct International Committee for Prostitutes; Rights (ICPR).

94. Ngwena supra note 79.

95. Miller, 'Sexual but Not Reproductive: Exploring the Junction and Disjunction of Sexual and Reproductive Rights', (2000) 4 *Health and Human Rights* 69.

96. *Ibid.*

97. CEDAW, General Recommendation 19 on Violence Against Women, UN GAOR, 1992, Doc.No.A/47/38 Para 15.

98. Concluding Observation of the Committee on CEDAW: regarding China 3/2/99 , CEDAW/C/1999/I/L.I/ADD.7

99. *Banana v The State* 2000) 8 BHRC 345

100. Universal Declaration on Human Rights (UDHR) adopted on 10 December 1948. GA res.217A(III) U.N Doc A.

101. International Covenant on Civil and Political Rights supra note 86.

102. Ibid.

103. Michael 'Privacy' in David Harris and Sarah Joseph (eds) *The International Covenant on Civil and Political Right and United Kingdom* (Oxford, Clarendon Press, 1995).

104. Joseph, Shultz and Castan , The International Covenant on Civil and Political Rights : Cases , Materials and Commentary (Oxford: Oxford University Press, 2004)

105. Human Rights Committee General Comment 16: The Right to Respect of Privacy, Family, Home and Correspondence and Protection of Honour and Reputation on Article 17 of the Covenant, U.N. Doc. HRI/GEN/1/Rev.6 at 142 (2003).

106. Decision of the European Commission of Human Rights, Application No 6825/74 in *Decisions and Reports*, Vol. 5 at p. 87.

107. (1994) UN GOAR, Human Rights Committee 15th Sess,. Case no 488/92 UN Doc. CCPR/C/D/488/92.

108. See the minority judgment in *Hertzberg et al v Finland* 61/79.

109. *Norris v Ireland* (1988) 13 ECHR 186.

110. 1999 (1) SA 6 (CC); 1998 (12) BCLR 1517 (CC) Para 32.

111. Bowers v Hardwick 478 U.S 186 (1986).

112. *Ibid* at 196.

113. *Ibid* at 200.

114. *Paris Adult Theatre I v. Slaton*, 413 U.S. 49, 63 (1973);

115. *Lawrence v. Texas*, 539 U.S. 558, 579 (2003).

116. 319 U.S. 624, 641 -642 (1943).

117. See *Dudgeon v The United Kingdom* Judgment of 22 October, 1991 Series A NO. 45, 41.

118. See Bronit 'The Right to Sexual Privacy , Sado -machonismand the Human Rights (Sexual Conduct) Act 1994 (1995) *Australian Journal on Human Rights*, 4.

119. Universal Declaration on Human Rights (UDHR) supra note 99.

120. *Ibid.*

121. Art 3 of the Women's Protocol supra note 90

122. Margalit , *The Ethics of Memory* (Cambridge Mass:: Harvard University Press, 2003).114

123. Donelly, Human Rights in Theory and Practice (Ithaca: Cornell University Press, 2003) 7.

124. Pazczolay, The Prohibition of Discrimination by the Constitutional Court of Hungary, A paper delivered at an International Legal Training Workshop on Effective Case Management, Effective Decision Understanding the ECHR at Sarajevo between 12-13 February 2004.

125. National Coalition of Gay and Lesbians v Minister Justice South Africa, CCT 11/98; [1999] (1) SA 6 (CC).

126. *John k. Modise v Botswana* Communication 97/93 decided in 1997.

127. See Shalev, Rights to Sexual and Reproductive Health: The ICPD and the Convention on the Elimination of All Forms of Discrimination Against Women, (2000). 4(2) *Health and Human Rights* 39

128. See art 2 of the African Charter on Human and Peoples' Rights; see also article 3 of the African Charter which provides for equality before the law and the equal protection of the law.

129. Dworking *Taking Rights Seriously* (Cambridge Mass.: Harvard University Press,1977)2.09

130. Rawls, *A Theory of Justice* (Cambridge Mass: Harvard University Press, 1971).

131. Section 42 of the Nigerian Constitution 1999, the equivalence of equality clause, forbids discrimination against anyone based on religious belief, sex, political belief, birth or ethnicity. This provision of the Constitution has not been well evaluated by Nigerian courts.

132. See General Comment 28 (2000) on the Universal Declaration of Human Rights para 2.

133. *Jordan v The State* [2002] (6) SA 642(CC); [2002] (11) BCLR 1117 (CC).

134. *Ibid* para 74.

135. *Ibid* para 17

136. Kruger supra note 9 at 146.

137. *Smeaton v. Secretary of State for Health* [2002] 2 Family Law Reports 146, para 48.

138. *Harksen v Lane NO & Ors* (1997) (11) BCLR 1489 (CC).In that case the Constitutional Court laid down the test to be adopted in ascertaining whether unfair discrimination has been established underthe equality clause of the Constitution. These include the following:

    (a) The position of the victim in the society

    (b) The purpose sought to be achieved by the discrimination

    (c) The extent to which the rights and interest of the victims of discrimination has been affected and

    (d) Whether the discrimination has impaired the human dignity of the victim.

    This test was not considered in *Jordan* case.

139. *National Coalition of Gay and Lesbians* case supra note 122.

140. It is provided under section 6 of the Nigerian Constitution that all the provisions contained in chapter 2 of the Constitution shall be unjusticiable before any court of law.

141. Nevada, 'Sex Trade: A Gamble for the Workers' (1998).69 *Yale Journal of Law and Feminism,* 88.

142. Bindman Redifing Prostitution as Sex Work on the International Agenda (1997) available at *www.walnet.org/csis/papers/redefining*. Accessed on 31 July 2007. Network of Sex Work Projects. In order to give recognition to sex work the author has suggested a new definition for sex work in this way:

    Negotiation and performance of sexual services for remuneration

    i. with or without intervention by a third party

    ii. where those services are advertised or generally recognised as available from a specific location

    iii. where the price of services reflects the pressures of supply and demand.

143. *Ibid.*

144. *Ibid.*

145. International Labor Organization (ILO) See Sex work as a Sector: Economic Incentives and Hardship fuels Growth *World of Work* No 26 September/October 1998.

146. *Ibid.*

147. International Covenant on Economic, Social and Cultural Rights, supra note 87.

148. The Right to the Highest Attainable Standard of Health; UN Committee on ESCR General Comment No 14, UN Doc E/C/12/2000/4 at para 3.

149. *Ibid* at para 12.

150. *Ibid.*

151. Convention on the Elimination of All Forms of Discrimination Against Women supra 88.

152. *Ibid.*

153. General Recommendation 24 of CEDAW on Women and Health UN GAOR, 1999, Doc A/54/38 Rev. 1.

154. African Charter on Human and Peoples' Rights OAU Doc CAB/LEG/67/3/Rev 5, adopted by the Organisation of African Unity, 27 June 1981, entered into force 21 October 1986.

155. Communication 241/2001 decided at the 33rd Ordinary Session of the African Commission held from 15th –29th in Niamey, Niger May 2003 ..

156. Women's Protocol supra note 91

157. *Festus Odaife and Ors V Attorney General of the Federation and Ors* Unreported suit no FHC/PH/CS/680/2003(Federal High Court

158. Fidler, International Law and Infectious Diseases (Oxford: Oxford University Press, 1999).12.

159. See for instance Evans, 'A Human Rights to Health?' (2002);23 *Third World Quarterly* 197 see also Fuller, 'The Forms and Limits of Adjudication' (1978) 92 *Harvard Law Review* 353-409.

160. See Byrne 'Making the Right to Health a Reality: Legal Strategies for Effective Implementation' a paper delivered at Commonwealth Conference, London September 2005.

161. Cook and Ngwena , 'Women's Access to Health Care: The Legal Framework (2006)94 *International Journal of Gynecology Obstetrics*, 216-225.

162. Commission on Human Rights 'Report submitted by the Special Rapporteur on the right of everyone to the highest attainable standard of physical and mental health, Paul Hunt: Addendum—Mission to Romania' (21 February 2005) UN Doc No E/CN.4/2005/51/Add.4 at paras. 42, 47-54.

163. CEDAW Committee Concluding Observation regarding Cameroun 26/06/2000. CEDAW/C/2000/II/Add.2 (2000) at para 23.

164. One of the objectives of the Policy is to 'Ensure that prevention programmes are developed and targeted at vulnerable groups such as women and children, adolescents and young adults, sex workers, long distance commercial vehicle drivers, prison inmates, migrant labour etc'.

"Protection of Human Rights, Act 1993– Human Rights Courts in India"

Sujesh Somanathan*

INTRODUCTION

We hold these truths to be self-evident; that all men are created equal, that they are endowed by their creator with certain unalienable rights, that, among these are life, liberty and the pursuit of happiness[1].

The concept of human rights has existed under several names in European thought for many centuries, at least since the time of King John of England. After the king violated a number of ancient laws and customs by which England had been governed, his subjects forced him to sign the *Magna Carta*, or Great Charter, which enumerates a number of what later, came to be thought of as human rights. Among them were, the right of the church to be free from governmental interference, the rights of all free citizens to own and inherit property and be free from excessive taxes. It established the right of widows who owned property to choose not to remarry, and established principles of due process and equality before the law. It also contained provisions forbidding bribery and official misconduct. The political and religious traditions in other parts of the world also proclaimed what have come to be called human rights, calling on rulers to rule justly and compassionately, and delineating limits on their power over the lives, property, and activities of their citizens.

In the eighteenth and nineteenth centuries in Europe several philosophers proposed the concept of "natural rights," rights belonging to a person by nature and because he was a human being, not by virtue of his citizenship in a particular country or membership in a particular religious or ethnic group. This concept was vigorously debated and rejected by some philosophers as baseless. Others saw it as a formulation of, the underlying principle on which all ideas of citizens' rights and political and religious liberty were based. In the late 1700s two revolutions occurred which drew heavily on this concept. In 1776 most of the British colonies in North America proclaimed their

* *Final Year (IInd) Student, Pursuing LL.M at Hidayatullah National Law University, Raipur.*

independence from the British Empire in a document which still stirs feelings, and debate, the U.S. Declaration of Independence. In 1789 the people of France overthrew their monarchy and established the first French Republic. Out of the revolution came the "Declaration of the Rights of Man."

The term natural rights eventually fell into disfavor, but the concept of universal rights took root. Philosophers such as Thomas Paine, John Stuart Mill, and Henry David Thoreau expanded the concept. Thoreau is the first philosopher I know of to use the term, "human rights", and does so in his treatise, *Civil Disobedience.* This work has been extremely influential on individuals as different as Leo Tolstoy, Mahatma Gandhi, and Martin Luther King. Gandhi and King, in particular, developed their ideas on non-violent resistance to unethical government actions from this work. Other early proponents of human rights were English philosopher John Stuart Mill, in his *Essay on Liberty,* and American political theorist Thomas Paine in his essay, *The Rights of Man.*

The middle and late 19th century saw a number of issues take center stage, many of them issues we in the late 20th century would consider human rights issues. They included slavery, serfdom, brutal working conditions, starvation wages, child labor, and, in the Americas, the "Indian Problem", as it was known at the time. In the United States, a bloody war over slavery came close to destroying a country founded only eighty years earlier on the premise that, "all men are created equal." Russia freed its serfs the year that war began. Neither the emancipated American slaves nor the freed Russian serfs saw any real degree of freedom or basic rights for many more decades, however. For the last part of the nineteenth and first half of the twentieth century, though, human rights activism remained largely tied to political and religious groups and beliefs. Revolutionaries pointed at the atrocities of governments as proof that their ideology was necessary to bring about change and end the government's abuses. Many people, disgusted with the actions of governments in power, first got involved with revolutionary groups because of this. The governments then pointed at bombings, strike-related violence, and growth in violent crime and social disorder as reasons why a stern approach toward dissent was necessary.

Neither group had any credibility with the other and most had little or no credibility with uninvolved citizens, because their concerns were generally political, not humanitarian. Politically partisan protests often just encouraged more oppression, and uninvolved citizens who got caught in the crossfire usually cursed both sides and made no effort to listen to the reasons given by either. Nonetheless many specific civil rights and human rights movements managed to affect profound social changes during this time. Labor unions brought about laws granting workers the right to strike, establishing minimum work conditions, forbidding or regulating child labor, establishing a forty hour work week in the United States and many European countries, etc. The women's rights movement succeeded in gaining for many women the right to vote. National liberation movements in many countries succeeded in driving out colonial powers. One of the most influential was Mahatma Gandhi's movement to free his native India from British rule. Movements by long-oppressed racial and religious minorities succeeded in many parts of the world, among them the U.S. Civil Rights movement.

In 1961 a group of lawyers, journalists, writers, and others, offended and frustrated by the sentencing of two Portugese college students to twenty years in prison for having raised their glasses in a toast to "freedom" in a bar, formed *Appeal for Amnesty,* 1961. The appeal was announced on May 28 in the London Observer's Sunday Supplement. The appeal told the stories of six "prisoners of conscience" from different countries and of different political and religious backgrounds, all jailed for peacefully expressing their political or religious beliefs, and called on governments everywhere to free such prisoners. It set forth a simple plan of action, calling for strictly impartial, non-partisan appeals to be made on behalf of these prisoners and any who, like them, had been imprisoned for peacefully expressed beliefs. The response to this appeal was larger than anyone had expected. The one-year appeal grew, was extended beyond the year, and *Amnesty International* and the modern human rights movement were both born. The modern human rights movement didn't invent any new principles. It was different from what preceded it primarily in its explicit rejection of political ideology and partisanship, and its demand that governments everywhere, regardless of ideology, adhere to certain basic principles of human rights in their treatment of their citizens.

Recognition for the human rights movement, and Amnesty International in particular, grew during the 1970s. Amnesty gained permanent observer status as an NGO at the United Nations. Its reports became mandatory reading in legislatures, state departments and foreign ministries around the world. Its press releases received respectful attention, even when its recommendations were ignored by the governments involved. In 1977 it was awarded the Nobel Peace prize for its work. If we look at the chronology of events that led to the development of Human Rights in the Indian perspective we can see a whole lot of events that actually led and promoted or we can say prompted the development of Human Rights in India. This starts rights from the 1800's when the *'sati'*[2] system was abolished and went on to secure the abolition of child marriage to the rights granted to the Scheduled Castes and Scheduled Tribes[3]. All this eventually led to the passing of the Protection of Human Rights Act, 1993[4] and a special provision in it for the creation of Special Human Rights Courts to specifically deal with Human Rights violation cases. The situation of Human Rights in India is a complex one, as a result of the country being large in size and the tremendous diversity, its status as a developing country and its history as a former colonial territory. It is often held, particularly by the Indian Human Rights groups and activists that the members of the Dalit community or the untouchable caste as they are commonly referred to, have suffered and continue to suffer substantial discrimination. Although Human Rights problems do exist in India the country is generally not considered as dangerous as are some other South-Asian countries and also the media in the country is pretty vibrant, influential and independent which has played a crucial role in upholding Human Rights in India.

Apart from the basic introduction to the topic, the paper comprises of four chapters. The first chapter deals with the evolution of Human Rights in the international context and has a subdivision on the evolution and present scenario in India. The second chapter deals with the mapping of the common human rights issues that can be seen in the Indian context. The third chapter deals with the critical analysis of the Act and includes the latest amendment made to it in 2006. The fourth chapter includes the details on Human Rights courts which is the actual centre of research. This is followed by the conclusion.

EVOLUTION OF HUMAN RIGHTS

The concept of human rights is, historically, the flower of a European plant. It has now received the support of world nations. The term has come into common currency during the 20th century though the idea of 'human rights' is essentially the product of 17th and 18th century European thought. Respect for human rights is becoming a universal principle of good government. Human rights are rights possessed by people as human beings. They include all fundamental freedoms and are based on mankind's demand for a life in which the inherent dignity and worth of each human being will receive respect and protection. Human Rights were seen as fundamental to the well-being of society, under the influence of philosophers such as Grotius, Hobbes and Locke. Then, these rights were called 'natural' rights, or 'the rights of man'. These natural or moral rights became part of the political agenda.

The great religions of the world - Judaism, Hinduism, Christianity, Buddhism, Taoism, Islam, and others contribute profound ideas on the dignity of the human being, and are concerned with the duties and obligations of man to his fellow human beings. Though the international concept of human rights can be traced back to the twentieth century, the western idea has its origins in the ancient Greek period. Plato stressed the equality of men and women in all walks of life. The notion of rights and man-centered ideas were in a stage of infancy during this period which gradually got eroded and eclipsed during the Middle Ages.

The conception of human rights transcended the boundaries and acquired utmost importance after the Universal Declaration of Human Rights (UDHR) on 10th December, 1948 which is also known as the Magna Carta of all mankind. The declaration set forth a comprehensive and a common standard of achievements for all by bringing the entire humanity under the uniform cover of the human rights umbrella. Subsequently the Unites Nations General

Assembly adopted two covenants of rights in 1966 which were the International Covenant on Civil and Political Rights (ICCPR) and the Covenant on Economic, Social, and Cultural Rights (CESCR). The stress of these covenants and declarations is not only to put restraints on the power of the state but also to evolve opportunities and positive environment for the fulfillment and dignified development of all human beings.

Defining Human Rights may be both simple and complex at the same time. Simple in the sense that one can argue that human rights implies a universal ethic which claims that certain rights ought to be believed and observed everywhere by everyone. They are possessed by human beings simply because they are human beings. It is complex because when an attempt is made to list those rights, geographical diversities, cultural variances and differences in social values make the attempt a near impossibility to agree upon a universally accepted list of rights. Any action which would affect, distort or violate the inherent dignity of a human being would amount to violation of the human rights of the person. Keeping this aspect in mind one may conclude that human rights are the basic rights of a person which are essential for the realization of the persons personality as an individual as well as a member of the society in which the person lives. They are based upon the belief that all persons are born free and with equal dignity and natural rights. Moreover the concept of human rights is closely associated with the worth and dignity of the individual and accords the highest respect to human personality without any discrimination on grounds of race, religion, caste, creed etc. It is self evident that human rights primarily aim to protect the human dignity of an individual.

Human rights are indivisible and interrelated. And they are inclusive. This inclusiveness makes human rights an excellent tool; a compass by which to navigate in the new state of the world, where borders are torn down. Human Rights are available to man in peaceful environment. Violence and human rights are incompatible. Violence and state sponsored terrorism is quite common in international areas. The leviathan countries play gimmicks and tricks on the pretext of human rights and even thrust wars upon weal nations to achieve their vested interests and spread their hegemonic tentacles. Though United Nations has adopted the UDHR yet it lacks universal applicability. Different countries have different set of rights depending upon their cultural specialties and perceptions.

The history of human rights may be traced to early slave revolts. Later on liberalism, Marxism, socialism and anti-colonial freedom struggles shaped the human rights perspective. Some important events, which have contributed for the growth of human rights movement, are the Renaissance, the 'Glorious Revolution' of 1688 that led to the English Bill of Rights, in 1689, the American and French Revolutions, the Bolshevik Revolution, the Industrial Revolution (1930) and the World War II. Human Rights have been intricately tied to the laws, customs and religions throughout the ages.

The prime contribution to Human Rights could be seen from the efforts of Hammurabi, the Sumerian king. One of the first examples of a codification of laws that contain references to individual rights is the tablet of Hammurabi. The Sumerian king Hammurabi created the tablet about 4000 years ago. Hammurabi's laws created a precedent for a legal system. This kind of precedent and legally binding document protects the people from arbitrary persecution and punishment. The problems with Hammurabi's code were mostly due to its cause and effect nature, it held no protection on more abstract ideas such as race, religion, beliefs, and individual freedoms. It is commonly known as the laws that were created against arbitrary persecution[5].

In ancient Greece, the concept of human rights began to take a greater meaning than the prevention of arbitrary persecution. Human rights became synonymous with natural rights, rights that spring from natural law. According to the Greek tradition of Socrates and Plato, natural law is a law that reflects the natural order of the universe, essentially the will of the gods who control nature. Plato first made a systematic attempt to protect the citizens and non-citizens of ancient Greece in his grand scheme of justice. Aristotle discussed virtue, justice and rights for individuals in the contemporary Greek society. However, Cicero "provided the philosophical foundations for later theories of natural law..."[6]. Later, religious Universalists like Thomas Aquinas based their religious arguments on the fundamental value of human dignity and universality of natural law.

This idea of natural rights continued in ancient Rome, where the Roman jurist Ulpian believed that natural rights belonged to every person, whether they were a Roman citizen or not. These writings, however, had oblique reference to human rights thinking rather than the one we find in the subsequent contributions. Despite this principle, there are fundamental differences between human rights today and natural rights of the past. For example, it was seen as perfectly natural to keep slaves, and such a practice goes counter to the ideas of freedom and equality that we associate with human rights today. In the middle ages and later the renaissance, the decline in power of the church led society to place more of an emphasis on the individual, which in turn caused the shift away from feudal and monarchist societies, letting individual expression flourish.

The next fundamental contribution to the philosophy of human rights arose from the idea of positive law. Thomas Hobbes saw natural law as being very vague and hollow and too open to vast differences of interpretation. Hobbes wanted to make the Leviathan all-powerful to protect individuals from, the anarchical state of nature through contract. For, he believed that human beings were basically greedy and violent creatures who lived on anarchy in their natural state[7]. He was, however, conscious of the need to ensure the right to security to the individuals to thwart the exploitation by the rulers; and state came into being because of the recognition of this basic need. The individuals in the civil society acquired certain rights that are inalienable and inviolable that the ruler has to protect those rights. In case the ruler does not perform the task of protecting those rights he has to go. This is the essence of Hobbes contribution in empowering individuals against the Leviathan who might be all powerful.

Locke's ideas laid the foundation for human rights. He believed that in the state of nature humans were basically good, peaceful and mercantile. He felt that the need for the protection of right to life and property necessitates the creation of a state. He insisted on having a ruler who might act as an arbiter to settle dispute that might arise over trade and property. Rousseau "saw the first virtue of the social contract as its capacity to organize in collective defence of liberty and order. The social contract establishes a community with a potential for doing justice, thereby giving the citizens the morality which had been wanting in the state of nature"[8].

Kant made human rights distinct from other rights like civil rights, international rights, and cosmopolitan rights. He believed in the oneness of human race. To quote him: "the right to resort, for all men are entitled to present themselves in the society of others by virtue of their tight to communal possession of the earth's surface. Since the earth is a globe, they cannot disperse over an infinite area, but must necessarily tolerate one another's."[9] Thomas Paine believed in the sovereignty of individual and argued for the minimal interference of the state. Like Locke he was deeply committed to the inalienable rights of man – rights of mind and rights of happiness and freedom. Whereas, Karl Marx was highly critical of, the natural rights of individuals. He argued that these rights were idealistic and ahistorical. To him, in the society where the capitalist monopolizes the means of production and distribution, ideas like individual rights are illusory. These rights are meant to cater to the interest of the ruling bourgeois class only. The proletariats would have nothing but their chains. This Marxist paradigm is considered to be one of the most formidable theoretical tools to analyze the human rights abuses.

The most important contribution to the contemporary thinking on human rights is that of John Rawls' *A Theory of Justice*. Rawls's idea of justice consists of two principles: The First Principle is that, "each person is to have an equal right to the most extensive total system of equal basic liberties compatible with similar system of liberty for all". This implies equality of political rights to all citizens in a democratic country. These rights are necessary for the development of individual liberty. Rawls may not have enumerated the basic liberties in detail though, by and large, they include political liberty, freedom of speech and assembly and liberty of conscience and thought, freedom of the person and freedom from arbitrary arrest and seizure. The second principle of Rawls' justice deals with distributive justice. According to this, ' Social and economic inequalities are to be arranged so that they are both (a) to the greatest benefit of the least advantaged, consistent with a just saving principle and (b) attached to positions and offices open to all under condition of fair equality of which include rights and liberties.

Abstract ideas regarding human rights and their relation to the will of nature have been transformed into concrete laws by various legal documents – British Magna Carta, the English Bill of Rights, French Declaration of the Rights of Man, American Bill of Rights, the Geneva Convention and the Universal Declaration of Human Rights etc. that specifically described these rights in details. The English Bill of Rights made the King subject to the rule of law, like any citizen, instead of claiming to be the law's (divine) source. It protected some basic rights to justice and guaranteed juries, impartial courts and independent judges. The American Declaration of Independence in 1776 asserted that governments were established by the consent of the people to protect rights. Governments that did not carry out their protective role could be overthrown. The Declaration did not, in fact, extend human rights to all human beings. The first US Constitution expressly preserved the institution of slavery and did not recognize the equal rights of women. Many 'rights' were added to the US Constitution over the years.

In 1788, as a result of the French Revolution, the Declaration of the Rights of man and of Citizens asserted the primacy of natural rights in similarly inspirational terms to the US Declaration of Independence. Yet in the Terror that soon followed the Revolution, with all its hopes, thousands unjustly lost their lives or suffered greatly in the name of 'Liberty.' In 1945, leaders of the world's nations met in San Francisco to form the United Nations. Inspired by the great South African pre-apartheid leader Field- Marshall Smuts, they included in the preamble to the Charter of the UN, an important reference to human rights[10].

In addition, largely as a result of pressure brought to bear on the political leaders by some 42 United States non-government organizations, Article 68 was included. It required the Economic and Social Council to set up commissions in the human rights and economic and social fields. The outcome was the establishment of a Commission on Human Rights. Thus the Commission is one of the very few bodies to draw its authority directly from the Charter of the United Nations. The Commission then turned to formulating the declaration. It decided to name it the Universal Declaration of Human Rights (UDHR). The very name emphasizes the UDHR to set a standard of rights for all people everywhere - whether male or female, black or white, communist or capitalist, victor or vanquished, rich or poor, for members of a majority or a minority in the community[11]. Even though it was initially not that effective but subsequently it has become the most powerful document in the human rights field which is followed by almost all members of the United Nations, at least on paper.

EVOLUTION OF HUMAN RIGHTS IN INDIA

Ancient Indian thinkers like Manu, Parasar and Kautilya had tried meticulously to protect the rights and dignity of individuals from the rapacity of the rulers. These Indian thinkers prescribed many duties to the rulers to protect the dignity of the citizens. Human rights create space for life and living. They foster respect for one self and for others. Human rights are inclusive - a dynamic relationship of give-and-take between cultures and human beings finding their particular room and space in society. Human rights help to create a society where diversity and difference is respected and they help to remind us to include the weak and the vulnerable in state policies.

Human Rights are available to man in peaceful environment. Violence and human rights are incompatible. Violence and state sponsored terrorism is quite common in international areas. The leviathan countries play gimmicks and tricks on the pretext of human rights and even thrust wars upon weal nations to achieve their vested interests and spread their hegemonic tentacles. Though United Nations has adopted the UDHR yet it lacks universal applicability. Different countries have different set of rights depending upon their cultural specialties and perceptions.

In the long history of Indian civilization the freedom of speech and thought, the freedom of one's life and the beliefs held by the person were all taken together to form the natural foundations of human relationships. Where the freedom of man was secured after a long and bitter struggle between the state and the church, in India it was seen as the very substance of human existence. Thus the influence of the ancient scriptures and the ancient beliefs tends to underscore the reality that the concept of right is not a gift from the west and that its origins are very much rooted in the ancient Hindu civilization. The Indian vision of rights emphasizes not only on the individual but also the total person. The Indian intellectuals generally accept the view that rights are not over and above the state; rather they are gift from the state itself. The rights of the individual must be balanced with the interest of the society as a whole. The good of each must contribute to the good of all.

Indian society has largely been a tolerant society embracing and respecting the dignity of its friends and foes alike. India has always welcomed and accommodated foreigners from alien societies. In a way Indian culture has emphasized some of the fundamental principles of modern day philosophy of human rights from a long time back. Human Rights cannot exist in a cultural and economic vaccum. The chances of being understood and respected, increases with the, increase or improvement in the educational and economic level of the society. It is a notable maxim that it is better for a man to go wrong in freedom than go right in chains. The categories of human rights are never closed. But we must guard against the devaluation of human rights by proliferation. The primary idea of human rights involves the idea of the rights against the government. There should be a clear distinction between the terms "Human Rights" and "Human Needs".

Even though there are many lofty postulations and novel ideas in the Indian philosophical outlook concerning the development and progress of man, however one cannot overlook the plethora of social evils like intolerant casteism, female infanticide, religious orthodoxy etc. Various reformers like Dayanand Sarawati, Swami Vivekananda, Raja Ram Mohan Roy etc. strived to eradicate these evils completely from the society.

Indian system of human rights protection is unique where human rights are constitutionally guaranteed and judicially protected. It was perhaps the first among **UN** member nations where right to enforce fundamental rights was also a fundamental right (Art. 32 of the Constitution). This was in sharp contrast to international system where the Human right Committee appointed under Art.28 of the International Covenant on Civil and Political Rights, acts as advisory and monitoring body, which studies reports and formulates comments. It works as a conciliatory body in relation to communications from member states and as inquiring and investigating body in relation to complaint from individuals. Inspite of it, the world community was not satisfied with the results of the Indian system and always accused India of human rights violations. Even Indian intellectuals and human rights activity were not satisfied and pleaded for a better system that may effectively protect human rights of even the rural illiterates and living below the poverty line.

The criminals and the government are the two potential violators of human rights. The government is set up to protect man from criminals and constitution is written to protect man from government. Under a proper social system the individual is legally free top take any action he pleases as long as he does not violate the rights of any other individual. A government official is bound to act by the laws in every official act he does. The proper functions, of the government fall into three broad categories, all of them involving the issues of physical force and the protection of human rights. The Constitution is a limitation on the government, not on individuals that it does not prescribe the conduct of the individual and only the conduct of the government has been prescribed. Today all these principles and duties are forgotten, ignored and evaded with mankind's retrogression to the lawlessness of absolutist tyranny to the primitive savagery of rule by brute force.

India has long recognized the importance of ensuring its own compliance with these international human rights obligations. While international treaties do not automatically become part of domestic law upon ratification, the Constitution provides, as a Directive Principle of State Policy, that the government "shall endeavor to foster respect for international law and treaty obligations in the dealings of organized people with one another," and also authorizes the central government to enact legislation implementing its international law obligations without regard to the ordinary division of central and state government powers[12]. The Indian judiciary has been an independent and vibrant forum for human rights discourse in Indian society. While the enforcement of human rights and the effectiveness of judicial institutions in India are far from perfect, the courts' – particularly the Supreme Court of India and various state High Courts – scrutiny of human rights under the Indian Constitution has been fairly effective.

The Supreme Court of India has frequently emphasized that constitutional and statutory provisions should be interpreted in light of India's international law obligations and has looked for guidance when interpreting the Constitution's fundamental rights provisions to the UDHR, which was adopted while the Constitution was being drafted. India also is bound by customary international law norms, to the extent it has not persistently objected to those norms, and is absolutely bound by norms that have attained the status of jus cogens[13].

The Protection of Human Rights Act of 1993[14] established India's National Human Rights Commission (NHRC) in 1993. The NHRC is empowered to receive complaints broadly relating to any human rights violations[15]. To conduct these activities, the NHRC has the powers of a civil court, including the ability to compel appearance of witnesses, examine witnesses under oath, compel discovery and production of documents, and order production of records from courts and government agencies. The NHRC only may investigate alleged violations within the previous year and may not investigate allegations against the armed forces.

Over the years, the NHRC has developed a good reputation both nationally and internationally with regard to intervention on human rights matters. NHRC's opinions on numerous matters are inconsistent with the Indian government's position. The NHRC also engages state governments on various human rights and law reform matters, the most important of which is ensuring that legislation conforms to the human rights obligations in the Indian Constitution and other laws. The NHRC's moral legitimacy is based on its members' impartiality and integrity, and not on its institutional independence or its guaranteed powers in the Protection of Human Rights Act of 1993. In addition, there have been serious attempts to create accountability mechanisms for human rights violations in different levels of the Indian government to help ensure that human rights remain the central focus of Indian political and government discourse. The NHRC remains a forum in which people can seek justice for human rights violations. The United Nations has encouraged the formation of national human rights institutions worldwide to promote institutionalization of human rights.

MAPPING OF HUMAN RIGHTS ISSUES

In India, the last quarter of the 20th century has been witness to a growing recognition of the place and relevance of human rights. It is axiomatic that this interest in human rights is rooted in the denial of life and liberty that was a pervasive aspect of the Emergency (1975-77). The mass arrests of the leaders of the opposition and the targeted apprehension of those who could present a challenge to an authoritarian state are one of the dominant images that have survived. The involuntary disappearance of Rajan in Kerala is more than a symbol of the excesses of unbridled power[16]. Forced evictions carried out in Delhi in what is known as 'Turkman Gate' conjures up visions of large scale razing of dwellings of those without economic clout, and of their displacement into what were the outlying areas of the city. The catastrophic programme of mass sterilization is an indelible part of emergency memory. The civil liberties movement was a product of the emergency. Arbitrary detention, custodial violence, prisons and the use of the judicial process were on the agenda of the civil liberties movement[17].

In the late '70s, but more definitively in the early '80s, the Supreme Court devised an institutional mechanism in public interest litigation (PIL). PIL opened up the court to issues concerning violations of rights, and non realization of even bare non-negotiables[18] by diluting the rule of *locus standi*; any person could move the court on behalf of a class of persons who, due to indigence, illiteracy or incapacity of any other kind were unable to reach out for their rights. In its attempt to make the court process less intimidating, the procedure was simplified, and even a letter to the court could be converted into a petition[19]. Individuals, groups and movements have since used the court as a situs for struggle and contest, with varying effect on the defining what constitutes human rights, and prioritizing when rights appear to be in conflict.

The right to natural resources is another human right which is one of the violated rights. Though it was one of the most violated rights during the initial years, the violation has come down considerably now. The right of the people to access forest produce for their subsistence and in acknowledgment of the traditional relationship between forests and dwellers in and around forests were agitated in the early years. Environmentalists and those espousing the dwellers and forest user's causes have spoken together, parted company and found meeting points again, over the years. The right to resources is vigorously contested terrain.

Movements for self-determination, militancy, dissent and the naxalite movement have provoked various extraordinary measures which have, in turn, prompted human rights groups into protest and challenge. The Terrorist and Disruptive Activities (Prevention) Act (TADA) is an instance[20]. The Armed Forces Special Powers Act (AFSPA) continues. Encounter killings, disappearances and the ineffectiveness of the judicial system in places where 'extraordinary' situations of conflict prevail, characterize the human rights-related scenario. A jurisprudence of human rights has emerged in these contexts.

Custody deaths, torture in custody and custodial rape have been subjects of much concern. Custodial violence has been on the agenda of civil rights groups for over two decades, and reports documenting instances of violence and its systemic occurrence, have been instrumental in the campaigns against custodial violence. Project displacements, for the construction of large dams or for power projects, for instance, have led to protest movements directly involving the affected people. Human rights issues that arise include displacement, per se, the poverty of rehabilitation and often the impossibility of rehabilitation, the impoverishment that results from displacement and the non-reckoning of cultural and community identity and of rights.

The displacement of the slum dwellers and the pavement hawkers is another area of human rights violation because they are not given any other alternative by which they can get back their lives. The government is too keen on removing them and not keen on giving them the basic human facilities that are actually constitutional rights guaranteed to every citizen of this country. Sexual harassment[21], rape, harassment at workplace [sexual or non-sexual] all constitute violation of the human rights guaranteed to the women. The civil liberties movement has been consistent in its opposition to the death penalty. The argument put forward is that it is against the human rights concept and that the state does not have the right to deprive a person of the right to live when, the right actually has not been granted by the state and that it is an inherent right obtained by the virtue of being a human being. Civil liberties groups, journalists and lawyers have consistently challenged the practice of extra-judicial killings or encounter killings as they are commonly referred to over the past two decades. The human rights community has had to contend with the issue of impunity which is immediately seen as arising from the non-registration and the non-investigation of cases where encounter killings took place. Involuntary Disappearances appear to be a pattern where there is militant resistance to the state. Case law speaks of this phenomenon in the Northeast. In fact, the first major case of compensation for disappearance after being picked up by the armed forces was from the Northeast[22].

When the Constitution came into being in 1950, preventive detention laws were avowedly intended to be a transient measure. During the emergency, the Maintenance of Internal Security Act 1971 (MISA) was among the more infamous laws which allowed for preventive detention of persons in the avowed interest of maintenance of internal security. There are now a number of legislations which permit preventive detention, in the states and at the centre. The National Security Act 1980 (NSA) is an instance of the latter. The A.P Prevention of Dangerous Activities of Bootleggers, Dacoits, Drug Offenders, Goondas, Immoral Traffic Offenders & Land Grabbers Act 1986 is an example of the former. Unlike the challenge to the TADA, preventive detention laws have not engaged the human rights community in any sustained manner.

In the early 1980s, India began to face a crisis of politicized violence that prompted the government to enact sweeping criminal antiterrorism laws. Since then, these laws have been enacted and repealed in a cyclical pattern that replicates the pattern established by the British and maintained after independence for emergency and preventive detention laws. The major antiterrorism laws that India has enacted since 1980- the Terrorist and Disruptive Activities (Prevention) Act, the Prevention of Terrorism Act, and the Unlawful Activities (Prevention) Amendment Act - all have raised human rights concerns under the Indian Constitution and international human rights treaties such as the ICCPR. To be sure, public debate over these laws has been vigorous and ongoing, and in part as a result, each subsequent law has incrementally improved upon its immediate predecessor. Nevertheless, the human rights concerns raised by these laws have been significant, and a number persist to this day.

Child labor, child marriage, abandoning of children, illegal adoption of children etc. are some of the other issues where actually human rights groups and organizations are doing the good work of protecting the human rights of these kids where no one even cares about them leave alone their rights. Tourism's contribution to the violation of human rights has become an area of increasing concern. The growth of the sex industry, including the use of children for sexual pleasure is most disturbing. The displacement and exclusion of people from forest areas, and the introduction of elite tourism is passed off as 'eco-tourism'. The taking over of agricultural land to create hotel resorts, as is happening in the Diamond Harbor area in West Bengal, is opposed as being inherently unjust and environmentally unfriendly. The images of the reservoir in the Tehri and at the Sardar Sarovar being converted into lake resorts, militates particularly against equity.

In approaching the court, or when an activist is drawn into the judicial process, a question of representation of a political or an ideological position often rises. Illustratively, a feminist litigating for getting custody of her child may be faced with two choices: either to assert the stereotype - the mother as the primary carer of the child, and the child needing the care and attention that only the mother can give - and increase the probability of getting custody, or staying within the politics of feminism and reject such stereotyping which, in turn, may drastically reduce the chances of getting a favourable order from the court. An instance, again, is in matters of contempt of court, where activists may be advised to tone down their honest opposition to a court order which is patently unjust, even unconstitutional, or perhaps to tender an apology which would serve the requirement of the court, but which may compromise the politics of the contemnor. Difficulties abound where activists are picked up by the police, and there are apprehensions that they may be subjected to torture, or even be killed in a fake encounter.

PROTECTION OF HUMAN RIGHTS ACT, 1993

The first demand for fundamental rights appeared in the constitution of India Bill. The bill envisaged for India a constitution on guaranteeing to everyone of her citizen freedom of expression, inviolability of one's house, right to equality before law, right to property, right to personal liberty and right to free education, etc. Resolutions adopted by Congress in between 1917 to 1919 repeated the demand for civil rights and equality of status with Englishmen. On Dec. 22, 1927 the expression for human rights came into policy form for the first time at the 43rd session of the Congress in Madras (now Chennai). In the session a resolution was passed regarding the future of religion and linguistic minorities in India. The resolution in Section 4 of all political rights emphasized that in the constitution of free India, liberty of conscience shall be guaranteed and no legislature, central or provincial shall have power to make any law interfering with this. But in August 1931, All India Congress Committee amended this resolution.

Most of these resolutions are adopted in Indian Constitution as a part of fundamental rights and directive principles. In the new constitution after independence, a declaration of rights, the most elaborate in the world, was incorporated. The spirit if human rights can be seen in our constitution through the various articles such as 330, 331 and 338. Our country has made the sincere efforts for the promotion and protection of human rights in the third world.

The country as a whole felt the necessity for better protection of Human Rights during emergency in 1975 when late Shri Jai Prakash Narain voiced his opposition to the then existing regime of repression and exploitation and formed the people's Union for Civil Liberties and Democratic Rights. In 1977, the Janta Party promised through its election manifesto to set up an independent and autonomous Civil Rights Commission headed by a person of status of Supreme Court Judge to secure civil rights of minorities, schedule castes and schedule tribes. Even the Congress Party through its manifesto released in 1991, promised to set-up a Human Right Commission to investigate and adjudicate complaints of human rights violations.

In the context of this growing demand of an effective human right protection programme, the Central Government introduced "Human Rights Commission Bill, 1992" in the Lok Sabha on 14th May, 1992. Since this bill was referred to the Standing Committee, of Parliament on Home Affairs, it could not become the law and considering the urgency of the matter, the President promulgated "The Protection of Human Rights Ordinance, 1993" on 28th September 1993 which was subsequently replaced by the *Protection of Human Rights Act, 1993*[23] which forms the basis of modem human rights protection regime in the country.

Preamble or long title of the Act informs that it aims providing for the constitution of a National Human Rights Commission at the national level and State Human Rights Commissions in states and Human Right courts for better protection of human rights and for matter connected therewith or incidental thereto. The words better protection should justify the conclusion that even the Parliament was not satisfied with the earlier human rights protection regime and wanted to make it better. In a country where about half of its population be illiterate and about 1/3rd of it be living below the poverty line, nothing better could be thought of. There should, therefore, be no doubt that better protection of human right is sought through human rights commission and human rights courts. But, in the context of growing number of complaints relating to human rights violations, it is doubted if the present system is capable of ensuring better protection of human rights, particularly of weaker sections of society.

Functions of Human rights Commissions are enumerated in a simple and lucid manner in the Act[24] and may be summarized as under, viz.

(i) Enquiry into complaints or violations of human rights or abatement thereof or negligence in prevention of such violations by a public servant;

(ii) Visiting institutions for suggesting reforms;

(iii) Promoting research and spreading human rights literacy;

(iv) Promotion of awareness about human rights;

(v) Encouraging NGOs and institutions working in the field of human rights.

The National Commission is in addition to the aforesaid, expected to study treaties and other international instruments on human rights and make recommendations for their effective implementation. The procedure to be followed while, making enquiries in complaints of human rights violations[25] and confers powers of a Civil Court trying a suit in relation to such enquiries[26]. The Act is however silent about powers of the Commission while visiting institutions or promoting research in the field of human rights. The National Commissions right to, make enquiries into complaints of human rights violations by members of armed forces wherein the National Commission is obliged to act on the report of the Central Government[27].

As regards complaints, the Commissions are authorized to enquire and investigate matters relating thereto and if on such inquiry a violation is detected, recommend prosecution or departmental action[28] and payment of interim compensation[29] of the Act. In case the Government differs with the Commission, the Commission may only publish its recommendations and the reaction of the government thereupon and forget about it. In suitable cases, the Commission may approach the Supreme Court or the High Court for necessary directions[30] of the Act. Since remedy in the Supreme Court or the-High Court was available to the aggrieved person even in the earlier regime, this procedure is considered 'unjust' and time consuming. Such persons assert that Commission's recommendations should have some binding effect. Because of these provisions, Commissions called "toothless tigers". There are, however, many satisfied with the present arrangement.

The Act secures appointment of persons of known status, proven ability and long experience by a committee consisting of persons equally high in status and ability. Once members, including chairperson, are appointed, they work in accordance with the provisions of the Act and not under any one by his or her sweet will. The procedure for their removal is almost the same as in relation to a judge of the Supreme Court. The Commission's finances are subject to audit by the Comptroller and Auditor General of India and hence there is financial autonomy also. The commission is authorised to develop its own procedure UIS 10 (2) of the Act which indicates its working independence also. Because of these provisions the Supreme Court in *Paramjit Kaur's Case*[31] held it to be an expert investigative body. It is thus possible to hold that these commissions are, in terms of law, autonomous and independent. But in actual practice, the autonomy and independence of these Commissions is a myth, for the following reasons viz.

(i) Administrative control of the Commission through an IAS Secretary General or the Secretary working with Central or the State Government;

(ii) Investigation in relation to complaints of human rights violations being done by police officials working under the control of an IPS Officer belonging to the cadre;.

(iii) Posting of staff required for efficient performance of Commissions' work to be done by the central Government in relation to National Commission[32] and State Commission[33];

(iv) Exclusive privilege of the Central and the State Governments to fix quantum of financial grant to be given to the Commission, there being no statutory guideline given in the Act for the purpose;·

(v) Controlling financial expenditures of the Commission by extra judicial means; and

(vi) Ignoring reports and recommendations of the Commission by not tabling the same in the parliament or the State legislature.

Section 30 of the Act which empowers the State Government to establish Human Rights Courts for trial of offences relating to violations of human rights also gives the impression that the legislature wanted these courts to be an integral part of the new system. But this provision stops at creating human rights courts and does not prescribe trial procedure, court's powers and sentence. It also does not define offences. No efforts are made by the Central Government in this direction. Unless the offence is not defined the courts cannot take cognizance of the offences and try them. Till then the Human Rights Courts will remain only for namesake. It is not possible to treat every violation of human rights a criminal offence. Even if it was so, those offences would require definition. It would also require presenting sentence to which the offence would lie punishable.

Another problem is who can take cognizance of the offences. What the Act says is in each district, one Sessions Court has to be specified for trying "offences arising out of human rights violation". It is silent about taking of cognizance of the offence. Sessions Court of the district concerned is considered as the Human Rights Court. Under the Criminal Procedure Code, 1973 a Sessions Judge cannot take cognizance of the offence. He can only try the cases committed to him by the magistrate under Section 193 of the Cr.P.C.

Apart from the above, the Special Courts will face yet another question whether provisions of Section 197 of Cr.P.C. are applicable for taking cognizance of the offences under the Protection of Human Rights Act, 1993. In most of the cases of violation of human rights it is the police and other public officers who will be accused. The offence relate to commission or omission of the public servants in discharge of their duties. Definitely the accused facing trial under the Act will raise the objection. There are a plethora of precedents in favour of dispensing with the applicability of Section 197 of Cr.P.C. on the ground that such acts (like the ones which result in violation of human rights) do not come within the purview of the duties of public servants. But there is scope for speculation as long as there is no specific provision in the Act dispensing with the applicability of Section 197 of Cr.P.C.

An effective adjudicatory system supporting recommendatory human rights commissions would strengthen the working of the new system. But a weak adjudicatory system even through newly constituted human rights courts would weaken it further. The wisdom may therefore require suitable modification of section 30 of the Act to make human rights courts effective. Because, the object of establishment of such Courts at district level is, to ensure speedy disposal of cases relating to offences arising out of violation of human rights. Unless the lawmakers take note of the above anomalies and remove them by proper amendments the aim for which provisions are made for establishment of special courts will not be achieved.

Some of the recommendations that have been made over the years as part of the self evaluatory process of the commission are quite interesting, considering that these changes if incorporated could bring about a very important and long due change in the Human Rights Act. Some of these are, Section 30 of the Act provides for setting up of Human Rights Courts. The existing provisions may be deleted and a new proviso made as follows: "Provided that until there is adequate work, the Human Rights Courts may be entrusted with normal criminal work." The Act provides for a National Human rights commission and the State Human Rights Commission. There is no specific mention in the statute on the setting up of Commissions at the level of Union Territories. The presumption could be that the Commission at the national level will serve the Union Territories as well. However, this militates against the concept of decentralized grievance redressal machinery through the State Commissions.

The Commission therefore feels that the Union Territories as well as the National Capital Territory of Delhi should have their own arrangements for the discharge of certain of the Government of India take steps for evolving suitable institutional mechanism for protection and promotion of human rights in Union Territories including National Capital Territory. In its previous Annual Report, the Commission had recommended amendments to section 36 of the Protection of Human Rights Act with a view to establish a clear functional relationship between National Human Rights Commission on one hand, and the State Human Rights Commission that have already come into existence or that are likely to be established imminently.

HUMAN RIGHTS COURTS IN INDIA

One of the objects of the Protection of Human Rights Act, 1993 as stated in the preamble of the Act, is the establishment of human rights courts at district level. The creation of Human Rights Courts at the district level has a great potential to protect and realize human rights at the grassroots. The Protection of Human Rights Act, 1993[34] provides for establishment Human Rights Courts for the purpose of providing speedy trial of offences arising out of violation of human rights. It provides that the state Government may, with the concurrence of the Chief Justice of the High Court, by notification, specify for each district a Court of Sessions to be a Human Rights Court to try the said offences. The object of establishment of such Courts at district level is to ensure speedy disposal of cases relating to offences arising out of violation of human rights.

The Act refers to the offences arising out of violations of human rights. But it does not define or explain the meaning of "offences arising out of violations of human rights". It is vague. The Act does not give any clear indication or clarification as to what type of offences, actually are to be tried by the Human Rights Courts. No efforts are made by the Central Government in this direction. Unless the offence is not defined the courts cannot take cognizance of the offences and try them. Till then the Human Rights Courts will remain only for namesake. Even if "offences arising out of violations of human rights" are defined and clarified or classified, another problem arises in the working of the Human Rights courts in India. The problem is who can take cognizance of the offences. What the Act says is in each district, one Sessions Court has to be specified for trying "offences arising out of human rights violation". It is silent about taking of cognizance of the offence. The Prevention of Corruption Act, 1988 is another law, which provides for appointment of a Sessions Judge in each district as Special Judge to try the offence under the said Act. Provision has been made in section 5 of the Prevention of Corruption Act, 1988 empowering the Special Judge to take cognizance of the offences under the said Act. In the Protection of Human Rights Act, 1993 it is not so.

Sessions Court of the district concerned is considered as the Human Rights Court. Under the Criminal Procedure Code, 1973 a Sessions Judge cannot take cognizance of the offence. He can only try the cases committed to him by the magistrate under Section 193 of the Cr.P.C. Similar problem had arisen in working of the Scheduled Castes and Scheduled Tribes (Prevention of Atrocities) Act, 1989 in the beginning. The Special Judges used to take cognizance of the offences. In Potluri Purna Chandra Prabhakara Rao V. State of A.P.[35], Ujjagar singh & others V. State of Haryana & another[36], and some other cases it was held that the Special Court (Court of Session) does not get jurisdiction to try the offence under the Act without committal by the Magistrate. The Supreme Court also held same view in Moly & another V. State of Kerala[37]. Consequently, the trial of, all the cases under the Prevention of Atrocities Act were stopped and all the cases were sent to the Courts of jurisdictional Magistrates. Thereafter the respective Magistrates took cognizance of the cases and committed them to the Special Courts. The Special Courts started trying the cases after they were committed to them. The Act was later amended giving the Special Courts the power to take cognizance of the offences under Act.

The situation in respect of the Human Rights courts under the Protection of Human Rights Act, 1993 is not different. Apart from the above, the Special Courts will face yet another question whether provisions of Section 197 of Cr.P.C. are applicable for taking cognizance of the offences under the Protection of Human Rights Act, 1993. In most of the cases of violation of human rights it is the police and other public officers who will be accused. The offence relate to commission or omission of the public servants in discharge of their duties. Definitely the accused facing the trial under the Act raise the objection. There are a plethora of precedents in favour of dispensing with the applicability of Section 197 of Cr.P.C. on the ground that such acts (like the ones which result in violation of human rights) do not come within the purview of the duties of public servants. But there is scope for speculation as long as there is no specific provision in the Act dispensing with the applicability of Section 197 of Cr.P.C.

The object of establishment of such Courts at district level is to ensure speedy disposal of cases relating to offences arising out of violation of human rights. Unless the lawmakers take note of the above anomalies and remove them by proper amendments the aim for which provisions are made for establishment of special courts will not be achieved. The setting up of human rights courts at the district level has begun, and activists have engaged with the process of establishing rules and guidelines in terms of the procedure to be adopted by these courts. These don't seem to have become functional yet, and they remain sidelined and hazily constructed within the dominant judicial system. Also, activists in Tamil Nadu said that human rights courts were restricting themselves to civil and political rights; it will lead to a defining of what constitutes human rights in this lexicon, they said[38].

As far as other new developments in this area are concerned, Human Rights Courts have now been notified in the States of Assam and Sikkim. The commission has also expressed its belief in the preceding annual report that the section pertaining to human rights courts would be soon amended and a new proviso is added to it which would in short be that until there is enough work for human rights courts in terms of human rights violation matter they should be designated as normal criminal courts and should be entrusted with normal criminal matters[39].

The amendment that was made to the Protection of Human Rights Act, 1993 in 2006 specifies that nothing about the Sessions Court being given additional power shall be applicable if separate courts have already been constituted or if such courts have already been notified by the government. The other amendments that have been introduced are relating to procedural formalities and the rules and regulations to be followed by the National and State Commissions.

CONCLUSION

"Liberty is itself the gift of the law and may by the law be forfeited or abridged."[40] "The principle that no one shall be deprived of his life and liberty without the authority of law was not the gift of the Constitution. It was a necessary corollary of the concept relating to sanctity of life and liberty; it existed and was in force before the coming into force of the Constitution."[41]

Human security means protecting fundamental freedoms – freedoms that are the essence of life. It means protecting people from critical (severe) and pervasive (widespread) threats and situations. It means using processes that build on people's strengths and aspirations. It means creating political, social, environmental, economic, military and cultural systems that together give people the building blocks of survival, livelihood and dignity. In this new millennium, the work of the United Nations must move our world closer to the day when all people have the freedom to choose the kind of lives they would like to live, the access to the resources that would make those choices meaningful and the security to ensure that they can be enjoyed in peace"

Human rights in all its ramifications have acquired social and political legitimacy in the contemporary world. While nations have made efforts to protect and promote human rights, there have been numerous challenges that confront the enforcement of human rights. Terrorism is probably the greatest danger to human rights one can think of, but unwise reactions and responses to it can itself lead to human rights violations. Mahatma Gandhi said, "An eye for an eye will only end up making the whole world blind."

A balance between creation of various laws and promoting human rights is attainable as long as a "reasonable" constitutional provision is developed and Indian law evolves in conjunction with the efforts of the inter- governmental and non-governmental organizations in protecting civil liberties. We need to underline the fact that through valuing human rights and promoting civil liberties, deliberative democracies like India and other countries create a place for meaningful dialogue, debate, and dissent within civil and political society.

It has always been paramount that we promote and protect human rights. And even though this word cannot be conjugated I would argue that it is even more paramount now. Human rights are under pressure from many angles – increased surveillance, further restrictions on travel, and extraditions without any protection. The prohibition of torture is – in no uncertain terms - absolute, but never the less torture is still common in prisons and police stations in many parts of the world; and worse: there is a tendency to revive and legitimize torture in the name of peace, stability and national security.

Human rights create space for life and living. They foster respect for one self and for others. Human rights are inclusive - a dynamic relationship of give-and-take between cultures and human beings finding their particular room and space in society. Human rights help to create a society where diversity and difference is respected and they help to remind us to include the weak and the vulnerable in state policies.

The Human Rights act has been analyzed above is a great piece of legislation but it still needs to be fine tuned a lot to actually achieve the purpose that it was created for in the beginning. There is lack of awareness which needs to be remedied immediately and which is the duty of the government of the day both at the Centre and the State and also the NGO's should take it up as a service to the society by actually helping in spreading the awareness.

Enhancing the power that is given to the National and State Human Right Commissions would actually convert them from being "paper tigers" to actual tigers and increase their effectiveness. Creation of Human Rights Courts is another area where the general opinion is in its favour but not in the way it has been proposed in the act. The idea is creation of separate courts which are exclusively devoted to dealing with Human Rights violation matters and are not doing it in the midst of dealing with a million other cases.

The creation of the Human Right Courts and the drastic amendment of the Protection of Human Rights Act, 1993 which has already been amended in 2006 is the need of the hour. The 2006 amendment though introduces a few new clauses but they do nothing to actually remedy the above stated problems and in fact seems to be, a mere eye wash. So the major provisions that cover the powers of the Commissions needs revamping and the state governments should seriously consider creating separate and independent Human Rights Courts.

Notes

1. See, *Civil Disobedience,* Henry David Thoreau.
2. The practice of, wife setting herself on fire on the pyre of the dead husband which, was prevalent among the Hindus.

3. See, Scheduled Caste and Scheduled Tribe (Prevention of Atrocities) Act, 1989.
4. The National Human Rights Commission, an autonomous body has been constituted under this enactment to protect Human Rights in India.
5. *Key Contributions on the Concept of Human Rights*, Dr. P.V.V. Subrahmanyam, Ph.D, *www.scribd.com*, Last Visited on 23rd March, 2009, at p. 1.
6. *Ibid.*
7. See, supra note 5 at p. 2.
8. See, supra note 5 at p. 2.
9. See, supra note 5 at p. 3.
10. See, supra note 5 at p. 3.
11. See, supra note 5 at p. 4.
12. See, C. Raj Kumar, National Human Rights Institutions: Good Governance Perspectives on Institutionalization of Human Rights, 19 *Am. U. Int'l L. Rev.*, 259 (2003).
13. *Ibid.*
14. As amended by the Protection of Human Rights (Amendment) Act, 2006-No. 43 of 2006.
15. See, C. Raj Kumar, Role and Contribution of National Human Rights Commissions in Promoting National and International Human Rights Norms in the National Context, 47, *Ind. J. Pub. Admin.*, 222 (2001).
16. *Niyamavedi* v. *CBI* (1999) 1 Ker LT 56, here the disappearance of an engineering student was in question and the matter is still shrouded with mystery.
17. *A.D.M.Jabalpur* v. *Shiv Kant Shukla* (1976) 2 SCC 521 had been a blow to civil liberties.
18. *Bandhua Mukti Morcha* v.*Union of India* (1984) 3 SCC 161; *Hussainara Khatoon* v. *Home Secretary, State of Bihar* (1980) 1 SCC 81.
19. Called 'epistolary' jurisdiction.
20. This Act was first enacted in 1985, reenacted in 1987 and for further periods of two years each time, till it lapsed in 1995. Interestingly, the National Human Rights Commission (NHRC) was among the TADA's most vocal opponents.
21. *Vishaka v. State of Rajasthan* (1997) 6 SCC 241.
22. *Sebastian Hongray v. Union of India* (1984) 1 SCC 339 and (1984) 3 SCC 82.
23. As amended by the Protection of Human Rights (Amendment) Act, 2006-No. 43 of 2006.
24. See, Sec. 12 of the Act.
25. See, Sec. 17 of the Act.
26. See, Sec. 13 of the Act.
27. See, Sec. 19 of the Act.
28. See, Sec. 18 (1) of the Act.
29. See, Sec. 18 (3) of the Act.
30. See, Sec. 18 (2) of the Act.
31. AIR 1999 SC 340

32. See, Sec. 11(2) of the Act.

33. See, Sec. 27(2) of the Act.

34. As amended by the Protection of Human Rights (Amendment) Act, 2006-No. 43 of 2006.

35. 2002(1) Criminal Court cases 150.

36. 2003(1) Criminal Court Cases 406.

37. 2004(2) Criminal Court Cases 514

38. See, Usha Ramanathan, *Human Rights in India, http://www.ielrc.org/content/w0103.pdf,* last visited on 26th March, 2009.

39. See, N.Chandrashekharayya, Human Rights Courts in India, *http://www.legalservicesindia.com,* last visited on 26th March, 2009.

40. A.D.M. Jabalpur v. Shiv Kant Shukla, 1976 1 S.C.R. 172 (lines quoted by Ray, C.J.).

41. *Ibid* (lines quoted by Khanna, J., in his dissenting opinion.).

"Consumer Right Transcending into a Human Right"

Arya Tripathy & Astha Sharma*

INTRODUCTION

The prominent feature of our time is not so much the wars and the dictatorship which have disfigured it, but the impact of different cultures on one another, their interaction and the emergence of new civilization based on the truths of spirit and the unity of mankind.[1] This brings out the spirit that all human beings are born free and equal in dignity and rights and endowed with reason and conscience and should act towards one another in a spirit of brotherhood.[2] The ever increasing pace of globalization and the resonating cruel violation of rights urge the necessity for taking a holistic perspective on human rights[3] which is not merely being faithful to the intellectual and political history of the human rights idea; it reflects the relationship in principle , in law and in fact, between national and international human rights in today's world and would trace the standing of human rights in lives of billions of people in an international political legal system of states in the 21st century.[4] The article is an attempt to bring forth the significance of transforming consumer right into the universal accepted stature of a human right. It elucidates and throws some light upon the expressions which form the building blocks of the proposition that consumer right is to be shaped as a human right. Further it brings out the various human rights that tend to protect the innocent consumer in the open markets. Subsequently it makes an honest attempt to provide justifications for making consumer right a human right.

CONSUMER - AN OVERVIEW

Consumer movement has come to stay as one of the most important social movements of our time responding in a very innovative way in which society responds to the problems of exploitation of the weaker group by the stronger, a factor that accompanies the progress of the human race. Claims of consumer can be traced as definite claims on society imposing an obligation upon the society to ensure that scarce resources are utilized in a way to provide ultimate

* *IVth Year and III year students at Hidayatullah National Law University, Raipur, (E-mail: arya.hnlu@gmail.com)*

satisfaction to the consumers. The consumer is the supreme in a welfare state and they exert a great deal of influence and regulation of the economic activities in modern economic structures.[5] But the sovereignty enjoyed by consumers is limited by various restraints.[6]

Consumer and Consumerism

This is an undisputed affirmation that every human being qualifies as a consumer and it is integral to his survival.[7] According to Mahatma Gandhi- "A consumer is the most important visitor on our premises; he is not dependant upon us, we are on him; he is not interruption to our work, he is the purpose of it. We are not doing a favor to a consumer by giving him an opportunity; he is doing us a favor by giving an opportunity to serve him."[8] Consumer means a person who consumes, especially one who uses a product or a purchaser of product with a relatively long useful life.[9] In simple parlance, a consumer is one who consumes.[10] *"Consumer"* means any person who—

(i) buys any goods for a consideration which has been paid or promised or partly paid and partly promised, or under any system of deferred payment and includes any user of such goods other than the person who buys such goods for consideration paid or promised or partly paid or partly promised, or under any system of deferred payment when such use is made with the approval of such person, but does not include a person who obtains such goods for resale or for any commercial purpose; or

(ii) hires or avails of any services for a consideration which has been paid or promised or partly paid and partly prom-ised, or under any system of deferred payment and includes any beneficiary of such services other than the person who "hires or avails of the services for consideration paid or promised, or partly paid and partly promised, or under any system of deferred payment, when such services are availed of with the approval of the first mentioned person but does not include a person who avails of such services for any commercial purposes.[11]

Consumerism means the welfare of the consumers by safeguarding their rights, by protecting them from unfair trade practices and from the articles injurious to public health and to save them from exploitation from the well organized world of sellers of goods and services.[12] This indicates that consumerism will help the consumers to get more satisfaction from the purchase of goods and services with given money by getting the goods at competitive and fair rates.

Consumers: Receiving End of Exploitation

Consumer sovereignty[13] has been viewed as a reality on the basis that consumers do affect the policies of the producers but there is another chain of thought that consumer sovereignty is a myth in view of vast economic inequalities in the globalized economy and the ever startling rates of white collar crimes.[14] Moving away from Sutherland's vision of white collar crimes[15] these are also phrased in many welfare societies as "socio-economic crimes" which are a departure from the conventional conceptualization of crimes.[16] Socio-economic crimes may be defined as illegal acts committed by means, which are not violent, by concealment and the purpose being to obtain money or property or business or personal gain or profit and some salient features of these new forms of crime are: (i) there is no social sanction against them (ii) commission of these crimes is done by organized groups equipped with information and technology (iii) these crop up and find shelter from the adulterous relationship between politicians, law enforcing agencies and the offenders (iv) there is lack of organized public opinion against them and (v) they have become a part and parcel of the society.[17] Adulteration[18], corruption[19], deceptive advertising[20], misbranding articles[21], monopolistic trade practices[22], restricted trade practices[23], spurious goods[24], violation of standards of weighs and measures[25] are some socio-economic crimes.

Consumer Right–A Socio-economic Right

Rights have figured prominently in moral, legal and political theory and in contemporary philosophical literature the idea of rights is often considered an alternative to various brands of utilitarianism.[26] Socio-economic rights include rights to social security, to work with just compensation, to rest and leisure, to an adequate standard of living including food, clothing, housing, health care and social services, to education, to participation in cultural life[27] and there has been continued insistence to give the second generation rights the equal status that is enjoyed by the first generation civil and political rights. Jeremy Waldron says that a moral theory of individual dignity is plainly inadequate if it regards socio-economic needs as less important than civil and political rights and rights to decent subsistence are fundamental to the conception of the dignity and inherent claims of individuals in a world that contains the resources that might (if others let them) enable them to live.[28]

Recognition of socio-economic rights as rights does not require that it be given constitutional status for the only requirement is that the state should stand as a guarantor if basic human needs are not met by personal resources and forms of contract.[29] The language of rights which many critiques portray to be instable , indeterminate ,and an empty abstraction[30] have failed to undermine the growing importance of socio-economic rights ensuring a vital content to the entire regime of rights. A consumer is an innocent victim left without any effective redressal mechanism if his claims and rights are considered to be outside the sphere of socio-economic rights. There are various human rights enjoyed by the consumers for they have a legitimate claim against the society as a whole to have protection of moral and material interest[31] and a minimum standard of living.[32] Thus consumers form a major class of right-holders and there rights in the same capacity would become the concern of the rule of socio-economic rights fulfillment of which would enable the achievement of socio-economic justice for justice is the first virtue of social institutions, as truth is of systems of thought.[33] Theories of justice and theories of human rights often neglect to recognize that markets are inevitable consequences of the protection of human rights.[34]

For the purpose of contesting that consumer right be made a socio-economic human right it is important at this juncture to settle down on an acceptable definition of "consumer right" which would present not a segregated viewpoint but would immensely concern itself with the major problems encountered by the innocent and in most developing countries the illiterate and ignorant consumers. Having contemplated on the plight of consumers all over the world, it would be wise to accept that consumer right is a conglomerated right comprising of the right to safety, the right to be informed, the right to choose, and the right to be heard and the right to satisfaction of basic needs.

CONSUMER AND THE RIGHTS

Every person is a consumer and this in the 21st century has become a vital aspect of human existence. The earlier times had the barter system where there was exchange of goods and the risks of deception were comparatively less but in the present scenario where trade and commerce has transcended territorial boundaries and multinational corporations have become the torch- bearer of the modern economic order, the consumer needs an entire system of legislations and protections at national as also international level to receive quality and quantity for a fair price paid.

It is undeniable that every consumer enjoys certain human rights from which following may be derived:

(i) the right to have information regarding quality, purity and the price of various articles to make proper choices[35]

(ii) the right to be assured that the weights and measures being used are standard and correct[36]

(iii) the right to have fair distribution of the essential goods and services at reasonable rates[37]

(iv) the right to be protected form goods and services which are hazardous to life and property[38]

(v) the right to be protected from the unfair trade practice or from other unscrupulous exploitations[39]

(vi) the right to have pollution free environment bestowed upon him by nature[40]

(vii) the right to consumer education and awareness[41] and

(viii) the right to be heard and to get speedy justice qua the enforcement of the basic human rights of the consumers in case of their infringement.[42]

To further bring forth the magnitude of the issue it is required to peruse through the UN General Assembly Resolution of 1985 whereby the rights of consumer got international recognition which took into account the interest and needs of consumers in all countries particularly the developing countries; recognizing that consumers often face imbalances in economic terms, educational levels and bargaining power, bearing in mind that consumers should have the right to access to non-hazardous products, as well as the right to promote just, equitable and sustainable economic and social development.[43] the protection to consumers with regards to health and safety risks, liability for defective products and checking on unfair clauses in standard contracts is emphasized whereby national courts can pass orders for withdrawal of such defective product or services.[44] The Council of Europe's 1973 Consumer Protection Charter focuses on the redressal mechanisms for violation and infringement of consumer rights and recognition of consumers' and citizens' organizations.[45] The 1980 Rome Convention provides for the applicable law in case of resolution of any dispute between any consumer and business enterprise with a flexibility involved to exercise the freedom to choose the law to be applied in such situations[46] at the same time it ensures that the consumer is not deprived of the protection afforded to him by the mandatory rules of the law of the country in which he has his habitual residence.[47]

The above deliberation presents the fact that consumer rights have been derived from a plethora of human rights and it is universally accepted that in an era of globalization consumers should be imparted adequate level of education to become aware consumers and exercise sovereignty in the true sense of the term. This strengthens the proposition that consumer right should be made a human right and be incorporated in various international human right instruments and be enforced by various institutions.

WHY CONSUMER RIGHT BE MADE A HUMAN RIGHT?

The principle difficulty lies in the non-availability of an adequate substantive definition of human rights. The definition that one ought to be able to claim as entitlements (as human rights) those minimal things without which it is impossible to develop one's capability and live life as human being fails as an insufficient and simplistic definition bringing out imprecision, unenforceability, unmanageability of the concept as a whole and the difficulty of achieving the full justiciability of rights in question[48]. The term Human Rights in its normal usage comprises the rights of the individual in all spheres of social life.[49] This has given rise to strained opinions regarding the entire set of human rights. Zygmunt Bauman asserts that human rights have "become a war-cry and blackmail weapon in the hands of aspiring 'community leaders' wishing to pick up powers that the state has dropped."[50]. Responsible critiques of human rights are concerned with (a) the modes of production of human rights; (b) the problems posed by the politics of universality of human rights and the politics of identity/difference; and (c) the arguments from relativism and multiculturalism. But what may constitute the future of human rights depends on how imaginatively one defines, both in theory and movement, the challenges posed by the processes of globalization for one needs to relocate human rights in the current passage of change.[51] The "contemporary rights" have at its essence the conversion of needs into rights and in its spirit speaks about self determination[52]and this has been its hall mark this emphasizes the claim of consumer right to become a separate and distinct human right to maintain the future of human rights and give more meaning to the socio-economic rights system for consumer stands as the focal point of the present times despite the criticisms that come forward for over production of human rights for the case of human rights is so strong that it argues for itself and is *res ipso loquitur*.[53]

The fact that the claims of consumers for protection against various deceptive practices adopted by profit hungry enterprises providing sub standard goods and services is being enforced in various nations as fundamental rights , as constitutional mandate or as statutory rights. The traditional doctrine of *"caveat emptor"*[54] which placed seller at higher pedestal has remained an old medieval concept. In its place the State has come up with legislations to provide remedy to aggrieved and disadvantaged consumers in the national limits. A plethora of consumer protection laws are in force in various developing and developed countries.[55] But this has an inherent problem that under the national laws it becomes difficult to trap the socially irresponsible multi-national corporations who are the major propellers of consumer apathy and victimization. The national judicial system fails to nail down the trans-national corporations due to the fact that consumer right is either a legal right or constitutional right that can be enforced within the territorial boundaries.

Law is indeed a regulator of human conduct but no law can effectively work unless there is an element of acceptance by the people and the society and the law works out with less fiction if there is voluntary interaction which calls for awareness which means that steps should be taken to make people cognizant of the indispensable necessity of their conduct being oriented in accordance with the law and this in turn would ensure that the social level is kept up. However in developing countries where multi national corporations find adequate scope for harnessing of profits the level of awareness about rights and duties is restricted by oppressive periods of history marked by traits of imperialism, colonialism, and vast economic disparities. In such a predicament, human rights act as an universal obligation upon all kinds of actors taking it out from the limited enforceability that rights suffer by virtue of it being a statutory right protected by a national legislation. The modern universal recognition of human rights limits the various theories of justice by recognizing common moral and legal core values (e.g., respect for human dignity, equal human worth, democratic self-governance, and access to courts) which, as legal entitlements of every human being independent from the benevolence of governments.[56]

Justice is becoming a matter of universal and inalienable human rights, democratic governance, and positive national and international constitutional law in order to empower and protect individual and democratic self-development across frontiers.[57] The legal definition of justice in terms of equal human rights is becoming ever more precise, and the legal justification for inequalities in the distribution of benefits and burdens is becoming ever more demanding. Even though democratic legislation defining, balancing, and implementing human rights and constitutional rights may differ legitimately from country to country, there is an inalienable core of human rights that can no longer be lawfully taken away by governments or new actors who deny their responsibilities making benefit of innocent an ignorant consumer. this ultimate aim of justice calls for acceptance of consumer right as human right.

Business and social responsibility go hand in hand and it has been argues that an international entity must take the conscientiousness to define the corporation's social responsibility towards human rights for until this is done corporations would continue to bear a piecemeal approach towards promoting and protecting human rights in the countries in which they do business. Human rights advocates now assert that corporations, particularly transnational corporations are the entities to fill the human rights protection void left by the public sector[58] for TNC's have greater power and influence upon the national governments and this power naturally stems from wealth.[59] Twenty-five per cent of the world's productive assets are controlled by the 300 largest TNCs.[60] Direct investment by TNCs in developing countries is greater than both the inflows from official aid and the net lending by international banks.[61] Furthermore, "the economies of most U.N. Member States are smaller than the annual revenues of the largest TNCs".[62] A TNC could use its power to positively affect a country's international human rights practices by refusing to invest in or deal with countries violating human rights standards.[63]

Despite the professed potential for a TNC to influence a particular country's human rights practices, some commentators reject placing such a burden on corporations. Economists like Milton Friedman argue that a human rights victim should look to government to alleviate human rights violations,[64] these economists simply assert that corporations are not in the business of international human rights, but in making a profit. The goal of the corporation is the maximization of profit for the benefit of its stakeholders; therefore, any action resulting in a deviation from this objective is improper because it decreases a shareholder's return on his or her investment.[65] This theory limits a corporation's social responsibility obligations to obey the law, abide by prevalent ethical customs, and promote good public relations. The primary focus of these activities, unlike promoting human rights, is to contribute to profit maximization.[66] Because a corporation will only face legal liability if it disobeys the domestic laws of the countries within which it does business, outside corporate human rights regulation can be accomplished in three ways.[67] They are: (1) direct regulation[68] (2) international regulation[69] (3) private action by private groups of human rights.[70] this portrays with full potential the protection that can be provided to consumers an their legitimate demands by giving it the color of a socio-economic human right strengthening the concept of corporate social responsibility and increasing there accountability transgressing the limits of territorial application.

Increasingly over the past thirty years, corporations have individually addressed human rights issues by adopting "global human rights codes of conduct and policies for their operations and contractors."[71] Theories of justice and theories of human rights often neglect the aspects of market but there has been a tremendous shift where by corporations who are responsible for the utilization of material resources which are scarce to ensure that the goals of a welfare society of promotion of equality and fostering well being. Various firms and corporations have voluntarily adopted codes of conduct[72] and the main motive seems to be consumer pressure.[73] Some studies did find a positive link between socially responsible behavior and profit; however, others found no such link.[74] No study has found that socially responsible behavior decreases profit.[75] Corporations might argue that a voluntary code of conduct would result in putting them in a disadvantageous position legally and in comparison to corporations that do not accept it bringing upon them legal and moral obligation to conform with it these codes keeping in view the growing universality of human rights make the consumers aware that they have complied with the need to preserve human dignity and human respect and are not violative of human rights. If consumer rights are given the status of human rights then the code of conducts would act as an self imposed consciousness whereby corporations would make certain that they in the process of earning profits and expanding demand for their commodities and services also perform there obligations of providing proper information so that the consumer can exercise its right to choose , provide quality and quantity goods to consumers for the right to safety of consumers, and may also have a responsive redressal system. Corporations should have a responsibility to protect and promote human rights. However, the definition of these responsibilities through adoption of voluntary codes of conduct should not be left to the corporations themselves, because the incentive to make a profit and remain competitive will potentially persuade a corporation to disregard the principles within such a code. An international organization such as the United Nations must promulgate the human rights standards by which companies shall abide, and the standards must have legal effect. Only through such efforts will human rights truly be safeguarded from corporate exploitation.

CONCLUSION

As the power and influence of Transnational Corporations (TNC) continues to grow, and as they overtake national governments in their dominance over the global economy, the role of TNCs in the realm of human rights will inevitably expand as well. Corporate codes of conduct have been advanced in lieu of direct regulation as the most promising prospect despite the absence of an enforcement mechanism to ensure compliance. For decades, the role of private actors has remained at the periphery of the debate and out of contemplation as a far fetched prospect while topics such as the scope of government responsibility and the extent of the consequences when governments violate their human rights obligations have taken center stage. As the level of social responsibility expected of TNCs continues to rise, corporations are increasingly pressured to adopt human rights policies to satisfy consumer demands and to preemptively defend against accusations of abuse and apathy. Words would be meaningless unless transnational corporations turn their promises into reality. If large segments of the market stress the importance of consumer right practices in their purchasing decisions, TNCs will find it impossible to forego, or to soften, their corporate codes. If we fail to recognize the importance then we would over look am important aspect of human existence and dignity that is inherent and needs due acknowledgement.

Notes

1. Statement given by Dr. S. Radhakrishnan quoted in "Foundation of Human Rights, A Critical Appraisal of the Theories of Maritain and Radhakrishnan" by Dr. Kusum Jain, University Book House Pvt. Ltd., 1st ed. , p. vii.
2. Article 1 of Universal Declaration of Human Rights 1948.
3. Human rights are the rights of individuals in society which are legitimate ,valid and justified claims upon the society. The holistic approach suggests that they are not abstract or inchoate nor mere assertions or aspirations rather are definite claims that need to be enforced and assured in every society.
4. Louis Henkin, Gerald L. Neuman, Diane F. Orentlicher, David W. Leeborn, "Human Rights", University Casebook Series, New York Foundation Series, 2nd ed., 1999, p. viii.
5. The producers of goods and services have to take into account the requirements of the consumers, their nature, tastes and preferences so as to ensure that the production activities satisfy them ultimately for example the price mechanism reveals the taste and preferences of the consumer resulting in an impact upon the demand and supply of commodities in a market structure.
6. The limitations can be of varied types for example scarcity of natural resources and equipments in the country, the technical knowledge of the goods, the low purchasing power and imposition of restrictions by the states in form of regulations and policies, taxation and market monopolies.
7. See J.N.Barowalia, "Commentary on the Consumer Protection Act 1986", Universal Law Publishing Pvt. Ltd., 2nd ed., (2002).

8. *Ibid* at p. 349
9. See "Concise Oxford Dictionary", 8th ed., (1919), p. 247.
10. See Bryan A. Garner, "Black's Law Dictionary", West Group Publication, 7th ed., (1999).
11. Section 2(1)(d) of the Consumer Protection Act, 1986. (India).
12. *Supra Note* 8 at p. 34.
13. It means that consumer is the master whilst the producer is the servant in a capitalist society.
14. Crime arising out of the exploitation of the innocent consumer through unfair trade practices or the sale of adulterated goods or injurious articles by the unscrupulous traders is a white collar crime.
15. Sutherland defines a crime committed by a person of responsibility and high social status in course of his occupation as a white collar crime.
16. Conventionally criminal act comprises of two vital elements "actus reus" and "mens rea". The simultaneous institution of both these elements would be a mandate for imposition of penal liability or criminal liability but with newer forms of crime emerging the traditional stereotype concept has undergone changes whereby the element of mens rea is given a set back and losing significance in affixing liability. Furthermore it is not associated with the traditional social and personal pathologies of the individual criminal
17. *Supra* Note 8 at p. 34
18. In ordinary sense the term means to debase or make impure by adding a foreign or inferior substance in order to make gain or illegitimate profit (See Bryan A. Garner, "Black's Law Dictionary", West Group Publication, 7th ed., 1999).
19. There is a intimate nexus between social problems and corruption and every social problem is a state of corruption but it generally refers to depravity, perversion or taint; an impairment of public official's duty and its integrity by bribery. (See Supra Note 18 at p. 349).
20. An advertisement is considered to be deceptive if it satisfies three elements. First, there must be a representation, omission or practice vis-à-vis the consumer population. Second, the representation, omission or practice must be likely to mislead consumers acting reasonably under the circumstances. And third, the representation, omission or practice must be misleading in a material respect. (See section 5 Federal Trade Commission Act, 15 U.S.C.S. § 45 (1999)).
21. It means to branding falsely or in a misleading way. (For a comprehensive definition of "misbrand" refer Food Adulteration Act 1954; Drugs and Cosmetics Act 1940).
22. It is that which represents abuse of market power in the production and marketing of goods and services by eliminating potential competitors from market and taking advantage of the control over the market by charging unreasonably high prices, preventing or reducing competition, limiting technology and development, deteriorating production quality or by adopting unfair or deceptive trade practices. (See MRTP Act 1969 for a comprehensive idea).
23. It means a trade practice which has or may have the effect of preventing , distorting or restricting competition in any manner and in any particular way which tends to obstruct the flow of capital or resources into the stream of production or which tends to bring about manipulation of prices pr conditions of delivery or to effect the flow of supplies in the market related to goods or services in such manner as to impose on the

consumers unjustified costs or restrictions.(See Section 2(1)(nnn) of Consumer Protection Act 1986).

24. Spurious goods and services mean such goods and services which are claimed to be genuine but they are actually not so (See section 2(oo) of Consumer Protection Act 1986).
25. A standard is intended to maintain quantity or quality of anything to maintain reliability in trade and commerce. For this purpose various countries do have specific legislations for instance in India it is Violation of weights and Measures Act 1976.
26. *Supra* Note 8 at p. 2.
27. See Article 22-28 of Universal Declaration of Human Rights 1948 (henceforth UDHR 1948).
28. *Supra* Note 8 at pp. 84-85.
29. See Louis Henkin, *"Economic and Social Rights as "Rights": A United States Perspective"*, 2 *Hum Rts. L.J.*, 223 (1981).
30. Mark Tushnet, *"An Essay on Rights"*, 62 *Tex. L. Rev.*, 1363 (1984) at pp. 1370-75.
31. Article 27(2) of UDHR 1948.
32. Article 11 of International Covenant on Economic,Social and Cultural Rights 1976 (henceforth ICESCR 1976).
33. Professor Doctor Ernst-Ulrich Petersmann, *"Theories of Justice, Human Rights and the Constitution of International Markets"*, 37 *Loy. L.A. L. Rev.*, 407.
34. *Ibid.*
35. Derived from Freedom of thought and expression under Art 18 of ICCPR 1966 and art 19 of UDHR, Art 9 of African Charter on Human and People's Right 1981, Art 13 of American Convention on Human Rights 1969.
36. Derived from Right to protection of Moral and Material Interest under Art 27(2) of UDHR
37. Derived from Right to equality , equal protection before the law and non-discrimination Article 7 of UDHR; Article 2, 3, 14, and 26 of ICCPR 1966.
38. Derived from Right to a standard of living adequate for health and well-being under Article 25 of UDHR.
39. *Ibid.*
40. *Supra* Note 39.
41. Derived from Right to education Article 26 of UDHR, Article 13 and 14 of ICSCER.
42. Derived from Right to approach justice system Art 8 of UDHR.
43. Resolution adopted by the United Nations General Assembly meeting in its 39th session (item no.12-A/res/39/248 dated 16th April 1985.)
44. Joao M.da Silva Miguel (deputy prosecutor general ,Portugal) , *"Tthe role of Public Prosecution in the Protection of Human rights and Public Interests outside the Criminal Law field"*; presentation made at Conference of Prosecutors General of Europe , St. Petersburg from 2-3 July 2008
45. The Council of Europe's 1973 Consumer Protection Charter.
46. Article 3, 4 of 1980 Rome Convention on the Law Applicable to Contractual Obligations.
47. Article 5.2 and 5.3 of Rome Convention 1980 (*ibid*). See also Art 13 of the Brussels Convention .

48. Richard Wassser Storm *"The International Law Association Wars: A conference"* cf. Gokulesh Sharma, "Huiman Rights and Legal Remedies", Deep and Deep Publications Pvt. Ltd., 1st ed., 2003.

49. V. M. Tarkunde J., *"Human Rights in Changing World"*, (*ibid.*)

50. See Zygmunt Bauman *"Post modern Ethics"*, cf Upendra Baxi, *"Voices of Suffering and The Future of Human Rights"*, 8 *Transnat'l L. & Contemp. Probs.* 125.

51. *The Realization of Economic, Social and Cultural rights. Final Report on the Question of the Impunity of Perpetrators of Human Rights Violations (economic, social and cultural rights)*, (prepared by El Hadji Guissé, Special Rapporteur).

52. Self-determination insists that every person has a right to a voice, the right to bear witness to violation, and a right to immunity against "disarticulation" by concentrations of economic, social, and political formations.

53. It means things that speak for themselves.

54. It means that let the buyer be aware.

55. Consumer Protection Act, 1986 (India).

56. *Supra* Note 33.

57. *Ibid.*

58. See Diane F. Orentlicher & Timothy A. Gelatt, *"Public Law, Private Actors: The Impact of Human Rights on Business Investors in China"*, 14, *Nw. J. Int'l L. & Bus.*, 66, 87 (1993).

59. See Barbara Frey, *"The Legal and Ethical Responsibilities of Transnational Corporations in the Protection of International Human Rights"*, 6 Minn. J. Global Trade, 153, 153 (1997); see also Su-Ping Lu, *"Corporate Codes of Conduct and the FTC: Advancing Human Rights through Deceptive Advertising Law"*, 38 Colum. *J. Transnat'l L.*, 603, 606 (2000).

60. *Ibid.*

61. Ann-Marie Erb-Leoncavallo, *"The Road from Seattle"*, UN Chronicle, Jan. 1, 2000 available at 2000 WL 25574281.

62. *Ibid.*

63. *Supra* Note 60.

64. Douglass Cassel, *"Corporate Initiatives: A Second Human Rights Revolution?"*, 19 Fordham *Int'l L.J.* 1963, 1977 (1996) (stating that the logical conclusion of Friedman's view that the only social responsibility of business is to increase profits within the rules of the game is that doing public good is the responsibility of government, not business).

65. Joel Makower, "Beyond the Bottom Line", (1994) cf Erin Elizabeth Macek, *"Scratching the Corporate Back: Why Corporations have No Incentive to Define Human Rights"*, 11 Minn. *J. Global Trade*, 101.

66. Wesley Cragg, "Human Rights and Business Ethics: Fashioning a New Social Contract", at *http:// www.yorku.ca/dreed/cragg.htm* (last visited Nov. 10, 2000) (describing a state's government as the focus of the United Nations Declaration of Human Rights).cf *Supra* Note 65.

67. *Supra* Note 60.

68. The country where the corporation is headquartered can regulate the foreign activities of its corporations. For instance, the United States could apply domestic laws such as

the Fair Labor Standards Act to the activities of U.S. corporations overseas. Criticism levels that it is inadequate for it lacks universality in terms of application.

69. This points to the role that has to be played by an international institution to regulate the regime of human rights. For example, the International Labor Organization (ILO) focuses on the promotion of human rights mainly through developing and monitoring compliance with international labor standards which are in the form of various human rights.

70. There efforts are often limited in terms of effect.

71. Douglass Cassel, "*Corporate Initiatives: A Second Human Rights Revolution?*", 19 Fordham *Int'l L.J.*, 1963, 1977 (1996).

72. *Ibid.*

73. *Supra* Note 65.

74. Thomas F. McMahon, "Socio-Ethical Issues: Two Conceptual Frameworks, in Profit and Responsibility", (Patricia Werhane & Kendall D'Andrade eds., 1985).

75. *Ibid.*

Female Criminality and Prisonisation in Karnataka

NANDINI G. DEVARMANI* & M. G. HUDDAR**

INTRODUCTION

Men and women are born equal; both play a vital role in creation and development of family in particular, and society in general. Inspite of this principle of equality between the two; it is an accepted fact that women all over the world have not only been denied justice; socially, economically and politically; they are used, abused, ill treated, exploited and discarded to lead immoral, vagrant and destitute life. They have been deprived of their due share of reward and respect. Equality is a relative term, but does have philosophical, sociological, economic, legal and political ramifications. In the social context it is understood that "men and women are equal". The Universal Declaration of Human Rights adopted by United Nations General Assembly 1948 claims that all human beings are born free and equal in dignity and rights, for egalitarianism men and women are equal before the law and there should be equality of opportunity.

In the history of mankind at some point we find assertions as "Yatra Naarayasu Poojyante Ramante Tatra Devatah," meaning 'where women are respected, divine grace adores that place'. Women were adored, respected and recognized. She had her own identity and received same respect as that of men. Woman's status today has undergone a drastic change from what it was in the past. A popular saying goes; "Man is born free but everywhere he is in chains" has been crafted keeping a woman in mind. She is born free but is answerable to either her family or society while making important decisions.

Here she doesn't need to fight for equality to prove that she is worthy enough, she should be given more opportunities in various areas so that she is able to show her talent. The status of women in Indian society has changed from time to time; position of women in society is the index to the standard of social organization.

---

* *Research Scholar perusing Ph.D, Department of Criminology & Forensic Science, Karnatak University, Dharwad, Karnataka, (India).*

* *Associate Professor, Karnatak University's Karnatak Science College, Dharwad-580001, Karnataka, (India).*

The term 'status' includes not only personal and proprietary rights but also duties, liabilities and disabilities *vis-à-vis* the society and her family members (Nirupama Prakash). We may study the status of women in India in three phases viz: Ancient, Medieval and Modern period.

In ancient India women enjoyed equal status with men in all fields of life; she received the same education like man. Many Hindu religious books like Vedas, Upanishads, Ramayana, and Mahabharata have mentioned the names of women who were great scholars, poets, philosophers of the time. According to Atharva Veda "the success of a woman in her married life was depended on the training she received during the Brahmacharya". Some of the revered Vedic women are Lopamudra, Viswavara, Sikata, Nivavari Gosha and Aswalayana. Gargi and Maitraye were the great Brahmavadinis who were enriched with deep knowledge of philosophy. The female had the right to select their life partner. In Mahabharata it is mentioned that "The sweet-speeched wives are their husband's friends on the occasion of joy; they are as their (husband's) fathers on occasions of religious acts; and they are as their mothers in hours of illness and woe". It may thus be said that in Vedic phase the status of woman was high.

After the Ancient phase the refulgent golden age of women and all round supreme progress and perfection there was deterioration in the status of women which is referred as the *medieval phase*. It was considered as the 'dark age'. Decline in the status of women in Indian society begins with the Muslim rule in India. Manu, the progenitor of Hindu race, stated that a woman should be kept day and night in subordination by males of the family - woman has to be protected by her father in childhood, by her husband in young age and by the sons in the old age. Social evils like purdah system, sati,, prostitution, child marriage, ban of widow remarriage, practice of jauhar, sexual exploitation of devadasis polygamy were part of social life during this period. Megasthenes opined that "women were treated as a commodity for bargaining and they were sold and purchased freely. The joint ownership of property by both husband and wife prevailing earlier was withdrawn. According to Altekar (1978):"Women were denied the benefits of education, brought up in the authoritarian atmosphere, having no opportunities to develop their natural capacities; women became helpless, illiterate, narrow minded and peevish..."

The position of women in *modern India* has changed significantly in the nineteenth century. India began to discover her long cherished ideals and self consciousness which is popularly known as the period of "Renaissance"- reawakening, process of rediscovery and reform of one self. Raja Ram Mohan Roy is considered as the father of Renaissance. Gandhi (1869) appreciating the qualities of women says that "To call women the weaker sex is a libel; it is mans injustice to women. If by strength is meant moral power, then woman is immeasurably superior to man. Has she not greater intuition? Is she not more self sacrificing? Has she not greater powers of endurance? And has she not greater courage? Without her man could not be. If non-violence is the law of our being, the future is with women. The various women organizations like Bharat Mahila Parishad, Bharat Stri Mahamandal, Women's Indian Association, and National Council for Women and a host of others are working for promoting modern ideals among women. They are also working for working for women education, abolition of social evils, and various awareness programs.

Hindu law reform, moral and material progress of women, equality of rights and opportunities to women for employment in different fields have made the society to treat them equally on par with men. Women's position in modern Indian society is equal to that of men; socially, economically, educationally, politically and legally. Her sufferings from Sati system, Child marriage, and Institution of Temple prostitution no longer exist. Legislations have been brought in force to deal effectively for unfair practices. Now, she has the right to receive education, inherit and own property, participate in public life and political life. She is becoming economically independent. She can seek employment anywhere and has become free from domestic slavery. She is undoubtedly enjoying the equal status with men in all respects. She is protected in every walk of life due to enactment and implementation of various legislations. To name a few legislations are Hindu Remarriage Act 1856, The Child Marriage Restraint Act1929, The Hindu Women Right Property Act 1937, The Hindu Marriage Act 1955,The Hindu Succession Act 1956,Immoral Traffic (Prevention) Act 1956,The Dowry Prohibition Act 1961,Commission of Sati (prevention) Act 1987, Protection of Women from Domestic Violence Act 2005 etc. Women in India in these days are gaining better status, recognition, honour and respect.

In the wake of industrialization, westernization and urbanization, Indian society has been fleeting through drastic and fundamental changes in structures, socio-economic and cultural spheres which resulted in changed physical environment; a new form of economic organization also affected social order, solidarity, and human conduct and thought (Patanaik, 2002). Traditionally women were confined to domestic work, but now are shifted from domestic work to productivity. The women are actively participating in spheres of professional life along with the male counterpart. The urbanization, industrialization, liberalization, globalization, and market friendly policies have increased the employment opportunities to women. Involvement of women in the work outside the house have resulted in some domestic problems due to confusion of roles, misunderstanding between the members of the family specially between husband and wife regarding their roles, status and responsibilities.

Sutherland E H and Donald Cressey (1965) say that "Crime is a social phenomenon." Crime is universal and committed by all sections of the society regardless age, sex, caste, religion and status. In the words of Durkheim crime is a common thing and society cannot be free from it. Since from the period of Cesear Lombroso it was believed by many Criminologists that Women

Criminals are very small proportion of the criminal world. It was Pollock (1950) who by his study stated that the women's participation in criminal activity is equal to that of men but are less brought to the notice due to the reasons like: Crimes committed by women are less likely to be detected; if detected less likely to be reported; if reported they have better chance of avoiding arrest/ conviction due to the double standard role shown to the women.

According to Paul Tappan, (1978) "crime is an intentional act or omission in violation of criminal law (statutory and case law) committed without defence or justification, and sanctioned by the state as a felony or misdemeanor". Further, he states that "Crime is an act of violation of law, and criminal is a person who does an act in violation of law". The concept of crime is an unusually difficult one, since it is difficult to find any definition of crime that does not have a large element of circularity. In general, crimes are committed as events and actions that are prescribed by the criminal law of a particular country. It is not easy to sociologically define crime particularly because of its implicit roots in the concept of crime. Crime is considered as a deviant behaviour, because it is an act of human against prevailing norms of the society. Emile Durkheim (1897) opines that a society without crime is impossibility. Durkheim believes that those who engage in criminal behavior also play a definitely positive role in normal social life. He further states that "Crime is the violation of the rules and regulations enforced by the society from time to time for which definite punishment is prescribed by law". Members in every society are expected to act according to its established norms and laws. But when an individual finds it difficult or impossible to satisfy his wants and desires in a direct and socially acceptable manner, he encounters the alternative of renouncing his motive or attempting to find a substitute satisfaction. When good solutions are not available, he engages himself in anti-social behaviour of criminal nature. According to Lombroso, C (1958) "Women shared many traits with children and that they were morally deficient and their lack of intelligence was the main reason of their relatively small participation in crime" Pollack, O (1961) found that women's involvement in crime was not significantly less than men and women are alleged greater conformity to social order, norms and law is a myth. Freud S (1962) opines that women who are not passive and content with their traditional roles as mothers and wives are maladjusted. Bonger W (1967) believed in the socio- economic determination of female criminality. Crimes committed by women need to be paid more attention because of the pivotal role played by them. Their participation in criminal activities leads continuous deterioration effecting not only to herself but also to her husband and children. The criminality of the women is masked by the role she plays as mother, wife, nurse, care taker etc. The society values this concept and looks sympathetically towards the acts of the women.

With the change in the status of the women due to education and liberty/ freedom, crimes are reported against women and detection of crimes against women goes difficult due to her masked role. Crimes committed by women are usually of domestic or sexual in nature i.e. theft, infanticide, receiving stolen property, poisoning etc. Earlier we could rarely hear of women indulging in economic offences like theft, extortion, robbery, dacoity, smuggling etc, but now it has become common feature to hear the involvement of women in such offences. The increasing crime trend among women not only disturbs the social equilibrium but also makes life difficult to the women folk in general. Therefore, it is most essential to devise ways and means to prevent such crimes.

The individual theories of crime phenomenon have been given by scholars like Sutherland, Freud and Dollard, W.J. Thomas and others. The application of Sutherland's 'Differential Association' theory to women is particularly helpful in emphasizing the criminal behaviour is learnt by interaction with other persons in a process of communication and is not psychologically or biologically determined. Sutherland (1960) thus emphasized on sociological factors which causes to female criminality, explaining individual's crime in terms of her past experiences rather than situations. A few criminologists have used 'Role Theory' in explaining female criminality in terms of sex roles, other than biological or psychological variables (Heidensohn, 1968, Hoffmann Bustamante 1973, Klein, 1973, Rosenblum, 1975).

Eminent experts in the field of criminology have developed various theoretical models on women criminality. Highlighting the strain theory of criminality based on tension or pressure of work; Merton (1949) states that "social structures and society were equally responsible for crime causation". He said that women are prone to commit crimes when they fail to attain 'culturally defined goals' through 'institutional means'. Over emphasis on cultural goals at the expense of institutions means create a tendency towards anomie. Durkheim (1897) while linking crime with social change has viewed that 'crime is a social fact and considered it essential for social change'. Therefore, it is functionally inevitable to the society to tolerate criminality and to find out ways and means to minimize it. Fernald (1920) found that two influences are related to female delinquency i.e. poor economic background, lack of education or training and inferior mentality. Bishop (1931) argued that due to emancipation movement more women became 'criminal minded'. While expanding the biological and psychosomatic condition of female criminality, Fernald (1931) states that "women who turn to crime do so as a form of rebellion against their natural feminine roles and because they are maladjusted to their biological limitations". But liberation model on the other hand argues that liberation is responsible for involving women in criminal activities. It has brought about two things. Firstly, competitive instincts; women are now more assertive, more aggressive and more masculine. Secondly, it has opened up structural opportunity for women to offend.

Taylor (1999) is of the view that the following social changes are responsible for increase in both crime rates and fear of victimization: Job crisis, Crisis of material poverty and social inequality, Fear of falling and fear of others, Crisis of nation and state, Crisis of inclusion and exclusion, Crisis in culture, Crisis of masculinity and gender order, Crisis of family and parenting, and Size of market society. The studies by Silberei and Walper, (1989) have proved that unemployment fosters intra family conflicts and tensions and even violent behavior. Significantly, globalization process with its concomitant (related) integration at economic, technological and cultural levels contribute to the globalization of crime which also appear in the form of terrorism; drug trafficking, money laundering and organized crime with international dimensions.

There are in all 1,155 prisons in India. These prisons are categorized as Central Jails, District Jails, Sub - Jails, Borstal Institutions/Juvenile Jails, open Jails/Camps/Farms, Women's Jails, and some specialized Institutions The Karnataka state has a total of 100 prisons with an authorized total capacity of 12213 prisoners. Out of which 923 are female prisoners and 11290 are male prisoners. Central Prison Bijapur is the oldest one and dates back to 1593 A.D. constructed during the regime of Adil Shah; Ramanagara Sub Jail is of 18th century and was built in 1783 A.D. and 25 Jails are of 19th Century.

Karnataka is one of the pioneering state to introduce production of UTPs through the Video Conferencing System from the date of inception of the Video Conferencing facilities i.e., from April 2003 up to December 2008, 1,51,317 under trial prisoners (both men and women) were produced before the Courts thus effecting savings of about Rs. 3,35,64,915.00. Prisons in Karnataka are classified as Central Prisons, District Prisons, District Head Quarter Sub-Jails, and Special Sub-Jails. There are eight central prisons, thirteen district prisons, four District Head Quarter Sub-Jails, two Special Sub- Jails, and seventy Taluka Sub- Jails. Out of these 29 sub-jails are functioning under department control and 41 are functioning under revenue department control. There is one Borstal School, one Jail and one Open Air Jail. The Borstal School at Dharwad till recently was functioning only as Borstal School and also a place to detain the undertrials; but now, this institution is also functioning as a Central Prison.

CRIME AND WOMEN

Opening the door on the subject of Women Prisoners is like standing at the threshold of an immense dark chambers cracking down with pain, but with hope of protest which will hinder the increasing rate of crime in turn the women prisoners.

Elizabeth Windschuttle (1981) found that women who live in restrictive, more anonymous urban environments, who are more independent of the male protectors but more dependent on the labour market and thus are more subject to the vagaries of the industrial economy, are more likely to turn to crime. According to her finding, women criminality was more in the urban areas than rural areas. Women criminality also accounted for a much higher proportion of the total crime in the city than in the countryside. Sohoni (1989) found that 60 per cent of women criminals belong to the age group of 22 to 41 years, while those below 22 years and above 41 years accounted for 20 per cent each; 93.33 per cent were married. Nagla (1991) revealed that 60 per cent female offenders belong to the age-group of 30 to 50 years. The study conducted by him showed that a large number of female offenders are young and adult at the time of committing crimes, which means that the interpersonal relations in the family after marriage create adjustment problems for women and sometimes force them to indulge in deviant behaviour. Saxena (1994) found that women offenders had stressful relations with their husbands. Their marital life had undergone severe conflicting situations involving oppression, cruelty, rejection and humiliation. Adultery by husband, his illicit affairs with other women, his immoral behaviour contributed significantly as a motivating factor among the married women to resort to crimes of murderous violence. The majority of the women offenders convicted for homicidal activities were poorly adjusted to the family settings.*The studies conducted by the researcher revealed that* 28 % of women belong to the age group of 30-40 years who comprise the maximum number followed by the age group 20-30 who are of 25 % .The study showed that there is equal participation of the women belonging to the age group 40-50 & 50-60 which is of 20 %.The remaining 7 % are the women above 60 years.

Women Prisoners – A Review: Women prisoners suffer from greater disabilities than men. The psychological stress caused by separation from children, the unhelpful attitude of close relatives, uncertainty about the future are all factors which make their life miserable in jail. The All India Committee on Jail Reforms, (1980-83) observed that "women in prison, as we have witnessed during our visits to various jails in different States and Union Territories suffer from unhealthy living conditions, exploitation, unnecessary prolonged severance from their families and lack of gainful and purposeful employment." The Committee laid emphasis on training of custodial staff in prisons to handle women prisoners with a reformative attitude. Finally, the Expert Committee on 'Women Prisoners' constituted by the Government of India in 1986-87 under the Chairmanship of Mr. Justice V.R.Krishna Iyer made a number of very useful recommendations for women prisoners and suggested a National Policy for Custodial Justice for Women. It laid particular emphasis on the need for adoption of a specialized approach towards handling, treatment and rehabilitation of women prisoners. The various dimensions of women and crime have recently been developed into a broad field of research in the areas of Social Work, Sociology, Criminology and Women Studies. Starting from Pollak (1950), Smith (1962), Sharma (1965), Ahuja (1969), Eliott and Voss (1974), Elizabeth Windshuttle (1981), Nagla (1982), Rani (1983), Khosh (1986) Joseph (1992), Saxena (1994), etc. are notable researchers who could contribute to the knowledge of women and crime. The Supreme Court outlined seven guidelines to come to the aid of women in custody, viz., exclusive police lock-ups for female suspects, interrogation of women prisoners in the presence of a female police officer, arrestee being informed of the grounds of arrest immediately, provision for legal aid, surprise visits to police lock-ups, communication to the nearest relatives or friends of arrested women, immediate enquiry by the Magistrate about any torture meted out to the woman arrestee and her right to medical examination etc. All these have become a part of the law itself.

As on 31st January 2009 there are 573 women prisoners in Karnataka out of which 177 are convicts, 379 undertrials 16 arrested under NDP'S Act and 1 under TADA. There are 30 children (17 male and 13 female) below the age of 6 years staying with their mothers. Government of Karnataka has accorded the sanction to establish a separate prison for women at Tumkur and it is yet to start functioning.

Facilities provided to the women prisoners - According to Wines. F (1919) "The most terrible moment in a convict's life is not that in which prison door closes upon her, shutting her out of the world, but that in which it opens to admit of her to return to the world, having lost her character and standing among women, having suffered for months or years from the deprivation of pleasure to which she was accustomed, and having little if any money in her pocket to meet necessary expenses." Women prisoners are provided with the facilities of maintaining contacts with their families through letters, visits from relatives. They are also permitted to go on leave on specific occasions. Apart from these facilities the other facilities like radio; TV, cassette player etc. are also provided to the women prisoners for their recreation in some prisons. Suitable clothing including sanitary pads are provided to the women prisoners along with the adequate quantity of washing and toilet soaps in order to maintain proper cleanliness and hygiene while in prisons.

Education: According to Tappan, P. (1951) "The objective of prison education in its broadest sense should be the socialization of the inmates through varied impressional and expressional activities with emphasis on individual inmate's needs. The objective of this programme shall be the return of these inmates to society with a desire to conduct themselves as good citizens and with the skill and knowledge which will give them a reasonable chance to maintain themselves and their dependents through honest labour".

In order to achieve the above objective the prison education in prisons of Karnataka is framed to acquire:

- Fundamental academic education designed to provide intellectual tools and training.
- Vocational educational designed to give training for an occupation.
- Health education designed to create awareness regarding personal and community hygiene.

- Cultural education for intellectual and aesthetic satisfaction.
- Social education for reformation and help the prisoner to adjust with the society after the release.

In different prisons of Karnataka it is observed that no restriction is imposed on prisoner for reading the books. The prisoners are allowed to use material for their recreation or improvement of their skills and development of personality including their capacity to pursue education while in jail. They can pursue their studies through open universities and classes are being conducted inside the prisons to educate the illiterate prisoners. Prisoners have enrolled for various courses through IGNOU (Indira Gandhi National Open University) and get through in the respective courses. The budgetary provisions are made to the effect in the prison budget. Fifty nine prisoners have enrolled for different higher education courses like B.A, M.A, Diploma in Journalism, Post Graduate Diploma in Business Administration from 2005 to 2007 and Rs. 1, 93,055.00 is paid towards the fees. Bangalore University has started a novel programme to impart formal education to prisoners in distance mode. The Directorate of Distance Education and correspondence courses of Bangalore University in association with prisons department has taken the responsibility of extending benefits of its different courses to 500 prisoners free of cost. The university started this scheme in October 2006. This scheme is implemented it in Bangalore, Belgaum, Gulbarga, Bellary and Bijapur. According this programme prisoner may pursue their studies and enroll to different Graduation and Post Graduation Courses. Apart from the above, they are also provided with daily newspapers, periodicals, magazines in all the regional languages along with TV/Radio and World Space Radio for their recreation and as well as to link their mind with outside society. Suvarna Akshara Andolana and Akshara Kalika Sibhira in coordination with District Literacy Committee 18 day's literacy camps Adult Education Programme, English Teaching Camp, have been organized for the benefit of inmates at central prison.

	2006	*2007*
Elementary Education	473	633
Adult Education	612	798
Higher Education	16	43
Computer Course	7	11

Food and medical care: The female prisoners are served cooked nutritious food as per the scale prescribed in the Prison Manual 1978 and Rules and the children of women prisoners are also provided the food as per the scale recommended by the Medical Officer depending on their age. On the festival day they are served with special extra diet. Inmates are provided with good medical facilities and treatment with suitable medical diet to the sick prisoners on the recommendation of the medical officer. The sick prisoners who are in need of higher medical investigation, care, treatment and surgery are referred to higher medical centers for specialized treatment. In major jail's minilabs, Urinary Analysis kits, Ophthalmic Scopes, X-ray and ECG machines are set up for better medical treatment of sick female prisoners. Ambulance vans are also maintained to take serious sick prisoners to the out side hospitals round the clock. Besides the medical facilities as enumerated above, Health Camps are organized every month with the help of non-governmental organizations such as Rotary Club and Lions Club. So far health camps are organized on screening of tuberculosis, eye camp, dental camp and hearing aid to the needy prisoners. The prisoners who are in need of the treatment for skin disease, gastro, ENT, Cardiac, Ortho and HIV are also taken care and the necessary treatment is provided to them.

Extra Nutritious food to the Lactating and Pregnant women prisoners. Extra clothing to the women prisoners. Nutritious diet to the children's with women prisoners of age group 0-6 years. Issue of clothing, bedding and utensils etc to the children's with women prisoners. Amendment to the Rule 86 of Karnataka Prison Rules 1974. Incorporation of a new chapter- for treatment of Children and Pregnant and Lactating Women Prisoners in Karnataka Prison Manual 1978.The daily average jail population during the past 3 years and average cost per prisoner are as under:

Year	*Avg. No. of Convicts*	*Avg. No. of Under trials*	*Average cost per prisoner per annum (In Rupees)*	*Avg. Adm. cost per prisoner per day (In Rupees)*	*Avg cost for food per day per prisoner (in Rupees)*
2005-06	3905	7995	37538.99	102.84	16.65
2006-07	3952	8489	31532.56	86.39	22.68
2007-08	3933	9224	35911.688	98.388	23.64

Training: The purpose of prison labour are

- To develop discipline and help the inmates to lead self disciplined life
- To maintain both - physical and mental health of the inmates
- To make the prisoners fit to earn their livelihood after their release
- To give a punitive value for punishment.

Training in Knitting, Tailoring, Embroidery, Basket making, Dress designing, Fabric Painting, Candle Making, Agarbatti manufacturing, bag making, preparation of bakery products, leaf cup making, Midwife and Home Nursing Training etc., are given by the jail authorities in association with Non Governmental Organizations. Sewing machines have been issued to jails under modernization of prison administration.

Legal Assistance : In coordination with the District Legal Services Authorities, Free Legal Aid Camps have been organized regularly in the jails to bring legal awareness among the prison inmates and also to assist them to defend their cases with a view to provide Legal Services to the prison inmates, a Legal Service Center has been started at Central Prison, Bangalore in association with Karnataka State Legal Service Authority, District Legal Service Authority, Bangalore Rural and Bangalore Advocates Association.

Counseling – Counseling is done by NGOs both individually and in groups, allowing prisoners to bring out their inner feeling of anger and hate to enable them to accept the realities of their present situation in life, giving them hope and courage to face the challenges in their future life.

Recreation – Periodical meditation courses, cultural programmes, recreation through TV/ Radio, etc., legal aid to the needy prisoners, better toilets, Hygiene facilities in the barracks, providing hot water, separate kitchen to cook their food. Literacy programmes, to the children of women prisoners in coordination with the NGO's are some of the important reformative measures adopted by the department for improving the living conditions of prisoners. Prisoners are also trained in theatre art and also encouraged to stage dramas. Measures have been taken to incorporate in the jail routine to facilitate the inmates to reform and rehabilitate themselves as good citizens on their release. To make the inmate economically self-dependent training is given to them in various vocational and trade crafts and brings out their latent skills.

Rehabilitation of Released Inmates: According to the All India Committee on jail reforms 1980-83 "The women offenders in India face peculiar problems of rehabilitation during their post release period. Indian social customs make women ex-offenders more vulnerable.

The details of premature release during the past three years are as under:

	No. of prisoners released				
Year	*M*	*F*	*T*	*Occasion*	*Date of Release*
2004	91	4	95	Republic day Celebration on 26-1-2004	26-1-2004
2005	51	6	57	Republic day Celebration	26.01.2005
	102	4	106	Independence Day Celebration	15.08.2005
2006	57	4	61	Republic day Celebration	26.01.2006
	297	12	309	Independence Day Celebration	15-08-2006
Total	598	30	628		

Karnataka State Government was pleased to order for premature release of 309 well behaved convict prisoners on the occasion of Suvarna Karnataka on 15.8.2006. Out of the 309 prisoners, 251 prisoners have been identified by the SC & ST Development Corporation Ltd, Backward Classes Development Corporation Ltd and Minority Development Corporation Limited for granting them the financial assistances under different schemes and facilitate them to be economically self reliant in their post released life. Out of the 251 prisoners, 106prisoners have been sanctioned loans amounting to Rs. 22, 73,455.00 as detailed below:

Name of the Corporation	*No. of Beneficiaries*	*Total Loan Amount Sanctioned*
Karnataka Minorities Development Corporation Ltd.	16	Rs. 3,55,705.00
D DevRaj Urs Backward Classes Development Corporation Ltd.	51	Rs. 13,44,550.00
Dr. B. R. Ambedkar Development Corporation Ltd.	39	Rs. 5,73,200.00
Total	106	Rs. 22,73,455.00

3 female prisoners who have been released prematurely has got appointment as Anganwadi Workers and Assistants.

OBSERVATIONS

After visiting all the eight central prisons of Karnataka the information collected was analysed on the bases of the social background of the inmates considering the age-wise distribution, educational status, religion, marital status, place of residence. The analysis reveals that 28 % of women belong to the age group of 30-40 years who comprise the maximum number followed by the age group 20-30 who are of 25 % .The study showed that there is equal participation of the women belonging to the age group 40-50 & 50-60 which is of 20 %.The remaining 7 % are the women above 60 years.

Since, majority of the women prisoners are young, it is interesting to concentrate on their educational status. It is understood that the educational status plays a vital role in the study as it is found to be very much influential in terms of attitude.

As we know that India is still a developing country, and Karnataka though ranked fourth in the literacy level in our country we find 55 % of the women convicts are illiterate. 18 % are below SSLC 17 % passed SSLC, 4 %completed PUC, 3 % graduates and 3 % are technical graduates. The analysis clearly shows the part played by education in making women criminal and shaking the base of the family is handled by the women. The maximum numbers of women prisoners belong to the Hindu religion are 83%. The respondents belonging to Muslim and Christian religion are about10 % and 7% respectively. The analysis of the place of residence of the respondents depicts that majority of respondents reside in rural areas, 73 and 27 per cent residing in urban area. Place of origin and place of residence are also influential factors in moulding an individual's character and behaviour.

The marital status of the respondents as per the analysis shows that 93 per cent of the respondents are married. Only 7 per cent of the respondents are unmarried. This clearly shows that the married woman, due to the family responsibility, over burden of work, and adjustment problems and ill treatment by in-laws develop frustration and conflict in her by which she take the extreme step to commit suicide or she may commit crime on others.

The economic profile of the respondents is analysed by the occupation of the respondent. A majority of the respondents were housewives who comprised of the 39 percentage followed by the women working as coolie 30%. It was amazing to find a specific group of women i.e. women working in the Garment sector formed 8%. Apart from these groups the researcher has found government employees 6% and women who carried on other business were 17%.

One of the important analysis made by the researcher was to know the sections under which the respondents were convicted which also pictured the grievousness of the crime committed by the women. The study showed most of the crimes committed by women were covered under Sec. 302 IPC44%, followed by Sec.498 IPC 11%, Sec. 309 IPC 6% Sec. 448 IPC 6%, Sec 120B IPC 4%, Sec. 395IPC 4 %, Sec. 380 IPC 4%, 3% each of Sec. 392, 364,149, 397 and 1.5% each were under Sec. 342, 304, 409, 138, 307, 427, 396 IPC.

The above analysis clearly shows that women criminals though in small number compared to men are involved in cognizable crime which is the point to be taken into consideration.

SUGGESTIONS

The following measures may be implemented either as preventive steps to curb crime as well as to help women criminals to alter their life in a wholesome approach at all levels.

Since, majority of prisoners belong to the middle aged group, they can be easily redeemed through counseling. They have the stamina and strength to work hard, the details of job opportunities and small business avenues may be explained to them and necessary help may be extended to them through prison aid societies.

- Measures may be taken for free and compulsory education to the girls and also provide adult education to the adult women. Lectures on moral, ethical, and human values be arranged at regular intervals to convert the mind of the convicted persons that crime does not pay.
- Since majority of the prisoners are married, counseling may be given to the members of the inmate's family to treat the woman with respect and dignity after her return from the prison.
- Awareness should be created among the rural people about the severe consequences of commission of crime and its adverse impact on the family.

- Women prisoners - like men - should be informed of their rights under the law. On being brought to the prison, the arrested women must be informed of the grounds of arrest and communication in that respect should also be sent to the nearest relatives of arrested women.
- Women prisoners should also be allowed to contact their families and communicate with their lawyers, women social workers, and voluntary organizations.
- Women Voluntary Organizations should be encouraged to be associated with women prisoners to express the problems they facing in the jails.
- Separate jails should be provided for women.
- The hardened criminals should not be clubbed with other inmates
- The prison administration should associate the students of Law Colleges to render legal assistance to women, follow-up cases for bail and other procedures to get relief from the courts.
- The prisoners should be aware of the amount earned by them and, they should have bank accounts where the amount earned by them during the conviction period could be deposited and they should be provided pass book of their bank accounts.
- Measures like premature release/remission of sentences of women prisoners suffering from serious ailments like Cancer, AIDS, TB, mental breakdown and depression and those above 60 years of age should be implemented.

CONCLUSION

Criminality among women is viewed as a serious problem and is on an increasing trend. The study reflected that the women criminals are generally young, married and illiterate and are of poor socio-economic background. It is also found that the main causes for their criminality are maladjustment in the family, emotional frustration, confusion of roles, and sense of insecurity. The study also revealed that the stress situation in the family influences on the criminality by the women. Free and compulsory education, awareness about the harmful consequences of criminality, Moral and ethical lectures, family counseling are some measures which may help in the reduction of criminality among women in general.

References

Ahuja, Ram(1969), "Female Offenders in India", India: Meenakshi Prakashan, Meerut.

Anderson, C. M. (1967), "The Female Criminal Offender", *American Journal of Correction*, Vol. 29, No. 6.

Ashish Virk & Aman A. Cheema (2009), Gendering Criminology to Discern Other Genders Criminality: An Analysis of Jagged Justice Behind Bars in a Lone Women Jail of State of Punjab, Ludhiana.

Bonger, A.W. (1916), "Criminality and Economic Conditions", Boston: Little Brown & Co.

Chadha, Kumkum (1983), "The Indian Jail: A Contemporary Document", Vikas Publishing House, New Delhi.

Chattoraj, B. N. (2000), " A Study on Children of Women Prisoners in Indian Jails", National Institute of Criminology and Forensic Sciences, Delhi.

Devasia,V.V. and Devasia, L. (1982), Prison as a Treatment Institution, *Nagpur Times*, Nov.. 9th.

Indian Journal of Human Rights and the Law. Vol. 6, No. 1-2, Jan.-Dec. 2009, ISSN: 0973-0818.

Ghosh, S. K. (1984), "Women in a Changing Society", New Delhi, Ashish Publishing House.

Ghosh, S. (1986), "Female Criminals in India", New Delhi, Uppal Publishing House.

Kawale, K. G. (1982), "Nature of Crimes Committed by Women in Nanded Readings in Criminology", News Bulleting, ISC, Calcutta.

Karnataka Prison Manual 1978 - Published by Government of Karnataka.

Madan, G. R. (1978), "Social Change and Problems of Development in India". Bombay: Allied Publishers Private Limited.

Orland, L. (1975), "Prison: Houses of Darkness", New York: The Free Press.

Sanyal, S. (1975), "An Empirical Study of Certain Personality Characteristics & Attitudes of 25 Female Convicts of Nari Bandi Niketan, Lucknow", *Social Defence*, Vol. XI, No. 41, July.

Sharma, R. K. (1965), "Women Offender of U.P.: A Psychological Social Study of Women Convicts and Undertrials Prisoners in U.P. Jails", Unpublished Ph.D. Thesis, Lko. University.

Sutherland, E. H. (1939), "Principles of Criminology", Lippincott.

Reports

Report of National Expert Committee on Women Prisoners, 1986-87.

Report of the All India Jail Reforms Committee, 1980-83.

Report of the Indian Jails Committee, 1919.

Report of the Women's Jail Committee, 1946.

Report of the All India Jail Manual Committee, 1955.

Report of the Jail Reforms Committee, Maharashtra, 1948. 9. Report of the Jail Reforms Commission, Rajasthan, 1964.

Women Behind Bars and their Rights – An Evaluation

NANDINI G. DEVARMANI* & M. G. HUDDAR**

INTRODUCTION

Traditionally, the Indian woman has been the foundation stone of the family and society in general. She creates life, nurtures it, guards and strengthens it. She plays various roles, as mother, as wife - committed to serve the family, but she is also its center, for it is through her that the family is perpetuated and in this lies the pride of her status in society at large. She is the transmitter of tradition, the instrument by which Indian culture is preserved. If the foundation is not solid or carefully maintained by those responsible for her protection, not merely the family but the society itself is bound to crack and dismember. Modernization, industrialization and urbanization have been invoked to account for the upsurge of female delinquency because they correlate closely with each other. As urbanization increases traditional roles decrease with increased mobility, people loose stability and continuous personal relationships are disrupted. There is a great need to study women in crime because the place and role of women in the Indian society has undergone considerable changes during the last two decades leading to a greater participation in the criminal activities by them.

Concept of Human Rights : Other than the basic human needs, which have now been included in the arena of right to life under the Indian constitution due to the brilliant humanistic judgments of the Supreme Court, right to life, also enables a person to avail the guarantee of protection in cases of criminal justice administration. The said humanistic approach has not stopped to the basic necessities of life like right to live with dignity, right to education, health, labour welfare etc., but it has also highlighted the other essential rights to live a dignified human life. The right to life includes the right to justice which

* *Research Scholar perusing Ph.D, Department of Criminology & Forensic Science, Karnatak University, Dharwad, Karnataka, (India).*

* *Associate Professor, Karnatak University's Karnatak Science College, Dharwad-580001, Karnataka, (India).*

includes fair trial. The human rights afforded to an individual are not a favour done to him but a matter of norm accepted in a civil society.

The Constitution of India is one of the most rights-based constitutions in the world. Drafted around the same time as the Universal Declaration of Human Rights (1948), the Indian Constitution captures the essence of human rights in its Preamble, and the sections on Fundamental Rights and the Directive Principles of State Policy. The constitution of India aims to establish a modern, developed egalitarian, democratic policy where every citizen enjoys a good life with ample opportunities for personal growth and well being. It guarantees fundamental rights to its citizens based on the rule of law. In jurisprudence and law, a right is the legal entitlement to do/refrain from doing something or to obtain/refrain from obtaining an action, thing or recognition in civil society. Rights serve as rules of interaction between people and as such they place constraints and obligations upon the actions of individuals/groups. Modern conception of rights are universalistic and egalitarian (Rights Wikipedia 2008). Human rights refer to the basic rights of freedom to which all humans are entitled without any discrimination of caste, creed, age, sex etc. Karl Vasak (Human Rights Wikipedia 2008) opines that there are three generations of human rights ,the first generation includes civil and political rights, second economic, social and cultural rights and third generation solidarity rights such as the right to peace and clean environment (ibid)[Indian Journal of Gender studies, 16:2 (2009): 253-271] India is a State signatory to various International instruments of human rights, like the Universal Declaration of Human Rights which states that: "No one shall be subject to torture or cruel, inhuman or degrading treatment of punishment" and the United Nations Covenant on Civil and Political Rights which states in part: "All persons deprived of their liberty shall be treated with humanity and with respect for the inherent dignity of the human person". Therefore, both under national as well as international human rights law, the state are obliged to uphold and ensure basic human rights.

Article 14 of the Indian constitution says that the state shall not only deny to any person equality before the law or the equal protection of laws within the territory of India. This Article is further strengthened/supported by Article 15 & 16. Article 39 contains certain principles of policy to be followed by the state in particular, direct its policy towards securing - that the citizen's men and women equally have the right to an adequate means of livelihood and that there is equal pay for equal work for both men and women. Women's rights have been a social problem rather than a problem of sex. The image of women as frivolous sex object has changed to some extent when their involvement in the workforce has become indispensable. But when they really engaged themselves in the workforce they started facing problems of discrimination and inequalities which was visible in jobs, pay etc. and was also found deeply rooted in our cultural definitions of males and females.

Women in revolt – A women having identity of her own is a concept totally alien to Indian culture. A woman with superior educational qualification threatens the masculinity of man. It has been observed that a position which brings a woman more remuneration than the husband is generally a disaster for domestic happiness. The main role of the traditional female is how to be at the service of the emotional and physical needs of others – mainly those of children, husband and elders. The wishes and feelings of others are prior over her own .Change is possible, not inevitable, change must be won against the inertia of past traditions and this course is precisely what motivates the contemporary Indian women. When the entire social, cultural, Political, educational. Economic, legal and religious milieu is steeped overwhelmingly in the tradition of women's total subjugation to men, when our atrocious cultural traditions continue to stand as a Himalayan peak, which women are mere objects for pleasure there can be no hope for a positive change in the condition of women. The position of women especially in urban areas has changed drastically after independence. The image of women has changed tremendously since 1980's. Modernisation and industrialization transformed the process of the socio-economic environment. Sonalde Desai (1985) in Gender Inequalities and Demographic Behavior asserts that "parents' reluctance to educate daughters has its roots in the situation of women. Parents have several incentives for not educating their daughters. Foremost is the view that education of girls brings no returns to parents and that their future roles, being mainly reproductive and perhaps including agricultural labor, require no formal education. As more and more boys are engaged in education, there is a growing reliance on the labor of girls. Girls are increasingly replacing their brothers on the farm while carrying on their usual responsibilities in housework. A large proportion of the roughly 40 million "nonworking" girls who are not in school are kept at home because of responsibilities in housework." Women work longer hours and their work is more arduous than men's. Still, men report that "women, like children, eat and do nothing." Women work roughly twice as many as many hours as men. Women's contribution to agriculture - whether it is subsistence farming or commercial agriculture - when measured in terms of the number of tasks performed and time spent, is greater than men. "The extent of women's contribution is aptly highlighted by a micro study conducted in the Indian Himalayas which found that on a one-hectare farm, a pair of bullocks' works 1,064 hours, a man 1,212 hours and a woman 3,485 hours in a year." Women's work is rarely recognized.

RIGHTS OF PRISONERS

Karnataka is one of the progressive states where attempts have been made for reforming the Jail administration. Considerable strides have been made towards achieving objectives of Reformation, Correction and Rehabilitation of Prison inmates and transforming the prison into curative centers. Prisoners' rights have become important from the viewpoint of prison reforms which is due to two important principles. *Firstly,* the prisoner "is no longer regarded as an object, a ward, or a 'slave of the state', who the law would leave at the prison entrance and who would be condemned to 'civil death'." It is recognized that a citizen does not cease to be a citizen just because he has become a prisoner. The Supreme Court has made it very clear in many judgments that except for the fact that the compulsion to live in a prison entails by its own force the deprivation of certain rights, like the right to move freely or to practice a profession of ones choice, a prisoner is otherwise entitled to the basic freedoms guaranteed by the Constitution. *Secondly,* the convicted persons go to prisons as punishment and not for punishment. Prison sentence has to be carried out as per court's orders and no additional punishment can be inflicted by the prison authorities without sanction. Prison authorities have to be, therefore, accountable for the manner in which they exercise their custody over persons in their care, especially as regards their wide discretionary powers.

FACTS AND MYTHS OF RIGHTS OF ACCUSED.

(I) *Constitutional rights :* Article 14, 15, 20, 21, 22.

(II) *Rights under CrPC:* 1973 and Indian Evidence Act 1872.

*Right to grounds of arrest - Sec. 50, 55 & 75.*Right of being produced before a magistrate - Sec. 56,76 *No unnecessary restraint 49 *Right to be examined by medical practitioner - 54 *Right to counsel *Statement to police not to be signed- use of statement in evidence - 162 CrPC *Right to trial in presence *Right to public trials *Interpretation of Evidence to the accused ?her pleader - 279(1) *Accused person to be competent witness - 315(1) *No influence to be used to induce disclosure - 316 *Magistrate may dispense with personal attendance of accused - 205 *Right of being presumed innocent through out the trial - 105 of Indian Evidence Act 1872 *Burden of proof - 101 *Recording of confession and statements *Release of accused when evidence deficient- 169 *Transfer on application of the accused - 191 *Supply copy of police report and other documents to the accused - 207 *Framing of charge - 228 & 240(2) *Sentence hearing *Right to produce and examine defense witnesses *Record of evidence in absence of accused - 299 *Right against double jeopardy.*Right of sanction for prosecution *Release of lunatic pending investigation of trial- 328 & 329 *Right to cross examine prosecution witnesses- 137, 138, 141, 142, 143.145 Indian Evidence Act .*Right to witnesses her own hostile witness - 154 Indian Evidence Act .*Right to bail - 436 & 437 CrPC *Judgment copy to be given to accused after judgment and right to appeal–363 & 382.

The object of legal system is to punish the guilty and protect the innocent. While punishing the criminals is necessary, their reform after imprisonment is equally if not more necessary, in order to prevent them from turning to crime again. It is necessary to build a suitable environment in jails to provide opportunities to the prisoners to reform themselves and change their mindset so that after their release from prison, they are prevented from venturing again towards the world of crime out of either force or compulsion of circumstances or lack of choice. Effort should be geared up to ensure that the released prisoner rather compensates for earlier wrongs by making a positive contribution towards the society's members. Maxims that "every saint has a past and every sinner has a future" and that "hate the sin and not the sinner" are well known and well founded. Reforming prisoners is not a mere ideal but has become an integral part of their Right to Life and is also necessary from the point of view of larger public interest. Reforms like providing vocational training, legal awareness camps, yoga, chanting and meditation sessions for physical, psychological and spiritual - upliftment, rehabilitation counseling have proved to bring positive results and need greater emphasis. The Supreme Court has observed in a catena of judgments that the purpose of prisons is not to avenge but to reform. Some of the prisoner's rights are:

- Right to free legal services and other statutory rights such as bail, parole etc.
- Right of prisoners to access to a prisoners' handbook in local language to be informed of their legal rights and placing of a grievance box in premises to enable prisoners to express their grievances.
- Right to food, hygiene, healthcare, clothing, protection against torture and vices, parole, visits by relatives and quicker justice.
- Right to opportunity for interviews with legal advisor of choice.
- Duty of District Magistrates and Sessions Judges to visit prisons and listening to and remedying and grievances of the prisoners, including approaching the High Court or Supreme Court where appropriate.
- Constitution of Visitors' Board to ensure that prisoners are up to date with cross section of latest developments in society, Sessions Judge should be given acknowledged position as a visitor and not as a casual visitor.
- Separating place of hardened criminals and juvenile delinquents.
- Providing religious teachings in jails.
- Right to drug therapy instead of chaining system for prisoners who are unruly or not physically controllable.
- Duty of State to ensure that Mental health Authority established and all steps provided in the Mental Health Act, 1987 to be implemented.
- Protect rights of pregnant women and children born to or accompanying female prisoners under incarceration.
- Right to equitable wages for prison labour and constitution of welfare fund for victims.

- Right of prisoners to approach High Court or Supreme Court under Art. 226/32 and Art. 21 for enforcement of their fundamental rights through a simple letter itself and for filing contempt petition in case of violation of the courts' orders 34.

The *International Covenant on Economic, Social and Cultural Rights (ICESC)* recognizes the right of everyone to the enjoyment of the highest attainable standard of physical and mental health. The UN Committee on Economic, Social and Cultural Rights has described this right as: "An inclusive right extending not only to timely and appropriate health care but also to the underlying determinants of health, such as access to safe and potable water and adequate sanitation, an adequate supply of safe food, nutrition and housing, healthy occupational and environmental conditions, and access to health-related education and information, including on sexual and reproductive health".

The UN Standard Minimum Rules for Treatment of Prisoners recommends measures to safeguard prisoners' health with regard to accommodation, personal hygiene, clothing and bedding, food, medical services, discipline and punishment, work and education and recreation. Prison overcrowding endangers the basic rights of prisoners, including the right to an adequate standard of living and the right to the highest attainable standards of physical and mental health. These are guaranteed by Article 25 of Universal Declaration of Human Rights and Articles 11 and 12 of the International Convent on Economic Social and Cultural Rights.

Even though right to life under Indian constitution has been broaden enough to include wide prison rights to the prisoners, unfortunate situation still prevails in the area of women prisoners. The Prison Act and the Prison Rules do talk about the segregation of the convicts on gender basis and certain rights to women convicts, yet the area needs special attention Prisoners in a jail are of three kinds: - (a) convicts (b) under trials. (c) Detunes under preventive laws. They are human being and the mere fact that they have been convicted in a criminal case which is pending in a court of law does not mean that they have lost all their constitutional rights or their basic and elementary rights as human beings.

Some of these rights which are based on Article 14 and 21 of the Constitution are:

1. Right against solitary confinement [Sunil Batra - 1978 (4) SSC 494].
2. Right against iron fetters on the legs [Charles Shobraj 1978(4) SSC 104].
3. Right against handcuffing (Prem Shanker Shukla 1980 3 SSC526).
4. Right against custodial violence (Shela Barse 1983 2 SSC 96).
5. Delayed Execution of death Sentence (Vaheeswaran 1983 2 SSC 68).
6. Custodial Death (1995 4 SSC 262; D.K. Basu 1997 1 SCC 416).
7. Medical aid hygienic living conditions, dean drinking water and food.

The Supreme Court issued directions regarding the procedure to be followed when a person is arrested. The Court refereed to the National Police Commission's finding that 60% of all arrests were either unnecessary or unjustified and laid down requirements to be strictly followed i.e.

(i) The right of the arrested person to request that a friend, relative or other persons be informed of his arrest and the place where he is detained.

(ii) The duty of the police officer to inform the arrested person of this right.

(iii) An entry to be made in the police station diary as to who was informed of the arrest.

(iv) The duty of the Magistrate before whom the arrested person is produced, to satisfy himself that these requirements have been complied with.

(v) A police officer making an arrest should record in the case diary the reasons for making the arrest, implying there by that every arrest by the police has to be justified.

The *Mulla Committee, the National Police Commission, Justice Krishna Iyer's Committee, and the National Human Rights Commission* have made various valuable recommendations to bring about not only improvements and reform in the jail administration but in the entire criminal justice system itself. Unless there are ample reforms of the criminal justice, change is not possible. The present status pictures severe damage caused to basic humanitarian considerations, the rule of law and public confidence in the entire system has been shaken. The results are that the society is disturbed by losing faith in the system of justice which has led to a major threat to a free and democratic society The courts in India have also laid down specific rules end guidelines in regard to matters like the right to physical protection; protection against physical assault ; restrictions on handcuffing and bar fetters ; on solitary confinement ; the right to a speedy trail (in Hussainara Khattum's case) Sheela Barse (AIR 1983 SC 378),; freedom of expression; and press interviews etc.The Supreme Court on 13th April 2006 has delivered a set of guidelines to protect the rights of women prisoners and their children in jail asking the Centre and state governments to amend and incorporate the new directions within three months. Among the important guidelines, the apex court directed the authorities that pregnant under trials should be taken to hospitals outside the jail premises for delivery and the birth certificate of the child should not mention jail as the place of birth. Ensuring that the children of women prisoners are not condemned, a bench comprising Chief Justice Y K Sabharwal, Justice C K Thakker and Justice P K Balasubramaniyan directed the authorities to follow its guidelines in letter and spirit so that the fundamental rights of children to education and healthy living are not violated when they are staying with their under trial or convicted mother in the jail.

Prisoners Rights: Some Landmark Judgements

Recently we have witnessed an increasing consciousness about the popularity of prison reforms, it is now being recognized that a reformative philosophy and a rehabilitative strategy must become a part of prison justice.

Maneka Gandhi's case was a landmark in Indian jurisprudence. The Maneka principle was extended to prison conditions and particularly to the plight of under-trials.

The Supreme Court again in a separate writ petition filed by Sunil Batra and Charles Sobharaj, two priso-ners in Delhi's Tihar jail, made an effort to humanize jail conditions. Sunil Batra, sentenced to death had challenged his incarcera-tion in solitary confinement and Charles Sobhraj had challenged his confinement with bar-fetters.

In another case of "Prem Shankar Shukla Vs. Delhi Administration," the Supreme Court struck down the provisions of the Panjab Police rules which discrimina-ted between the rich and the poor prisoner in determining who was to be handcuffed. The procedure of handcuffing is a violation of Article 21.

In another recent landmark judgement in the case of "Francies Corale Mullin vs. the Administrator, Union Territory of Delhi & others", the Supreme Court explained the ingredients of personal liberty under Article 21. The case arose out of the rights of a detainee under COFEPOSA to have an interview with his family members and lawyers. The meeting with family members was restricted to one a month and the lawyer could be met only in the presence of an officer of the customs department. The Supreme Court ruled that the right to life and liberty included his right to live with human dignity and therefore a detainee would be entitled to have interviews with family members, friends and lawyers without these severe restrictions.

The Universal Declaration of Human Rights : Everyone is entitled to all the rights and freedoms set forth in this Declaration, without distinction of any kind, such as race, colour, sex, language, religion, political or other opinion, national or social origin, property, birth or other status.

Out of the total prison population of 166054 in the country as on 2007, 77871 (2707 Females)were undertrials.[1] Thus 46.89 % of the prison population is not even convicted of any crime. Secondly, even those who are convicts, a large number of them are first time offenders involved in technical or minor violations of law. Very few are recidivists or hardened criminals. According to the report of Mulla Committee, a majority of the inmates come from the "underprivileged sections of the society, as persons with the means and influence generally manage to remain beyond the reach of law even if they are involved in violation of law." As mentioned earlier some important rights of prisoners are *Right to Live with Human Dignity, Right to Punishment as Prescribed by Law, Right to be Free of Fetters or Handcuffs, Right to Communication and Information, Right to Counsel, Right to Writ of Habeas Corpus and the Right to Air Grievances.*

Women Jail

Women jails exclusively for women prisoners exist only in 12 States/UTs (Tamil Nadu has 3 women jails followed by Andhra Pradesh and Rajasthan (2 each), Bihar, Kerala, Maharashtra, Orissa, Punjab, Tripura, Uttar Pradesh, West Bengal and Delhi (1each). The total capacity of women inmates was highest in Tamil Nadu (1,013) followed by Delhi (400), Rajasthan (350), Andhra Pradesh, Punjab (320 each), Maharashtra (262), West Bengal (100), Uttar Pradesh (90), Bihar (83), Orissa (55), Tripura (30) and Kerala (24) (Two more to be added as they are ready but still to start functioning - One each in Karnataka - Tumkur and Rajasthan) Karnataka state has a total number of 100 prisons of various classifications with an authorized capacity of 12213. Out of which 11290 for male and 993 for female prisoners. As on 30.9.2008 there are 534 women prisoners in various jails of the State. Out of them 166 Convicts, 354 Undertrials and 14NDPS. There are 25 (12 Male + 13 Female) children's below the age of 6 years along with their mother prisoners in this state.

Women, due to their ignorance, are not even getting the benefit of proviso to Section 437 Cr.P.C, according to which they can be released on bail even in non-bailable cases. The Commission has now insisted on the prison authorities to take up the cases of women undertrials with courts so that they can be released on bail "It paints a very grim picture," said Margaret Alva, Minister of State for Human Resources in Prime Minister Rajiv Gandhi's Government. Mrs. Alva, who commissioned the report, stated that she had found that many women prisoners were "ignorant of their rights, and unaware that they could get bail." Justice Seth opines that women should be allowed to return to their families for delivery, as that time they need special support and care which they cannot get in prisons. We also find there is the problem of rehabilitation of women prisoners Women suffer from a low social and economic status within their own families and it is hard to get back into society after release. Rehabilitation of inmates will be meaningful only if they are employed after release and for that purpose educational facilities should be introduced or upgraded.

Mrs. Alva, a prominent spokeswoman for women's rights in India, said the stigma of a jail term sometimes ruined a woman's life because her family would refuse to take her back even after her release. Often, women preferred to stay in prison even after they were released because of social ostracism, the report said. Indian law permits women who are destitute or mental patients to be kept in jail until alternative accommodation is found for them. The number of women in Indian jails is small compared to the total prison population. Women prisoners constitute a small minority and are often a neglected group. Some of the major problems faced by women prisoners are: separation from their families, mental and emotional health problems (including experiences of trauma), and issues related to child care and pregnancy, violation of human rights and limited access to health care and other services. Health care is an issue in most women's prisons. The women in prisons come from the poorest sections of society and they come to prison with a range of untreated physical and mental health problems. Work to improve the health care in women's prisons is needed as well as drug counseling, mental health care, and programmes to help women deal with a past of abuse and violence. *('Reforming Women's Prisons', ICPS, 2004).*

Open Air Prison : India's first open jail for women was inaugurated at the Yerawada Central Prison on Sunday 8th March 2010 by Maharashtra Home Minister R.R. Patil. Addressing a gathering of prisoners, politicians and police officials, Principal Secretary (Home) of the Prisons department Medha Gadgil termed the measure a "historic moment" unfolding in the centenary year of the International Women's Day. It was MLC Mohan Joshi who had raised the question of starting it during the last years Assembly of winter session. Women in the open jail would be made to do agricultural work on the 17 acres of land adjoining the prison. This would improve their physical and mental wellbeing. They would also be eligible for remission in their punishment; for every one year served in the open jail, a year of their sentence would be reduced. It is also proposed to start open prison for women at Yerawada very shortly. Male prisoners had the facilities of an open jail at the prisons in Yerawada, Aurangabad, Paithan and Morshi.

VIOLATIONS AND DEPRIVATIONS OF THE PRISONERS' RIGHTS

Prison conditions remained deplorable. According to NHRC, 56 cases of deaths in judicial custody were registered in Karnataka during 1 April 2006 - 31 March 2007. The jails in the state did not have proper facilities to allow prisoners to meet and discuss legal matters with their lawyers. In October 2007, the Karnataka State Human Rights Commission directed the Director-General of Police (Prisons) of Karnataka "to provide a suitable and conducive place where advocates and other visitors meet the prisoners" following a complaint that about 35 to 40 under-trial prisoners meet their advocates in a small room and the time allowed for meeting was not sufficient to facilitate legal access.

Formulation and adoption of National Policy on Custodial Justice to Women:

- Formation of a statutory autonomous body to be designated as the National Authority on Custodial Justice to Women (NACJW).
- Specialized courts must be set up to dispense justice separately and speedily to women. In addition to the separate Women's Courts or Family Courts it is recommended that Nari Bandigriha Adalats be held in the nature of mobile judicial camps. Its objectives should be to provide speedy justice.

- Prison should be brought into the concurrent Lists of the Seventh Schedule of the Indian Constitution in order to strengthen the process of standardized and uniform national approaches to reform of custodial conditions.
- There is need to have a Comprehensive Prison and Prisoners Act.
- A widespread code which will include the administration of all custodial institutions and the treatment of inmates of such institutions, with special provisions for the treatment and handling of women.
- A critical assessment of the effectiveness and relevance of various legislations bearing on women's status in custody and their criminality should be undertaken by the Law Commission.
- On an immediate basis, appropriate amendments and additional provisions should be introduced in the IPC and Cr. PC as well as in the Prisons Act, 1894 to reflect the special needs of women in custody.
- The rights of dependent children of custodialized women also need to be clearly stated.
- Apart from female staff in women's jails, there should be women D.I.G. in the state Headquarters preferably from the prison services, particularly to look after the work relating to women prisons, women prison staff and women prisoners.
- Released Prisoners' Aid Societies should operate in every district which can provide single-window assistance toward the habilitation and mainstreaming of the released prisoners. Counseling cells should be attached to every custodial centre.
- Separate police lock-ups for female arrestees should be established.
- A special unit known as women's Assistance Police Unit (WAPU) should be created which should be combined cadre of men and women police, to deal specifically with crime preventive work and assistance to women at the time of arrest and in custody.

CONCLUSION

The basic amenities of right to life in case of prison rights which are guaranteed under arts, 21 and 22 are the oxygen tubes for the convicts and the victims as well."Right to life" under Art 21 of the Indian Constitution is a broad concept which has covered every possible right to be guaranteed to the prisoners, under trials and convicts of any democratic country.. But a big black hole still exists in the case of women offenders. Even though right to life under Indian constitution has been broaden enough to include wide prison rights to the prisoners, unfortunate situation still prevails in the area of women prisoners. The Prison Act and the Prison Rules do talk about the segregation of the convicts on gender basis and certain rights to women convicts, yet the area needs special attention.

In a patriarchal society like India, women prisoners are seen as worse than witches. In most cases, they are denied access to their homes, family and children after their release. But undoubtedly, women prisoners are mostly victims of circumstances. Broader outlook and wider views are still wanted to uplift the condition of women prisoners in India. Even though right to equality is guaranteed to every Indian citizen irrespective of their sex; legislation needs to work on the safeguards to be guaranteed to the women offenders. New amendments should be brought in the concept of prison rights under the broad arena of Right to life. the National Human Rights Commission (NHRC) said that rights such as medical assistance and contact with family members must be respected. Illegal detention, the commission added, was still one of the biggest challenges that they were countering. a report by the National Police Commission (NPC), Patel said: "As per the third report by the NPC, 60 per cent of arrests are unjustified or unnecessary and such arrests leads to 42.3 per cent of the expenditure of the jails - which can be avoided."

To conclude, Indian constitution is a growing constitution and hence the concept of right to life should be amended along with the global change of ideologies. Newly improved rules of prison management and criminal psychology should be considered to give way to a broader idea of right to life for the convicts and under trials for the betterment of prison life in India successfully.

References

Ahuja Ram (1969), Female Offenders in India, Meenakshi Prakashan, Meerut.

Devasia Leelamma and V.V. Devasia (1989), Female Criminals and Female Victims, Nagpur: Dattasons.

Human Rights Wikipedia, *http://en.wikipedia.org/wiki/Human Rights.*

Prisoners Rights Wikipedia, *http://en.wikipedia.org/wiki/Prisoners Rights.*

Report of National Expert Committee on Women Prisoners Vol. I & II Government of India, Department of Women & Child Development, New Delhi, 1990.

Rights Wikipedia *http://en.wikipedia.org/wiki/Rights*

Sohani,Neera Kukreja (1989), Women Behind Bars,New Delhi,Vikas Publication.

Tamil Nadu Prison Department, *http://www.prison.tn.nic.in*

The Unlawful Activities Prevention (Amendment) Act, 2008:
Anarchy Codified?

Akshaya Iyer*

INTRODUCTION

> *"It is important that the legal structure enables the prosecution of people who attack the sovereignty of the nation and interfere with its secular social fabric."*[1]

Every individual, irrespective of caste, creed, age, sex and race, has a right to live. The liberty and prosperity of every individual is the prime concern of the global community at this point in time. The autonomy of the individual and the social and psychological welfare of mankind is taking centre-stage as news of terrorist attacks, wars and human rights violations across the globe fight for newspaper space and threaten to demolish the very basis on which mankind is founded-peace and mutual respect.

The startling rise of insurgency and terrorism in regions across the world has left many areas torn by war and in desperate need of support and financial and moral aid. These regions are in dire need of support from the international community and restoration of peace and harmony is the primordial requirement of these war-torn nations, where peace is a utopian concept and normalcy an unknown term. The situation at present has forced the world to sit up and take notice of the fact that the very existence of the human race is at stake as hostilities and tensions between nations and communities grow to such an extent that mutual destruction has risen to become the order of the day.

The growing terrorism stands to make a mockery of the religious and political ideals that they supposedly stand for, and attempts to destroy the very social fabric of the nation by putting the people at mortal peril to serve their so-called larger purposes.

---

* ....

In the wake of the current situation across the world, where even superpowers like the USA are vulnerable to such terrorist attacks, it is imperative that special legislation be enforced in order to control the onslaught of terrorism and ensure the harshest punishment to the destructors of civil society.

It has been postulated that counter-terrorism has four aspects – preventive through timely intelligence, physical security to thwart terrorist attacks if intelligence fails, crisis management if physical security too fails and deterrence through investigation and prosecution.[2] India's counter-terrorism capability is hindered by lack of adequate measures in terms of deterrence through legal action against terrorists and their organisations.[3]

A study conducted by the Committee on International Human Rights of The Association of The Bar of New York indicates that Indian anti-terrorism laws raise the following concerns:

- Overly broad and ambiguous definitions of terrorism that fail to satisfy the principle of legality;
- Pre-trial investigation and detention procedures which infringe upon due process, personal liberty, and limits on the length of pre-trial detention;
- Special courts and procedural rules infringe upon judicial independence and right to a fair trial;
- Provisions that require courts to draw adverse inferences against the accused in a manner that infringes upon the presumption of innocence;
- Lack of sufficient oversight of police and prosecutorial decision making to prevent arbitrary, discriminatory application; and
- Broad immunities from prosecution for government officials.

This paper examines these concerns and the impact it has on civil liberties and discusses anti-terrorism legislation in India today, emerging from the amendments to the Unlawful Activities (Prevention) Act in 2008, vis-à-vis the human rights concerns that surrounds this legislation, and puts a perspective to the national security versus human rights debate that has been raging in the world since the dawn of democracy.

AMENDMENTS TO THE UAPA IN 2008: DRACONIAN LEGISLATION?

In November 2008, following the terrorist attack on Mumbai, the Union Government proposed,in addition to the enactment of new legislations such as the National Investigation Agency Act, further amendments to the Unlawful Activities (Prevention) Act, 1967, in an attempt to make anti-terror legislation in the country more authoritarian and effective.

The amendments were in accordance with the recommendations made by the Administrative Reforms Commission in its Report 'Combating Terrorism-Protecting by Righteousness[4]', as highlighted above.

The government, in its statement of objects and reasons, stated:" The Government is of the view that further provisions are required to be made in the law to cover various facets of terrorism and terrorist activities, including financing of terrorism, which are not fully covered in the present law, and to make further provisions with the aim of strengthening the arrangements for speedy investigation, prosecution and trial of cases related to terrorism related offences, while at the same time ensuring against any possible misuse of such provisions."[5]

The amendment was a result of India's adherence to the United Nations Resolutions 1267 (1999), 1333 (2000), 1363 (2001), 1390 (2002), 1455 (2003), 1526 (2004), 1566 (2004), 1617 (2005), 1735 (2006) and 1822 (2008), which "require the States to take action against certain terrorists and terrorist organisations, to freeze the assets and other economic resources, to prevent the entry into or the transit through their territory, and prevent the direct or indirect supply, sale or transfer of arms and ammunitions to the individuals or entities".[6]

Section 15 of the UAPA has been amended to include within the definition of 'terrorist act', the words- "*...or by any other means of whatever nature..*"

This indicates that any physical act could be deemed a terrorist act, if the government could satisfy the very low burden of proof threshold – that the act was *likely* to cause terror in the people.[7] Such an ambiguous definition allows a wide range of acts to be deemed 'terrorist acts', bestowing upon the authorities the freedom to interpret any act to be a potential 'terrorist act' and carrying on investigation under such presumption, which undermines the requirement of a formal procedure being followed for prosecution and circumvents the due process of law, hence appearing to be extremely arbitrary and prone to widespread misuse, by providing legal sanction to authorities to exercise power beyond their competence, and allowing arbitrary persecution of innocent individuals.

The 2008 amendments maintain the stand taken by previous anti-terrorism legislation in regard to presumption of innocence, allowing a person to be considered guilty until proven innocent if any evidence is found linking the accused to the terrorist act under question. This is a clear violation of the Principles of Natural Justice which form the basis of the entire legal system.

The amendment in the definition, together with this denial of presumption of innocence, allows the government to exercise authority beyond its legitimate capacity to construe anything as a terrorist act and prove it without difficulty in the courts. This is a dangerous development that threatens not only genuine terrorists, but also ordinary citizens who may be prosecuted under the amended UAPA if it is politically convenient.[8]

Other seemingly draconian provisions included by the 2008 Amendment Act are as follows:

(a) It further broadens the purview of the intention clause in POTA, by introducing the words *likely* to threaten the unity, integrity, security or sovereignty of India, expanding the ambit of the definition and providing it with extra-territorial applicability.

(b) It extends the maximum period of pre-charge detention to 180 days, if after 90 days the progress in investigation is shown and more time demanded. This again poses the same problem as was faced due to the detention period specified in TADA and POTA, and the 2004 UAPA amendments (which had shortened the tenure) have been done away with by way of this clause. This provision is in contravention to the ICCPR,[9] which requires all arrested persons to be informed of the charges against them and that they be entitled to trial within a reasonable time or release.

(c) The Amendments deny an accused person bail if the court believes that, based on the evidence so far, the accusations against him/ her are prima facie true.[10] This is in clear contravention of established criminal procedure wherein the judge is not authorised to consider the guilt of the accused in the granting of bail.

Moreover, the 2008 UAPA amendments also deny bail to all non-citizens who have entered India "illegally", thus denying bail to all asylum seekers or refugees not recognised by the government.[11]

(d) Section 51A of the Act provides powers to the Central Government to take action against individuals or entities listed in the Schedule to the Order, or any other person engaged in *or suspected to be engaged in terrorism*[12] and bestows upon the government excessive powers to seize the property or prevent entry/ transit of people who are even suspected to be terrorists. This power is criticised to be excessively broad[13] and is extremely prone to misuse, and may be used to fulfil communal and political agendas, thus causing destruction of the democracy.

OMISSIONS IN THE 2008 AMENDMENTS: WHAT WAS REALLY REQUIRED

Certain provisions that were required to be incorporated in the UAPA were not addressed by the 2008 amendment. Inclusion of these provisions in an anti-terrorism legislation, as highlighted below, is of utmost importance in the interest of justice and social welfare, in addition to protection of law and order in the nation, since they may be able to successfully safeguard the interests of all sections of society, while ensuring adequate punishment to offenders under the legislation.

According to the UN's Special Rapporteur on The Promotion and Protection of Human Rights while countering terrorism, "at the national level, the specificity of terrorist crimes is defined by the presence of three cumulative conditions:

(i) the means used...

(ii) the intent... and

(iii) the aim, which is to further an underlying political or ideological goal."[14]

The special rapporteur observed that without all three elements the prohibited act could not be considered a terrorist act because it fails to distinguish itself from an ordinary criminal act.

Therefore, the multidimensional nature of terrorism and the distinctive rationale is required to be addressed[15], which has not been mentioned in the recent amendments to the UAPA.

The UAPA amendments do not address the issue of the presumption of innocence of the accused, which has been expressly denied in all anti-terror legislations to be enacted till date in India. This, as has been previously highlighted, is in contravention to Article 14 of the Constitution of India, which ensures a free trial to all, as well as human rights as recognised by the United Nations over the years[16]. The presumption of innocence is a basic tenet of the principles of natural justice. On the contrary, it reinstates and emphasises upon the notion that a person accused of a terrorist act is guilty until proven otherwise. The amended UAPA, when read *in toto*, indicates that a person arrested on the ground that he is *likely* to be involved under terrorist activities may also be tried on the presumption of guilt, thus completely eliminating any possibility of fair trial to the accused, and increased manifold the possibility of its misuse.

The issue was also highlighted in the Parliamentary Debate preceding the passing of the Unlawful Activities (Prevention) Amendment Bill:

> *"The Bill places the burden of proof on the accused under two specific conditions. If arms or explosives are recovered from the possession of the accused and there is reason to believe that such arms and explosives were used for the commission of the offence, finger prints or any other definitive evidence are found at the site of the offence, under such conditions the courts shall presume that the accused has committed such offence unless contrary is shown. This is more stringent than the provisions of the POTA which stated that the court shall draw adverse inference against the accused. There are three broad parameters for judging guilt. Most laws require the evidence to be proved beyond reasonable doubt. This Bill assumes guilt unless innocence is proven..."*[17]

This presumption of guilt is highlighted by various provisions of the 2008 Amendment Act, the most manifest of which reads:

Presumption as to Offence Under Section 15

43E. In a prosecution for an offence under section 15, if it is proved –

(a) that the arms or explosives or any other substances specified in the said section were recovered from the possession of the accused and there is reason to believe that such arms or explosives or other substances of a similar nature were used in the commission of such offence; or

(b) *that by the evidence of the expert the finger-prints of the accused or any other definitive evidence suggesting the involvement of the accused in the offence were found at the site of the offence or on anything including arms and vehicles used in connection with the commission of such offence, the Court shall presume, unless the contrary is shown, that the accused has committed such offence.*

Moreover, the Amendment Act does not include a sunset clause, unlike the TADA and POTA, which makes the UAPA an integral part of the criminal justice system. The TADA and POTA contained sunset clauses which ensured limited operation of the law and made the legislations extraordinary in their operation. However, the incorporation of the repressive provisions of the TADA and POTA in the UAPA without provision of a specified period of operation makes these provisions part of established criminal law, designating to the UAPA the position of an ordinary legislation.

The amendments do not specify any pre-trial safeguards against torture and other cruel, inhuman or degrading treatment or punishment of detainees. Such lack of safeguards, combined with the other draconian provisions of the UAPA, makes detainees extremely vulnerable to abuse undermines basic human rights of detainees. Such agrave omission also highlights the lack of deliberation of the legislature regarding the human rights concerns surrounding the issue, and their inability to include adequate safeguards in the amendments, despite their claims to the contrary.[18]

Scholars cite four primary factors that make the UAPA Amendment draconian in its operation:[19]

> Firstly, the amendment cites 10 Resolutions of the United Nations Security Council passed from 1999 to 2007 as justification for this undemocratic amendment, thus taking a negative approach to the UN standards and undermining the "form and spirit of international vision".[20]

The second reason is the lack of a sunset clause in the UAPA, as has been elucidated above.

The third factor is that these amendments were brought about in a hurry under pressure from the electronic media, which presented a very one-sided view of the situation during the 26/11 attacks. Owing to the urgency under which the Amendment Act was passed, a holistic view was not developed for the framing of the legislation and, lacking adequate review, the legislation passed seemed to be an attempt to appease the masses and provide only a short-term solution.

The fourth reason is one that has been the primary concern of the intelligentsia and human rights activists, and makes the legislation draconian and contrary to established law-the abuse of the provisions, elucidated above, which may arguably be the root of the national security versus human rights debate.

However, justification for these 'draconian provisions' is derived from the Supreme Court judgment upholding the validity of TADA,[21] stating that stringency and harshness of such provisions was seen as a matter of legislative wisdom, and the court cannot question it if it was based on a reasonable classification of offences and offenders for separate treatment.

Argument favouring the passing of the amendment to the UAPA also asserted that *"nearly because power may sometimes be abused, it is not ground for denying the existence of power. The wisdom of man has not yet been able to conceive of a Government with power sufficient to answer all the legitimate needs and at the same time incapable of mischief."*[22]

This argument is indicative of the lack of incentive on part of the legislature to incorporate appropriate safeguards to prevent misuse and abuse, and also displays the legislature's preference for national security over human rights.

CONCLUSION

A detailed analysis of the provisions of the UAPA Amendment Act highlights the extreme potential of misuse of this legislation, and puts at stake the lives of millions of people who may stand to be implicated without sufficient cause under this Act.

The root of the issue continues to be the same in the case of every anti-terrorism legislation, be it the POTA, TADA or the UAPA- the humans rights versus national security debate.

The proposition of enacting a legislation that will comprehensively deal with the issue of national security while upholding human rights may be the ideal solution, but is also, given the situation, a very improbable notion. Since the idea of not compromising on either remains a relatively utopian concept, a trade-off of sorts is necessitated. In the maintenance of national security, a certain level of conciliation is required as far as the preservation of human rights is concerned. This does not, however, imply that national security should be given more prominence than human rights- the argument put forth is that a certain amount of exclusion of human rights is unavoidable, and correspondingly, some leeway is required to be given in matters of national security in order to uphold the basic rights of the people and to ensure that they are not indiscriminately subjugated to suffering. Hence, a certain balance or equilibrium is required to be arrived at in the drafting of anti-terrorism legislation, and a more balanced view is required to be taken by the legislature, and the current trend of proclivity towards national security rather than human rights is in need of reversal.

Hence, in summary, it is submitted that immediate review of the current legislation is required in order to analyse its effectiveness in not only persecuting perpetrators, but also preventing the onslaught of terrorism, as well as to determine the level of misuse of the legislation and the promptly addressing the human rights concerns that surround the UAPA currently.

Notes

1. Francis Fanthome, Nominated member of the Lok Sabha, during Parliamentary Debate on the Unlawful Activities (Prevention) Amendment Bill, 2008 on 17th December 2008.
2. B. Raman, Evolution of India's Counter-Terrorism Capabilities, International Terrorism Monitor, South Asia Analysis Group, 2006.
3. *Id.*
4. 8th Report of the Administrative Reforms Commission, Combatting Terrorism-Protecting By Righteousness, [*http://arc.gov.in/8threport/ARC_8th_report.htm*]. See also, Brief on Combatting Terrorism [*http://arc.gov.in/8threport/ARC_8th_report.htm*]
5. P. Chidambaram, Unlawful Activities (Prevention) Amendment Bill, 2008.
6. Preamble to the Unlawful Activities (Prevention) Amendment Bill, 2008.
7. Ravi Nair, The Unlawful Activities (Prevention) Amendment Act 2008: Repeating Past Mistakes, *Economics and Political Weekly*, January 24, 2009.
8. Ravi Nair, The Unlawful Activities (Prevention) Amendment Act 2008: Repeating Past Mistakes, *Economics and Political Weekly*, January 24, 2009.
9. Articles 9(2) and 9(3) of the International Convention on Civil and Political Rights (ICCPR).
10. S.43D (5), Unlawful Activities (Prevention) Amendment Act, 2008.
11. Ravi Nair, The Unlawful Activities (Prevention) Amendment Act 2008: Repeating Past Mistakes, *Economics and Political Weekly*, January 24, 2009.
12. Text of Section 51A.
13. Asaduddin Owaisi, member of the Lok Sabha, during the Parliamentary Debate on the Unlawful Activities (Prevention) Amendment Bill, 2008 on 17th December 2008.
14. Special Rapporteur, "Protection of Human Rights and Fundamental Freedoms while Countering Terrorism" (2008), UNGA Doc A/63/223.
15. UK Terrorism Act, 2000: s.1(1)(c) the use or threat is made for the purpose of advancing a political, religious [, racial] or ideological cause., Canada: Anti-Terrorism Act: 83.01(b) an act or omission...(i) that is committed (A) in whole or in part for a political, religious or ideological purpose, objective or cause.
16. Special Rapporteur, "Protection of Human Rights and Fundamental Freedoms while Countering Terrorism" (2008), UNGA Doc A/63/223, p 5. :"[t]he right to a fair trial is one of the fundamental guarantees of human rights and the rule of law"
17. Prof. Ramadass, member of the Lok Sabha, during Parliamentary Debate on the Unlawful Activities (Prevention) Amendment Bill, 2008 on 17th December 2008.
18. "What is being presented here is a fair balance of all the views without compromising the ability of the agency to prosecute the offence and, at the same time, without disregarding what are considered fundamental, basic human rights. I have tried to make the best possible balance of these two competing, two equally important values and virtues which we cherish in life." -Home Minister Shri P. Chidambaram, Parliamentary Debate on 17th Dec. 2008.
19. G Haragopal, B Jagannatham, Terrorism and Human Rights:Indian Experience with Repressive Laws, *Economics and Political Weekly*, Vol. xliv, No. 28, July 11, 2009.
20. *Id.*
21. Kartar Singh v. State of Punjab (1994) 3 SCC 569.
22. Moily Commission Report, quoted by LK Advani in Parliamentary Debate on the Unlawful Activities (Prevention) Amendment Bill, 2008 on 17th Dec 2008.

Educational Development of Muslims in Maharashtra: Analysis from Policies, Commissions and Educational Schemes in India

DHANESWAR BHOI*

INTRODUCTION

Educational development is one of the needy key indicators for development of human index. Being India a secular country the state should take care of equally developed human index and social capital of the country. From the sociological point of view, one of the important objectives of the education is to equalise opportunity to all sections of the society. In a demographic setup, every individual should have equal opportunity to getting education for personal development. We must take all the efforts to increase the educational facilities to the weaker sections of the society and simultaneously to the minorities of the society. In our country, the minority community is formed on the basis of religion, caste, language and tribes. There are several communities those are falling the minority community in our country. They are Muslim, scheduled caste, scheduled tribe, unban slum people and linguistic minorities. The Muslims are also lagging behind in access to education. There are many causes which hinders the education of Muslims generally in India and more particularly in Maharashtra. The Muslims are falling lag behind in education in our society. We are unable to provide to bring the Muslims to our mainstream society as well as education. There is a challenging task in the educational development of the minority communities in forthcoming years. If education has to play an important role in socio-economic development of our economy, then there is an urgent need for increasing our efforts to develop the education of minority communities. To promote equality it will be necessary to provide opportunities to the minority community and religious groups for the development of nation. Evidence reveals that the plight of minorities in regards to education and development had not receive serious attention until eighties, even if indigenous education period. More particularly Muslims are depriving to access education since long back in Maharashtra.

* *PhD. Scholar, Centre for Studies in Sociology of Education, Tata Institute of Social Sciences, Mumbai, (E-mail: dhaneswar.bhoi@gmail.com)*

OBJECTIVES

1. To find out the socio-economic causes behind the educational backwardness of Muslims.
2. To study the efforts of government for developing the Muslims at different level of education.
3. To examine the Policy and Programmes towards the development of Muslim education.

METHODOLOGY

In methodological part, the content analysis method is applied to analyse the data from secondary sources. This paper is based on the report of 'Sachar Committee, 2006,' data of National commission for Minorities, Seventh All India School Educatiional Survey, different government reports, UGC reports and different website data are the major content of this paper. In quintessence, the paper gathers different ideas from many of the books and journals. Basically this paper analysed the role government and policies to strengthen education of Muslims in India especially in Maharashtra.

MUSLIM AND THEIR EDUCATION IN MAHARASHTRA

The population of Muslims in Maharashtra is 9.7 per cent as compare to 81.1 per cent Hindus according to Census 2001. In the same way the population of Muslims is 13.4 per cent as compare to 80.5 per cent Hindus in India. The participation of Muslims is very low in comparison to other category students of Maharashtra. Here we can easily guess the educational status of Muslims of Maharashtra through these following Tables.

Table 1
Primary and Middle Educational Enrolment of Muslims in Maharashtra

	Enrolment in Primary level (Class: I-V)		*Enrolment in Middle Education level (Class: VI-VIII)*	
	Muslims	*All Category*	*Muslims*	*All Category*
Boys	612312	5,709484	321908	3186828
Girls	595061	5182651	310002	2761495
Total	1207373	10,892135	631910	5948323

Sourse: Seventh All India School Educatiional Survey.

This table shows the muslim educational enrolment which is over all 1207373 as compare to 10892135 of all category enrolment at primary level. Again the total enrolment of muslims is 631910 against 5948323 at Middle education level. The educational enrolment of Muslim girls is 595061 and 310002 as compare to 5182651 and 2761495 of all catagory students both at primary and middle education level. It clearly shows that the muslims are suffring a lot to getting education both primary and middle education level in Maharashtra.

Table 2
Secondary and Higher Secondary Enrolment of Muslims in Maharashtra

	Enrolment in Secondary (Class: I-X)		*Enrolment in Higher Secondary (Class: XI-XII)*	
	Muslims	*All Category*	*Muslims*	*All Category*
Boys	140526	1562224	48189	557596
Girls	130974	1262384	44879	427940
Total	271500	2824608	93068	985536

Sourse: Seventh All India School Educatiional Survey.

This table shows the muslim educational enrolment which is over all at secondary level is 271500 as compare to 2824608 of all category enrolment. Again the total enrolment of muslims is 93068 against 985536 at higher secondary education level. The educational enrolment of Muslim girls is 130974 and 1262384 as compare to 44879 and 427940 of all catagory students. It clearly shows that the muslims are in worse order to getting education both secondary and higher secondary level in Maharashtra.

Table 3
Muslim Educational Enrolment Retention Rate in Maharashtra

	Enrolment of Muslims in Class I to X against the Enrolment of 100 in Class I			
Sex	*Class: I*	*Class: V*	*Class: VIII*	*Class: X*
Boys	100	90	80	55
Girls	100	89	73	49
Total	100	90	76	52

Sourse: Seventh All India School Educatiional Survey.

This table shows the educational retaiontion of Muslim students at different education level in Maharashtra. The number of enrolment of muslim students are 100 at class 'I' when they reached in class 'V' that are reduced to 90 and the number of student are 76 when they reached the calss 'VIII', finally the number of them are 52 when they reach in class X. So it clearly indicates the existance of droup out and retention of Muslims students at different educational level in Maharashtra.

Table 4
Comparative Higher Educational Enrolment of Muslims in India

Religion	*Enrolment (%)*
Hindu	12.00
Muslims	8.19
Others	30.87

Source: National Sample Survey, 2003-04.

This table shows the rate of Muslim high educational enrolment in India which is only 8.12 per cent in comparison to 12.00 per cent of Hindu and 30, 87 per cent of religions out of total enrolment.

POLICY AND PROGRAMMES FOR MUSLIM EDUCATION

There are different educational substantive measures are taken to strengthen the Muslim education in India. Except the Prime Minister's new 15 Point Programme for the welfare of the Minorities, the ministry took several steps to implement the recommendations of the Prime Minister's high level committee on social, economic and educational status of the Muslim Community of India (Sachar Committee, 2006). Again the University Grants Commission is also working out modalities so that all universities could be encouraged to recognize qualifications from Madrassas for the purposes of enrolment on the pattern followed by Jamia Millia Islamia, Aligarh Muslim University, Maulana Azad National Urdu University and Jamia Hamdard, in appropriate courses and programmes of study. Academics have been established thee Central Universities; Jamila Millia Islamia University, Aligarh Muslim University and Maulana Azad National Urdu University for training of teachers to teach in Urdu medium at higher education level. Madarsas can be linked with a higher secondary school board so that students wanting to shift to a regular/ mainstream education can do so after having passed from a Madarsa (Sachar Committee, 2006).

STATE MINORITIES COMMISSIONS

Thirteen State Governments of Andhra Pradesh, Assam, Bihar, Chhattisgarh, Delhi, Jharkhand, Karnataka, Maharashtra, Madhya Pradesh, Rajasthan, Uttar Pradesh, Tamil Nadu and West Bengal have set up statutory State Minorities Commissions. The State Governments of Manipur and Uttarakhand have set up non-statutory Commissions. The Ministry has also requested the remaining State Governments/Union Territory Administrations to set up such Commissions.

NATIONAL POLICY AND MINORITY EDUCATION: AN OVERVIEW

The National Policy on Education (NPE) -1986 and updated Programme of Action in 1992 (POA-1992) spells out the concept of a national system of education, in which all students irrespective of caste, creed, location or sex have access to education of comparable quality. The policy lays special emphasis on the removal of disparities and seeks to equalise educational opportunities by attending to the specific needs of those who have remained educationally backward so far. Suitable incentives, therefore, have to be provided to educationally backward sections of society. Government has always shown concern for the education of these groups in the interest of equality and social justice.

NATIONAL MONITORING COMMITTEE FOR MINORITIES EDUCATION

A National Monitoring Committee for Minorities Education has been constituted on 7.8.2004 under the Chairmanship of Minister of Human Resource Development. Two meetings have so far been held i.e. first on 27.08.2004 and second on 17.11.2005. A Standing Committee of this Committee also been constituted on 3rd September, 2004. Its Chairperson is Sh. Jafar Ali Naqvi. The Standing Committee had held a number of meetings and had visited Uttar Pradesh, Maharashtra, Andhra Pradesh, Karnataka and Kerala in the first year of its constitution and submitted its report in the second meeting of the NMCME held on 17.11.2005. The Committee considered the report of the Standing Committee. Action points which emerged from the 'Standing Committee' report have been circulated to all the states and concerned departments/organisations for their comments/views. In the next phase, the 'Standing Committee' had visited West Bengal and Assam, Haryana, Punjab and Chandigarh Administration, Tamil Nadu and Pondicherry.

NATIONAL COMMISSION FOR MINORITY EDUCATIONAL INSTITUTIONS

A Commission with the name of "National Commission for Minority Educational Institutions- 2004" has been established through an Act of Parliament. The functions of the commission would be as follows: 1) Advise the Central Government or any State Government on any question relating to the education of minorities, that may be referred to it; 2) Look into specific complaints regarding deprivation or violation of the rights of minorities to establish and administer educational institutions of their choice, and any dispute regarding affiliation to a scheduled university and report its findings to the Central Government for implementation; and 3) To do such acts and things as may be necessary, incidental or conducive to the attainment of all or any of the objects of the commission.

PRIME MINISTER'S NEW 15 POINT PROGRAMME FOR WELFARE OF MINORITIES

Enhancing opportunities for Education: Under the subject of enhancing opportunity for education "Prime Minister's New 15 Point Programme" is taking care the educational interest of minorities with providing these facilities. The main points of 'Enhancing opportunities for Education' are (1) Equitable availability of ICDS Services (2) Improving access to School Education (3) Greater resources for teaching Urdu (4) Modernizing Madarsa Education (5) Scholarships for meritorious students from minority communities (6) Improving educational infrastructure through the Maulana Azad Education Foundation.

Equitable Share in Economic Activities and Employment: Under this main point "Prime Minister's New 15 Point Programme" taking care the employment interest of minorities with providing these facilities. The major points of 'Equitable Share in Economic Activities and Employment' are (7) Self-Employment and Wage Employment for the poor (8) Up-gradation of skill through technical training (9) Enhancing credit support for economic activities (10) Recruitment to State and Central Services.

Improving the living conditions of minorities: To seeking the interest of living conditions of minorities the "Prime Minister's New 15 Point Programme" emphasises upon these points. The major points of 'Improving the living conditions of minorities' are (11) Equitable share in rural housing scheme (12) Improvement in condition of slums inhabited by minority communities.

Prevention & Control of Communal Riots; finally these are the points of "Prime Minister's New 15 Point Programme" which are meant for controlling communal riots under these heads, (13) Prevention of communal incidents (14) Prosecution for communal offences (15) Rehabilitation of victims of communal riots.

MERIT-CUM-MEANS SCHOLARSHIP SCHEME FOR MINORITY COMMUNITIES STUDENTS

The 'Merit-cum-Means Scholarship' is a government substantive scheme for development of Muslim higher education in India. The objective of the 'Merit-cum-Means Scholarship' Scheme for Minority Communities Students is to provide financial assistance to the poor and meritorious students belonging to minority communities to enable them to pursue professional and technical courses. These scholarships are available for studies in India only and will be awarded through an Agency designated by the State government/union territory administration for this purpose.

MAJOR FINDINGS

Discrimination and Social Security in Education

The security is matter for hampering the education of Muslims at different education level. The feeling of insecure affects the education of Muslims in different state of India. Hundreds of communal riots have taken place after independence. Communal politics has taken its toll. Many Muslims live on past glory and many Hindus on complex it being in majority and hence chauvinism. Lack of a sense of security and a discriminatory attitude towards Muslims is felt widely.

Women Education and Marriage

In Muslim society, the social attitudes towards the education women are still remain same as earlier. The education is controlled by the social tradition and some blind believes. Due to the social norms in the Muslim community most of the women are deprived of to getting education in general and higher education in particularly. The disadvantages that Muslim children face vis-à-vis education can be broadly seen as educational, economic and social. This is particularly true when it comes to girls' education. The concept of educational disadvantage with respect to children from these communities can be seen from the point of view of sheer absence of facilities in terms of exclusive girls schools for which there is a preference in the community, combined with economic disadvantage which is an additional factor inhibiting girls participation in education. Apart from the household chores, and responsibility of siblings, the Muslim girl child very often does not experience the transition from child to girl, and girl to woman. Chronological age has no bearing on age for marriage. In another point of view the marriageable age also directly affect the education of Muslim women in our country in term of accessibility.

Low Retaliation Rate at Different Educational Level in Maharashtra

The educational retention of Muslim students at different education level in Maharashtra vary according to the promotion of classes beginning from class I to X. The number of enrolment of muslim students are 100 at class 'I' when they reached in class 'V' that are reduced to 90 and the number of student are 76 when they reached the calss 'VIII', finally the number of them are 52 when they reach in class X. So it clearly indicates the existance of drop out and retention of Muslims students at different educational level in Maharashtra. (Seventh All India School Educational Survey)

Employment and Job Assurance of Muslims

Muslims routinely argue that despite possessing adequate educational qualifications they are not employed in government services, and point out that Muslim representation in the services are lesser than that warranted by their population. What is the use, many Muslims ask, of investing in their children higher education if they are refused government employment simply because of their religion? In the private sector, too, Muslims, like Dalits, believe that discrimination continues unabated, further dampening their enthusiasm for higher education. This has led to demands by some Muslim organisations for reservations for Muslims, either as a single category or for backward caste Muslims, in government jobs and educational institutions.

Population and Educational Sustainability

The Muslims population increased rapidly from 47 million to 138 million. This amounts to an increase of 194 per cent just short of trebling and much higher than the average increase of 134 per cent. The Muslim population growth has been close to 30 per cent in each of the four inter censual decades since 1961, with the latest decade showing fall to a level just below 30 per cent. In 1961 Muslim population in the country was 10.7 per cent, which has now increased to 13.4 per cent as per 2001 census. This excess of 2.7 per cent growth is large by due to higher growth rate of Muslims, which is directly to illiteracy, poverty and conservatism.

Educational Backwardness and Illiteracy

The enrolment of Muslims in educational institutes is lesser than others. A high dropout rate in addition among Muslim students is worrisome. The main reason for educational backwardness of Muslims is abject poverty due to which children are forced to drop out after the first few classes. The incidence of the same is more in OBC Muslims because of poor back-up support. This is particularly true for Muslims girls. Small children are expected to provide for their families by working in small workshops as domestic helper or by looking after the sibling while their mothers go to work. The incidence of child labour is much higher among OBC Muslims as compared to others. Again very low participation of Muslim women compared to all other socio-religious communities in economic activity is one of the important highlights of the Sachar Committee Report. While overall about 44 per cent of women are engaged in economic activity, the figure for Muslim women is 25 per cent overall and as low as 18 per cent in urban areas. This is bound to adversely affect the overall economic status of the community (Sachar Committee Report, 2006, Pg. 89). The economy of the Muslim community indirectly affects the education of Muslims at higher education level.

Medium of Instruction in Educational Institutions

The discriminatory policies of various state governments towards Urdu, which was unfairly branded as a language, hit north Indian Muslims particularly badly, dampening their enthusiasm for sending their children to school, where Hindi, and in some states Sanskrit as well, was made compulsory for all students. The Medium of instruction is also a major factor in the way of educational assessment and retention. But in case of Maharashtra the medium of instruction is also a problem for educational development of Muslims. Sometimes students are also not comfortable with regional language. They are comfortable with their mother tongue only. So the mother tongue is essential for developing the curriculum, medium of instruction for examination and avail that language teacher in respective educational institutions.

Lack of Supportive Curriculum System

The curriculum frame work is not support to the Muslim students at different educational level. Basically our curriculum at higher education level which falls under general higher education does not have practical importance. The contents of different general courses are highly subjective which are unable to give employment in Indian market for sustain the livelihood. Today, the selection of subject matter for the curriculum, especially in higher education, is obviously driven by utilitarian and holistic way rather than by Islamic educational goals. Again, national economic development overrides holistic human development. The notion of the university as merely a factory producing products for national development was acutely felt when a directive was issued by the Indian higher educational authority to shorten the length of study from four to three years as a step to accelerate the production of manpower for national development. The present curriculum system does not favour the earning based education which is required to maintain the future livelihood of Muslims in true sense.

Lack of good Scholarship Facilities for Muslims

To study at higher educational level is a difficult job for lower economical background students. In Indian higher education, there are different scholarship schemes and facilities for the higher education of different categories of students. But there is no such good amount of scholarship system for the Muslims higher education. The Muslims are backward in term of higher education due to lack of better scholarship facilities in higher education level. Even if the Indian government started some schemes for the minorities to assist students by way of special coaching for professional courses and Post-Matric scholarship for minorities that is not fully substantiates Muslim education at higher education level.

Less Implementation Success and Lack of State Level Schemes

Implementation is another major part of any type of policies and programmes. There are different educational programmes are implemented in national and state level, but there are lacuna in successive programmes. In the state like Maharashtra, there is a commission for Muslim minorities but there are no such substantive programmes particularly in primary secondary education level have been implemented for the development of Muslims. The major issues for the centrally sponsored scheme are gaps in policy programme and implementation, fewer initiatives for primary and secondary education in Maharashtra.

CONCLUSION

A number of warfare programmes have been initiated and lunched since independence, particularly last 25 years at various levels to light on the status of minority in regards to educational development. Efforts have been made to mitigate the magnitude of educational backwardness and economic difficulties of minority communities. In spite of number of programmes for the welfare of Muslims, the condition and accessibility of education of Muslims continues to pathetic in India as well as in Maharashtra. The government should have ensured the effective and proper implementation of different policies and programmes towards the development of Muslims in education. The government should initiate the programme for educational assessment and retention in India with a special attention to the Maharashtra. To develop the educational status of Muslims in Maharashtra there is a need to initiate different state level programmes in all level of education. The implementation part is the major issue which would be the focus area of Muslim for educational development.

References

Ahmad, A. (1995), Muslims in India. Inter India Publications, New Delhi.

Ashraf, A. (1982), Muslim Elite. Atlantic Publishers, New Delhi.

Al-Shamat, H. A. (2009), Educational Divide across Religious Groups in Nineteenth Century Lebanon: Institutional Effects on the Demand for Curricular Modernization. *Journal of Islamic Studies,* 20: 317-351.

Alesina, A. F., Easterly, W. and Baqir, R. (999), Public Goods and Ethnic Divisions. *Quarterly Journal of Economics,* 114 (40): 1243-1284.

Anderson, M. S. (1998), The Experience of Being in Graduate School: An Exploration: New Directions for Higher Education. Jossey-Bass, New York.

Apple, M. W. (1995), Education and Power. Routledge, New York.

Bell,L., Neary, M. & Stevenson, H. (2009), Future of Higher Education: Policy, Pedagogy and the Student Experience. Continuum, London.

Betancourt, R. and S. Gleason (2000), The Allocation of Publicly Provided Goods to Rural Households in India: On Some Consequences of Caste, Religion and Democracy. World Development, 28: 2169-2182.

Banerjee, A.V., L. Iyer and R. Somanathan (2005), History, Social Divisions and Public Goods in Rural India. *Journal of the European Economic Association,* 3(2-3): 639-647.

Dostie, B. and Jayaraman, R. (2006), Determinants of School Enrollments in Indian Villages. Economic Development and Cultural Change, 54 (2): 405-21.

Dreze, J. and Sen, A. (1997), Indian Development: Selected Regional Perspectives. Oxford University Press, New Delhi.

Dutta, P. V. (2006), Returns to Education: New Evidence for India, 1983-1999. Education Economics, 14(4): 431-451.

Government of India (2006), Social, Economic and Educational Status of the Muslim Community of India: A Report. Government of India Publication, New Delhi.

Imam, Z. (1975), (ed.), Muslims in India. Oriental Longman, New Delhi.

Jain, R. (1992), Minority Rights in Education in Bombay: an exploration. Project Report, T.I.S.S., Mumbai.

Jain, R. (2005), Minority Rights in Education: Reflections on Article 30 of the Indian Constitution. *Economic and Political Weekly,* 40 (24): 2430-2438.

Kingdon, G. G. (2007), The Progress of School Education in India. *Oxford Review of Economic Policy,* 23(2): 168–95.

Kochar, A. (2004), Urban Influences on Rural Schooling in India. *Journal of Development Economics*, 74 (1): 113-36.

Mohammad, N. (1999), (ed.), Indian Muslims: Precepts & Practice. Rawat Publication, New Delhi.

PROBE (1999l), Public Report on Basic Education in India. Oxford University Press, New Delhi.

Puniyani, R. (2000), Minorities and Human Rights. Perspectives in Social Work, 15 (3): 14-21.

Sachar, R. (2006), Social, Economic and Educational Status of the Muslim Community of India: A Report. Prime Minister's High Level Committee Cabinet Secretariat, Government of India, New Delhi.

Yaqin, A. (1986), Constitutional Protection of Minority Educational Institutions in India. Deep & Deep Publications, New Delhi.

Problems of Women Entrepreneurs in Karwar Taluka of Uttar Kannada District

MAYA S. GAONKAR*

INTRODUCTION

Entrepreneurship is a multidimensional activity and is basically innovative and dynamic. Entrepreneurship among women is a recent phenomenon. There has been a rapid growth of women entrepreneurs all over the world. In India only 5.2 per cent of women were self employed in 1981; but as per census 2001 this figure has risen to 11.2 per cent and if prevailing trend continues it is likely that in another 10 years women will comprise 20 per cent of the entrepreneurial force.

PROBLEMS OF WOMEN ENTREPRENEURS IN INDIA

Women entrepreneurs in India face some formidable problems.

(i) The patriarchal family system which is the dominant social order works as a deterrent to women entrepreneurship. . Banks and other financial institutions consider women loanees as higher risks than men loanees.

(ii) Women entrepreneurs are less mobile, have low level of education and possess low level of management skill. They lack encouragement and motivation from others.

(iii) The domestic duties of women entrepreneurs are always a hindrance to their success in business.

(iv) Women entrepreneurs lack knowledge of latest technological changes and know how. They are factors that affect business of women entrepreneurs.

Despite the various problems faced by them women entrepreneurs have been experiencing success in life and moving a step closer to their dreams of being self dependent.

The hidden entrepreneurial potential of women has gradually been changing with the growing sensitivity to the role of economic status in the

* *Principal and SGL in Commerce Mahasatee Arts, Commerce and Science College Ulga Karwar.*

society. Today women entrepreneurs represent a group of women who have broken away from the beaten track and are exploring new avenues of economic participation.

GOVERNMENT SUPPORT

Central and state governments have initiated a number of measures for giving fillip to the cause of women entrepreneurial development. These measures include, granting a variety of special concessions, Incentives, Subsidies, Assistance of varied nature - financial, technical, organizational and managerial.

The incentive schemes of the central government are executed and implemented through commercial banks, lead banks, state financial corporations, khadi and village industries, cooperatives and district industries centers etc.

State government have special subsidy schemes to women entrepreneurs for establishing electronic industries, leather industries, automobile spare parts, drugs and pharmaceuticals, jute industries and export oriented gold jewellery, etc. In the past 10 years on an average 6.8 per cent of women entrepreneurs alone had availed and utilized special subsidy. Institutional support is given through various programme implemented through institutions like:

- Federation of Societies of Women Entrepreneurship (FSWE)
- Small Entrepreneurship Development Institute of India (SDII)
- District Industries Centre (DIC)
- Development of Women and Children in Rural Areas (DWCRA)
- Integrated Rural Development Programme (IRDP)
- Prime Minister's Rojgar Yojana (PMRY)
- Training of Rural Youth for Self Employment (TRYSEM)
- Women's Cooperative Finance Corporation (WCFC)
- Financial Assistance through Women's Development Corporation (FAWDC)
- National Backward Classes Finance and Development Corporation (NBCFDC)
- National Safary Karamchari Finance and Development Corporation (NSKFDC)
- Mahila Udyog Nidhi (MUN) of Small Industries Development Bank of India (SIDBI)
- Stree Shakti Package (SSP) of SBI.

SCOPE AND STATEMENT OF THE PROBLEMS

Though women remained in the four walls of house during pre independence period, with the active participation of women in the various socio economic and political areas in the post independence period there has been a substantial shift in the mind set of people regarding the new role of women .Emergence of women entrepreneurs is traced with keen interest and support measures from government and non government as equal partner in the socio economic areas. Despite of this problems are confronting the women entrepreneurship and the growth is slow and halting.

The study addresses the various constraints and problems affecting the women enterprises. The study has covered areas like personal and family profile of the selected women entrepreneurs, social and financial dimensions and problem areas of women entrepreneurs in Karwar Taluka. In view of the scope, research problem is stated as problems of women entrepreneurs in Karwar Taluka.

OBJECTIVES

(1) To study the profile of the selected women entrepreneurs.

(2) To study the problems faced by the women entrepreneurs covered under the study.

(3) To make suitable suggestions for improvements of the enterprises managed by the women entrepreneurs.

HYPOTHESIS

(1) Husbands have been the motivating factors for the women entrepreneurs in takingn up the entrepreneurial activity.

(2) Attitude of the family members have not been encouraging for the women entrepreneurs.

(3) Women entrepreneurs have been confined to local markets only .

(4) Low level of education has not been considered as managerial problem by the women entrepreneurs.

METHODOLOGY

The present study is empirical survey based on both primary and secondary data. Primary data is of 70 selected entrepreneurs having their units in Karwar Taluka of Uttar Kannada District. The units covered include those belonging to manufacturing, services and trade organizations. Secondary data have been used from published records. The data have been collected through structured questionnaires from the selected women entrepreneurs.

REVIEW OF LITERATURE

Reviews of some contemporary writings on women entrepreneurship have revealed some areas of problems and useful remedial measures for promoting the women entrepreneurship have been made. Major areas of concern indicated by writers relate to lack of family support, shortage of finance, lack of practical knowledge, lack of self confidence, lack of marketing facility, stiff competition and lack of training, etc.

The remedial measures suggested by writers include special incentive to women entrepreneurs by government, ear marking certain percentage of credit to women entrepreneurs by banks, speedy release of subsidies. Women entrepreneurs should be made conversant with advanced information technology and effective publicity. They should be assured of adequate raw material and power supply. Adequate training in the area of entrepreneurship, financial management, etc. should be imparted to women entrepreneurs.

PROFILE OF WOMEN ENTREPRENUERS COVERED BY THE STUDY

The profile of the selected women entrepreneurs in the study provides details regarding age composition, religious affiliations, marital status, educational details, size of the family, income level of the family, business profile, etc.

(1) The data obtained through field survey has revealed that majority (78.57%) of the women entrepreneurs were in the young age group of 30-45 years. This leads to the conclusion that large majority of women entrepreneurs were in the economically active age groups.

(2) Religious affiliation of the women entrepreneurs covered by the study is largely in conformity with the overall religious distribution pattern of population in the study area. Accordingly women entrepreneurs belonging to the Hindu religion constituted the largest religious group accounting for 88.57 per cent

(3) Entrepreneurship among the married women is more predominant compared to unmarried women. Married women entrepreneurs accounted for 84.29%.

(4) Education has a direct and significant influence on entrepreneurship. The study indicate that majority of the women entrepreneurs (58.57%) had secondary +level education.

(5) The family size of the women entrepreneurs indicates that majority of them (60%) belonged to nuclear family. A small size of the family is advantageous since the entrepreneurs can devote more time for the business work.

(6) A large number of women entrepreneurs had their family income in the range of Rs. 10000-50000(80%) per year each.

(7) Manufacturing and trading activities have attracted maximum number of 28 women entrepreneurs (40%) each.

(8) High profitability (27.14%) and Low investment of capital (24.29%) has made women entrepreneurs to take up their entrepreneurial activity.

(9) Organizational pattern of the units managed by women entrepreneurs indicates the predominance of 'sole trading' type of organization as indicated by maximum of 62.86% of them.

(10) It is found from the field survey that maximum number of women entrepreneurs (58.57%) had been running their units for the last 5-10 years.

(11) The employment position of male and female workers in the enterprises run by women entrepreneurs indicates some trends. Women entrepreneurs (50%) had employed women employees while 50%women entrepreneurs each had employed less than three male employees.

PROBLEM AREAS AND WOMEN ENTREPRENEURS IN THE STUDY AREA-AN ANALYSIS

The focus of analysis is on the problem areas confronted by the women entrepreneurs covered by the study. The following aspects of the problems faced by the entrepreneurs have been analyzed

- Problems of raw materials
- Labour problems
- Markets and marketing problems
- Problem of power supply
- Government schemes and the problem of awareness
- Problem of discrimination
- Problems of management
- Relief measures needed from the government

The various problems encountered by the women entrepreneurs have been analyzed based on their responses in the study area.

PROBLEMS ENCOUNTERED BY WOMEN ENTREPRENEURS

Problems Relating to Raw Materials

Majority of 43 women entrepreneurs (61.43%) did not face any difficulty in getting raw materials. However it was difficult for 24 respondents (34.29%) in obtaining their required raw materials while for 3 women entrepreneurs

(4.29%) it was very difficult to obtain raw materials. The following table provides the details.

Table 1
Problems of Raw Materials

Problems Related to get Raw Materials	*No. of Respondents*	*% of Respondents*
Difficult	24	34.29
Very Difficult	3	4.29
Not Difficult	43	61.43
Total	70	100.00

Problems of Labour for Women Entrepreneurs

Getting suitable labour was found difficult for majority of 37 women entrepreneurs (52.86%). However a small number of 4 women entrepreneurs (5.71%) found it very difficult to get suitable labour for their units. It is significant to note that a substantial number of 29 women entrepreneurs (41.43%) did not find any difficulty in obtaining labour. The following table provides the details.

Table 2
Problems of Labour Faced by Women Entrepreneurs

Problems Related to Labour	*No. of Respondents*	*% of Respondents*
Difficult	37	52.86
Very Difficult	4	5.71
Not Difficult	29	41.43
Total	70	100.00

Consumers (Buyers) for the Enterprises

Majority of 39 respondent entrepreneurs (55.71%) indicated that their consumers / buyers consisted low, middle and high income groups. However for 19 women entrepreneurs (27.14%) buyers or consumers included only middle class people and for 8 women entrepreneurs high income people were the buyers, low income group consisted of buyers for the products of 4 respondent entrepreneurs (5.71%) belonged to low income group. The following table provides the details.

Table 3
Type of Consumers for the Enterprises

Consumers	*No. of Respondents*	*% of Respondents*
Low Income Group	4	5.71
Middle Class	19	27.14
Higher Class	8	11.43
All	39	55.71
Total	70	100.00

Market for the Products of Women Entrepreneurs

Local and state level markets absorb the products of the units organized by the respondent women entrepreneurs. Large majority of 60 women entrepreneurs (85.71%) sold their products at local market while only 10 women entrepreneurs (14.29%) sold their products in the state level market. None of them were found selling their products at national or international markets. The following table provides the details.

Table 4
Markets for the Products of Women Entrepreneurs

Market	*No. of Respondents*	*% of Respondents*
Local	60	85.71
State	10	14.29
National	0	0
International	0	0
Total	70	100.00

Channels of Distribution (Method of Dealing)

Direct selling to buyers of the products was practiced by large majority of 56 women entrepreneurs (80%), sales through agent was practiced by 6 women entrepreneurs (8.57%). Cooperatives were the channel of sales for 5 women entrepreneurs (7.14%) and 3 women entrepreneurs (4.29%) sold their products to government agencies. The following table provides the details.

Table 5
Channels of Distribution

Method of Dealing	*No. of Respondents*	*% of Respondents*
Direct	56	80.00
Agents	6	8.57
Government	3	4.29
Co-op	5	7.14
Others	0	0
Total	70	100.00

Difficulties in Marketing Encountered by Women Entrepreneurs

Stiff completion is the major difficulty of marketing of products encountered by majority of 29 women entrepreneurs (41.43%). Demand fluctuation has affected marketing of 16 women entrepreneurs (22.86%). Lack of storage facilities and lack of transportation facilities have affected marketing of 10 (14.29%) and 6 (8.57%) of women entrepreneurs untrained salesman and choice of improper channel of distribution has affected marketing of 6 (8.57%) and 2 (2.86%) of entrepreneurs. The following table provides the details.

Table 6
Marketing Problems Faced by Women Entrepreneurs

Difficulties in Market	*No. of Respondents*	*% of Respondents*
Competition	29	41.43
Demand fluctuation	16	22.86
Lack of transport facilities	6	8.57
Lack of storage	10	14.29
Untrained salesmen	6	8.57
Choice of improper channel	2	2.86
Other	1	1.43
Total	70	100.00

Problems of Power Supply

A good number of 35 respondent women entrepreneurs (50%) encountered power cut sometimes. A substantial number of 34 entrepreneurs (48.57%) faced power cut often. However one entrepreneurs did not face any problem of power supply. The details of responses are given in the following table.

Table 7
Problem of Power Supply

Problem Concerned with Power Supply	*No. of Respondents*	*% of Respondents*
No problem of power supply	1	1.43
Faced power cut (often)	34	48.57
Sometimes faced power cut	35	50.00
Total	70	100.00

Method of Quality Control

Majority of 22 women entrepreneurs (31.43%) have not followed any measure for quality control of their products. Quality control on sample basis is enforced by 21 respondents (30%) while 18 entrepreneurs (25.71%) have resorted to inspection of each item towards quality control. There is a system of automatic quality control system in case of 9 enterprises. The following table provides the details.

Table 8
Method of Quality Control

Method of Quality	*No. of Respondents*	*% of Respondents*
Inspection of each item followed	18	25.71
Quality control on sample basis enforced	21	30.00
Automatic quality control followed	9	12.86
No measure followed for quality control	22	31.43
Total	70	100.00

Conflict between Domestic Work and Entrepreneurial Activity of Women Entrepreneurs

Majority of 23 women entrepreneurs (32.86%) felt that domestic work suffered because of their involvement in entrepreneurial activity. A less number of 18 respondents (25.71%) indicated that they had less time to spend with their family. A small number of 12 women entrepreneurs (17.14%) felt that they were overloaded with the work at home and the enterprise. Further education of children is affected according to 10 respondents (14.29%) and entrepreneurship was inconvenienced the family members according to 9 women entrepreneurs (12.86%). The following table provides the details.

Table 9

Conflict Between Domestic Work and Entrepreneurial Activity

Conflict	*No. of Respondents*	*% of Respondents*
Domestic work suffered	23	32.86
Entrepreneurship is inconvenient to family	9	12.86
Less time to spend with family	18	25.71
Education of children is affected	10	14.29
Overloaded with work at home & enterprise	12	17.14
Total	70	100.00

Rate of Return on Investment

The rate of return on investment by the women entrepreneurs has been 5-10% according to majority of 35 women entrepreneurs (50%) while 26 women entrepreneurs (37.14%) indicated that the rate of return on their investment was 10-20%. Rate of return on investment was 0-5% and 20-30% in case of 3 and 5 women entrepreneurs respectively. A lone women entrepreneur mentioned that the rate of return on investment was more than 30%. The following table provides the details.

Table 10

Rate of Return on Investment

Rate of Return	*No. of Respondents*	*% of Respondents*
0-5%	3	4.29
5-10%	35	50.00
10-20%	26	37.14
20-30%	5	7.14
More than 30%	1	1.43
Total	70	100.00

Awareness about Government Schemes

Majority of 47 women entrepreneurs were aware of the government scheme of PMRY while 42 women entrepreneurs were aware of DIC and 19 women entrepreneurs were aware of bank facilities. The following table provides the details.

Table 11
Awareness About Government Facilities

Aware of Government Schemes	*No. of Respondents*	*% of Respondents*
DIC	42	60.00
PMRY	47	67.14
Bank Facilities	19	27.14
Total	70	100.00

Discriminative towards Women Enterprises

Buyers showed aversion toward women enterprises according to majority of 27 respondents (38.57%). However a substantial number of 31 women entrepreneurs (44.29%) did not find any discrimination towards women entrepreneurs. Discrimination by government and by bank against women entrepreneurs was indicated by 7 (10%) and 5 (7.14%) entrepreneurs respectively. The following table provides the details.

Table 12
Discrimination Towards Women Entrepreneurs

Discrimination Faced	*No. of Respondents*	*% of Respondents*
No discrimination	31	44.29
Buyers aversion towards women entrepreneurs	27	38.57
Discrimination towards women entrepreneurs by government	7	10.00
Discrimination by banks against women entrepreneurs	5	7.14
Total	70	100.00

MANAGERIAL PROBLEMS AND GOVERNMENT APPROACH TOWARDS WOMEN ENTERPRISES

Managerial Problems of Women Enterprises

Low level of education has led to managerial problems in women enterprises according to 8 respondents (11.43%). However majority of women entrepreneurs (35.71%) felt that managerial deficiencies were experienced because of their over involvement in domestic and business activities. Lack of confidence among women entrepreneurs had caused managerial problems according to 24 women entrepreneurs (34.29%). It is significant to find that lack of professional training had led to managerial problems as mentioned by 13 women entrepreneurs (18.57%). The following table provides the details.

Table 13
Causes for Managerial Problems

Managerial Problems	*No. of Respondents*	*% of Respondents*
Lack of professional training	13	18.57
Low level of education	8	11.43
Over involvement in domestic activities	25	35.71
Lack of confidence	24	34.29
Total	70	100.00

Maintenance of Accounts

Women entrepreneurs have been widely using manual operations of accounts maintenance. This has been indicated by large majority of 60 women entrepreneurs (85.71%). However a small number of 10 women entrepreneurs (14.29%) have been using computer for their accounts maintenance in their business firms. The following table provides the details.

Table 14
Maintenance of Accounts

Maintain Account	*No. of Respondents*	*% of Respondents*
Manually	60	85.71
Use of Computer	10	14.29
Total	70	100.00

Government Steps Unfavourable to Women Entrepreneurs

The government insistence on strict implementation of factory administration as per the rules and regulations has been felt as unfavourable government policy according to large majority of 65 women entrepreneurs (92.86%). The following table provides the details.

Table 15
Unfavourable Government Steps

Government Steps	*No. of Respondents*	*% of Respondents*
Implementation of Factory Act	65	92.86
None	5	7.14
Total	70	100.00

Favourable Steps taken by Government towards Women Entrepreneurs

Majority of women entrepreneurs (43) constituting 61.43 per cent of the total have found the loan subsidy as the major favourable step taken by the Government in favour of women entrepreneurs. Providing of financial security by the government has been mentioned as a favourable step according to 6 entrepreneurs (8.57%). Low interest on loan and moral support to women enterprises are other favourable steps taken by government according to 2 women entrepreneurs each (2.86%). Providing of loan is considered as a favourable step taken by the Government by one women entrepreneur. The following table provides the details.

Table 16
Favourable Steps Taken by Government

Favourable Steps Taken by Government	*No. of Respondents*	*% of Respondents*
None	15	21.43
Financial Security	6	8.57
Loan	1	1.43
Low Interest Rate	2	2.86
Moral Support	2	2.86
No Help	1	1.43
Subsidy	43	61.43
Total	70	100.00

Expectation of Assistance by the Government

Moral support to women entrepreneurs from the government is expected by majority of 26 women entrepreneurs (37.14%) followed by 23 entrepreneurs who expected financial support on easy terms. Bulk purchases by the government from enterprises run by women entrepreneurs was expected by 19 respondent entrepreneurs (27.14%). Establishment of women corporation and establishment of raw material bank by the government was indicated by 9 and 5 respondent women entrepreneurs respectively. The following table provides the details.

Table 17
Expectation of Assistance

Assistance	*No. of Respondents*	*% of Respondents*
Financial Support on Easy Term	23	32.86
Establishment of Raw Material Bank	5	7.14
Establishment of Women Corporate	9	12.86
Encouragement of Bulk Purchases	19	27.14
Moral Support	26	37.14
Other Assistance	0	0
Total	70	100.00

Suggestions for Improvement of Women Entrepreneurship

Majority of 31 respondent women entrepreneurs (44.29%) have suggested for adequate and timely credit to their enterprises. Making available of modern technology and quality innovation and consumer satisfactions are the two suggestions made by 22 respondent women entrepreneurs each. Hard work on the part of women entrepreneurs and SWOT analysis by the women entrepreneurs have been suggested by 7 and 5 respondent women entrepreneurs respectively. The following table provides the details.

Table 18
Suggestions for Improvement of Women Entrepreneurs

Suggestions	*No. of Respondents*	*% of Respondents*
Adequate and Timely Credit	31	44.29
Modern Technology to be Made Available	22	31.43
Quality Innovation & Consumer Satisfaction	22	31.43
SWOT Analysis	5	7.14
Hard work	7	10.00
Increase in No. of Entrepreneurs	0	0
Total	70	100.00

SUMMARY, FINDINGS AND SUGGESTION

(1) Some women entrepreneurs have faced the problem of getting raw materials and also labor in the study area.which has its impact on the performance and sustenance of the entrepreneurship in general and women entrepreneurs in particular.

(2) The consumers for the women entrepreneurs belong to low income group, middle class and higher class and Large majority of women entrepreneurs sale their products in the local market. Besides the channels of distribution is again highly concentrated directly to the buyers.

(3) Competition from rival units has been the major problem of marketing the products as indicated by majority of women entrepreneurs. Shortage of power supply has been faced by women entrepreneurs. Majority of women entrepreneurs have indicated that they did not follow any measure for quality control in their enterprises,

(4) Involvement in entrepreneurship has affected the domestic work in case of majority of women entrepreneurs Education of children has suffered due to involvement in entrepreneurship and have indicated that they were overloaded with the work at home and at the enterprise. The above responses indicate the social impact of the women entrepreneurship.

(5) The rate of return on the investment made by majority of women entrepreneurs has been quite low at 5-10 per cent. Entrepreneurs could manage their business venture successfully by taking advantage of financial and other facilities provided by government. Further majority of women entrepreneurs expressed their awareness about the financial facilities provided by banks.

(6) Women entrepreneurship is faced with the problem of discrimination at different level - buyers, government bank officials.

(7) Managerial problems of women entrepreneurs have been faced due to varied reasons like involvement in domestic work,. lack of confidence, Lack of professional training and Low level of education are the cause for managerial problems according to women entrepreneurs.

(8) Maintenance of accounts has still not been computerized largely. Implementation of Factory Act has been considered as an unfavorable step by the Government as such steps affect the functioning of the women managed enterprises. Government has taken some steps in favour of the women entrepreneurship in the state. Major step favoring the women entrepreneurs is the subsidy.

(9) The women entrepreneurs covered by the study have indicated some assistance programme like moral support and financial support, adequate and timely credit, availability of modern technology and quality innovation for consumer satisfaction. Other suggestions included incorporation of SWOT analysis and hard work by the entrepreneurs.

HYPOTHESES AND FINDINGS OF THE RESEARCH STUDY

(1) The first hypothesis that husband has been the motivating factor for the women entrepreneurs in taking up their entrepreneurial activity has been partially vindicated by the responses of women entrepreneurs.

(2) The second hypothesis that the attitude of the family members has not been encouraging for the women entrepreneurs is largely vindicated. It is found from the field survey that only 37.14% of the women entrepreneurs have mentioned that the attitude of family members has been encouraging and large majority of 62.86% of the women entrepreneurs could not find the attitude of family members as encouraging.

(3) The third hypothesis that women entrepreneurs have confined to local market only for the sale of their products is largely true as indicated by large majority of 83.71% of women entrepreneurs in the study area.

(4) The fourth hypothesis that low level of education has not been considered as a managerial problem by women entrepreneurs is largely vindicated by the responses of the women entrepreneurs. Large majority of 88.57% of the women entrepreneurs have indicated other factors causing managerial problems.

SUGGESTIONS

Following measures are needed towards achieving the above objectives.

- Conducting gender analysis for all entrepreneurial support programme.
- Using targeted approaches for priority categories in order to provide additional 'push' to women entrepreneurs to the next level of growth.

- Promoting more flexible and innovative financial products by banks.
- Policies, laws and overall regulatory environment are frequently seen as barriers to expansion and growth. They need to be removed.
- Taking account of the social and cultural context affecting policy implementation and redress inequalities and abnormalities.
- Making use of IT and associations so as to minimize the administrative burdens on women entrepreneurs.
- Encouraging and rewarding dynamic representative associations of women entrepreneurs.
- Profiling the economic and social contributors among women entrepreneurs to the national economy.
- Ensuring synergies between (a) women related ministry, (b) economic ministry, (c) welfare and social development ministry in the government.
- Government and other voluntary organizations should conduct financial management training programme for women entrepreneurs.

Marketing problems of women entrepreneurs need to be addressed by the government and NGOs.

The problem of price competition has to be addressed by giving subsidies and concessions to the women entrepreneurs. Purchase preference for the products of the women entrepreneurs and reservation of certain products for the women entrepreneurs would also be of help to them. Shopping complex for women entrepreneurs for marketing their products

Forming of 'Women Entrepreneurs Association' at the district level would be useful as it would provide a forum and a common platform for discussing their problems and for a collective approach for findings ways and means to solve them.

(i) Training on professional competence and leadership skill should be extended to women entrepreneurs.

(ii) Training and counseling on a large scale of existing women entrepreneurs should be initiated to remove psychic causes like lack of self confidence and fear of success.

(iii) Vocational training should be extended to women entrepreneurs that enable them to understand the production process and production management.

(iv) Skill development should be given priority in women's polytechnics and industrial training institutes.

(v) Training in entrepreneurial attitudes should start at the high school level through well designed courses, which build confidence through behavioural games.

(vi) Continuous monitoring and improvement of training programmes should be conducted.

Short term courses should be organized for women entrepreneurs to make them proficient in the areas of working capital management, costing techniques, sales promotion, marketing management, etc.

Women entrepreneurs should be fully conversant with computers, documentation, account and book keeping, communication, etc. must be carried out systematically.

Women entrepreneurs should experiment and innovate continuously and implement new technology so as to achieve cost efficiency and competitiveness.

There is need for counseling through committed NGOs, psychologists, managerial experts and technical personnel to women entrepreneurs - existing and emerging.

There is also need for special programmes, training, symposium, seminar, workshop, seed capital and incentive for women entrepreneurs on entrepreneurship.

Women are not into business for survival but to satisfy their inner urge of creativity and to prove their capabilities. Women education is contributing to a great extent to the social transformation. Women are increasingly making their mark in the typically male dominated workplace. However they comprise a very meager portion of entrepreneurs in India. Women in India still need to be courageous, risk taking, challenge seeking and above all they are required to be independent. They need to break themselves free from the confines of the four wall of the home which is traditionally recognized role of women in our country and to come out of the cocoon of a subservient living provided by male family members. This requires cultural ethos and training the male mindset to recognize women as equals and not inferior to them through a multipronged action of legislative, admini.

References

B. N. Singh (1989), "Women Workforce–Problems and Prospects", *Yojana*, March, p. 15.

C. Swarajyalakshmi , "Development of Women Entrepreneurship in India" - Problems and Prospects, Discovery Publishing House, New Delhi.

Dileepkumar M. (2006), Problems of Women Entrepreneurs in India.

Dr. Vasantgopal and Santa S., "Women Entrepreneurship in India". New Century Publication, New Delhi.

Jose P. Ajith Kumar and Paul T.M. (1994), "Entrepreneurship Development". Himalaya Publishing, New Delhi.

Pooja Nayyar et al. (2007), Causes and Constraints Faced by Women Entrepreneurs in Entrepreneurial Process. *J. Soc. Sc., www.krepublishers.com/02*

S.P. Mishra, "Factors Affecting Women Entrepreneurship in Small and Cottage Industries in India. *http://www.ilo.org*

Sabita Mishra and Ashok Baran Das, Women Entrepreneurship for Self Employment–Employment News, 2006, p. 4.

Sanjay Tiwar, Anshuja Tiwar, "Women Entrepreneurship and Economic Development".

Sankaran A. (2009), Trend and Problems of Rural Women Entrepreneurs in India, *Southern Economist,* June 15, 2009.

Shilpee Adhikari (2009), Women Entrepreneur – New Face of Women.

Uttar Kannada District at a Glance 2005-06.

Valasamma Antony (2007), Women Entrepreneurs on the Upbeat–A Study. *Southern Economist,* March 1, 2007.

Vikas – Problems of Women Entreprenerus in India. *http://www.123eng.com*

Right to Education and Problems in it's Implementation: A Case Study of Women's Education in Jammu and Kashmir

FAYAZ AHMAD BHAT* & FOUZIA KHURSHID**

INTRODUCTION

Education has been the main instrument of human development as it helps men and women to claim their rights and realise their potential in economic, political and social arenas. This emphasis on education is because of the fact that in the modern world it is considered as an important and powerful instrument of economic development, social transformation and mobilization of human resources. The progress and prosperity of a nation as well of a community is determined by the level of education. Education plays a significant role in the dissemination of modern attitudes, values, approaches and outlook. This remarkable modernizing potential of education needs to be realized by every individual and community and must go in for it (Ahmad, 1987: 201).

The importance of education has been emphasized through fundamental rights, principles, statutes/acts in a number of countries. At the international level, attempts have been made at various conferences to focus on aspects of education as a part of fundamental human right. According to the Article 26 of the Universal Declaration of Human Rights (UDHR).

> *'Everyone has the right to education. Education shall be free, at least in the elementary and fundamental stages. Elementary education shall be compulsory... Education shall be directed to the full development of human personality and to the strengthening of respect for human rights and fundamental freedoms.'*
>
> *(Universal Declaration of Human Rights, Article 26)*

This right is also repeated in the UN Declaration of the Rights of the child which seeks to ensure, 'Right to free and compulsory education at least in the elementary stages and education to promote general culture, abilities, judgment

* Research Scholars, Department of Sociology and Social Work, Aligarh Muslim University, Aligarh, India, (E-mail: *fayazbht8@gmail.com & **fouzia.khurshid@gmail.com

and sense of responsibility to become a useful member of society and opportunity to recreation, and play to attain the same purpose as of education'. The right to education has also been enshrined in International Covenant on Economic, Social and Cultural Rights (ICESCR, 1966), Convention on the Elimination of All Forms of Discrimination against Women (CEDAW, 1979) and more recently in Convention on the Rights of the Child (CRC, 1989). While the right to education is universally recognised, the way it is interpreted at the national level differs substantially.

India has ratified the above, and these have thus the power of domestic laws. The 86th Constitutional Amendment Act 2002 made education in India a Fundamental Right for children in the age group of 6-14 years by stating that

> *'the State shall provide free and compulsory education to all children of the age of six to fourteen years in such manner as the State may, by law, determine'.*

Right to education has been a part of the directive principles of the State Policy under the Article 45 of the Constitution, which is part of Chapter 4 of the Constitution and rights in Chapter 4 are not enforceable. For the first time in the history of India, this right has been made enforceable by putting it in Chapter 3 of the Constitution as the Article 21. After sixty-three years of independence, the Right of children to Free and Compulsory Education Act has come into force in the whole of India except the state of Jammu and Kashmir from April 1, 2010. From this day the right to education will be accorded the same legal status as the right to life as provided by the Article 21(A) of the Indian Constitution. This entitles children to have the right to education enforced as a fundamental right.

Right to Education Act (RTE) promises that every child in the age group of 6-14 years will be provided 8 years of elementary education in an age appropriate classroom in the vicinity of his/her neighbourhood. Any cost that prevents a child from accessing school will be borne by the State which shall have the responsibility of enrolling the child as well as ensuring attendance and completion of 8 years of schooling. No child shall be denied admission for want of documents; no child shall be turned away if the admission cycle in the school is over and no child shall be asked to take admission through admission test. Children with disabilities will also be educated in the mainstream schools. All private schools shall be required to enrol children from weaker sections and disadvantaged communities in their incoming class to the extent of 25% of their enrolment, by simple random selection. Financial burden will be shared between state and central government on the basis of Sarva Shiksha Abhiyan (SSA). The National Commission for Protection of Child Rights (NCPCR) has been mandated to monitor the implementation of this historic Right together with Commissions to be set up by the states.

Despite of the widespread agreement on that all people have the fundamental human right to education, millions of children, most of them girls, do not have access to primary education and are still unaware of the fact that this is the right they can demand. Women continue to face discrimination at all levels of education, a fact which poses tremendous obstacles to their advancement. Cultural and traditional values stand between women and their prospects for education. They have not been able to enjoy the rights available to them because of sheer ignorance and lack of knowledge, the undercurrent of this being illiteracy. The right of girls to education is one of the most critical of all rights because education plays an important role in enabling girls and women to secure other rights.

Women education has assumed special significance in the context of the country's planned development. This is because women represent a valuable human resource, and play an important role in the development of the community and the nation. Education is widely perceived as a key factor in improving the status of women and even more importantly, as an agent for developing modern attitudes, values, approach and rational outlook. Lack of education among women hinders their ability to bring about economic development and social transformation of the community and of the nation as a whole (Srivastava, 2005: 7). Improving educational opportunities for women helps them to develop skills that allow them to make decisions and influence community change in key areas. Education is crucial in empowering women to participate in economic, social and political life of their societies. It not only unlocks their potential but also assists in improving health, nutrition, and well-being of themselves as well as of their families. However, despite this significance of education, the participation of women in the field of education is not very satisfactory. There is a wide gender gap in literacy rate, not only in India but also in the state of Jammu and Kashmir.

The current paper is an attempt to trace the growth and expansion of women's education in Jammu and Kashmir and is based on secondary data. It also focuses on governmental policies and programmes laid down for the development of education among women in the State. The paper also stresses the need of the Right to Education (RTE) Act to be extended to the state of Jammu and Kashmir.

JAMMU AND KASHMIR AT A GLANCE

The State of Jammu and Kashmir is one of the largest States of the Indian Union. It lies between 32°-15′ and 37°-05′ North latitude and 72°-35′ and 83°-20′ East longitude. The total area of the state is about 222236 sq.km of which 78114 sq.km. are under the illegal occupation of Pakistan and 37555 sq.km under China. In addition to this, 5180 sq.km of Jammu and Kashmir were illegally handed over by Pakistan to China. This leaves the State with an area of 101387 sq.km. The Indian state of Jammu and Kashmir comprises three natural regions: Jammu, Kashmir and Ladakh. The total population of the state is 10143700 persons with its density being 99 and sex ratio 900 in Census 2001. Further, sex wise break-up of the population shows that 5,300,574 are male and 4,769,343 are female.

HISTORY OF WOMEN'S EDUCATION IN JAMMU AND KASHMIR

The educational status of women in Kashmir like their equivalents elsewhere in the country is also depressing and quite dismal. There is a scarcity of comprehensive sociological studies covering the various aspects of women's life in Jammu and Kashmir. Women in the traditional Kashmiri society were generally subjected to discrimination, inequality and oppression. They were considered unequal and inferior to men both physically and mentally. Kashmiri woman had no role in the decision making process and all important decisions, including decisions about them, were exclusively sanctioned by male members of the family. The role of women remained confined to domestic affairs and so they were also debarred from education. (Dabla, 2007: 43-44). Thus the life of woman in traditional Kashmiri society was characterized mainly by dependency, inequality, ignorance and pervasive and severe gender discrimination. People were highly conservative and the realization that women need to be educated was totally lacking.

The first effort to educate Kashmiri women who were living in suppression and oppression came from the missionaries. They realized the need to dispel ignorance for improvement in the condition in which Kashmiri women were living. It struck them that they should do something to teach them at least the rudiments of learning. The education of women was a sensitive social question as such a thing was never heard of. It was sometime between 1893 and 1895 that a missionary school for girls was started by the Church Missionary Society. There was a strong opposition to this school as it aroused suspicion in the minds of people who were conservative in their outlook. They feared that in the school the minds of their women would be polluted by the impure ideas from foreign lands which would lead them astray (Bazaz, 1959: 211). Due to the conservative attitude of people and their general indifference and apathy to the education of women, the school could not become popular, as it shocked the prejudices of the traditional conservative Kashmiri society. Only a few girls attended the school and their parents were somewhat on the shake, as the public opinion was very much against them (Biscoe, 1998: 257). After some initial opposition, the school managed to establish itself and to get the students. The dedication and personal efforts of the missionary ladies who laid the foundation of this school, encouraged parents to enrol their daughters in this school (Khan, 2005: 160).

Keeping into consideration the people's attitudes and the mode of their thinking, the State Council adopted a very cautious policy and did not took any step towards the opening of schools for the education of girls. However, it favoured helping private efforts. In 1904, for the first time the State Council provided funds for the establishment of two girls' schools at Srinagar, one for

Hindu girls and the other for Muslim girls, which were to be managed by separate committees of the leading men of the two communities under the guidance of State educational authorities. It was in 1912, that the first attempt was witnessed at imparting secondary education to women.

In 1926, Women's Welfare Trust was established with some prominent citizens as its trustees and members. It made a significant contribution in the promotion of women's education. Within a period of four years the Trust was running ten schools with an enrolment of 575 girls. The Education Reorganization Committee (1938-39) under the chairman-ship of G.K. Saiyidain, with regard to promotion of girls' education recommended the opening of more primary and middle schools and provision of incentives in the form of increase in scholarships and distribution of free books. Other recommendations included the appointment of two woman inspectors one for each region, reorganization of the curriculum for girls and provision of accommodation for women teachers (Khan, 2005: 158-161).

With the partition of the country, the Jammu and Kashmir National Conference formed the first elected government in the State. The Party prepared the Draft of the future constitution of the State which was given the name of "Naya Kashmir" in which education in the State of Jammu and Kashmir was a major and important demand. The Draft provides special arrangements for women's education in accordance with the provision of the Women's Charter.

The Women's Charter

Realizing that educational facilities are essential and a pre-requisite for any large scale upliftment of women, the Jammu and Kashmir National Conference calls for more intensive work and schemes for women's education based on the following:

(a) Compulsory free primary education for women. Travelling schools to be provided for nomad women, boat schools for boat women, and other special arrangements to be made for other classes of women who find it impossible to attend ordinary schools.

(b) Equal educational rights and privileges in liberal and technical education, women's study to be encouraged by the grant of special scholarships at every stage.

(c) Separate colleges for women, liberal and technical and domestic to be established. Women also to be given the right to join men's colleges.

(d) Recognition of the special needs of women in the drawing up of educational curricula.

(e) Schemes for adult education among women to be put forward, these schemes to include not only the three Rs. but also hygienic and elementary child welfare (Khan, 1973: 13-14).

The first college in the State was established in 1905 in Srinagar. Although it was open to both men and women, it remained predominantly a male institution. Being a conservative society, attending men's college was not acceptable for women. However, the college had some girls on its rolls who were mostly daughters of non-Kashmiri or of Kashmiri families who had lived outside the state. A major obstacle to women's education was the absence of any institution of higher education exclusively for women. A breakthrough in women's education came in the year 1950, which saw the establishment of the first women's college, on Maulana Azad Road, Srinagar and the higher education among women started to gain popularity with the establishment of this college. In 1961, another college (Nawa Kadal College) for women was established. With the establishment of institutions of higher education exclusively for women, there was change in the attitude of women, and their consciousness rose. (Khan, 2005: 150-160).

TREND IN DEVELOPMENT OF WOMEN'S EDUCATION IN JAMMU AND KASHMIR

An analysis of census figures reveals that there is an increase in the literacy levels in general and male-female literacy in particular from 1961-2008. However gender gap in literacy rate still exists which is an issue of grave concern.

It is depicted by Table 1 that there is a substantial progress in the general literacy rate of the state. According to census 2001, the literacy level climbed up from 12.95 per cent in 1961 to 54.46 per cent in 2001 but it still lags far behind the national average of 65.38 per cent (65.67 per cent in 2008 according to Economic Survey 2008-09 of the State). Further account of the male-female literacy rates shows that the male literacy rate is higher than female literacy rate in all the years. The male literacy rate reached to 73.30 per cent in 2008 which was only 19.75 per cent in 1961, whereas the female literacy rate increased from 5.05 per cent in 1961 to 57.11 per cent in 2008. There is a continuous rise in the literacy rate of females. Nevertheless, it did not exceed over the male literacy rate. In the delineation of above figures, it can be argued that though there is a considerable progress in female literacy rate but gender disparity in literacy rate still prevails in the state.

Table 1

Trends in Literacy Rates by Sex in Jammu and Kashmir: 1961-81 and 2001.

Particulars	*1961*	*1971*	*1981*	*2001*	*2008**
Male	19.75	31.01	41.46	65.75	73.30
Female	5.05	10.94	18.73	41.82	57.11
Total	12.95	21.71	30.64	54.46	65.67
Gap (Male-Female)	14.7	20.07	23.09	23.93	16.19

Note: *The figures under the year 2008 are Estimated Literacy Rates.

Source: Census of India (a) J & K 2001, Paper-2 of 2001, Rural-Urban Distribution of Population and Government of J& K (2008-09) Economic Survey.

The progress made in the literacy rate is not uniform and it varies across rural and urban areas. The differentials in literacy rates in rural and urban areas have been illustrated in Table 2. The data shows that the literacy rate in rural areas has increased from 25.01 per cent in 1981 to 61.91 per cent in 2008 whereas in case of urban areas, the literacy rate has increased from 51.12 per cent in 1981 to 77.08 per cent in 2008.

It can be observed from Table 2 that literacy rate in rural areas is lower than urban areas. Since 1981 census, the literacy rate in rural areas has increased by 36.9 per cent against 25.96 per cent in urban areas. Further analysis of the table depicts that since 1981 census, the literacy rate among males has increased by 33.73 per cent and 23.28 per cent in rural and urban areas respectively. Similarly, the progress in literacy rate among the females is reported higher in rural areas in comparison to urban areas as it has jumped from 12.19 per cent to 52.70 per cent since 1981, which is almost a four-fold increase. In urban areas, the female literacy has increased from 41.05 per cent in 1981 to 70.37 per cent in 2008. Thus during the period 1981-2008, female literacy rate in rural areas has increased by 40.51 per cent against 29.32 per cent in urban areas.

The analysis clearly shows that the progress in literacy rate is noticed higher in rural areas than urban areas both in case of male and female. Rural males have taken lead over urban males by 3.56 per cent and 6.89 per cent during the period 1981-2001 and 2001-08 respectively. Similarly, the progress in literacy rate among the rural females is higher by 1.73 per cent and 9.46 per cent than urban females during the period 1981-2001 and 2001-08 respectively. Further analysis reveals that female literacy rate is lower than male literacy rate in both rural and urban areas.

Table 3 aptly shows that in the past few years, a continuous increase in the enrolment ratio has been achieved in the state of Jammu and Kashmir. From 1996-97 to 2000-01 enrolment ratio saw an increase of 24.19 per cent.

It can be noted from Table 3 that enrolment ratio increased to 91.79 in 2000-01 as against 67.6 in 1996-97. It can be observed from the table that enrolment ratio of girls has increased to 80.11 as against 104.05 for boys in 2000-01. This variation is due to high dropout rate in girls in comparison to boys. The goal of Right to Education Act or universalisation of elementary education cannot be achieved till the dropout rate is brought down to the minimum level possible. Dropout rate is defined as the percentage of students who drop out of a class in a year. Dropout rate is a very important indicator about enrolment status to capture the flow aspect of educational attainment in any context. Table 3 also depicts the picture of dropout rate at primary level in the past couple of years in Jammu and Kashmir. The table clearly indicates that the dropout rate at Primary level in 1996-97 was 34.08 which came down to 22.39 in 1998-99. It saw a decrease of 11.69 per cent within a very short span of time. However in 2000-01 it increased to 33.18 depicting an increase of 10.79

Table 2

Percentage of Male-Female Literacy Rates in Rural/ Urban Population, 1981, 2001 and 2008 In Jammu and Kashmir

	Literacy Rate																	
	Persons			*Variation*			*Males*			*Variation*			*Females*			*Variation*		
Rural/ Urban	*1981*	*2001*	*2008**	*1981-2001*	*2001-08*	*1981-2008*	*1981*	*2001*	*2008**	*1981-2001*	*2001-08*	*1981-2008*	*1981*	*2001*	*2008**	*1981-2001*	*2001-08*	*1981-2008*
Rural	25.01	48.22	61.91	23.21	13.69	36.9	36.35	60.34	70.08	23.99	9.74	33.73	12.19	35.09	52.70	22.9	17.61	40.51
Urban	51.12	72.17	77.08	21.05	4.91	25.96	59.87	80.3	83.15	20.43	2.85	23.28	41.05	62.22	70.37	21.17	8.15	29.32

Note: *The calculated figures under the year 2008 are Estimated Literacy Rates.

Source: Census of India (a) J & K 2001, Paper-2 of 2001, Rural-Urban Distribution of Population and Government of J& K (2008-09) Economic Survey.

Table 3
Enrolment Ratio and Dropout Ratio: I-V

	Enrolment Ratio			*Drop Out Ratio*		
Year	*Boys*	*Girls*	*Total*	*Boys*	*Girls*	*Total*
1996-97	84	53.1	67.6	34.4	33.63	34.08
1998-99	93.38	66.63	79.95	24.01	20.20	22.39
2000-01*	104.05	80.11	91.79	34.35	31.67	33.18

Note: * Selected Educational Statistics 2000-2001.
Source: Annual Report on Educational Profile (School Stream) of J&K for 2000-2001. Education Department.

per cent. In case of boys the dropout rate increased by 10.34 per cent as against 11.47 per cent for girls during the same period. Increase in the dropout rate of girls resulted in the widening of gap between male and female literacy rates. This gender disparity in literacy rate is also revealed by the census figures.

Since independence the state government has been expanding the provision of education to realize the goal of universal education for all children up to the age of fourteen years. This resulted in the gradual expansion of institutions at all levels and their number started increasing. As a result there was a phenomenal progress in terms of the expansion of number of institutions, enrolment and number of teachers at all the three levels i.e. Primary, Middle and High/Higher Secondary levels.

Table 4
No. of Educational Institutions, Enrolment and Number of Teachers in Primary Schools

	No. of Institutions			*No. of Students on roll (Lacs)*			*No. of Teachers*		
Years	*T*	*M*	*F*	*T*	*M*	*F*	*T*	*M*	*F*
1968-69	4955	3524	1431	2.7	2.59	0.11	6340	4596	1744
1979-80	7034	4473	2561	5.21	3.35	1.86	9885	6132	3753
1989-90	8990	6007	2983	6.77	4.6	2.97	15406	9090	6316
1999-00	10860	7878	2982	11.05	6.11	4.94	25369	15433	9936
2007-08 (P)	11395	9333	2062	11.36	5.93	5.43	36718	21082	15636

Note: P: Provisional; T: Total; M: Male; F: Female.
Source: Government of J& K, Digest of Statistics, 2007-08.

Table 4 gives a comprehensive picture of primary schools in terms of enrolment, number of teachers and institutions in the State. The table indicates that the number of Primary schools in the year 1968-69 was 4955, which increased to 11395 in 2007-08, indicating an increase of 6440 schools during this period. The number of students on roll in Primary schools during 1968-69 was 2.70 lac which increased to 11.36 lac during 2007-08. This shows that there was a steady increase in the enrolment of girl students. The number of girl students at the Primary level which was 0.11 lac during 1968-69 reached to 5.43 lacs in 2007-08 i.e., an increase of 5.32 lac girl students during the said period of time. The number of boys increased by 3.34 lacs during this period. This shows that the number of students in Primary schools has gone up. Further analysis of the table clearly depicts that the female enrolment ratio has remained lower than the males throughout these years. The growth in the number of teachers at the Primary level also seems to be phenomenal. The number of teachers reached to 36718 in 2007-08 from 6340 in 1968-69. Thus there was an increase of 30378 teachers during this period. During the same period, the number of male teachers increased by 16486 as against 13892 for female teachers. The increase in the number of teachers is not proportionate with the number of students which showed an increase of 8.66 lacs during the same period. The shortage of teachers in the State forced the State government to open new institutions to fulfil the gaps. During the Eighth Five-Year Plan, 14 District Institute of Educational Training (DIET) were opened to overcome the shortage of teachers at the Primary level.

Table 5
No. of Educational Institutions, Enrolment and Number of Teachers in Middle Schools

	No. of Institutions			*No. of Students on roll (Lacs)*			*No. of Teachers*		
Years	T	M	F	T	M	F	T	M	F
1968-69	1309	1017	292	1.05	0.75	0.3	5964	4765	1199
1979-80	1997	1465	532	1.67	1.1	0.52	12306	8482	3824
1989-90	2368	1799	569	3.03	1.95	1.08	17185	10957	6228
1999-00	3487	2836	651	4.24	2.35	1.89	30054	18784	11270
2007-08 (P)	5464	4412	1052	7.26	4.12	3.14	36573	21026	15547

Note: P: Provisional; T: Total; M: Male; F: Female.
Source: Government of J& K, Digest of Statistics, 2007-08.

Table 5 gives a comprehensive picture of middle schools in terms of enrolment, number of teachers and institutions in the State. The number of institutions which was 1309 during 1968-69 reached to 5464 during 2007-08. Thus there was an increase of 4155 schools during this period .The number of teachers reached to 36573 during 2007-08 as against 5964 during 1968-69. During the same period of time, the number of male teachers increased by 16261 as against 14348 for female teachers. The figures in the Table 5 reveal that the enrolment at the middle school level was 1.05 lacs during the period 1968-69. These figures reached to 7.26 lacs during 2007-08. There was an increase of students by 6.21 lac during this period. During this period, the number of both male and female students increased by 3.37 lacs and 2.84 lacs respectively. Stage wise enrolment in general education up to school standard is depicted in Table 6.

Table 6
Stage Wise Enrolment in General Education Up to School Standard (Lacs)

	Pre-primary Stage			*Primary stage (I-IV Classes)*			*Middle Stage (V-VIII Classes)*		
	T	*M*	*F*	*T*	*M*	*F*	*T*	*M*	*F*
1968-69	0.08	0.2	0.6	2.62	2.57	0.05	1.05	0.75	0.3
1979-80	0.10	0.06	0.04	5.11	3.28	1.83	1.62	1.10	0.52
1989-90	0.15	0.09	0.06	7.43	4.52	2.91	3.03	1.95	1.08
1999-00	0.42	0.23	0.19	10.63	5.88	4.75	4.25	2.36	1.89
2007-08 (P)	1.37	0.76	0.61	10.52	5.61	4.91	5.19	2.86	2.33

P: Provisional; T: Total; M: Male; F: Female

Source: Government of J& K, Digest of Statistics, 2007-08.

It can be observed from Table 6 that there has been a continuous rise in enrolment during the period in observation i.e., 1968-69 to 2007-08 at Pre-primary stage. However, there has been decrease in the enrolment of girls from 0.060 lacs in 1968-69 to 0.058 in 1989-90. From 1989-90 onwards, a phenomenal growth in the enrolment of girls was seen and their number increased to 0.612 lacs in 2007-08. Thus there was an increase of 0.554 lacs from 1989-90 to 2007-08. In the enrolment of boys at Pre-primary stage there has been a continuous rise and their number increased to 0.761 lacs in 2007-08 from 0.020 in 1968-69.

At Primary stage (I-V classes), it has been noticed from Table 6 that total enrolment increased from 2.620 lacs in 1968-69 to 10.630 in 1999-00. However, in 2007-08, it decreased to 10.519 showing a decrease of 0.111 lacs during this period. The number of boys on roll increased from 2.570 in 1968-69 to 5.879 in 1999-00 and then decreased to 5.612 in 2007-08 showing a decrease of 0.267 lacs from 1999-00 to 2007-08. In case of girls there has been continuous rise in their enrolment which increased to 4.907 in 2007-08 as against 0.050 in 1968-69 thereby showing an increase of 4.857 lacs. A glance at Table 6 reveals that there has been a continuous increase in the enrolment of both boys and girls at both Middle stage and Secondary stage during 1968-69 to 2007-08. However, it can be observed from the table that there exists variation in the enrolment of boys and girls across all the four stages i.e., Pre-primary stage, Primary stage (I-V) classes and Middle stage (VI-VIII) classes. The enrolment of girls is found to be low when compared to the enrolment of boys at all the four stages.

With low female enrolment, and high dropout rates, achieving universal elementary education is an enormous challenge that is why state government has launched various interventions to improve the education among women.

GOVERNMENT POLICIES

The Article 43 of the constitution set the goal of free and compulsory education for all children through age fourteen and gave States the power to set standards for education within their jurisdictions. High priority has been accorded to the education of women in the Five Year Plans. During these Plans, greater thrust was laid on UEE (Universalisation of Elementary Education) and UPE (Universalisation of Primary Education). In order to achieve it the government of India launched the District Primary Education Programme (DPEP) (Srivastava, 2005: 125-129). Based on the Fourth Educational Survey, the Sixth Plan emphasized that achieving elementary education was a major problem not due to non-availability of schools but socio-economic reasons in rural areas. The Sixth Plan stated the programme of Universalisation of Elementary Education (UEE) would be specially directed towards high enrolment and retention of girls in schools. The Seventh Five Year Plan (1985-90), stressed on enrolment and retention of girls at the elementary stage specially belonging to rural areas, the Scheduled Castes/Scheduled Tribes and other weaker sections. The key issue which characterized the Seventh Plan was the economic independence of women and this was followed by the evolution of beneficiary oriented programmes for their development. The Eighth Five Year Plan (1992-97) tried to ensure that the benefits of development do not bypass women especially in education, health and employment. The Ninth Five Year Plan (1997-2002) and the Tenth Five Year Plan (2002-2007), took up empowering women as agents of socio-economic change and development as a major commitment. Education was considered to be the most important factor leading to their empowerment (Das and Sagar, 2007: 52).

Table 7
Distribution of Outlay to Education in Various Plans

Plans	*Total plan outlay (in Lacs)*	*Allocation to Education (in Lacs)*	*Actual Expenditure on Education*	*Total Outlay (%)*	*Actual Expenditure (%)*
1st Plan	1274.15	66.06	48.86 Lacs	5.18	3.83
2nd Plan	5127	281.68	235.51 Lacs	5.49	4.49
3rd Plan	7514.84	612.75	557.64 Lacs	8.15	7.42
4th Plan	15740	794	827.11 Lacs	5.04	5.25
5th Plan	36340	2318	1694 Lacs	6.37	4.66
6th Plan	900*	4030	5052.55 Lacs	4.47	5.61
7th Plan	1400*	8262	141.57 Lacs	5.90	10.11
8th Plan	5200*	483.43*	-	9.29	-
9th Plan	1000000	100066.5	87781.57 Lacs	10.006	8.79
10th Plan	1450000	136612.8	36669.46 Lacs	9.42	2.53
11th Plan	2583400	216037	NA	8.36	NA

Note: * Figures in Crores; NA-Not Available.
Source: Government of J & K, Digest of Statistics, 2008-09.

The 11th Plan (2007-2012) will focus on bridging gender disparities in educational access, focusing specifically on Schedule Caste, Schedule Tribe, Tribal and Muslim communities through allocation of greater resources and more context-specific programming, including a sub-plan on Muslim girls' education. As a result of these interventions there has been a continuous rise in rate of literacy among women which can be ascertained on the basis of statistics available on women education. Having a glance at Table 7 shows that the total out lay incurred on education increased from Rs. 1274.15 lac to Rs. 216037 lacs in the first plan to Eleventh Plan respectively. Similarly the total expenditure on education increased from 48.86 Lacs to 36669.46 lacs in the first plan to Tenth Plan respectively. With the result the literacy level raised from 12.95 per cent in 1961 to 65.67 per cent in 2008. However, the gender disparity in education continues to be an area of concern. Thus we find that despite significant policy initiatives there exist gender disparities. This has once again made the Policy planners to look into the policies formulated by the government.

From the foregoing discussion and the data base regarding educational indicators it is depicted that there exist gender disparities in education in state. The disparity in educational attainments between men and women has been so wide despite the fact that women have been entitled equal rights in the constitution. The Article 42 of the constitution, an amendment added in 1976, transferred education from the State list of responsibilities to the concurrent list for which both central and state governments are responsible. Despite this joint responsibility for education by State and central governments, the central government has the preponderant role in formulating education policies to be implemented by the state governments. Various policies and programmes that have been initiated by the central government for education of women and implemented in Jammu and Kashmir are given below.

POLICIES FOR PROMOTING EDUCATION OF GIRLS

Various policies and programmes that have been initiated by the central government for education of women and implemented in Jammu and Kashmir are given below.

Sarva Shiksha Abhiyan (SSA)

The Sarva Shiksha Abhiyan was launched in accordance to the Eighty Sixth Constitutional Amendment for Universal Elementary Education (UEE) towards the end of the Ninth Five Year Plan in 2001 and was integrated with the District Primary Education Programme (DPEP). It was intended to ensure that all children were enrolled into the schooling system by 2003. All initially enrolled children were to complete five years of schooling by 2007 and eight years by 2010. By 2010, the Sarva Shiksha Abhiyan aimed to achieve universal retention. It was also an attempt to bridge gender and social disparities at the primary level by 2007 and at the elementary level by 2010. Needless to say, these ambitious objectives were not fulfilled. However, according to the Mid-Term Appraisal of the Tenth Five Year Plan, out of school children between the ages

6-14 were reduced from 42 million in 2002 to 8.1 million in 2004, which is rather dramatic. Though this figure has been accepted by the Planning Commission, the effectiveness of the Sarva Shiksha Abhiyan even with reference to initial enrolment is doubtful.

Sarva Shiksha Abhiyan promotes girls education to equalize educational opportunities and eliminate gender disparities .The targeted provision for girls under Sarva Shiksha Abhiyan include: Free textbooks to all girls up to Class VIII; Separate toilets for girls; Back to school camps for out-of-school girls; Bridge courses for older girls; Recruitment of 50 per cent women teachers; Early childhood care and Education centers in/near schools; Convergence with ICDS (Integrated Child Development Services) programme; Teachers' sensitization programmes to promote equitable learning opportunities; Gender-sensitive teaching-learning materials including textbooks Intensive community mobilization efforts; and Innovation fund per district for need based interventions for ensuring girls' attendance and retention (Department of School Education and Literacy, MoHRD, GoI, 2008).

The State of Jammu and Kashmir joined Sarva Shiksha Abhiyan a little late in 2003 owing to its circumstances particularly disturbance due to militancy and typical topography having sparsely populated habitations. The State has two State Institutes of Education (SIE) and 14 District Institute of Education & Training (DIETs) which work in collaboration with Sarva Shiksha Abhiyan. In the year 2005-2006 and 2006-2007 the expenditure on Sarva Shiksha Abhiyan interventions in Jammu and Kashmir was Rs. 13630.23 lacs and Rs. 19908.09 lacs, respectively. Until the 31st December, 2007 a sum of Rs. 7140.60 lacs has been spent against the total out lay of 31655.69 lacs. During 2006-07, 148 primary schools were upgraded to upper primary schools. There were 108560 out of school children in which 20702 have been provided with educational opportunity through Non-Residential Bridge Courses (NRBC). The gender gap appears to be closed as against 930476 boys enrolled, there were 804837 girls amounting to 46.62 per cent. Gender disparities still persist in rural areas and among disadvantaged communities (J&K State Report: 2008).

National Programme for Education of Girls at the Elementary Education Level (NPEGEL)

The National Programme for Education of Girls at the Elementary Level (NPEGEL) is a focused intervention of Government of India, to reach the 'Hardest to Reach' girls, especially those not in school. Launched in July 2003, it is an important component of Sarva Shiksha Abhiyan, which provides additional support for enhancing girls' education over and above the investments for girls' education through normal Sarva Shiksha Abhiyan interventions. The programme provides for development of a 'model school' in every cluster with more intense community mobilization and supervision of girls enrolment in schools. Gender sensitisation of teachers, development of gender-sensitive learning materials, and provision of need-based incentives like escorts, stationery, workbooks and uniforms are some of the endeavours under the Programme. The scheme is being implemented in educationally backward blocks (EBBs) where the level of rural female literacy is less than the national average (46.13 per cent) and the gender gap is above the national average (21.67 per cent); in blocks of districts which are not covered under educationally backward blocks but having at least 5 per cent Schedule castes/ Schedule Tribes population and where Scheduled Caste/Scheduled Tribe female literacy is below 10 per cent; and also in selected urban slums.

The idea behind free textbooks and uniforms is to reduce the costs of schooling for the girl child. It is generally seen that when there are economic constraints, the girl child is the first of the children in a family, to be taken out of school. This is because the opportunity cost of educating a girl is generally high. In case of economic constraints, the daughter of the house must do housework and various odd jobs. The sons are kept at school since they can be counted upon as a future investment while the girls are to be married off (Department of School Education and Literacy, MoHRD, GoI, 2008).

The National Programme for Education of Girls at Elementary Level (NPEGEL) was sanctioned for the State of Jammu and Kashmir in 2003-04. In view of the financial constraints of the state it was decided that model schools should be adopted at the block level rather than the cluster level where the number of cluster schools would have been 1592. Table 8 depicts the numbers of model schools taken up in each district during the years 2004-05 and 2005-06.

Table 8

Numbers of Model Schools Taken up in Each District during 2004-05 and 2005-06 under National Programme for Education of Girls at Elementary Level in Jammu & Kashmir

District	*Number*
Anantnag	46
Baramulla	39
Budgam	16
Kargil	14
Kupwara	13
Leh	10
Pulwama	18
Doda	22
Kathua	21
Poonch	11
Rajouri	15
Udhampur	62
Total	287

Source: Annual Works Plan and Budget 2007-08, SSA for Jammu and Kashmir.

The total amount sanctioned for this component was of the order of Rs. 787.12 lacs during 2005-06. For the year 2006-07 Government of India has furnished a new list of Educationally Backward Blocks as per the Census 2001. National Programme for Education of Girls at Elementary Level had been initiated in 104 blocks in the 12 districts of Jammu and Kashmir. Now only 84 blocks qualify as per Census 2001. It was decided that ongoing activities would be allowed in those blocks that do not figure in the new list. Fresh activities under National Programme for Education of Girls at Elementary Level would be confined to the 84 Educationally Backward Blocks (Annual Works Plan and Budget 2007-08, SSA for J&K) .The State has about 302 Model Cluster Schools (MCS) in operation. Further 261 Model Cluster Schools have also been sanctioned during 2007-08 which are yet to be operationalised (J&K State Report: 2008).

Kasturba Gandhi Balika Vidyalaya (KGBV)

Kasturba Gandhi Balika Vidyalaya (KGBV), a girls' school scheme in the memory of Kasturba Gandhi, wife of Mahatma Gandhi, launched in July 2004, was designed to encourage greater participation of girls in education at the upper primary level.

The Kasturba Gandhi Balika Vidyalaya scheme was launched, for setting up residential schools at upper primary level for girls belonging predominantly to the Schedule castes, Schedule Tribes, Other Backward Classes and minority communities. The scheme is being implemented in educationally backward blocks of the country where female rural literacy is below the national average (46.13 per cent) and gender gap in literacy is above the national average (21.67 per cent). The scheme provides for a minimum reservation of 75 per cent of the seats for girls belonging to Scheduled Castes, Scheduled Tribes, Other Backward Classes or minority communities. For the remaining 25 per cent, priority is accorded to girls from families below poverty line. The Kasturba Gandhi Balika Vidyalaya scheme has been merged with Sarva Shiksha Abhiyan in the XIth Plan with effect from the 1st April, 2007. The Government of India has sanctioned 2180 Kasturba Gandhi Balika Vidyalayas up to March 2007 (Department of Elementary Education and Literacy, MoHRD, GoI).

The Project Approval Board of Sarva Shiksha Abhiyan Mission in its 64th meeting held under the chairmanship of Ms. Kumud Bansal, Secretary (EE&L) on the 22nd February, 2005 approved the Kasturba Gandhi Balika Vidyalaya plan for 14 blocks of the state of Jammu and Kashmir. The blocks approved for establishment of Kasturba Gandhi Balika Vidyalaya blocks are Ramnagar, Chenani Ghordi, Surankote, Gurez, Uri, Keller, Tral, as modal-I (New schools + residential facility for 100 girls) and Billawar, Dongi, Budhal, Khansahib and Khag as model-II (New schools + residential facility for 50 girls). One model school each for Leh and Kargil districts was also approved for which the block and the model were to be selected by the state itself. Accordingly model II was selected for both the districts by taking into consideration block Nobra for Leh district and block Taisuru for Kargil district.

The district wise details for establishment of 13 KGBVs during 2007-08 are depicted in Table 9. All the places where the establishment of 13 KGBVs in the 12 districts has been proposed fall in the genuinely educationally backward blocks (EBBs). No centre has been proposed for district Jammu as the said district does not qualify for opening of KGBV. Similarly projections have not been made for district Kathua in view of the fact that district has not projected any requirement of KGBV during 2007-08. Given the OOSC (out of school children) in the above mentioned 12 districts, seven schools of model I with an intake capacity of 100 girls shall be established in the districts of Anantnag, Baramulla, Pulwama, Udhampur, Poonch, and Srinagar while as in respect of left over districts of Kupwara, Rajouri, Budgam, Leh and Kargil KGBVs under model II with an intake capacity of 50 students shall be opened by debit to appropriate head of account of the Budget of the respective districts (Annual Works Plan and Budget 2007-08, SSA for Jammu and Kashmir).

Table 9
District Wise Details for Establishment of KGBVs during 2007-08 in Jammu and Kashmir

Disrict	*CD Block*	*Educational Zone*	*Village*	*ST/SC/OBC/ OOSC(11-14)*
Budgam	Nagam	Charar-e-sharief	Naidnar Gogjipathri	-
Pulwama	Lorgam	Lorgam	Shaladraman	191
Kupwara	Kralpora	Aloosa	Aloosa	192
Rajouri	Darhal	Thanamandi	Lowerbangi	200
Doda	Bhagwa	Bhagwa	Bhagwa	103
Poonch	Mandi	Loran	Loran	115
Srinagar	Nishat	Nishat	Nishat	112
Kargil	Sankoo	Sankoo	Sankoo	139
Udhampur	Chenani	Chenani	Chenani	387
Baramulla	Watergam	Watergam	Watergam	112
Leh	Kharoo	Kharoo	Kharoo	83
Anantnag	1. Breng	Bidder & Vailoo	Vailoo	1696
	2. Devsar	Devsar	Devsar	1207

Source: Annual Works Plan and Budget 2007-08, SSA for Jammu and Kashmir.

Table 10 depicts the status of KGBVs sanctioned, operationalised and girls enrolled in the state of Jammu and Kashmir as on 31 January, 2008. It can be observed from the table that out of 51 KGBVs sanctioned only 13 are operational. Percentage of girls enrolled in these 13 operational KGBVs include 16.65 per cent of Scheduled Caste, 10.63 per cent of Scheduled Tribe, 2.30 per cent of Other Backward Class, 65.94 per cent of Muslims and 4.48 per cent of Below Poverty Level respectively.

Table 10
Status of KGBVS Sanctioned, Operationalised and Girls Enrolled in Jammu and Kashmir as on 31 January, 2008

			Total no. of girls enrolled									
Total No. of KGBV's Sanctioned	*No. of KGBV's Operational*	*% Operational*	*SC Girls*	*% of SC Girls*	*ST Girls*	*% of ST Girls*	*OBC Girls*	*% of OBC Girls*	*Muslim Girls*	*% of Muslim Girls*	*BPL*	*% of BPL Girls*
51	13	25.49	130	16.65	83	10.63	18	2.30	515	65.94	35	4.48

Source: http://ssa.nic.in/girlseducation/KGBV_enrolled_operational_15Jan08.pdf.

Besides these programmes, there are other centrally sponsored schemes for over all development of education in the state, which are as follows:

1. Operation Black Board
2. Border Area Development Education Programme
3. Improvement of Science Education
4. Education Technology
5. Vocationalisation of Education at +2 Level
6. Integrated Education of Disabled Children
7. Teacher Education.

PROBLEMS IN IMPLEMENTATION OF RIGHT TO EDUCATION IN JAMMU AND KASHMIR

The right to education is an enabling right. Education creates voice through which rights can be claimed and protected and without education people lack the capacity to 'achieve valuable functioning as part of the living'. If people have access to education, they can develop the skills, capacity and confidence to secure other rights.

People have not been able to act as free fellow human beings; to enjoy the rights available to them because of sheer ignorance and the undercurrent of this being illiteracy and lack of awareness. Financial constraints and over heads play a significant role in realization of the Right to Education (RTE). Other than these general challenges, the particular ones faced by the state to successfully implement the Right to Education (RTE) are:

1. Deprivation of the state from the benefits of the Act by not making it mandatory to the state.
2. Number of teachers is not in proportionate with the number of students.
3. Lack of educational infrastructure in far flung areas of the state.
4. Adoption of model schools at the block level rather than at the cluster level.

5. It can be observed from the table that out of 51 KGBVs sanctioned only 13 are operational. (Annual Works Plan and Budget 2007-08, SSA for Jammu and Kashmir).
6. It is generally seen that when there are economic constraints, the girl child is the first of the children in a family, to be taken out of school. This is because the opportunity cost of educating a girl is generally high. In case of economic constraints, the daughter of the house must do housework and various odd jobs. The sons are kept at school since they can be counted upon as a future investment while the girls are to be married off (Department of School Education and Literacy, MoHRD, GoI).
7. Lack of transparency and dedication on the part of governmental agencies.
8. Preference to son's education, and finally
9. Disturbances in the state due to militancy, typical topography and sparsely populated habitations.

CONCLUSION

Having discussed the educational scenario in Jammu and Kashmir it can be concluded that there exists gender disparity in education in general and in rural and among disadvantaged communities in particular. The efforts made by the government through legislative, constitutional and legal measures have no doubt proved fruitful in removing the gender gap in literacy to some extent but have not totally succeeded in fulfilling the cherished expectations and aspirations of women in the state. A major segment of women population is illiterate especially in the Kashmir province. The quality of education provided by the government system remains in question in the state as it suffers from shortages of teachers, infrastructural gaps and several habitations continue to lack schools altogether. Accountability by along with transparency in regard to decisions and actions taken by various authorities and people's participation is necessary to make the system more accountable and transparent. Further a significant improvement in the education of people in general and women in particular in Kashmir would only be possible if the "Right to Education Act" is extended to the State of Jammu and Kashmir. Withholding the extension of the "Right to Education Act" to the State reflects the general apathy of Central government towards the state. The Central government has legally/officially excluded the state of Jammu and Kashmir from the "Right to Education Act." Chapter 1 of the Act formally titled as the "Right of Children to Free and Compulsory Education Act 2009" states that "It shall extend to the rest of India except the State of Jammu and Kashmir." The problematic state of education in the Valley needs to be addressed in the proper forum and context. Thus, if the Central government is genuinely concerned with the importance of education in the Valley, it must toil and engage itself in the fundamental work of extending the "Right to Education Act" to the State of Jammu and Kashmir. In nutshell, sound policy and good governance can lead the state to a faster development in education.

ACKNOWLEDGEMENT

The authors are very grateful to Dr. P.K. Mathur, Associate Professor, Department of Sociology and Social Work, Aligarh Muslims University, Aligarh, for providing us with excellent guidance and tactical advice in the various phases of the present work.

References

Ahmad, I. (1987), Educational Development of Minorities in India: Future Perspective', Educational Planning and Administration, Vol. 1, No. 2, p. 201.

Bazaz, P. N. (1959), Daughters of the Vitasta: A History of Kashmiri Women from Early Times to the Present Day, Pamposh Publications, New Delhi, p. 211 and p. 219.

Census (2001), Census of India Jammu and Kashmir 2001, Paper -2 of 2001, Rural-Urban Distribution of Population, New Delhi.

Dabla, B.A. (2007), Multi-Dimensional Problems of Women in Kashmir. Gyan Publishing House, New Delhi, p. 43-44.

Das, N.M and S.V. Sagar (2007), Practical Utility of Gender Study, in L. Murthy, N, *et al.*, ed. Towards Gender Equality, Serial Publications, New Delhi, p. 52.

Government of Jammu and Kashmir (2007-08), Digest of Statistics, Directorate of Economics and Statistics, Srinagar, pp. 389-390, 393, 514, 516, 518, 520, 525-527 & 555-557.

Government of Jammu and Kashmir (2008-09), Economic Survey, Directorate of Economics and Statistics, Srinagar, p. 577.

Government of India (2009), The Gazette of India, New Delhi.

Government of India (GOI) (2007), Guidelines for Implementation of Kasturba Gandhi Balika Vidyalaya (KGBV). Dept of Elementary Education and Literacy (MoHRD), New Delhi, Retrieved December 11, 2007 from *http://education.nic.in/kgbv_guidelines.asp*

Government of India (2008), Department of School Education and Literacy (MoHRD), New Delhi, Retrieved June 21, 2010 from *http://ssa.nic.in/ssaframework/ssafram.asp#1.0.*

Government of India (2008), Dept of School Education and Literacy MoHRD), New Delhi, Retrieved April 3, 2008 from *http://planningcommission.nic.in/plans/stateplan/sdr_jandk/sdr_jkch3b.pdf.*

Government of Jammu and Kashmir (2008), Jammu and Kashmir State Report, January 21- February 5, 2008 Sarva Shiksha Abhiyan, Seventh Joint Review Mission, Retrieved June 12 2010 *http://www.ssa.nic.in/17pdf%20%20files/Microsoft%20Word%20-%20J&K_FINAL.pdf.*

Khan, F. A. (2005), Other Communities, Other Histories: A Study of Women and Education in Kashmir, in Zoya Hassan and Ritu Menon (ed.): In A Minority: Essays on Muslim Women in India. Oxford University Press, New Delhi, pp. 150-168.

Khan, G. H. (1973). The Kashmiri Musulman. Falah-e-aam Press Srinagar, Kashmir, pp. 13-14.

Social Sectors (2008), Education, Department of Education, Government of Jammu and Kashmir. The official Website of Jammu & Kashmir Government, India, Retrieved on April 3, 2008 *http://planningcommission.nic.in/plans/stateplan/sdr_jandk/sdr_jkch3b.pdf*.

Srivastava, Gouri (2005), Women Education in India-Issues and Dimensions. Academic Excellence, Delhi, p. 7 and pp. 125-129.

Status of KGBVs sanctioned, operationalised and girls enrolled category-wise as on 31 January, 2008, Retrieved on May 8, 2008 *http://ssa.nic.in/girlseducation/KGBV_enrolled_operational_15Jan08.pdf*

Tyndale Biscoe, C.E. (1998), Kashmir and Its Inhabitants, Shubhi Publications, Delhi, p. 257.

Yadav, Neelam. (2003), Education for Women. Reference Press, New Delhi.

Foeticide – A Threat to Society

NIRMALA DEVI*

INTRODUCTION

"Every child comes into this world with the message that God is not yet disappointed with man," said the great Noble Laureate Rabindranath Tagore. But alas! The girl child. She is hated even before her birth. Nay she is disliked even when only her idea comes to the mind. So is the taboo set for her in this land of Laxmi and Durga. On birth she is either killed or exploited.

The girl child in India is facing many torments in the form of sexual abuse, foeticide, infanticide and the like. The practice of female foeticide is really alarming in India[1].

Female infanticide and foeticide is one manifestation of male supremacy. From Womb to Tomb the story of girl in our society is a story of discrimination, contempt, utter disregard, oppression and cruelly. The practice of female infanticide, is killing of infants has been prevalented since ages. The girl who opens her eyes in our partiarchal world having escaped from female infanticide and recently foeticide is greeted (exceptions not withstanding) with glum faces by near and dear ones[2] and is frequently subjected to neglect.

After birth, a girl child gets less time breast milk and less nutritional supplements as grows up. This malnutrition and neglected upbringing may lead to many girls dying in their childhood[3].

The girl is the first and foremost need to humanity because her survival is essential for the continuation of the species. To kill her means to kill the coming generation. Denial of her right to live means denial of right to life to future generations[4].

BACKGROUND OF FOETICIDE

Killing of women exists in various forms in societies the world over. The unfavourable atmosphere that developed against women from Smriti age was further aggravated by customs that cropped up during the Mughal period.

* *Assistant Professor in Law, Regional Campus (G.N.D.U.) Ladhewale, Jalandhar.*

The custom of dowry added fuel to the fire. The birth of girl child never welcomed in the family because religiously it was duty ' of the father to get his daughter married; and to many her dowry was required, and to escape the problems in future started practice of killing the girl child soon after her birth. Due to lack of scientific methods the new born baby of unwanted sex was used to be killed.

The practice is still prevalent in Indian society; but in a changed form with the advancement of science and technology and development of medical science it is now possible to detect the sex of the child before birth and the foetus if turns to be a female then it got aborted. Thus, a girl child is not even allowed to get birth and she falls prey to violence even before they all born.

Female foetuses are selective aborted after pre natal sex determination, thus avoiding the birth of girl child. As a result of selective abortion between 35 and 40 million girls and women are missing from the Indian population. In some parts of the country, the sex ratio of girls to boy has dropped to less than 800: 1000. The united nation has expressed serious concern about the situation[5]. The united nation an estimated that 2000 unborn girls are illegibly aborted everyday in India[6]. The sex ratio has altered constantly in favour of boys, since the beginning of 20th century and the effect has been most pronounced in the state of Punjab, Haryana and Delhi. In these states private foetal sex determination clinic were first established and the practice of selective abortion became popular from the late 1970s. Worrying the trend is for stranger in urban rather than rural areas of among literate rather than illiterate women exploding the myth that growing influence and spread up of basic education along with result in the erosion of gender bias.

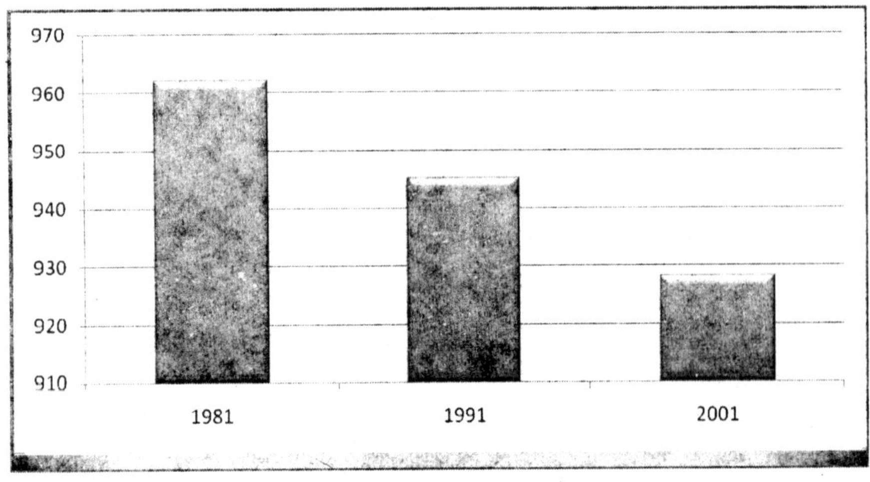

Graph 1: 0-6 Age Group Child Sex Ratio in India for the Year 1981, 1991 and 2001

The 0-6 child sex ratio 962 in 1981, 945 in 1991 and further declined to 928 in 2001. This age group reflects the most adverse sex ratio. The decline in the number of girl children can be inferred to be caused by high girl child mortality including female infanticide or due to female foeticide. Even though the biological sex ratio at birth is naturally masculine with 104-107 male live births per 100 females[7], a fall from this number and its continued fall after birth is indicative of the presence of unnatural factors. Data show that both female infant and girl child mortality is higher than that of the males. The presence of sex determination clinics and subsequent abortions, no doubt, has affected this child sex ratio.

As a result of high discrimination against female children, the status of Gujrat (878), Haryana (820) and Punjab (793) the highest percentage of missing female children aged group (0-6) year in 2001. In Punjab imbalance between male and female children increasing day by day.

To males, but that even fewer survive to the age of 6 years, suggesting clearly that the unwanted girl child is neglected in infancy.

It may be added that the inordinately low child sex-ratio of below 850 are recorded in 48 districts in India and include all districts of Punjab and Haryana. The finding of the census 2001 is in a sense explosive, showing clearly that female foeticide is widely prevalent in the state of Punjab.

MISSING GIRL CHILDREN AND RESPONSE FROM AUTHORITIES

Authorities in India belatedly awaken to the bargaining practice of sex selection abortion after the shocking results of 2001 census released in April. The fall in sex ratio is due to the routine practice of sex selection abortion or female foeticide.

Centre for Enquiry into Health and Allied Themes (CEHAT)[8] filed public interest litigation in Supreme Court citing the findings of the new census. They argued that the alarming drop in the female to male ratio was due to the unchecked practice of determining the sex of the foetus-as practice which is illegal in India. The CEHAT pointed to the particularly remarkable sex ratio in the state of Punjab, where there are only 874 women per 1000 men.

Anguished over the steady rise in female foeticide and citing the blatant abuse of modern medical techniques Supreme Court issued a May 4, 2001. Policy statement calling upon federal and state government to undertaken:

1. Vigorous media-campaigns against the practice. The court directed the governments.
2. To rally public opinion against sex-selection abortion and even against the practice of determining the sex of unborn child-through appropriate releases of mass-media.
3. To embark a serious effort to enforce a 1994 law that bans female foeticide.

4. To set up a central supervisory board which will be required to furnished quarterly reports on the implementation of that legislation?
5. To establish local committees to assist in publicity campaign.

On the same day as the courts announcement, Federal Health Minister C.P. Thakur issued a public caution to doctors, threatening them with revocation of their medical practice licenses if they continue to perform sex-selection abortions despite the legal ban on practice.

Almost simultaneously, the federal department of women and child development called for "immediate and serious" intervention by authorities at all levels of government to draw up an action plan to combat the trend.

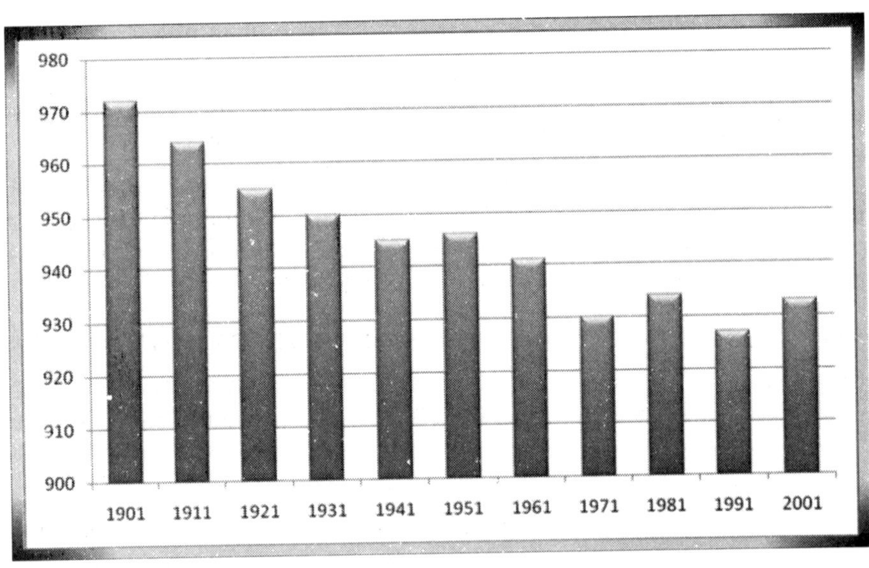

Graph 2: Sex Ratio of India from 1901-2001

India's sex ratio throughout the 20th century and in the 21st century reflects a masculine sex ratio. In fact, one that has declined from the natural sex ratio where females out number males. In 1901, India's sex ratio was 972, deficit in the number of females to proclaim intrusion of social factors in its disruption. The sex ratio decline steadily in the years 1901 to 1971 (with a negligible increase in 1951) to improve marginally to 934 and has hovered around 930. In 2001 it stands at 933 to affirm the presence of unfavourable conditions for women's survival[9].

CAUSES OF FEMALE INFANTICIDE AND FOETICIDE

Traditional Gender Bias

In the matrilineal society which was prevalent before the vedic period and Aryan civilization women were said to have enjoyed equal rights with men from education to inheritance. The patriarchal system which comes into practice later denied property right to women, they didn't have access to the means of production and had to depend on the male family members for existence. This highly deplorable gender discrimination which started then continues to be practiced today even more strongly. The first manifestation of this gender bias now begins before the birth. It is highly disheartening to hear about female foeticide or infanticide[10].

There exists a common belief that bringing up a girl is like watering the neighbour is plant. Hence the girl child is denied equal opportunities m terms of food, clothing and education, as a result she faces deterioration in health and knowledge. Also in literacy the girl child doesn't get a fair chance as a male child does. Whenever facility of amniocentesis is not available people turn to misusing the scanning facility to identify the sex by sixth or seventh month of pregnancy and undertaking 'Abortion' if it is a female. Those who can't afford these tests awaits the child's birth to do away with it if the baby is a girl.

Poverty

Poverty is another major cause of female infanticide Maranayer says, "I had ten babies. I killed seven daughters. I now have two sons and one daughter. Recently another case of female infanticide, a mother, unhappy over giving birth to a girl child Geeta killed her new born girl child, says she could not have afforded another girl child. She has been arrested by the police under section 302 of the IPC.

Another women narrates:

"I killed three daughters with poison. I am an agricultural labourer. If we need bangles for a daughter it now costs Rs. 20, A Sari Costs Rs. 200! How can we afford more children? People taunt us if we don't have a son. They don't invite for ceremonies. Why watch a daughter crying a being tortured? We must all die at some time! Why not when she is unmoulded earth? Best to do it before applying water or oil[11].

Fear of Sexual Abuse

Fear of sexual abuse of the girl child is also a major cause for female infanticide. A very condemnable practice that exists especially in Tamil Nadu is the sex practice of father-in-law with daughter-in-law and the husband's inability to do anything against the practice due to the fear that he would lose his share of the property from his father.

Also it has been found that due to the marriage taking place at an early age and with quite a few child deliveries, the husband loses interest in his wife and he finds it convenient to find a bride for his on to have his sexual "fulfillment" through her. These men don't want to go for another marriage because their existing property would be divided further with the addition of more children through the second marriage.

Dowry

Patriarchal society has developed into a tremendously greedy and materialistic society which strongly supports the notion of male supremacy and consequently justifies, even encourages demand for dowry. It has become a dowry nightmare for young women, there is a culture of criminality and immorality which has got inbuilt into the society there is almost no social ethics which can withstand this craze.

The question is as to who would bear the dowry expenditure for the girl. Expenses do it stop even after her marriage but continues till her death. Having a son is an asset as he brings more revenue to the family through his marriage. Also he would perform last rites of the parents.

It is an irony to see that even the schedule tribes community has started to consider the female as a liability because of dowry. Even a decade before in most of the tribal communities the bridegroom had to pay a bride price to get the hand of the girl and the expenditure for the girl's parents was only the feast on the wedding day. It is disheartening to see that the present day mores have an impact even on the tribal culture. This unhealthy custom of dowry is slowly sliding gradually into their culture also. To avoid to pay huge amount of money into dowry people eliminate their female infants. They know it is against the law but it matters them the least.

Domestic Violence/Mercy

Some mothers kill their babies as an act of 'mercy' that they may be saved from future excesses by husbands in the form of domestic violence[12].

Lust for Son

The birth of a male child makes one young again, while the birth of a female child makes one feel aged. The birth of a male child recognised in is patriarchal roles of a relevant source of financial dependence, provides of the family lineage, protected of the family and its status. Religious point of view son is must to perform last funeral rites etc.

LEGAL DIMENSIONS

Law regards a child in the womb as a person and law accords it equal protection as is accorded to other human beings.

The practice of sex determination by Amniocentesis followed by abortion in case of female child is not only illegal but constitutes criminal offence. With an object to tackle with this type of offences IPC included Sec. 312 to 318.

It is to be noted here that the term 'abortion' is no where used in law. Only miscarriage or termination of pregnancy is used for it. If may occur accidentally or spontaneously or be induced. Induced or artificial termination of pregnancy has extensive legal implications,

Indian Penal Code, Offences Relating to Miscarriage

The practice of sex determination by Amniocentesis followed by abortion in cases of a female child is not only illegal but constitutes a criminal offence.

The relevant sections of the Indian Penal Code are as follows:

Section	*Offence*	*Punishment*
Sec. 312	Causing miscarriage if the woman be quick with child (quick with child is not defined under the act but it can be interpreted to mean a child capable of being born alive	Imprisonment for 3 years or fine or both or imprisonment of 7 years and fine
Sec. 313	Causing miscarriage without women's consent	Imprisonment for life or imprisonment for 10 years and fine
Sec. 314	Death caused by an act done with intent to cause miscarriage if act done without women's consent	Imprisonment for life or imprisonment for 10 years and fine
Sec. 315	Act done with intent to prevent a child being born alive or to cause it to die after its birth	Imprisonment for 10 years or fine or both
Sec. 316	Causing death of a quick unborn child by on act amounting to culpable homicide	Imprisonment for 10 years and fine
Sec. 317	Child under 12 years by parents or persons having care of the child with intention of wholly abandoning it.	Imprisonment for 7 years or fine or both

The Medical Termination of Pregnancy Act, 9171

The India Penal Code, 1860 Which was enacted more than a century ago, on the basis of the then British Law, Contained some provisions regarding the termination of pregnancy. Sec. 312 to 316 of the Indian Penal Code punish the person Causing miscarriage, preventing a child being porn life or casing the death of quick unborn child. In spite of these penal provisions the practice of causing miscarriage continued in India for Various social and medical reasons. In order to save the pregnant women's health, strength and sometimes life the medical Termination of pregnancy Bill was introduced in Parliament.

The Medical Termination of Pregnancy Act, 1971 Provides for the termination of Creation pregnancy by registered medical practitioners and for matters Connected therewith or incidental there to. The Act Consist of 8 Sections dealing with various aspects like the time, place and Circumstances in which a pregnancy may be termination by medical practitioners legally. Here the 'Medical practitioner' means the persons who posses nay recognised medical qualification as defined in the India Medical Council Act, 1956 and Whose name has been entered in State medical Register. Such person must have experience or training in gynecology and obstetrics.

This Act has been amended by the parliament in 2002 by the Medical Termination of Pregnancy (Amendment) Act, 2002 (64 of 2002) and by the delegated legislation Provisions (Amendment) Act, 2004 (4 of 2005). By these amendments certain provisions of the Act has been amended[13].

Under this Act, all abortions carried out require the Consent of women and all abortions after twenty weeks are illegal. Pregnancy is allowed to be termination when the foetus is less than 12 weeks on the certificate of one registered gynecologist and obstetricians.

Where any one of above Conditions is satisfied, abortion may be allowed only if:

1. Pregnancy Would involve risks of life of the pregnant women or Cause grave injury to her physical or mental health,
2. There is a substantial risk that the child if born would suffer from physical or mental abnormal ties and would be handicapped, or
3. Abortion can be carried on anytime if it is immediately necessary to save the life of the pregnant woman.

So under MTP Act abortion is prohibited after 20 weeks of pregnancy.

Sec. 3(4) of the Act specifically provides that the pregnancy of a women who has not attained the age of 18 year can't be terminated except with the written Consent of her guardian is essential In every case of medical termination of absolutely essential.

Sec. 4 of the Act Stated that pregnancy can be terminated either at a hospital established or maintained by the Government or at a place which is approved the Government or district level committee constituted by that Government.

According to Sec. 8 of the Act, 1971 if any registered medical practitioner causes any.

Damage by anything Which is, in good faith, done or intended to be done under the medical Termination of Pregnancy Act, 1971, no suit or other legal proceedings can be instituted against him.

In State of Haryana Vs. Amrawati[14] the court held that if the operating doctor is not negligent on his part then petitioner can't be allowed. In

Chaman Bai Vs. State of M.P[15] Plaintiff become pregnant and gave birth to a child. Surgeon not liable to pay damages.

From the above discussion, it becomes clear that the Act 1971 is a Welfare legislation aimed at protecting the physical and mental health of a pregnant women and also of the child being carried in the womb of the mother.

The Pre-Conception and Pre-Natal Diagnostic Techniques (Prohibition of sex selection) Act, 1994 By The advancement in medical science and technology pre-natal sex determination technique has been widely and grossly misused in killing the girls in mother's womb. The Parliament realised the necessity of bringing the female foticide. The parliament passed the Pre- Natal Diagnostic techniques (Regulation and Prevention of Misuse) Act, 1994, which come into forcefrom1-1-1996.

By Section 3 of the Pre-natal Diagnostic Techniques Regulation and Prevention of Misuse) Amendment Act, 2002 (14 of 2003) the nomenclature of the Act has been amended and now it stands as the Pre Preconception and prenatal Diagnostic Techniques (Prohibition of sex selection) Act, 1994 (57 of 1994).

This Act regulates the use of prenatal sex determination technique. It permits the use of pre-natal sex determination technique for the purpose of detecting genetic or chromosomal disorders or certain congenital malformations or sex linked disorders and not for the purpose of killing the female child in the mother's womb.

The said Act has the following objectives:

(1) Prohibition of the misuse of pre-natal diagnostic techniques for determination of sex of foetus leading to female foeticide.

(2) Prohibition of advertisement of pre-natal diagnostic techniques for detection or determination of sex.

(3) Permission and regulation of the purpose of detection of specific genetic abnormalities or disorders,

(4) Permitting the use of such techniques only under Certain conditions by the registered institution and

(5) Punishment for violation of the provisions of the proposed legislation.

In Dr. Gurpreet Kaur Vs. State of Punjab[16]. The Court held that complaint under Sec. 4(1)(2)(3), (6) and 29 of the PNDT Act, 1994 are Criminal Complaint in their nature under the said Act.

This Act banned sex determination tests all over the country. This Act Carries a three year imprisonment and Rs. 10.000 fine offenders. But-the implementation of this Act is slow.

The Act has a Central and State levels Supervisory Board, An Appropriate Authority, Committee. The function of the Supervisory Board is to oversee, monitor and make amendments to the provisions of the Act. Appropriate to the provision of the Act. Appropriate Authority provides registration and Conducts the administrative work involved in inspection, investigation and te penalizing of defaulters. The Advisory committee provides expert and technical support to the Appropriate Authority. The Appropriate Authority in forms the Central or state medical council to take action against medical professionals, leading to suspension or the striking off of practitioners found guilty of contravening the provisions of the Act.

Before Conducting any prenatal diagnostic procedure the medical practitioner must attain a written consent from the pregnant women in a local language the she understands. Prenatal tests performed in various specified Circumstances, including risk of chromosomal abnormalities in the Case of women over 35, and genetic diseases evident in the family history of the Couple.

Inspire of these statutory or penal provisions female feticide is still common in India. India Parliament has enacted laws banning sex determination tests but aborting female fetuses that have been happening in several parts of the country.

The irony of the whole situation is that in the 10 years since India enacted the PNDT Act, 1994, not a single person was convicted till very recently and in the beginning of April 2006 only two people were Convicted fined and pronounced five years of rigorous imprisonment. Only 23 cases have been registered under this Act so far.

Other Preventive Measures: Law alone cannot stop the social evil of female Feticide. Indian Culture has been built in the Concept of male superiority and subordinate status of women. Religion can play important role to control this problem. Efforts in this direction have been made in past by religious personalities.

There was Hukam nama against female Feticide by Sikh high Priest of Akal Takhat Sahib in April 200. The Hukam Nama stated "the decreasing number of women in society can lead to social upheaval, so it is necessary that steps are to be taken to restrict the practice of female foeticide and a Sikh should not kill his daughter, nor should be maintain any relationship with the killer of a daughter."

Awareness drive can also help in such matters and medical can play important role. Girls must be educated so that they aware their rights.

CONCLUSION AND SUGGESTIONS

For the success of any campaign against the sex detection it has to be launched first on the social front and then the legal measures can succeed in bringing about desired change. In fact, social change is a complex process and to decide the direction of change either through measures or constitutional provisions alone cannot succeed, until and unless it is backed up by organised campaign of people directed towards bringing about social Cultural Revolution. To prevent female infanticide and foeticide here all some suggestions, this may be considered for an immediate action plan that may be adopted by the government in this respect. The suggestions are as follows:

1. Compulsory registration of the birth of girl child;
2. Speedy investigation of the causes leading to a girl child's death;
3. A female health officer must be associated with the investigations about the offence;
4. Continuous effort be made to educate the adult community which controls the lives of children;
5. There must be effective implementation of PND/Act punishment which carrying such business like sex-determination or abortion;
6. Governmental organisation and nongovernmental organisation must play an important role to prevent female infanticide and foeticide;
7. They must create social awareness among people that girls and boys are equal by the different non-governmental organisation. Conducting drama's, stage show or other methods which are necessary to aware and educate the people and tells the importance of girls;
8. Media plays an important role in society. People follow everything which media shows.

Notes

1. Azim Sherwani, The Girl Child in Crisis, A Sponsored Publication of Indian Social Institution, p. 2.
2. Indu Parkash Singh, "Indian Women, The Power Trapped", Intellectual Publishing House, 1991, p. 8.
3. Dr. Shams Shamsuddin, "Women Law and Social Change", Ashish Publishing Boose, New Delhi, 1991, p. 172.
4. Azim Sherwani, The Girl Child in Crisis, Indian Social Institutes, New Delhi, 1998, p. 47.
5. A Death Unsung: Female Foeticide in India. *http//theviewpaper.net/3 visited on 25 sept.2010*
6. Indu Grewal and J. Kishore, a Female Foeticide in India, *http//www.thev.org/female-foeticide-in India*
7. Renuka Dagar, Identifying and Controlling Female Feoticide and Infanticide in Punjab, Jan. 2002, Institute for Development and Communication, Chandigarh
8. Writ Petition (Civil) No. 301 of 2000.
9. Supra note 28, p. 2.
10. Vasant Fatima, "Preventing Condition of the Girl Child",
11. R. Venkatachalam and Vijay Srinivas, Female Infanticide, Har Anand Publications Chirage, Delhi, p. 59.
12. The Tribune, April 19th, 2003.
13. Section 3, sub section 2, Medical Termination of Pregnancy Act, 1971
14. 2008 (2) RCR (G) 989(PH)
15. 2008 (1) RCR 9 (G). 562 (M.P)
16. 2008 (2) RCR (G) 285 (P&H).

Index

A

Abolitionism, 190, 191
Acid Rain, 122
Active Euthanasia, 45
Adil Shah, 260
Administration, 169
Administrative Reforms Commission, 113, 284
Adulteration, 243
African
- Charter, 194, 199, 201, 203, 204, 206, 207
  - On Human and Peoples, 4
  - On Human Rights, 62
- Commission, 200
- Commission on Human and Peoples Rights, 206
- Society, 181

Agrarian Unrest, 111
Agricultural (re)
- Labor, 25, 273
- Sector, 31

AIDS, 268
- In Nigeria, 186
- Transmission, 190

Air Blasting, 12
Akshara Kalika Sibhira, 263
Alienation from – Society, 56
Aligarh Muslim Universitiy, 294
All India Committee on Jail Reforms, 265
American
- Convention on Human Rights, 4, 62
- Declaration of Independence, 224
- Indians, 172
- Slaves, 218

Amnesty International, 219
Amritsar Prison, 141
Ancient
- Greece, 222
- Laws and Customs, 217

Annan, UN Secy. Gen, 72
Anti-Social Elements, 106
Anti-Terrorism
- Funding, 110
- Laws, 229

AP Prevention of Dangerous – Land Grabbers Act, 229
Appeal for Amnesty, 219
Aquinas, Thomas, 222
Arab Charter of Human Rights, 62
Arbitrary Persecution and Punishment, 222
Aristotle, 222
Armed Forces Special Powers Act (AFSPA), 60, 61, 228
Asia Development Bank (ADB), 27
Assam – Goa, 112
Atharvaveda, 256
Atlantic Charter, 71
Augustine, 50
Australia, 191
Ayodhya, 56

B

Babri Masjid, 56
  Demolition in Ayodhya, 56
Backward Classes Development Corporation, 265
Balance of Power among Nations, 175
Balasubramanyam, Justice PK, 277
Balochistan, 29
Bamgbose Sex Work, 184
Bank Scams, 110
Basic
  Human Rights, 88, 137
  Rights, 65
Beedi and Cigar Workers Act, 164
Beijing Declaration, 85, 165
Belgium, 122
Below Line of Poverty, (BLP), 27
Bengal Coal Company, 11
Benue, 186
Berlin Conference, 1885, 171
Bharat
  Mahila Parishad, 257
  Stri Mahamandal, 257
Bhartiya Janta Party, 59
Bhikhim Shah Under-Trial, Death in Custody, 148
Bhogibhai case, 88
Bihar
  Police Bill, 1007, 112
  Police Commission, 106
Bihar – Rajasthan, 112
Bilaspuria Loaders, 13
Black Diamond, 12
Bodhisatva Gautam VS Subha Chakraborty, 89
Bombing over Lockerbie Scotland, 71
Bonded
  Child Labor, 34, 35
  Labor System Abolition Act, 29
Bosnia and Kosovo, 75
Brazil, 122
Bribery and Official Misconduct, 217
Brick Kiln Industry, 25
British
  Colonies in North America, 217
  Empire, 218
  Magna Carta, 224
  Museum, 171
  Rule, 219
Brothel Based Sex Workers, 187
Brothels, 185

C

Cairo Declaration on Human Rights in Islam, 2
Call Girls, 185
Cambridge University, 169
Carpet
  Industry in Amritsar, 17-23
  Weaving, 25
Cases (Of Child Labor) in-, 20
  Andhra Pradesh, 20
  Karnataka, 20
  Madhya Pradesh, 20
  Orissa, 20
  Rajasthan, 20
Casteism, 226
CEDAW (Convention on Elimination of the All Forms of Discrimination against Women), 85, 159, 162, 164, 193, 195, 201, 203, 206, 208, 322
Central Jail
  Bhatinda, 143
  Ferozepore, 143, 150
  Jalandhur, 148
  Ludhiana, 151

Charter of
International Court of Justice, 4
United Nations, 58
Chemical Industry, 25
Child
Carpet Weavers, Amritsar, 20
Labor and Female Literacy, 20
Labor Force, 17
Labor Legislation in Carpet Industry, 20
Labor Prohibition and Regulation Act, 17, 22
Labor, 17-23, 135, 218, 230
And Literacy, 19
Causes of-, 18
In Districts of Upper Sindh Pakistan, 25-41
In Donkey Cart Riding, 33
In Pakistan, 25-41
In Rural Areas, 17-23
Legislation in Pakistan, 30
Major Sectors, 25
Socio-Economic Aspects, 25-41
Socio-Economic Background, 32
Malnutrition, 131
Marriage, 131, 230
Mortality, 131
Pornography, 132, 135
Prostitution, 134
Rights, 131-140
Rights Convention, 136
Children Classification for Study, 32, 33
Children's Human Rights, 133
China, 195, 196, 323
Christian Traditions, 50
Church Missionary Society, 324
Civil
And Political Rights, 46
Code of Quebec, 121
Conflict in Liberia and Angola, 72
Disobedience, 218
Law, 121
Law System, 123
Liberties Groups, 229
Liberties Movement, 229
Rights Commission, 231
Rights Group, 59, 229
Rights of Minorities, 231
CMPF Act, 13
Coal
Fields India, 15
Industry, 11, 14
Mining Industry, 11, 13
Mining Society in West Bengal, 11-15
Mining Society, 13, 14
Code of Conduct, 248
Colonial Empires, 171
Colonialism, 169, 177, 183
Commercial Markets, 175
Commission
Bihar Police, 106
Punjab Police, 106
West Bengal Police, 106
Committee
Against Torture, 3
On CEDAW, 208
On Elimination of Discrimination against Women, 60
On Elimination of Racial Discrimination, 60
On Rights of Child, 135
Common Law, 121
Communal
Conflict, 55
Politics, 296
Violence for Political Gains, 106

Communicable Diseases, 142
Community Policing, 110
Comprehensive Environmental—Liability Act (CERCLA), 126
Concurrent List, 95
Condom Use, 187, 193
Confidence Building Measures, 110, 114
Congo, 169
Constitution of India, 45, 50, 95, 137
Consumer
  And Consumerism, Defined, 242
  Movement, 241
  Rights Details, 244
  Rights, 241-253
  Sovereignty, 242, 243
Continental European Philosophy, 171
Convention
  Against Torture and -Degradation Treatment Or Punishment, 2
  On Economic, Social and Cultural Rights (CESCR), 221
  On the Rights of the Child 1989 (CRC), 4, 11, 38, 131, 133, 135-137, 322
Conventional Human Rights Scheme, 68
Corporate Paternalism, 94
Correction, 273
Corruption, 243
Cottage Industry, 25
Council of Europe, 124
Council of Europe's 1973 Consumer Protection Charter, 245
Cradle to Grave Philosophy, 93
Crime
  And Women, 260
  Investigation Bureau (CBI)
  Situation in India, 109
Criminal
  Code, 190, 191
    Of Nigeria, (225A-225B), 189
  Exploitation, 19
  Investigation, 105
Criminal Justice System, 105, 107, 114, 277, 288
  Administration of-, 105
  Law Under-and its Loopholes, 107
Criminal Law, 258, 288
  Amendment Act, 1983, 86, 88
  Failure in Nigeria, 190
Criminal Procedure Code (Cr PC), 88, 105, 106, 107, 234, 236, 279, 281
Criminalization
  Of Female Sex Workers, 200
  Of Sex Work in Nigeria, 208
  Of Sex Work, 181, 190, 192
Crisis in Kosovo, 72
Cross Rivers, 186
Cultural
  Education, 263
  Transformation, 169
Custodial
  Deaths, 145-148
    Of Natha Singh, 148
  Violence, 228, 229
Custody Deaths, 228

D

Dacoity, 110
Dalit Community, 219
Dalits, 59
Dams, 229
Death Trap, 12
Deaths of Prisoners During Judicial Custody, 147
Decentralized Security System, 73
Deceptive Advertising, 243
Decision Making Process, 324

Declaration
- of the Rights of Child, 1824, 132
- of the Rights of Man, 218
- on the Protection of All Persons—Punishment, 2

De-Criminalization, 191
Defence of Human Rights, 66
Degrading Treatment, 1
Deportation, 188
DEVAW (Declaration on the Elimination of Violence against Women), 165
Diamond Harbor Area West Bengal, 230
Difficulties in Marketing, 309
Directive Principles of State Policy, 95, 136, 207, 226, 272
Distance Education, 263
District
- Institute of Education and Training (DIET), 334
- Jail Sangrur, 148
- Literacy Committee, 263
- Primary Education Program, (DPEP), 333
- Uttar Kannada, 303-319

Donkey Cart Riding, 25, 34, 35, 37, 39
Draconian
- Laws, 60
- Legislation, 284

Drug
- And Pharmaceuticals, 304
- Trafficking, 110

Durgapur Steel Plant, 14

E

ECL Management, 15
Ecological
- Damage, 122
- Incidents in France, 123

Economic
- Crimes, 110
- Crisis, 170
- Development, 18, 55, 103, 321
- Disparities, 246
- Inequalities, 224
- Injustices, 243
- Offences, 110, 259

Economy, 31
Ecosystem, 122
Education, 31, 35-37, 39, 321-341
- And Information, 3
- Reorganization Committee, 325

Educational
- Development, 291
  - Of Muslims in Maharashtra, 291-301
- Enrolment of Muslims in India, 293
- Infrastructure, 338
- Institutions, 39, 298, 329, 330
- Status of Women in Kashmir, 324

Employees
- Family Pension Scheme, 99
- Pension Scheme Benefit, (EPSB), 100
  - Children Pension/Orphan Pension, 100
  - Early Pension, 100
  - Permanent Total Disable Pension, 100
  - Superannuation Pension, 100
  - Widow's Pension, 100
- Provident Fund Organization, 102
- Provident Fund, 95, 98, 100
- State Insurance Corporation, 102

Employees'
- Deposit Linked Insurance Scheme, 99, 100
- Provident Fund Act, 99
- State Insurance At, 95, 97

Act, 102
Scheme 98
Employment of Children Act, 1991, 29, 30, 33
Enforcement
Agencies, 109
Of Economic and Social Legislation, 111
English Bill of Rights, 221, 224
Environmental
Actors, 121, 125, 127
Claims, 121, 122
Damage, 121-125
Protection, 121, 122, 125
Degradation, 126
Law, 122, 125
Protection and Regulation, 121
Regulation, 121-129
Equal Remuneration Act, 164
Equitable Coal Company, 11
Eradication of Child Labor, 21
Ethnic Conflict, 55
Europe Convention on Human Rights, 4, 5
European
Commission, 62, 122, 124
Convention on Human Rights, 48
Court of Human Rights, 199
Court of Justice, 122
Court on Human Rights, 197, 199
Union, 122
Union Organization, 165
Euthanasia, 43-54
Easeful Death, 43
Explained, 44
Indian Legal Perspectives, 45
Eve Teasing, 160
Act, 164
Expert Committee on Women Prisons, 261
Explosives Gas, 12
Carbon, 12
Methane, 12
Monoxide, 12
Extremists, 111

F

Factories Act, 1934, 29, 163
Factors Leading to Sexual Harassment, 158
Federal
Crimes, 113
Investigation Agency, 113
Law, 113
Republic of Yugoslavia, 72
Female
Child Laborers, 29
Criminalization, 259
Criminals, 255-269
Genital Cutting (FGC), 194
Infanticide, 226
Literacy, 326
Sex Workers, 187
Feudal Culture, 12
Fifteen Point Program, 295
Financial Institutions, 303
Fisheries, 25
Five Year Plan
(8th), 332
(9th), 332
(10th), 332, 333
Footwear Industry, 25
Forced Labor, 134
Forensic Science, 114
Forestry, 25
Forgery, 110
Fourth World Conference, 194

France, 218
Franklin Roosevelt Four Freedoms Address, 71
Free
  Legal Aid Camps, 264
  Market Crisis, 175
French
  Civil Code, 123
  Republic, 218
  Revolution, 224
Fundamental
  Human Rights of Women, 165
  Rights, 55, 59, 89, 137, 272
  Rights and Freedom, 194

G

Gandhi, Mahatma, 95, 173, 218, 219, 237, 242, 356
Gandhi, Rajiv, 279
Garokhpuria Loaders (GKP Loaders), 13
Gender Disparity in Education, 339
Geneva Convention, 224
Germany, 191
Ghajar Dynasty, 5
Gill, KPS, former DG Punjab Police, 161
Global Economic Order, 175
Globalized Economy, 243
Globalization, 257
Government
  Policies, 331
  Schemes, 311
Great Religions of the World, (GRW), 220
  Buddhism, 220
  Christianity, 220
  Hinduism, 220
  Islam, 220
  Judaism, 220
  Taoism, 220
Greek
  Society, 222
  Tradition of Socrates and Plato, 222

H

Haiti Election Results, 71
Hammurabi, Sumerian King, 222
  Code, 222
  Laws, 222
  Tablets of-, 222
Harassment of Jail Inmates, 149, 154
Haryana High Court, 142
Health
  And Shelter, 19
  And Social Welfare Activities, 39
  Camps, 264
  Cards, 191
  Education, 262
  Of Children, 38
Herbal Research Institute Gopeshwar Uttaranchal, 161
  High Court,
  Haryana, 142
  Himachal Pradesh, 46
  Rajasthan, 89
  Rajasthan, 89
Himachal Pradesh High Court, 46
Hindu
  Civilization, 225
  Law Reform, 257
  Race, 3256
Hinduism, 50
Hindus Marriage Act, 1958, 87
HIV, 182, 207
  Infection, 189
  Positive Prisoners, 208
  Prevention, 187
  Testing, 187

Transmission, 190

Transmission in Nigeria, 186

HIV/AIDS, 181-216

Epidemic, 186

In Nigeria, 182

Pandemic, 181

Prevention Program, 187, 191

Holy Roman Catholic Church, 172

Homosexual Fundamental Rights, 198

Homosexuality, 203

Human

Resource Development in Coal Industry, 12

Rights, 4, 57-60, 66, 67, 69, 72, 85, 169, 217-240

Abuses, 73

Act, 159

And Peace, 65-84

Commission, 59, 161, 232

Functions, 232

Committee, 197, 226

Courts, 220, 233, 234

Courts in India, 217-240

Defined, 221

Evolution, 220

Groups, 219, 230

In India, 219, 220

In India, Evolution, 225

In Indian Perspectives, 219

Infringement, 68

Instruments, 159, 204, 207

Issues, 229

Literacy, 143

Movement, 218, 219

Organization, 59

Philosophy, 222

Problems, 220

Protection, 69

Treaties, 57

Violation, 61, 67, 70-72, 85, 89, 143, 147, 182, 228, 229, 283

Human Security, 237

Humanitarian

Catastrophes in Kosovo, 72, 74

Intervention, 169

Intervention Defined, 65

Rule of Law, 170

I

ICDS (Integrated Child Development Services), 334

IGNOU, 263

In-alienation Rights, 132

Incentives, 304

Indecent

Dress Pattern, 167

Representation of Women Act, 163

India

And International Human Rights Instruments, 43-54

Labor Conference, 99

India's

Counter Terrorism, 284

Independence, 98

Indian

Civilization, 225

Constitution, 271, 272, 274, 281, 282, 322 see Constitution of India also

Counter-Terrorism Policy, 56

Evidence Act, 274

Panel Code, 1860, 46, 85-87, 163, 164, 167, 267, 281

Police Act, 1861, 108, 111

Security Forces, 61

Society, 160, 225, 255, 271

Tradition, 49

Women, 160, 271, 273

Industrial
- And Commercial Workers, 98
- Capitalism, 175
- Conflicts, 15
- Dispute Act, 1947, 13, 163
- Peace, 11
- Relation Culture, 11, 12, 14
- Relations, 11, 13, 14
- Revolution in Europe, 94
- Workers, 99

Industrialization, 14, 94, 96, 257, 271, 273

Industry
- Based Cooperatives, 126
- Brick Kiln, 25
- Chemical, 25
- Cottage, 25
- Electronic, 304
- Footwear, 25
- Footwear, 25
- Leather, 304
- Power Looms, 25
- Sport, 25
- Surgical Goods, 25

Infanticide, 259

Institutional Support Programs- Details, 304

Insurance Scheme, 96

Insurgency and Terrorism, 283

Integrated Social Security Scheme, 103

Inter-American Convention – against Women, 165

International
- Conference on Population and Development (ICPD), 194
- Convention on Civil and Political Rights (ICCPR), 2, 49, 57, 62, 72, 133, 134, 194, 196, 197, 201, 202, 221, 226, 230, 286
- Convention on the Rights of the Child, 29, 33
- Conventions and Agreements, 1
- Court of Justice, 68
- Covenant on Economic, Social and Cultural Rights, (ICESCR), 72, 133, 134, 194, 203, 205, 206, 276, 278, 322
- Disputes, 70
- Human Rights Regime, 68
- Labor Organization (ILO), 17, 26, 27, 95, 205
  - Convention, 93
  - Convention 182, 26
  - Convention No, 59, 137
- Law, 4, 65, 67, 69
- Peace and Security, 66, 67
- Women's Day, 280
- Year of the Child, 133

Intervention in Kosovo, 76

Inundation, Danger of -, 12

Investigating Officers, 108, 109
- Need for Separate Cadre, 108

Investigation Steps, 105-106

IPEC (International Program on Elimination of Child Labor), 26, 27

Iran
- Constitution, 1, 6-8
- Contra Affair, 172

Iran's
- Criminal Procedure Code, 6
- Legal Text, 1-9
- Legal Text, Concerning Prohibition of Torture, 1-9
- Principals Criminal Procedures, 7
- Supreme Court, 7

Iranian
- Commanders, 5
  - Amir Kabir's Command, 5
  - Command of Hajji Mirza Aghassi, 5

Command of Mirza Hussain Khan Sepahsalar, 5
Iron Shops, 25
Irregularities in Prisons, 150
Islamic
  Penal Code, 7
  Republic of Pakistan, 29

J

Jail
  Administration, 273, 277
  Conditions, 145, 146, 151-153
  Manual, 142
  Population in Punjab, 142
Jail's Minilabs, 264
Jails, 141, 260
  Central, 141
  District, 141
  Female, 141
  Open Air Agriculture Jail, 141
  Sub-Jail, 141
Jamia Millia Islamia University, 294
Jammu and Kashmir, 58, 61
  National Conference, 325
Jaswal, BS, Lt. Gen. 61
Jeffers, Robinson, American Poet, 170
Joint
  Families, 94
  Hindu Family, 94
  Special Task Force, 161
Jordan Case, 202
Judicial Custody, 145-147, 154
Judiciary, 85
Judiciary Procedure, 7
Justice Krishna Iyer's Committee, 277
Juvenile
  Delinquency, 136
  Justice, 137
  Justice Act, 136
  Justice System, (JJS), 136

K

Kant, 223
Karma, 50
Karnani Group, 11
Karnataka State Legal Service Authority, 265
Karwar Taluka, 303-319
Kashmir
  And Ladakh, 323
  Valley, 61
Kashmiri
  Society, 324
  Women, 324
Kautilya, 225
Kautilya Arthshastra, 94
KGBV (Kasturba Gandhi Balika Vidyalayas), 336-339
  Blocks, 336
Kharag Singh Vs State of Uttar Pradesh, 45
King John of England, 217
Kosovo, 169
  Crisis, 75
Krishna Iyer, VR, Justice, 261
Kurdish People in Iraq, 71

L

Labor
  Investigation Committee, 99
  Laws, 95
  Laws in India, 95
  Problems, 307, 308
Landless Farmers, 35
Landmark Judgements of Prisoners Rights, 278

Law
- And Order, 109
- Commission, 107, 111, 112
- Enforcement, 106
- Reformers, 227
- Restoration and Administration, 123

Lawrence Vs Texas, 198
Laws and Legal Strategies, 132
League of Nations, 132
Left Wing Extremism (LWE), 110
Legal
- Assistance, 264
- System, 136

Legalization and De-Criminalization, 191, 192
Legislations—to Combat Terrorism, 58
Legislative, Administrative and Judicial Measures, 2
Leo Tolstoy, 218
Liberalization, 257
Life Insurance Company, 94
Literacy, 14
- Rate, 327

Locke, 223

M

Macaulay, 86
- Economy, 183

Magna Carta or Great Charter, 217, 220
Maintenance of Internal Security Act, 1971, (MISA), 58, 229
Male Literacy, 326
Malinath Committee on Reforms of Criminal Justice System, 111, 113
Managerial Problems, 311
Mandatory Health Inspections, 191
Manu, 225, 256
Manusmriti, 94
Marital Rape, 85, 87
- A Domestic Violence, 87

Marketing Problems, 310, 317
Martin Luther King, 218
Marx, Karl, 223
Maternity Benefit Act, 95, 101, 103, 163
Mathura Rape Case, 88
Matrimonial Consent, 85
Maulana Azad National Urdu University, 294
Media, Electronic, 288
Medical Ethics, 50
Medical/Scientific Experiments, 2
Mental Harassment, 159
Mentally Disabled Children, 137
Migrant Sexual Workers, 188
Migration, 19
- Of Young Girls, 184

Military
- Interventions, 67, 70
- Operation, 77

Mill, JS, 218
Miners, 13
Mines Act, 1952, 13, 163
Minimum Wages Act, 13
Minority
- Community, 291, 295
- Development Corporation, 265
- Education, 294
- Linguistic, 291

Misbranding Articles, 243
Model Cluster Schools, 336
Modernization, 271, 273
- Madarsa Education, 295
- Of Police Forces, 113
- Of Women, 167

Mohalla Committees, 110

Molestation, 164
Monarchy, 218
Monica Lawinski Investigation, 172
Monopolistic Trade Practices, 243
Moral and Ethical Standards in India, 49
Mrs. Alva, 279
Mulla Committee, 277
Multinational Corporations, 246
Multi-Party Democratic System, 77
Mundra, Haridas, 11
Muslim (s), 291-301
  Community, 297, 298
  Education, 294
  Education in Maharashtra, 292
Mysteries Deaths in Jail, 142

N

Namibia, 177
Narain, Jai Prakash, 231
Narco-Terrorism, 110
Nari Bandigraha Adalats, 280
National
  Action Committee on AIDS, (NACA), 186
  And International Human Rights, 241
  Authority on Custodial Justice to Women (NACW), 280
  Child Labor
    Policy, 22
    Projects, 22
  Commission for
    Minorities Educational Institutions, 295
    Protection of Child Rights, 135
    Protection of Rights of Child (NCPCR), 322
    Women-Survey, 159
  Concensus List of Occupations, 26-27
  Council for Women, 257
  Economy, 317
  Human Rights Commission, 111, 142, 153, 161, 227, 231, 234, 235, 277, 282
  Investigation Agency Act, 284
  Laws—Child Labor, 29
  Liberation Movement, 219
  Monitoring Committee for Minorities Education, 295
  Police Commission (NPC), 107, 109, 110, 111, 277, 282
  Policy
    for Custodial Justice for Women, 261
    on Custodial Justice, 280
    on Education, 299
    on HIV/AIDS, 208
  Productivity Council, 109
  Program—Elementary Education (NPEGEL), 334, 335
  Rights, 217, 218
  Security, 113, 289
  Security Act (NSA), 58, 229, 58
NATO Member States, 74-76
NATO's Intervention and Kosovo, 69, 73
Natural Rights, 220
Naya Kashmir, 325
NDPS Act, 143, 262
Nehru, 95
Neo-Natal Deaths, 131
Netherlands, 191
New
  Environmentalism, 121
  Green Technologies, 121
  York's World Trade Centre, 59
Nigeria, 181-216
  Polarized Society, 192
Nigerian

Constitution, 200, 204, 207
Society, 187, 192
Night Brides, 185
Non-Government
Social Organization, 23
Organization (NGOs), 21, 26, 39, 40, 143, 166, 187, 219, 232, 238, 265, 317, 318
Sector, 39
Non-
Political Crimes, 1
Registration of Complaints, 152
Voluntary Euthanasia, 44, 45, 51
North West Frontier Provinces (NWFP), 29

O

Obama, Barak, US Pres., 176
Obasanjo's Administration, 186
OBC Muslims, 298
Offences of Rape, 85, 92
Old Prison Act, 1894, 141
Open Air Prison, 280
Optional Protocol, 133, 134, 135
Organized Crimes, 110, 113

P

Padmanabhaiah Committee, 111
Paine, Thomas, 218
Pakistan, 25, 323
Economy, 25
Agrarian Economy, 26
Child Labor in-, 27
Child Labor Legislation, 29
House Based Industry, 25
Member of ILO, 25\
Working Children, 28
Panchayat, 94
Parasar, 225
Paris Minimum Standards, 4
Partition of India, 56
Patel, Vallabhbhai, 95
Patriarchal
Family System, 303
Society, 282
Payment of Gratuity Act, 1972, 95, 101, 102, 103
Peace
And Security, 70, 71, 72
Conference, 71
Defined, 70
People's Union for Civil Liberties (PUCL), 59
Peoples' Union – Democratic Rights, 231
PEPFAR, 187
Perez de Cuellar, UN Secy Gen. 68, 70
Personnel Management, 11
Philanthropists, 40
Philosophers, 220
Grotius, 220
Hobbes, 220
Locke, 220
Physical Punishment, 39
Plantation Labor Act, 163
Plato, 220, 222
Police
Act, 112
Atrocities, 106
Commission Report, 111
Community Program, 114
Investigation in India, 106
Standards of-, 106
Reforms, 105-119
Judicial Approach, 112
Reforms Commission, 112
Political
And Economic Freedom, 56

Conflicts, 55
Disputes, 55
Parties, 58
Polluters, 123
Pollution, 123, 124, 127
POTA (Prevention of Terrorist Act), 2002, 58-60, 286, 287, 288, 289
Poverty
Alleviation Program, 22
And Social Inequality, 260
Reduction, 22
Power
Looms Industry, 25
Projects, 229
Presidential Committee on AIDS, 186
Prevention of
Corruption Act, 235
Terrorism Act and Unlawful Activities (Prevention) Amendment Act, 230
Primary
Education, 29
Schools, 329, 330
Principle of
Ahimsa, 50
Non-Intervention, 67
Prison
Act, 141
Administration, 268
Conditions, 141-155
Defined, 141
Education in Prisons of Karnataka, 262
Prisoners' Rights, 143, 144, 153, 280
In Punjab, 141-155
Prisons
in India, 260
in Punjab, 142
Private
Insurance, 94
Law, 121-129
Schooling System, 31
Program of Action, 294
Project Displacement, 229
Property Rights, 122
Prostitution, 182, 188
Protection of Human Rights
Act, 1993, 143, 152, 153, 217-240
Ordinance, 231
Protocol to African Charter, 195
Provident Fund of India, 98
Psychological Torture, 2
Public
Accounts Committee, 142
Legislation, 121
Safety Act, 58
Punjab, 59
Compulsory Education Act, 29
Jail Manual, 1996, 41
Police Commission, 106
State Human Rights Commission (PSHRC), 141-155
Role, 141-155
Purohit and Moore Vs Gambia, 206

Q

Quadruple Conventions, 4
Quality Control, 310

R

Rafiq Vs State of Uttar Pradesh, 88
Rajasthan High Court, 89
Ramayana and Mahabharata, 256
Rape, 85-92, 158, 165
Ad Relevancy of Consent, 85-92
Defined, 85
Rapid Urbanization, 184
RC Cooper Vs Union of India, 46

Reform Homes, 142
Reformers, 226
Dyanand Saraswati, 226
Raja Rammohun Roy, 226
Vivekananda, Swamy, 226
Reforms, 96, 273
Regulation and Licensing, 191
Rehabilitation of
Prison Inmates, 273
Released Inmates, 265
Relief Measures, 307
Religious
Minorities, 59
Orthodoxy, 226
Traditions, 217
Remuneration of Child Workers, 35
Renaissance 'the Glorious Revolution', 221
Revolutionaries, 218
Revolutions, 221
American, 221
Bolshevik, 221
France, 221
Industrial, 221
Ribeiro Committee, 111
Right to
Die, 44
Dignity, 199, 200
Education, 321-341
Education Act, 322, 323, 327, 339, 340
Education in J&K, 338
Education in J&K, Problems in Implementation, 338
Equality, 201
Food, 275
Free and Compulsory Education, 321, 322
Act, 339
Free Legal Services, 275
Health, 205, 206
Human Treatment, 4
Humanitarian Intervention, 65-84
Life, 44-46, 48, 57, 58, 73
Life – Liberty, 206
Privacy, 196
Privacy of Sexual Workers, 199
Sexual/Reproductive Health Care, 205
Social Security, 243
Rights of
Accused, 274
Custodial Rights, 274
Rights under Criminal Procedure Code, 274
Child, 132
Children, 39
Prisoners, 273
Prisoners Details, 276
Widows, 217
Rio Declaration, 1992, 125
Robbery, 110
Role Theory, 259
Roof Falling, 12
Rousseau, 223
Roy, Raja Rammohun, 256
Rural
Joint Families, 93
Migration, 184
Russia, 218
Russia, China, US, 175
Russian Serfs, 218
Rwanda, 169
Rwandan Genocide, 173

S

Sabharwal, Justice YK, 277
Sachar Committee Report, 298

Safe Drinking Water, 13
Saiyidain, GK, 325
Sakshi, NGO, 159
San Francisco Conference, 68
Sanitary Conditions, 147
Sardar Sarovar (Dam), 230
Sarva Shiksha Abhiyan, (SSA), 333, 334
    Mission, 336
Sati System, 219
Scandals and Embezzlements, 142
Scheduled Castes/Tribes, 55, 219, 291, 332, 336
    Act, 236
    Development Corporation, 265
    Female Literacy, 335
School Education, 295
Schooling Facilities, 37
Second
    Generation Rights, 243
    West Bengal Police Commission, 106
Sector,
    Agricultural, 25, 31
    Construction, 25
    Hospitality, 21
    Trade, 25
    Transport, 25
Security
    Council, 69, 71, 72
    Forces in Kashmir, 61
Sekhon, JS, Justiace, 151
Separate Colleges for Women, 325
Separatist Movement, 55
Serial Bomb Blasts in Mumbai, 56
Sex
    Relationship, 181
    Wars, 183
    Work, 181-216
        Economic Contribution, 205
            Indonesia, 205
            Malaysia, 205
            Philippines, 205
            Thailand, 205
    Work and Human Rights, 192
    Work Defined, 182
    Work in Nigeria, 183, 186
    Workers, 182, 184, 186, 187
Sexual
    Abuse, 29, 165
    Assault Incidents, 157
    Exploitation, 134
    Harassment, 145, 157-167, 229
        And Domestic Laws, 163
        Cases, 161
            Mrs. Rupeam Deol Bajaj, 161
            Ms Asha Rajora, 161
            Nalini Netto, 161
        Defined, 158
        Existing Laws in India, 162-163
        In Indian Society, 157
        Remedial Measures, 157
    Intercourse, 85-87, 90
    Offences Act, 202
    Rights as Human Rights, 194
    Rights in Africa, 181-216
    Rights, 193
    Violence, 194
        Physical, 87
    Workers, 188-190, 191, 200, 204, 205, 207
    Workers Rights, 208
Sexuality, 183, 193, 194
    Rights, 195
Sexually
    Abused Children, 131
    Transmitted Infection (STI), 186, 192, 206

SIE (State Institute of Education), 334
Sierra Leone, 177
Sindh, 29
SIT (Special Investigation Teams), 110
Slavery, 218
Slum Dwellers, 229
Smuts, Field Marshall, South African Pre-Apartheid Leader, 224
Social
  And Economic Rights, 204, 207
  Changes, 259
  Customs and Norms, 27
  Disintegration, 56
  Disorder, 218
  Education, 263
  Evils, 226, 256, 257
    Ban on Widow's Remarriage, 256
    Child Marriage, 256
    Devadasi, 256
    Polygamy, 256
    Practice of Jauhar, 256
    Prostitution, 256
    Purdah, 256
    Sati, 256
  Groups, 56
  Integration, 56
  Justice, 97
  Movement, 241
  Organization, 172
  Policy Development Centre, Karachi, 27
  Protection, 104
  Security, 93-104
    Evolution of-, 93-104
    In Education, 296
    In India, 93-104
    Legislations, 104
    Minimum Standards, 93
    Program, 95, 103
    Scheme, 95, 104
    System, 94
  Structure and Society, 259
  Structure, 94
  Transformation, 321
Socio-Economic
  Crimes, 243
  Development, 157, 291
  Factors, 27
  Human Rights, 244
  Justice, 243
  Rights, 243, 244
Sodomy, 196, 198, 204
Soli Sorabjee, former Attorney Gen., 111
Somalia, 71
Sorabjee Committee, 112
South
  Africa Domestic Racial Policy, 71
  African Constitutional Court, 202
Southern Rhodesia, 71
Sovereignty and Peace, 65
Soviet
  Forces, 73
  Union, 169, 175
Special
  Marriage Act, 1957, 87
  Subsidies Schemes, 304
Specialized Squads, 110
Sport Industry, 25
Sree Krishna, Justice, 56
Standing Labor Committee, 99
State
  Human Rights commission, 231, 234, 235
  Of Georgia, 197
  Of Himachal Pradesh Vs Umed Rani, 45

Of Jammu and Kashmir, 97, 98, 100, 320-341
Security Commission, 112
Sponsored Terrorism by Libya, 71
Stateless Areas, 55
States of Assam and Sikkim, 236
Stone Quarying, 25
Sudan, 169
Sugar Daddies, 185
Superpowers, USA, 284
Suppression of Immoral Traffic in Women and Girls Act, 136
Supreme Court of
Canada, 124
India, 227, 228
Surgical Good Industry, 25
Suvarna Akshara Andolan, 263

T

TADA (Terrorist and Disruptive Activities (Prevention) Act, 1985, 58, 59, 228, 229, 230, 262, 286, 288, 289
TAPASYA, NGO, 159
Taraba, 186
Teachers' Training Curricula, 39
Teaching-Learning Materials, 334
Technology, 11, 12
Tehru Reservoir, 230
Termination of Services, 102
Terrorism, 55-63, 108, 110, 113, 283, 287
And Human Rights, 56
Causes, 55
Terrorist Attacks, 55, 284
Thakkar, Justice CK, 277
Thangjam Manorama Rape Victim in Manipur, 60
Thapar, Karam Chand, 11
Thomas Aquinas, 50
Tort of Negligence, 121
Trade
Sector, 25
Union (s), 11, 26
Union Act, 13, 14
Unionism, 13
Traditional
Architecture, 121, 126
Kashmiri Society, 324
Trafficking of Girls, 186
Training, 109-110
In Knitting—Home Nursinig Training, 264
Of Law Enforcement Personnel, 3
On Professional Competence, 317
Transnational Corporations, 246

U

UEE (Universalization of Elementary Education), 332
UK House of Lords Select Committee, 50
UK Vs Lord Wolfenden Committee, 192
UK, 74, 75
UN (United Nations), 1, 3, 4, 8, 66-68, 72, 74, 131, 133, 191, 219, 221, 225, 226, 237
Charter, 132, 224
Charter Regime, 65-84
Committee on Economic, Social and Cultural Rights, 276
Convention for Suppression—Prostitution, 190
Commission on Human Rights, 135
Convention on Sexual Harassment, 164
Convention on Human Rights, 17
Right to Development, 17
Right to Participation, 17
Right to Protection, 17
Right to Survival, 17
Conventions, 29

Counter-Terrorism Committee, 62
Covenant on Civil, Political Rights, 272
Declaration, 135, 193
on Elimination of Violence against Women, 194
on Rights of Child, 321
Development Program, (UNDP), 27
Fourth World Conference on Women, 165
Framework, 172
General Assembly, 133, 220, 255
Human Rights Committee, 60
Resolutions, 285
Security Council, 65
Standard Minimum Rules for Treatment of Prisoners, 276
Universal Declaration of Human Rights, (UDHR), 1, 48, 57, 72, 95, 132, 133, 134, 196, 199, 203, 220, 221, 224, 225, 227, 255, 272, 276, 278, 321
Unlawful Activities Prevention (Amendment) Act, 283-290
Unsafe Sexual Intercourse, 186
Upanishads, 256
UPE (Universalization of Primary Education), 332
Urban and Industrial Centre, 93
Urbanization, 257, 271
US, 7, 122, 172, 174, 218
Case of Bowers Vs Hardwick, 197
Civil Rights Movement, 219
Constitution, 197, 224
Declaration of Independence, 218
Global HIV/AIDS Funding, 187
NGOs, 224
Patriot Act, 59
Supreme Court, 197, 198

V

Vedas, 256
Vedic Women, 256
Lopamudra, Viswavara, Sikala–Maitreya, 356
Venereal Infections, 190
Victims of Crimes, 107
Video Conferencing System, 260
Vienna Declaration, 165
Of Action, 194
Violation
Of Human Rights, 230
Against Women, 194
Of Human Rights, 194
Of Human Rights in Punjab, 143
Of Standards and Weights and Measures, 243
Physical, 158
Sexual, 159
Vishaka Vs State of Rajasthan, 158, 159
Vocational Training, 317
Voluntary Euthanasia, 44, 45, 51

W

War on Terrorism, 169
Wars and Dictatorships, 241
West
Bengal, 14, 15
Employee's Organization, 15
Police Commission, 106
Pakistan Shops and Establishment Ordinance, 1969, 29
Virginia Board of Education VS Barnette, 199
White Collar Crimes, 243
Women
Compulsory Free Primary Education for-, 325

Criminals, 261
Education, 323
History in J&K, 324
Education and Marriage, 296
Entrepreneurs, 303-319
Association, 317
Problems, 303, 307
Profile, 306
Equal Educational Rights, 325
In Ancient India, 256
In Modern India, 256
Jails, 279
Prisoners, 142, 260-264, 268, 281, 282
Protocol, 203, 204
Sexual Harassment at Workplace, 157-167
Voluntary Organizations, 268

Women's
Charter, 325
Courts, 280
Education in Jammu and Kashmir, 321-341
Education, 325
Indian Association, 257
Legislation details, 257
Participation in Criminal Activities, 258
Position in Modern Indian Society, 257
Protocol, 199, 200
Reproductive Health, 194
Sexuality, 85
Status Today, 255
Welfare Trust, 325

Working
Children, 28, 29, 36
Children in India, 17
Women, 159
Women (Prevention of Sexual Harassment at Workplace), Bill, 164

Workmen's Compensation Act, 1923, 31, 95, 96, 102, 103

World
Charter for Prostitution Rights (WCPR), 195
Conference on Human Rights in Vienna, 1993, 194
Health Organization (WHO), 193, 195
War I in Europe, 71, 169, 221
War II, 70

Y & Z

Yerawada Central Prison, 280
Zimbabwean Supreme Court, 196